Jews in the Russian Army, 1827–1917
Drafted into Modernity

This is the first study of the military experience of some one million to one-and-a-half million Jews who served in the Russian Army between 1827, the onset of the conscription of Jews in Russia, and 1917, the demise of the tsarist regime. The conscription integrated Jews into the state, transforming the repressed Jewish victims of the draft into modern imperial Russian Jews. The book contextualizes the reasons underlying the decision to draft Jews, the communal responses to the draft, the missionary initiatives directed toward Jews in the army, alleged Jewish draft evasion and Jewish military performance, and the strategies Jews used to endure military service. It also explores the growing antisemitism of the upper echelons of the military toward the Jews on the eve of World War I and the rise of Russian Jewish loyalty and patriotism.

Yohanan Petrovsky-Shtern teaches Early Modern, Modern, and East European Jewish history and culture at Northwestern University. He is the author of *The Anti-Imperial Choice: The Making and Unmaking of the Ukrainian Jew* (forthcoming). He has also published about forty scholarly essays in journals such as *East European Jewish Affairs*, *Jewish Social History*, *Jewish History*, *Jewish Quarterly Review*, *AJS Review*, *POLIN*, *KRITIKA*, *Ab Imperio*, and *The Ukrainian Quarterly*. He has been a Fellow at the Davis Center for Russian and Eurasian Studies at Harvard University, a Rothschild Fellow in Jerusalem, a Visiting Scholar at the Institute for Advanced Studies in Jerusalem, a Sensibar Visiting Professor at Spertus College in Chicago, a Visiting Scholar at École des Hautes Études en Sciences Sociales in Paris, and a recipient of multiple fellowships and grants, including the National Endowment for the Humanities and Fulbright.

Jews in the Russian Army, 1827–1917

Drafted into Modernity

YOHANAN PETROVSKY-SHTERN

Northwestern University

CAMBRIDGE
UNIVERSITY PRESS

CAMBRIDGE UNIVERSITY PRESS
Cambridge, New York, Melbourne, Madrid, Cape Town, Singapore, São Paulo, Delhi

Cambridge University Press
32 Avenue of the Americas, New York, NY 10013-2473, USA

www.cambridge.org
Information on this title: www.cambridge.org/9780521515733

First published 2009

Printed in the United States of America

A catalog record for this publication is available from the British Library.

Library of Congress Cataloging in Publication Data
Yohanan Petrovsky-Shtern.
  [Evrei v russkoi armii. English]
  Jews in the Russian army, 1827–1917 : drafted into modernity / Yohanan Petrovsky-Shtern.
     p.   cm.
  Includes bibliographical references and index.
  ISBN 978-0-521-51573-3 (hardback)
  1. Jews – Russia – History.   2. Jewish soldiers – Russia – History.
  3. Jewish children – Government policy – Russia – History – 19th century.
  4. Russia – Armed Forces – Recruiting, enlistment, etc. – History.
  5. Russia. Armiia – History.   6. Russia – Ethnic relations.   I. Title.
  DS134.84.P4813 2008
  355.0089'924047–dc22   2008008312

ISBN 978-0-521-51573-3 hardback

To the blessed memory of my grandfather
Semen Vasil'evich Petrovsky
(Shimon ben Meir Shtern)
1897–1972
World War I Russian Imperial Army Volunteer

Posle obiazannostei–prava
Khoteli my. No myslia zdravo
Obiazannosti vyshe prav.
Skazhite, razve ia ne prav?

The duty we fulfilled. And hence
The rights we sought. But common sense
Prompts duty overrides them all.
Now try to tell me I am wrong!
David Samoilov, "Iulii Klompus"

Contents

Illustrations

Tables

Acknowledgments

This study was a collective enterprise. To thank everybody to whom I owe gratitude is to tell my life story, a task that exceeds the capacities of the acknowledgments. My apology to all those who are not mentioned here: I hope to be able to catch up with you in my next book. Conversations with Henry (Hillel) Abramson, Benjamin Nathans, and Paul Radensky informed my decision to switch my focus from comparative literature to the study of Jewish history. Gershon Hundert, Moshe Rosman, and Shaul Stampfer made me into a historian of Jewish people with broad interests in social and quantitative history and comparative analysis. Arthur Green, Reuven Kimelman, and Jonathan Sarna turned my years at Brandeis into a rewarding spiritual journey. My Brandeis dissertation advisor, Antony Polonsky, has been amazingly generous intellectually. He read four, if not five, versions of my dissertation, helped me to reshape it into a book (first, Russian; later, English), and was a guardian angel for me and my family through our first years in the United States. Antony's adage "context is everything" has framed and is still framing my research. Notes of Gregory Freeze and Michael Stanislawski, the readers of my dissertation, provided me with excellent ideas leading toward this book. I am indebted to John Bushnell, a senior colleague, friend, and a connoisseur of Russian military history, whose suggestions and corrections in the margins of my manuscript deserve a separate publication.

Tatiana Burmistrova, Olga Edelman, Aleksei Litvin, Binyamin Lukin, Ludmila Uritsky, and Hanna Węgzynek took me through the labyrinths of Israeli, Polish, Russian, and Ukrainian archives; some of them should be credited for instructing me how legally to obtain twenty files per day whereas the rigid archival former Soviet Union rules allowed not more than five. Yaroslav Tynchenko and Alexei Vasiliev consulted with me on some murky aspects of military history. The staff of the Kyiv Judaica Institute – Leonid Finberg, Miron Petrovsky, and Galya Likhtenshtein – uncovered, scanned, and provided me with most of the illustrations for this book. My profound thanks to the annoyed reviewers of the Russian version of this book – I am glad I managed to find some valuable critical points in their aggressive escapades and used those points to improve my English narrative. Seymour Simckes was a great help as an editor on the first stages of this project, and Lisa Ferdman painstakingly edited the final version of the book. It was a rewarding experience to work with Angela Turnbull, my Cambridge University Press copy editor: her consistency and curiosity greatly contributed to polishing the final product. But I bear the entire responsibility for errors and misconceptions in this book.

The Rothschild Foundation, the Memorial Foundation for Jewish Culture, Ruth Ann Perlmutter, the National Endowment for the Humanities, and Northwestern University generously provided their support, which enabled me to conduct research for this book in five countries. My wife, Hanna, and children, Sara Sofiya and Shlomo Efraim, stoically endured my absences – overseas or at home – when I was working on this book.

Parts of Chapter 2 previously appeared in *The Military and Society in Russia, 1450 to 1917*, edited by Eric Lohr and Marshall Poe (Leiden: Brill, 2002), 413–434, and in *Jews in Russia and Eastern Europe*, no. 1 (2004): 130–144; parts of Chapters 5 and 6 in *KRITIKA: Explorations in Russian and Eurasian History*, no. 2 (2002): 217–254. I would like to thank the publishers who permitted me to use parts of my work for this book.

Lewis Bateman was an epitome of good taste, strategic planning, and efficiency: it took him two days to assess my manuscript and two months to obtain the reviewers' responses. I deeply regret I cannot thank the late John Doyle Klier: he read my dissertation, my Russian book, and the manuscript of this book, supported me at each and every stage of my career, and penned an enthusiastic review for the Press, which, among other things, suggested how to make my narrative tighter and my conceptualization more compelling. May John's memory be a blessing.

Note on Transliteration, Names, Figures, and Dates

Towns whose names have an accepted English-language form are given in that form; some examples are Warsaw, Kiev, and Moscow. The only exception is Vilna, used in its traditional form accepted in English-language historiography. In bibliographical references, abbreviations are used for the most frequent references, as, for instance, "M." for Moscow and "SPb." for St. Petersburg. Towns and cities of the Russian Empire, including western provinces of the Pale of Settlement (what today is Ukraine, Belorussia, and Lithuania), are given in contemporary Russian transliteration, as they appear in Russian military or governmental documentation of the nineteenth century. In most cases, but not in all, towns of the Kingdom of Poland and Polish towns in western provinces that had a majority Polish population are given in their official nineteenth-century Russian spelling, immediately followed by their original Polish spelling, for example, Lodz (Łódź). Small towns, shtetls, and villages of the Kingdom of Poland are given in their Polish spelling only. In cases when Polish, Lithuanian, or Ukrainian geographical names appear as the names of Russian army regiments, Russian spelling is retained, as for instance, Belostok (not Białystok) infantry regiment.

The Library of Congress system is used for Russian and Ukrainian languages. Russian geographical names are also spelled according to the system of the Library of Congress, except that they are spelled without a single prime for the soft sign. In the case of personal names of the well-known Russian Jewish public figures who have an established European form of name both names are given, as, for instance, Baron Gintsburg (Guenzburg). Transliteration of Yiddish follows the YIVO system, except for the names of the people, where the spelling they themselves used has been retained. In transliterating Hebrew words no distinction has been made between *aleph* and *ayin*. *Het* is written *h* except words that have an accepted English form; *khaf* is written *kh*; *yod* is written *y* when it functions as a consonant and *i* when it occurs as a vowel; *tsadi* is written *ts*; *kof* is written *k*. The *sheva na* is represented by an *e*. The *dagesh hazak* is not represented, except in words that have more or less acquired normative English spelling, as for instance, kaddish. Hebrew prefixes, prepositions, and conjunctions are followed by hyphens when they are transliterated, for instance, *Ha-Melits*. Capital letters are not used in the transliteration of Hebrew except for the first word and proper nouns in the titles of books and geographical names. The names of Jewish soldiers are given only in their Russian form as they appear in primary Russian military documents. No attempt to reestablish their original first or last name is made. Therefore, it is Itsik-Mordke Vulf, and not Isaac Mordekhai Wolf. However, if the name is mentioned in Hebrew or Yiddish-language primary sources, its respective Hebrew or Yiddish spelling is retained, as for instance, Yakov Yabets.

Figures in the tables appear as they are in the primary documents and reflect the contemporary Russian nineteenth-century sense of calculation. All dates follow the Julian calendar, which was twelve days behind the contemporary Gregorian calendar in the nineteenth century, when most of this study is set.

Abbreviations

AGAD	*Archiwum Główne Akt Dawnych* (Central Archive of Old Documents)
CAHJP	Central Archive of the History of the Jewish People
CMRS	*Cahiers du monde russe et soviétique*
ch.	*chast'* (part of the collection)
d.	*delo* (file)
DAVO	*Derzhavnyi arkhiv Vinnyts'koi oblasti* (State Archive of the Vinnitsa district)
f.	*fond* (collection)
GARF	*Gosudarstvennyi arkhiv Rossiiskoi Federatsii* (State Archive of the Russian Federation)
L.	Leningrad
l.	*list* (page)
M.	Moskva
NBU	*Natsional'na Biblioteka Ukrainy* (Vernadsky National Library of the Academy of Sciences of Ukraine)
op.	*opis'* (inventory)
Pb.	Peterburg
Pg.	Petrograd
PSS	*Polnoe sobranie sochinenii*
PSZ	*Polnoe sobranie zakonov Rossiiskoi imperii* (Complete Collection of the Laws of the Russian Empire)
r.	*razdel* (chapter)
RGME	*Russkii gosudarstvennyi muzei etnografii* (Russian State Museum of Ethnography)
RGAVMF	*Rossiiskii gosudarstvennyi arkhiv voenno-morskogo flota* (Russian State Archive of the Navy)
RGIA	*Rossiiskii gosudarstvennyi istoricheskii arkhiv* (Russian State Historical Archive)
RGVIA	*Rossiiskii gosudarstvennyi voenno-istoricheskii arkhiv* (Russian State Military History Archive)

SEER	*Slavonic and East European Review*
st.	*stol* (lit.: table; here: a Russian ministerial subdivision)
sv.	*sviazka* (lit.: bundle; here: a set of documents)
SVM	*Stoletiie voennogo ministerstva*
SPb.	St. Petersburg
SD	Socialist Democrats
SR	Socialist Revolutionaries
t.	*tom* (volume)
TsDIAU	*Tsentral'nyi derzhavnyi istorychnyi arkhiv Ukrainy* (Central State Historical Archive of Ukraine)
URP	Union of the Russian People

Jews in the Russian Army, 1827–1917
Drafted into Modernity

Introduction

On August 26, 1827, Nicholas I issued the Law on Conscription Duty, targeting Jews in the western provinces of the Russian Empire, known as the Pale of Jewish Settlement. He intended to make these Jews useful, and ended up making them imperial. The Pale of Settlement Jews feared that their induction into the military would transform them into Russian Christians; they did not expect that it would turn them into Russian Jews. In the long run, the army service wrought changes in the Jews' physical appearance, forged new forms of Jewish consciousness, facilitated the acquisition of new skills, ignited Jewish patriotic fervor, militarized Russian and Jewish public discourse, and opened for Jewish soldiers the doors to equality and emancipation. This volume examines the military service of the roughly million-and-a-half East European Jews who served in the Russian army between 1827 and 1917, tracing their evolution from tolerated aliens into His Majesty's loyal subjects.

Notwithstanding Catherine the Great's previous efforts to integrate Jews formally into society as merchants or urban dwellers, Jewish conscription constituted the autocratic Russian regime's first aggressive attempt to bring them into the empire. Unchallenged for some thirty years before Alexander II's Great Reforms, this measure had more dramatic ramifications than Nicholas I's later bid to acculturate Jews by means of state schooling or by subjecting their traditional communities to the authority of the Crown Rabbis (*kazennye ravviny*). Russia drafted its Jews into the empire before permitting them to educate themselves through it or to engage it politically.

While, elsewhere in Europe, the introduction of the draft put an end to the Jews' exclusion from society at large and from the body politic, the conscription of Russian Jews was a unique enterprise. In Austria, Prussia, and France, the army helped transform a society of subjects into a society of citizens, serving as an intensive school for the creation and training of a new man: the "citizen-soldier," to use the language of Jean-Paul Bertaud. Jews in these countries entered the draft pool either simultaneously with the extension to them of civil rights or immediately thereafter. Austria admitted Jews into the army in 1788–1789, France in 1792, and Prussia in 1813. European rulers saw

Jewish personal military duty as an essential precondition for full Jewish equality. If Jews sought civil parity, it seemed commonsensical that they should be required to fulfill their obligation to the state that conferred upon them the yearned-for privileges. The readiness of Jews to sacrifice their lives for their country demonstrated to Austrians, Prussians, and French that they deserved equal rights.

Unlike the way it happened in Europe, Russia simply and summarily drafted her Jews into the state. For nineteenth century Russian rulers duties superseded rights, and the obligations of the individual to the state overrode the state's responsibilities to the individual. Jews were required to serve for twenty-five years, obtaining no civil freedoms in exchange for this enormous, mandatory sacrifice. The moment they joined their regiments, their families and communities regarded them as dead. It was not until nearly a century after they had begun serving in the military that Russia emancipated its Jews; even then, the change occurred only as a result of the demise of the old regime, in February 1917.

Nourishing and Challenging Popular Legends

With the exception of pogroms, no other issue in nineteenth-century Russian history has aroused as much bitterness among East European Jewish historians as has Jewish conscription. Yiddish, Russian, and Hebrew historical narratives regard the conscripted Jew as the contemporary embodiment of the biblical Joseph, whose brothers sold him into Egyptian bondage. The traditional Jewish community, the merciless sons of Israel (Jacob's biblical name), sold their defenseless teenaged brothers to idol worshippers; that is to say, they allowed the *kahal*, or East European communal organization, to conscript their youth into the Russian army. Both professional and amateur Jewish historians invoke the story of a betrayed and abandoned Jewish boy, associating Jewish service in the Russian military with religiously conceived exile. The shtetl family is portrayed as the heartbroken Jacob and Rachel, bemoaning the untimely loss of their son. It comes as no surprise that dozens of stories and memoirs, generally regarded as trustworthy, tell the story of an alleged real figure captured by merciless *khapers*, the communal kidnappers: he was the only son of a neighbors' family, sometimes named Yossele, the Yiddish diminutive for Joseph, or Ierukhim, perhaps Hebrew for "God, have mercy."

The myth was so powerful that, as Yuri Lotman once observed, life began imitating literature; memoirists often accounted in their autobiographies for what they read, not for what they had experienced. In every shtetl there was a Jew claiming to have a widowed neighbor whose son had been captured by the *kahal* and dispatched to the army. This massive corpus of literary sources provided a convenient pool of images shaping Jewish memories. Only at the beginning of the twentieth century did the narrative change; the theme of exile gave way to the image of a captive Jew who became a soldier and succeeded in maintaining his Jewish identity, albeit no longer a purely religious one. This version, too, was prefigured by the biblical Joseph, who, *mutatis mutandis*, not only survived his exile but, due to his extraordinary talents, prevailed. The Siberian snows had replaced the Egyptian desert.

Students of East European Jewry found it difficult to free themselves from the grip of their traditional narratives. Jewish memory perceived current experience as a manifestation of the biblical narrative; "though the actors change, the scenario remains fundamentally the same."[1] The encounter of East European Jews with the Russian military fitted this paradigm perfectly. If it was not the treacherous sale of Joseph, it could be Rachel bemoaning the fate of her children, Hannah sacrificing her sons, or even Abraham offering Isaac. Appealing to Jewish collective memory, Jewish historians rarely considered the introduction of conscription for Russian Jews as part of a general European process of modernization. Instead, they depicted it in terms of exile, suffering, starvation, humiliation, and forced baptism, all of which are utterly alien to the enlightened spirit of modernity. They identified the military with the imperial administration, deeming both to be backward, intolerant, and anti-Jewish. The military acted precisely upon orders from the autocratic Russian Pharaoh. Conscription was a cruel device of Nicholas I, a noted antisemite, expressly designed to put an end to what he himself had described as "one of the most harmful religions."[2]

Jewish historians did not notice that, according to Nicholas I, religions were essentially harmful. Nicholas I's vision, as will be discussed later, betrayed a strong Enlightenment agenda, and therefore demanded a context of enlightened politics. But the collective memory could not conceive of Nicholas I in terms of the Enlightenment; Jewish history in Russia was uniformly regarded as a book of tears. The realities of the twentieth century shaped the Jewish vision of the nineteenth. The historical narratives of Russian Jews sought to instill a spirit of ethnic solidarity with suffering brethren. Narratives of Russian Jewish conscription were not appreciably different from medieval and early modern chronicles of Jewish martyrdom. The Temple in Jerusalem had been destroyed; Jews were exiled from the Holy Land; and new calamities replicated old ones. This cyclical vision of Jewish history defied modern historical sensibilities, but vividly conveyed genuine Jewish feelings about past events and the significance Jews adduced to them. The Russian army came to exemplify the evil realm of Esau. Ending up in the army signified spiritual, if not physical, death. New myths came to replace the old ones: a nineteenth-century Russian Jewish writer resorted to the romantic imagery of Goethe's *Erlkönig* (the Forest King) to tell the story of a Jewish boy who died out of fear of conscription.[3]

---

[1] Haim Yosef Yerushalmi, *Zakhor: Jewish History and Jewish Memory* (Seattle: University of Washington Press, 1982), 37.

[2] V. O. Levanda, ed., *Polnyi khronologicheskii sbornik zakonov i polozhenii kasaiushchikhsia evreev, ot ulozheniia Tsaria Alekseia Mikhailovicha do nastoiashchego vremeni, 1649–1873 g.* (SPb.: Tip. K. V. Trubnikova, 1874), 261–262.

[3] Yohanan Petrovsky-Shtern, *Evrei v russkoi armii, 1827–1914* (M.: Novoe literaturnoe obozrenie, 2003), 384–387.

The themes of exile and suffering, generally referred to in Yiddish as *golus* (in Hebrew, *galut*), permeated every important Jewish narrative of the past. In 1912, Joseph Boyarsky, an American Jew of East European origin and an amateur historian, related that, in 1827, Jews received the order to serve in the army. They had to undergo "actual service, twenty-five years, with very small pay, next to nothing." The authorities imposed "cruel treatment" upon them. Indeed, "[o]nly conversions saved them from suffering."[4] Simon Dubnow, a preeminent historian today regarded as the founder of East European Jewish historiography, wrote, in his three-volume history of Polish and Russian Jews, that the promulgated "military constitution" surpassed the Jews' worst expectations. Their conscription was received as a sudden blow that destroyed their lifestyle, their time-honored traditions, and their religious ideals. They endured their prolonged service amid extraordinary hardship. Their commanders beat and ridiculed them "because of their inability to express themselves in Russian, their refusal to eat *treifa*, and their general lack of adaptation to the strange environment and to the military mode of life."[5] Iulii Gessen, another prominent Russian Jewish historian much less well known in the West, argued that Nicholas I devised conscription in order to "effectively break the religious and national structure of Jewish life."[6] Echoing East European scholars such as Dubnow and Gessen, Louis Greenberg further dramatized this issue. In his view, military service concealed the malicious agenda of baptizing the Jews.[7]

Salo Baron, the first holder of a Jewish studies chair in the United States, repeatedly argued against what he dubbed the "lachrymose" concept of Jewish history that presented historical narratives as unremitting martyrdom. Ironically, Baron's otherwise acute sense of social context abandoned him in his analysis of conscription; there he bowed to the Jewish collective memory. It is perhaps because of his influence that subsequent historians described the draftees as "Jewish victims of the *rekrutchina*" (conscription).[8] Among the

---

[4] Joseph Boyarsky, *The Life and Suffering of the Jew in Russia: A Historical Review of Russia's Advancement Beginning with the Year 987 A.D. to the Close of the Nineteenth century; a Description of the Special Laws Enacted against the Jews and Reasons Thereof* (Los Angeles: Citizen Print Shop, 1912), 49.

[5] Simon Dubnow, *History of the Jews in Russia and Poland: From the Earliest Times until the Present Day*, trans. I. Friedlander (Philadelphia: The Jewish Publication Society of America, 1916–1920), 2:21, 28–29.

[6] Iulii Gessen, *Istoria evreev v Rossii* (SPb: L. Ia. Ganzburg, 1914), 200.

[7] Greenberg uses heavily charged language: "In addition to the sadism engendered by the military system, officials were led by their anxiety to please the monarch to employ the cruel means mentioned above to gain converts." In other words, there was no way out for a drafted Jew, whether a twelve-year-old cantonist or an adult, other than to be baptized. Those who resisted and who managed secretly to practice Judaism "were committed to prisons and monasteries and subjected to 'corrective' torments, which many of them endured for years without recanting their original faith." See Louis Greenberg, *The Jews in Russia: The Struggle for Emancipation* (New Haven: Yale University Press, 1944), 1:51–52.

[8] Salo W. Baron, *The Russian Jews under Tsar and Soviets* (New York: Macmillan, 1962), 35–38. Russian Jewish historians, surveying nineteenth-century East European Jewry, vividly depicted the suffering of Jewish soldiers, which improved the lives only of drafted children. See,

previous generation of Jewish historians, only Saul Ginsburg and Isaac Levitats, both known for their balanced and nuanced judgments, cautiously expressed some doubt about the received wisdom, noting that conversion may not have been entirely the motive for Jewish conscription.[9] However, the myth prevailed. Emulating the classics of the religiously shaped Jewish historiography such as *Zikhron Yaakov* by Jacob Lipmann Lipschitz, the collective memory of Russian Jews absorbed the story of Joseph's enslavement and exile into what Thomas Mann called the "Egyptian pit."

Fernand Braudel famously suggested that one consider geography for an understanding of historical continuities.[10] Unlike western and central Europe, where Jewish migration was sometimes limited but Jewish residence mostly was not, the kidney-shaped Pale of Jewish Settlement, occupying fifteen western provinces of the empire, seemed an impenetrable border. In the 1820s, only Jewish guild merchants and Jewish alcohol distillers were allowed into Russia's interior. For the one million Jews whom Russia inherited from Poland following the Polish Partitions of 1772–1795, the Pale was a swarming, albeit Jewish, place of residence, whereas Russia's interior was anything but a Jewish realm. At the end of the nineteenth century, no more than 4 percent of Jews resided beyond the Pale; as of 1820, this figure was so minuscule as to be inconsequential. Abolished de jure only in February 1917, the early nineteenth-century Pale circumscribed the settlement and legal inequality of the Russian Jews. Both imperial capitals were closed to Jews. Relatives of Jewish conscripts serving in Austria, France, or Prussia could visit them in their barracks, but Jews in the Pale were unable to do so, either legally or financially. The latter families bemoaned their losses because they felt that their sons were being sent away, outside the Pale, and into the army – forever. To a shtetl Jew, the Russian interior was comparable to the biblical Jew's Egypt: a vast, mighty land, immersed in idolatry, brimming with filth, and frighteningly non-Jewish. In this unimagined territory, family and community were both too remote to offer any assistance. Geography came to signify time.

Jewish narratives of the Russian Jewish military experience are colored by biblical and liturgical patterns of historical reconstruction and by a certain misleading reductionism. With all due respect to the religious sensibilities of traditional nineteenth-century East European Jews, one should question their claims that Jews on Russian army service should not be regarded as Jews. Contrary to the assumptions of Jewish historians, the Jews who served in the Russian army had much in common with their brethren in the Pale. Additionally, depressing stories about a twenty-five-year term of service obfuscate

among others, Henry Tobias, *The Jewish Bund in Russia: From Its Origins to 1905* (Stanford, Calif.: Stanford University Press, 1972), 2.

[9] Isaac Levitats, *The Jewish Community in Russia, 1772–1844* (New York: Columbia University Press, 1943), 59, n. 49.

[10] See Fernand Braudel, *The Mediterranean and the Mediterranean World in the Age of Philip II* (New York: Harper and Row, 1976), 23.

the fact that, beginning in the mid-1830s, this term was reduced to fifteen years for all recruits. Finally, being conscripted into the reformed army of 1874 differed considerably from being drafted into the pre-reform army of 1827; consequently, the service of Jewish soldiers also differed. Whatever the emphasis on change or continuity between the two Russian armies, pre-reform and reformed, it is misleading to discuss late nineteenth-century military duty in terms of the conscription of the 1820s. After 1874, the country was in flux, the army was different, and Jewish society underwent significant changes. Nonetheless, one should not dismiss altogether Jewish popular narratives; an object of study in their own right, they provide cultural historians with an opportunity to trace the history of feelings and meanings embedded in the writings of the founders of East European Jewish historiography, who resolutely disassociated European modernization from the Russian experience.

The first revision of the Russian Jewish military encounter belongs to Michael Stanislawski, although the Cold War cast a shadow on his research. While the American military historian William Fuller obtained access to Russian archives (despite anti-American animosity) and an American Slavicist, John Klier, obtained access to Jewish archival documents by pretending he was researching Russian history, Stanislawski could not access Jewish sources in the archives of the former USSR. Instead, he employed broad contextualization, placing Nicholas I among the enlightened European monarchs, exhausting the primary sources available in the United States, and ultimately arriving at the conclusion that still holds true thirty years later, in light of the thousands of newly available documents: Nicholas I did not intend to baptize the Jews through conscription; rather, he intended to integrate them into the larger Russian culture by "standardizing them through the military."[11] Yet, even if Nicholas I's intentions had become transparent when studied in context, Russian primary sources were required to describe Jewish experience in the army. Lacking these, Stanislawski drew heavily upon available Jewish narratives, according to which a Jew serving under Nicholas I had little alternative to converting to Christianity. Most recent English- and Hebrew-language books about Jews in the Russian army further elaborated this view. Its power is so pervasive that students of Russian Jewry working in Russia with access to archives were scandalized by a dissenting opinion. Indeed, their bias stemmed from a parochial community-focused approach to the Jewish conscription.[12]

This book seeks to further demythologize traditional historical narratives, drawing upon the writings of John Klier and other colleagues who described the

---

[11] Michael Stanislawski, *Tsar Nicholas I and the Jews* (Philadelphia: Jewish Publication Society of America, 1983), 15.

[12] See, for example, critical reviews of my Russian-language monograph on the Jews and the Russian army, such as Aleksandr Lokshin, *Ab Imperio*, no. 4 (2003): 659–666; Valerii Dymshits, "Igra v soldatiki," *Narod knigi v mire knig*, no. 2 (2004): 9–11; Mark Shteinberg, "Chto zhe delali evrei v russkoi armii?" *Mezhdunarodnaia evreiskaia gazeta*, no. 49 (2003). Some of the suggestions in these (and other) reviews convinced me to include in the English book a comparative account of Jewish combat performance and Jewish military acculturation.

Jewish encounter with the Russian military. Although this volume refutes Klier's assumption that Nicholas I "envisioned military service as an assault upon the religious beliefs of the Jews," it corroborates and elaborates upon other of his findings. Klier correctly claimed that raw statistics provide an indispensable source for a nuanced understanding of Russian Jewish conversion, and that the Russian Orthodox Church was reluctant to perform such conversions.[13] He also asserted that the large number of Jewish minors drafted, while a moral burden to their communities, was not the consequence of a criminal decision by the regime. *Jews in the Russian Army* concurs with Klier that, from the inception of the Great Reforms, Jewish conscription precipitated a perennial argument over Jewish emancipation between the Jewish enlightened leadership and Russian Judeophobes.[14] This study maintains that, until 1917, Russian Jews increasingly supported the imperial army. Their patriotism was evinced by the disproportionately large number of Jewish recruits, who proved their civic responsibility and their eligibility for full Russian citizenship. At the same time, Russia's conservative social institutions and her military hierarchy propagated the myth of Jewish draft dodging, primarily to forestall any discussion of Jewish civic equality. Consequently, Jewish soldiers became a central focus of the integrationist agenda; debate as to whether or not the Jews deserved the Russian version of modernity raged across the entire Russian political spectrum.

Benjamin Nathans undertook another significant step toward understanding the role of the military in modernizing the Russian Jewish political discourse. Although the army was not the focus of his groundbreaking research on Jews living outside the Pale of Settlement (that is to say, the most acculturated, integrated, and imperialized Russian Jews), Nathans made a number of observations that assist in demythologizing the encounter between Jews and the Russian army. He demonstrated the extent to which military service was part of Russian Jewish emancipation. Jewish deputies (*shtadlans*) in the capital spared no effort in convincing the authorities that Jews who completed military service should be accorded permission to settle outside the Pale of Settlement. Military authorities maintained that the empire's civil regulations should not affect Jews in the military or reserve soldiers. These and other observations of Nathans confirm that the military saw itself as a separate entity, with its own laws; that Jewish soldiers who finished their service (including the cantonists) became thoroughly Russified while still retaining their Jewish identity; and that restoring the imperial context corrects some misleading assumptions upon which previous scholarship had rested. *Jews in the Russian Army* further develops these ideas, demonstrating that, in a country as vast as Russia,

---

[13] John Klier, "State Policies and the Conversion of Jews in Imperial Russia," in Robert P. Gerachi and Michael Khodarkovsky, eds., *Of Religion and Empire: Missions, Conversion, and Tolerance in Tsarist Russia* (Ithaca and London: Cornell University Press, 2001), 93–112.

[14] John Klier, *Imperial Russia's Jewish Question, 1855–1881* (Cambridge: Cambridge University Press, 1995), 332–349 (Chapter 14, "Dead souls: Jews and the military reform of 1874").

permission to settle outside the Pale became the center of a debate in St. Petersburg, solved by the local administration and by military authorities elsewhere. Nineteenth-century Russian history was imperial but not homogeneous: local histories and grassroots reconstruction provide a more nuanced vision of Russian realities.

Unlike its Russian version, the present English edition virtually excludes literary references, and dispenses with a separate discussion of the image of the Jewish soldier in Russian Jewish literary discourse; Olga Litvak, in her monograph on the literary responses to conscription, has substantially addressed this topic.[15] Litvak explored the many traditional Jewish myths that shaped the portrayal of Jewish recruits in Hebrew, Yiddish, and Russian belles lettres. She represented the military experience in Russian Jewish discourse as a tension "between the ideological embrace of modernity and persistent anxiety about its disruptive social effects." Her approach suggested a promising prospect of exploring the Jewish encounter with the Russian army using the method of social imaginary – something that still remains a scholarly desideratum. It is particularly instructive that, as Litvak noted, the images of Jewish soldiers "mobilize the meaning of exile" in the Jewish imagination, not only for Jewish lay readers but also for Jewish historians of the early twentieth century.

Like Litvak's monograph, an extensive essay by Mordechai Zalkin shed light on yet other feedback to conscription: that of the rabbinic leadership.[16] Zalkin assembled a wide array of literary sources, rabbinic responsa and correspondence, memoirs, nineteenth-century Jewish historiography, and articles in the contemporary Yiddish and Hebrew press in order to reconstruct a complex, but by no means homogeneous, perception of the Jewish conscription by East European rabbis, including Hasidic. Although Zalkin's emphasis was on the contemporary criticism of the elitist approach of rabbinic leadership to the praxis of the draft, he pointed out the existing – and unbridgeable – gap between the grassroots reality of the conscription and the *halakhic* (related to Judaic Law) debates about "whom to have drafted." Zalkin is quite right assuming that in most cases East European rabbis, with all their good intentions, could not influence the communal decisions to exempt members of financial and intellectual elite from the conscription; as a result, the draftees came from poor families. However, both Litvak's and Zalkin's musings about "social effects" and "reality" need a much better comparative perspective and broader historical, social, military, and cultural context – exactly what *Jews in the Russian Army* seeks to recreate.

---

[15] Olga Litvak, *Conscription and the Search for Modern Russian Jewry* (Bloomington: Indiana University Press, 2006), cf. Petrovsky-Shtern, *Evrei v russkoi armii*, 357–413.

[16] Mordechai Zalkin, "Bein 'bnei elohim' li-'vnei adam': rabanim, behurei yeshivot ve-ha-giyus la-tsava ha-rusi ba-me'ah ha-19," in Bar-Levav, Avriel, ed., *Shalom u-milhamah ba-tarbut ha-yehudit* (Jerusalem: Zalman Shazar, 2006), 165–222.

Drafting European Jews

One of the key tools in the creation of modern European empires was the social transformation engendered by military service. The need to convert tolerated subjects into loyal citizens engaged in the defense of a state with which they had come to identify loomed large in the state-making agendas of European monarchs, ranging from Joseph II and Nicholas I to Napoleon and Friedrich Wilhelm III. They viewed military duty as a means of recasting feudal state members of disparate social, ethnic, or religious groups into the empire's mold. Standardizing the empire started with the standardization of loyalties. The military draft realized a multifaceted agenda: it replaced any loyalties to a corporate group with loyalty to the state and its institutions; it provided military training, enabling the troops to fight more effectively than did the mercenaries; it exerted control over the various groups who comprised the draft population; and it forged a military-based process of citizenship and state-building.

The state administrations asserted that the readiness of individuals to perform military duty manifested their loyalty and their preparedness for citizenship. Although making Jews useful was a top priority of various European programs for what French enlightened politicians called the regeneration of the Jews, the utilitarian agenda was not the only driving force behind their conscription. Sometimes Jews found themselves included in the draft pool because of a ruler's political or philosophical convictions, such as his devotion to the *Polizeistaat* (well-managed state) concept or to an Enlightenment agenda, rather than for practical reasons. In Austria, for example, Joseph II decided to draft Jews against the advice of his war ministry; his radical ideology prevailed over his pragmatism. He argued that "[a] Jew 'as a man and as a fellow-citizen' had duties that could not be palmed off, duties he was obligated to perform in person."[17]

Ten years before the French National Assembly concluded that the army was the ideal institution for promoting good citizenship, Joseph II resolved that military service was a pivotal crucible for forging useful subjects. Jews, seen through the prism of Enlightenment as nonproductive, if not parasitic, would have to undergo cultural Germanization, legal unification, and militarization. These three measures were crucial in transforming the Jews of Austria, devoted to their corporate groups, communities, and territory, into Habsburg Jews. Joseph's resolution to draft his Jewish subjects conformed to the utilitarian goals stated in his 1782 Edict of Tolerance, and resulted largely from his discovery that the partition of Poland had doubled his country's Jewish population. In 1788, he ordered the conscription of Jews, allowing their enlistment into the transportation and artillery corps as drivers and auxiliaries. In

---

[17] See Michael Silber, "From Tolerated Aliens to Citizen-Soldiers: Jewish Military Service in the Era of Joseph II," in Pieter M. Judson and Marsha L. Rozenblit, eds., *Constructing Nationalities in East Central Europe* (New York: Berghann Books, 2005), 19–36, here 25–26.

1789, the imperial administration extended obligatory military service first to traditional-minded Galician Jewry and then to Jews in the entire Austrian empire, who enrolled in the infantry.

Between 1790 and 1806, as Joseph's successor curtailed the enlightened Jewish policy, the war ministry allowed Jews to replace conscripts with ransom. But, with the campaign against Napoleon, Jews once again found themselves in the conscription pool. In Austria, some 36,200 Jews entered active service during the second decade of the nineteenth century. This number more than ten times exceeded the number of East European Jews to whom Russia extended the draft ten years later. Although the military bureaucracy rejected the idea of organizing Jewish conscripts into a single army unit to facilitate the observance of their religious rites, it did allow some important concessions. For instance, it commissioned new uniforms, manufactured so as to satisfy the requirements of the biblical laws of *sha'atnez*, which prohibited the interweaving of flax and wool.[18] The rabbinical leadership grudgingly supported the new social demands upon their brethren: Rabbi Ezekiel Landau of Prague praised Jewish obedience to the state, while Rabbi Ishmael Cohen, in his *Zerah Emet* collection of responsa, permitted the Jews of Mantova (which was then Austrian territory) to bear arms on the Sabbath.[19]

Perhaps as early as 1802, and certainly by 1815, the Austrian War Council allowed Jewish army privates to become officers. In 1825, it accepted Jewish doctors into the military at the officer rank. At the same time, it severely limited Jewish upward mobility in the territorial reserve and judicial corps. Before the formal emancipation of Austro-Hungarian Jews, in the 1850s–1860s, there were between 10,000 and 20,000 Jewish regular troops participating in military campaigns. Some of them, like Karl Strass of Bohemia, volunteered for a light infantry regiment. In 1849, at the age of twenty-one, he became the first Jewish lieutenant in the emperor's Hungarian hussar regiment.[20] Thanks to the emancipation of 1867, Austrian Jews liberated themselves from the last vestiges of medieval inequality. Grateful to the emperor, they welcomed the introduction of universal conscription. After 1867, the number of Jews in the army grew rapidly, reaching 60,000 in 1902, which constituted 4 percent of the army: a

---

[18] See Deut. 22: 11, and *Shulkhan Arukh*, Yoreh Deah 299: 4.

[19] See Lois C. Dubin, *The Port Jews of Habsburg Trieste: Absolutist Politics and Enlightenment Culture* (Stanford, Calif.: Stanford University Press, 1999), 149, and Shlomo See Simonsohn, *History of the Jews in the Duchy of Mantova* (Jerusalem: Kiryat Sefer, 1977), 96, n. 304. Significantly, the greater the level of Jewish acculturation, the more they were willing to serve in the military. Thus, Mantua and Trieste (ironically, both communities exempt from the conscription) supported the idea of obligatory Jewish service, whereas Galician Jews protested. See Simonsohn, *Jews in the Duchy of Mantova*, 475, n. 501. The letter of the Trieste Jewish community supporting the new civic duty as the way to teach Jews to "love labor and hate idleness" influenced the perception of Jewish military service among Jews in German-speaking lands. See Dubin, *The Port Jews*, 150–151.

[20] On his career, see István Deák, *Jewish Soldiers in Austro-Hungarian Society: Leo Baeck Memorial Lecture*, no. 34 (New York: Leo Baeck Institute, 1990), 8–9.

rather high figure, considering that Jews in toto comprised 4.5 percent of the overall population of the empire.

Jews made full use of every opportunity granted to them in the military to explore upward mobility. About 70 percent of the Jewish officers served in the infantry, while four Jewish medical officers attained the rank of army generals. Some twenty-three Jews became generals before 1911. Fourteen of them converted, for personal rather than career reasons. However, Major General Eduard von Schweitzer, who, at the peak of his career commanded an infantry brigade, remained a Jew.[21] Austrian military authorities vehemently defended the honor of Austrian officers, regardless of their religious persuasion. To reject a Jewish officer's challenge to a duel was an act unbecoming of an officer; an Austrian soldier who repudiated a Jewish colleague on racial grounds bore severe consequences and could lose his rank. The military also respected the spiritual needs of the cadre. As in the United States of America, Austrians, in 1866, endorsed Jewish chaplains. Before World War I, there were 178 career and 244 reserve Jewish chaplains. However, unlike France, Austria routinely excluded Jews from its General Staff. After 1914, some 320,000 Jewish soldiers participated in the Great War, sharing in the patriotic fervor of their Austro-Hungarian brethren. During World War I, Austria commissioned approximately 25,000 Jews as officers. Some of these Austrian Jewish officers, such as General Alexander von Eiss, became fervent Zionists and others, like Wolfgang von Weisl, became active in the Israeli army after the establishment of the Jewish state.[22] The loyalty to the military of grateful Habsburg Jews deeply penetrated the European cultural memory. One modern British author portrayed a group of soldiers from the Czech Corps in a forsaken Siberian town during the Russian Civil War under the command of a Lieutenant Joseph Mutz, a rational, pragmatic, and loyal Habsburg Jew with an allegiance to the new national military.[23]

[21] Jewish soldiers comprised 3 percent of the rank and file in the army, while (in 1897) the career military officials comprised about 12.7 percent of the total. At the same time, Jews constituted 18.7 percent of all reserve officers, "many more times than the proportion of Jews in the monarchy." The decline of these numbers by 1911 (although the number of Jewish officers in the army remained high) was the result of the decline of the overall Jewish population in the empire and of the rampant antisemitism from which even the Austrian military was not immune. See István Deák, *Beyond Nationalism: A Social and Political History of the Habsburg Officer Corps, 1848–1918* (New York and Oxford: Oxford University Press, 1990), 133, 171, 174–178 and idem., *Jewish Soldiers*, 11–16.

[22] Erwin A. Schmidl, "Jews in the Austro-Hungarian Armed Forces," in Stephen Fischer-Galati and Béla K. Király, eds., *Essays on War and Society in East Central Europe, 1740–1920* (Boulder, Colo.: Social Science Monographs; New York: distributed by Columbia University and Columbia University Press, 1987), 69–84. After the demise of the Austrian empire, the successor states abandoned tolerant policies toward Jewish officers in the military. István Deák, *Jewish Soldiers*, 23–24.

[23] James Meek, *The People's Act of Love: A Novel* (Toronto, Edinburgh, and New York: HarperCollins, 2005), 36–58.

Taking the Austrian Jewish experiment as a point of departure, enlightened French politicians declared that military service was a sine qua non precondition for the civil Jewish equality. (The notion of "emancipation," coined by Wilhelm Traugott Krug, became a buzzword only much later, in the late 1820s). Abbé Grégoire argued before the French National Assembly that contemporary Jews retained the seed of valor, since they descended from the Old Hebrews and therefore, once again, could become good soldiers. He asked rhetorically, "If I can make a husbandman of a Jew, why could I not make him a soldier?"[24] Revolutionary French society viewed the army as a school of citizenship, in which soldier-citizens had to accept stoically the reduction of their rights, become true champions of liberty and fraternity, and be ready to sacrifice their lives for the sake of the nation.[25]

Immediately after the Revolution, the more acculturated Sephardic Jews from Paris and southern France joined the National Guard. However, the more traditional and less integrated Ashkenazic Jews from Alsace resisted the imposition of this duty, and obtained exemption.[26] In the mid-1810s, the Grand Sanhedrin, convened by Napoleon Bonaparte to endorse his plan of enforced Jewish assimilation, argued for conscription and declared all Jews in the army exempt from religious and dietary observances; Jewish soldiers fulfilled the commandment to defend the state; hence, they were free from the obligation to fulfill other commandments. Following the 1808 Napoleonic decree that forbade the replacement of Jews with non-Jews and, as happened in Austria, made military service obligatory, the Jewish presence in the Napoleonic army was in direct proportion to their number in society at large.

Initially, all Jews were placed in a separate battalion, called the Corps Israelite, which the military expanded into a regiment. This was disbanded in 1810, after which Jews were transferred into the First light infantry regiment.[27] The Consistoires, the French Jewish umbrella institutions under state administration, used the network of communal rabbinical leaders to impress upon Jews the importance of French patriotism and of their sacred duty to perform

[24] For Abbé Grégoire's stance on military issues, see Ronald Schechter, *Obstinate Hebrews: Representation of Jews in France, 1715–1815* (Berkeley: University of California Press, 2003), 92.
[25] See a fundamental theoretical discussion in Jean-Paul Bertaud, "The Revolutionary Role of the Army: To Regenerate Man, to Form a Citizen, a Model for Civil Society?" in George Levitine, ed., *Culture and Revolution: Cultural Ramifications of the French Revolution* (College Park: University of Maryland at College Park, 1989), 18–39. The army draft and the process of naturalization/emancipation of Jews went hand-in-hand in the twentieth century, as well. For instance, the early years of the second decade of the twentieth century saw debates over the draft of refugee Russian Jews into the British army as part of the British naturalization process. See Eugene C. Black, *The Social Politics of Anglo-Jewry, 1880–1920* (New York: Basil Blackwell, 1988), 374–377, and Harold Shukman, *War or Revolution: Russian Jews and Conscription in Britain, 1917* (London and Portland, Oreg.: Valentine Mitchell, 2006), 6–8.
[26] Schechter, *Obstinate Hebrews*, 172–173, and documentary evidence he assembles in n. 42 (p. 284).
[27] John R. Elting, *Swords around a Throne: Napoleon's Grande Armée* (New York: Da Capo Press, 1997), 189, 325.

military service. Simultaneously, France allowed its Jews unrestricted upward mobility, equal to that of its other citizens. This strategy appears to have succeeded; a military career became a fad among French Jews. Indeed, disproportionate numbers of Jews joined the army, attempting to assimilate into the upper echelons of state bureaucracy and to join the imperial elite. During the Third Republic, the French army boasted about twenty-five Jewish generals in active service.[28] Born amid the fervor of the French Revolution, the idea of a citizen-soldier influenced many a French Jew, including young Alfred Dreyfus. Inspired by genuine French patriotism, he chose to join the army, the "school of duty and honor."[29] As in Austria, the loyalty of French Jews was duly noted by other Europeans; a popular Spanish writer portrayed Robert, a brave cavalryman in Napoleon's Grande Armée, passionately devoted to his emperor, and disguising the fact that he was actually Yossel Dorfman from Haguenau.[30]

As the Revolution unfolded in France, the French- and Austrian-controlled provinces of Italy saw their Jews debate the parameters of their service in the Guardia Civica, in light of their traditional observance and of their new political loyalties.[31] As elsewhere in Europe, after becoming fully emancipated in 1848, these Jews experienced a patriotic reawakening: 235 of them volunteered for the Sardinian and Piedmont armies. The forty-five Jews in Venice's Toscana battalion appointed two commanders, Treves and Levy, both of Jewish origin. In Florence, Captain Bacevi, a Jew, took command of the local Guardia Nazionale. Even before their emancipation, Jews volunteered in the militant underground Carbonari as early as 1820, while, in 1859, about 113 Jewish volunteers joined the Bersaglieri. Roughly 260 Jewish volunteers participated in the 1859–1860 Risorgimento campaign. The introduction of civil equality turned many Jews into patriots of the evolving nation-state: 127 Jewish soldiers fought under Garibaldi at Naples in 1860, and 236 of them entered Rome with the Royal Italian Army in 1870.

[28] See Paula Hyman, *The Jews of Modern France* (Berkeley: University of California Press, 1998), 44–45, 94.

[29] See Martin P. Johnson, *The Dreyfus Affair: Honour and Politics in the Belle Époque* (New York: St. Martin's Press, 1999), 20–21. The alleged French military antisemitism may not have been the reason for the Dreyfus affair. At any rate, it is obvious that Dreyfus was able to circumvent those who objected to a Jew on the General Staff; by deliberately lowering his qualifying grades, he managed to become a General Staff captain without having to convert. See Jean-Denis Bredin, *The Affair: The Case of Alfred Dreyfus*, trans. Jerry Mehlman (New York: George Braziller, 1986), 19–22. For the best revision of the Dreyfus case that convincingly proves a link to the counter-intelligence intrigue designed to cover groundbreaking French technological advances, see Robert Elliot Kaplan, "Making Sense of the Rennes Verdict: The Military Dimension of the Dreyfus Affair," *Journal of Contemporary History*, vol. 34, no. 4 (1999): 499–515.

[30] Antonio Benitez Rojo, *Mujer en traje de la batalla* (Madrid: Alfaguara, 2001), 81–85.

[31] See Shlomo Simonson, "Teguvot ahadot shel yehudey italiya al 'ha-emantsipatsiya ha-rishonah,'" in *Italia judaica: gli ebrei in Italia dalla segregazione alla prima emancipazione: atti del III convegno internazionale* (Rome: Ministerio per i beni culturali e ambientali, 1989), 47–68; for a discussion of the dichotomy "loyalty vs. observance" see ibid., 57–58.

In Italy, as in Austria and France, Jewish faith did not present any obstacle to promotion. In 1895, the Italian army enlisted 104 Jewish lieutenants, 42 captains, 8 majors, 2 colonels (Teodoro Debenedetti and Giacomo Segre), and 1 general. This general, Giuseppe Ottolenghi, graduated from Turin Military Academy; he participated in the 1859–1860 military campaign; received distinguished military decorations in 1864 and 1866; became the commander of the Turin Division in 1895; served as a war minister between 1902 and 1904; and, in 1903, obtained the rank of commander of the First Army Corps. Affluent Italian Jews considered it an honor to serve in the army. This value was typified by the noted Italian industrialist Federico Jarach, who graduated from the Naval Academy as a *guardiamarina*, and later served during the Italian-Turkish war of 1912 as the captain of an escort vessel. Italy's complete emancipation of this ethnic minority ignited the patriotic and military imagination of its Jews. At the turn of the nineteenth century, the proportion of Jews in the army was seventeen times greater than that in the general population. The Italian army accorded Jews the same unrestricted access to office and rank as they enjoyed in other facets of society, while at the same time they were able to retain their traditions.[32]

The Enlightenment informed not only the empires' approach toward the militarization of their ethnic minorities, but also their notion of the rank-and-file soldier. After the disastrous defeat of the Prussian troops at Jena, Gerhard Johann David von Scharnhorst, who eventually became the chief of Prussian General Staff, elaborated the concept of the "enlightened soldier" that reshaped the Prussian army, rendering it capable of defeating Napoleon's army relatively quickly. Prussia needed a new soldier, a loyal subject serving *Gott, Kaiser und Vaterland* – God, Monarch, and Fatherland. Scharnhorst argued that only *Bildung* – Enlightenment and education – could forge a new, thinking soldier, a conscientious, self-sacrificing patriot, whom he regarded as the foundation of the developing Prussian social order. Scharnhorst maintained that the army was an institution for the integration and mobilization of society into a new, hierarchical political entity: the sacred Prussian empire.[33] Like the rest of the Prussian population, the Jews were subjected to Scharnhorst's plan, which combined Enlightenment ideology, the modernization of the state, and the militarization of society.

---

[32] Salvatore Foà, *Gli ebrei nel Risorgimento italiano* (Assisi and Rome: Carucci, 1978), esp. 30–31, 51; Ilaria Pacan, *Il Comandante: la vita di Federico Jarach e la memoria di un'epoca, 1874–1951* (Milano: Proedi, 2001); see the letters Jarach wrote home while in the navy, ibid., 45–52; Alberto Rovighi, *I militari di origine ebraica nel primo secolo di vita dello stato italiano* (Rome: Stato maggiore dell'esercito, Ufficio storico, 1999), 14–15.

[33] See Charles Edward White, *The Enlightened Soldier: Scharnhorst and the Militärische Gesellschaft in Berlin, 1801–1815* (New York: Praeger, 1989), xii–iv, 56–86, 122–123. It is hard to believe that an admirer of the Prussian military such as Nicholas I was not familiar with his revolutionary ideas. The impact of the new military ideas of Klausevitz and Scharnhorst upon Nicholas is mentioned in Carl Van Dyke, *Russian Imperial Military Doctrine and Education, 1832–1914* (New York: Greenwood Press 1990), xiv.

The 1813 edict ushered in a new stage of Prussian emancipation, making newly introduced Jewish social freedoms contingent upon military duty. The determination of Friedrich Wilhelm III (who eventually became the father-in-law of Nicholas I) to make all Jews useful to the state was manifest in the exemption from military service of Jewish industrial entrepreneurs and merchants in Berlin, Breslau, and Potsdam. Exactly as in Austria, no specific regulation concerning Jewish military duty initially was introduced, but the kaiser himself decided upon a Jewish military draft. A statute to this effect was adopted only in 1815, when there already were hundreds of Jewish soldiers in the Prussian army. The 1813 edict generated Jewish-German patriotism; synagogue boards in towns such as Breslau commemorated the edict's first anniversary by organizing a party for new Jewish recruits. In Silesia, the communal leaders addressed the Jewish volunteers, praising the "holiness of the [soldier's] profession" and proclaiming the imminence of a war for "the King and the Fatherland." In Königsberg, a local rabbi called upon Jewish volunteers to sacrifice their "blood and possessions for our Fatherland." In addition to the 170 Jews who joined the draft after the publication, in 1812, of Edict no. 16, regarding the establishment of the *Jäger* regiments, about 561 volunteered and fought in the 1813–1816 campaign. More than half of these troops served in the infantry, while about 10 percent were in the cavalry. Significantly, the ratio of Jewish soldiers (731) to the Prussian Jewish population was greater than the average ratio of Jews among Prussians. Perhaps the nexus between civil equality and military duty had an invigorating effect; approximately eighty of the first Prussian Jewish soldiers were decorated, and forty promoted. In his 1814 catechism, Herz Homberg, one of the most radical German Jewish reformers, preached that the battlefield exempted Jews from religious observance and that there was no higher duty than service to the state, even if it required the violation of Jewish law.[34]

Jews in the Prussian military could not become officers; the Main Staff decreed that Jews should not command Christian soldiers. Later in the nineteenth century, the Russian Main Staff arrived at the same conclusion, for the same reason. With the exception of Meno Burg (1789–1853), Germany had no Jewish officers until 1914. Burg, in recognition of his excellent service, enjoyed the benevolence of a high-ranking German military bureaucrat, and became an artillery captain in 1832. The military ordered a differently colored uniform for him, to distinguish him from the Christian artillery officers.[35] Yet the emancipation of Prussian Jews, however partial, signified more to them than an officer's insignia; Prussia could never complain of a lack of Jewish soldiers eager to fight and die for their German *Vaterland*. In 1827, the standing army

---

[34] Horst Fischer, *Judentum, Staat und Heer in Preussen im frühen 19. Jahrhundert: Zur Geschichte der staatlichen Judenpolitik* (Tübinger: J. C. B. Mohr, 1968), 32–41.

[35] Michael Meyer, ed., *German-Jewish History in Modern Times*. In 4 vols. (New York: Columbia University Press, 1997), 3:259–261. For a detailed description of Meno Burg's military career, see Fischer, *Judentum, Staat und Heer*, 127–130.

comprised some 1,346 Jewish soldiers. Roughly 4,700 Jewish soldiers fought in the 1870–1871 Franco-Prussian War, 483 of whom perished or were wounded. After 1880, about 25,000–30,000 Jewish volunteers joined the ranks annually, for a one-year term of service. This number does not include those who were drafted. Between twelve and fifteen hundred Jews converted to Christianity in order to enhance their army careers.[36] Walther Rathenau, who eventually became the German foreign minister, felt particularly humiliated as a "second-rate citizen" when he was denied an officer's commission, and instead was discharged as a "lowly lance corporal."[37] Out of 30,000 Jews trained for the officer rank between 1885 and 1914, none received promotion. However, during the Great War, pragmatic considerations finally outweighed ideology, and the German military agreed to grant the Jews officers' commissions. In contrast, the Russian military resisted doing so until the empire's collapse. During World War I, German Jews were as patriotic as their fellow country-men; 100,000 of them fought in the German army between 1914 and 1918, and 12,000 perished at the front.[38]

Austria, France, Prussia, and Italy, not to mention the United States, offered their Jews various modernization packages, each of which presupposed military duty. As we will see in due course, Russia's reasons for drafting Jews into the army were similar to those of enlightened European monarchs. Yet Jewish historians preferred stressing the coercive and brutal nature of Russian military service while ignoring its modernizing European context and overlooking its integrating effect.

The Russian context, like the European one, clarifies many aspects of Jews' military draft. Jews served under virtually the same conditions as did other groups in the Russian empire; twenty-five years of service were not specifically a draconian anti-Jewish measure. None of the groups represented in the Russian conscription pool enjoyed civil freedoms; unemancipated Jews fulfilled their duty along with the unemancipated peasants who comprised more than 80 percent of the troops, and with colonized Poles who, especially after the 1830 Polish rebellion, were also forced into the Russian army. This volume argues that the legislation was neither impartial nor particularly cruel toward the Jews. After the Napoleonic Wars, the regime conducted a thorough administrative reform of the military, resulting in an expansion of the draft pool. Furthermore, Jews who served in the army of Nicholas I became part of what Benjamin Nathans referred to as the "selective integration." The draft effected a partial integration of the Jews, but only of those Jews who completed their terms of active service.

---

[36] *Ein Stuck von uns: deutsche Juden in deutsche Armeen 1813–1976: e. Dokumentation* (Mainz: v. Hase und Koehler, 1977), 27–28, 34–38.

[37] Amos Elon, *The Pity of It All: A History of Jews in Germany, 1743–1933* (New York: Henry Holt, 2002), 234.

[38] Israel Schwierz, *Für das Vaterland starben: Denkmäler und Gedenktafeln für jüdische Soldaten in Thüringen: Dokumentation* (Aschaffenburg/Main: Krem-Bardischewski, 1996), 18.

This volume investigates how the army fulfilled its mission to transform Jewish soldiers into physically fit, loyal, Russian-speaking citizens, accessing for some of them the economic and residential privileges unavailable to most of their Pale of Settlement brethren. It appears that the Jewish reserve soldiers already enjoyed, in the first half of the century, some of the elements of civil freedom granted to their co-religionists only later in the century, with the advent of educational and political reform, if not with the collapse of the regime. For the majority of East European Jews, only the abolition of the Pale of Settlement was coterminous with full emancipation, the epitome of Jewish modernization. Whether Russia drafted her Jews into modernity is the issue this study seeks to solve – as it tries to clarify the very specificity of Russian imperial modernization and its implications regarding Russia's Jews.

To avoid addressing, for the moment, the complex question of whether late imperial Russia was a premodern, early modern, or modern empire, *Jews in the Russian Army* regards modernity as a vantage point; it is an epistemological view of nineteenth-century Russia, rather than an immediate Russian onto-logical reality. To paraphrase Rogers Brubaker, modernity emerges from this book as a perspective on the world rather than as a reality in the world.[39] Although the abuse of the term has thoroughly blurred its meaning, this study perceives modernity as the capacity of a state to transform its elements, whether economic and technological patterns, political structures, legal institutions, social and religious groups, or individuals. Historians have proved that imperial Russia displayed an unusual capacity to imitate and emulate Western mod-ernization patterns. Russia emancipated its peasantry, introduced universal liability to conscription, implemented court reform, and created an industri-alized economy. Yet the empire also manifested a no less remarkable inability adequately to respond to the changes produced by its policies. Therefore one has to ask not only whether Jews became patriots for the Slavic cause but also whether Russia became the protector of her Jewish subjects.

Grappling with the Sources

Natan Eidelman once observed that historians would not have been able to reconstruct the nineteenth-century Russian past were it not for the Third Department of His Imperial Majesty's Chancellery, the imperial secret police, with its network of informers and its diligently amassed denunciations. By the same token, Jewish social historians would not have been able to reconstruct the details of Jewish army service if not for the bias and bigotry of the state administration. Suspicious of Jews, the regime generated a formidable body of military documents, scrutinizing this group far more systematically than it did any other religious or ethnic minority. *Jews in the Russian Army* relies heavily

---

[39] Rogers Brubaker, *Ethnicity without Groups* (Cambridge, Mass.: Harvard University Press, 2004), 79.

upon these Russian military archival documents, assesses them cautiously and critically, and balances them against external Russian and Jewish evidence.

The profusion of reports found in Russian military and state archives concerning Jewish recruits and the scarcity of similar reports about soldiers drafted from other ethnic groups appears to challenge any notion of Russian army service as a homogenizing effort. There were many ethnicities in the empire – and in the army – that were treated differently. One may even maintain that in comparison with the *inorodtsy* (people of alien, non-Christian beliefs) and most Muslims exempt from conscription, drafted Jews were in a better position as an ethnicity more desirable for integration into the empire. If Nicholas I, an enlightened monarch, sought to equate Jews with others, surely there would have been no need to so assiduously monitor, control, and report the behavior of Jewish soldiers. The archival evidence demonstrates that the military intended to follow the letter of imperial law, to take charge of the social engineering program targeting regeneration of the Jews, and to establish Jews on the same footing in the army as other enlisted personnel. This project's autocratic methods contravened its ostensibly enlightened spirit. The administration was quite content to send Jews into the army to make Russians of them, and then bombard the regiments and battalions with inquiries as to how profoundly Russian the Jewish recruits had become. Available data on Jewish military service reflects a continual conflict between regimental commanders and state officials; the latter commissioned the former to monitor Jewish soldiers in a manner that was not consonant with normal army protocol. Regimental commanders received orders to report the baptisms of Jewish soldiers in the 1830s to 1850s and, after 1874, to record Jewish population distribution and performance in the army. Whether or not the Jews were a burden upon the Russian military remains undetermined, although certainly the sheer quantity of commissioned reports was vexatious to the low-ranking and underpaid regimental clerks. The documents they prepared reflected not only the situation on the ground and grassroots attitudes toward Jewish soldiers, but also local military response to the imperial administration's annoying inquiries, and the latter's indignation that local commanders had misunderstood the government's intentions.

Military documents, especially data reports, reveal an unexpected dichotomy: while the army was part of the regime insofar as it served the autocracy rather than society, its interests did not necessarily coincide with those of the state. This study demonstrates the clashes in mentality between the imperial administration and the army. Historians have often failed to discern the Russian army's complex nature; in certain respects, the military displayed a commonality with society. The assembled Jewish data is testimony to an imperial ideology that initially patronized ethnic soldiers but that, by the end of the old regime, had grown increasingly xenophobic. The mere fact of the data's existence discloses the regime's bias, bigotry, and suspicion. Nevertheless, the substance of the reports, the analysis they furnished, and the insights they offered evinced the army's painstaking and often unbiased effort to gather and systematize the information. These reports therefore are deserving of scrutiny. The untrained and underpaid regimental clerks lacked the skill and sophistication to forge data or to mislead authorities;[40] when they tried to do so, their mistakes were so ill considered and transparent that Nicholas I immediately detected them, making angry notes in the margins.

Reliable statistical research was an unfamiliar concept in that epoch. Nicholas I stipulated that reports be dispatched to him directly, and he carefully read and corrected them. Virtually no one outside the restricted circle of high state bureaucrats had access to this data; before 1856, military statistics circulated exclusively internally. Access to military statistics was among the major achievements of Alexander II's Great Reforms.[41] The War Ministry of the 1870s considered two groups of military reforms: those that increased the military's financial efficiency and those that facilitated the collection of data.[42] Any discussion of statistics was distinctly political in character, apparently part of the public debate on Russian liberalism.[43] Post-reform Russia knew two kinds of military data: internal and external. Regarding Jews, the army and the War Ministry generated the first, while the Ministry of Interior produced the second. The internal army data, relating the numbers and characteristics of Jewish soldiers, sometimes found its way into the press, to the War Ministry's daily, *Russkii invalid*, although in partial and irregular fashion; it appeared more often in thick, scholarly journals such as *Voennyi sbornik*, *Voenno-statisticheskii sbornik*, and *Voenno-meditsinskii zhurnal*. Yet these reports had

---

[40] On the weakness of the Russian bureaucracy and its inability to think independently, see Marc Raeff, *Political Ideas and Institutions in Imperial Russia* (Boulder, Colo.: Westview Press, 1994), 76–87.

[41] For military reforms in the times of Alexander II, see Dietrich Beyrau, *Militär und Gesellschaft in Vorrevolutionären Russland* (Cologne: Bohlau Verlag, 1984), 254–308; W. Bruce Lincoln, *The Great Reforms: Autocracy, Bureaucracy, and the Politics of Change in Imperial Russia* (DeKalb: Northern Illinois University Press, 1990), 143–158; John L. Keep, *Soldiers of the Tsar: Army and Society in Russia, 1562–1874* (Oxford: Clarendon Press, 1985), 351–381; John D. Klier, "Dead souls: Jews and the military reform of 1874," in his *Imperial Russia's Jewish Question*, 332–349; Bruce W. Menning, *Bayonets before Bullets: The Imperial Russian Army, 1861–1914* (Bloomington: Indiana University Press, 1992), 6–50; Forest A. Miller, *Dmitrii Miliutin and the Reform Era in Russia* (Nashville, Tenn.: Vanderbilt University Press, 1968); Jacob Kipp, "The Grand Duke Konstantin Nikolaevich and the Epoch of the Great Reforms, 1855–1866," (Ph.D. diss., Pennsylvania State University, 1970); L. Beskrovnyi, *Russkaia armiia i flot v deviatnadtsatom veke. Voenno-ekonomicheskii potentsial Rossii* (M.: Nauka, 1973); P. Zaionchkovskii, *Voennye reformy 1860–1870 godov v Rossii* (M.: MGU, 1952); A. V. Fedorov, *Russkaia armiia v 50–70-kh gg. XIX veka* (L.: n. p., 1959).

[42] See David Rich, "Imperialism, Reform and Strategy: Russian Military Statistics, 1840–1890," *SEER*, no. 4 (1996): 636–637.

[43] On the paradoxical destiny of Russian liberalism, see Dietrich Geyer, *Russian Imperialism: The Interaction of Domestic and Foreign Policy, 1860–1914* (New Haven and London: Yale University Press, 1987), 17–32; W. Bruce Lincoln, *Nikolai Miliutin, an Enlightened Russian Bureaucrat* (Newtonville, Mass.: Oriental Research Partners, 1977), 101–109; Marc Raeff, *Political Ideas and Institutions in Imperial Russia* (Boulder, Colo.: Westview Press, 1994), 22–31, 32–41; Francis W. Wcislo, "Bureaucratic Reform in Tsarist Russia: State and Society, 1881–1914," (Ph.D. diss., Columbia University, 1984), 10–71.

little impact upon Russian public opinion. Conversely, external data reflecting Jewish attitudes to the draft were always a topic of public discussion. Statistics on Jewish draft dodgers were an especially hot topic in the Russian conservative press of the late 1870s and early 1880s.[44] The ongoing conflict between the War and the Interior ministries eventually evolved into a public debate between a liberal and a conservative institution and turned into a war of numbers, in which the more conservative Ministry of the Interior used Jewish draft statistics to argue against the more liberal War Ministry. In turn, Jewish statisticians used internal military data, which they considered more accurate, to prove to Russian readers that the inflated figures of draft dodgers and exorbitant Jewish arrears existed only on paper bearing the insignia of the Ministry of the Interior.[45]

Later, between the 1880s and 1910s, the counterreform administration made use of military statistics in its antiliberal policy toward various ethnicities.[46] Under pressure from the imperial administration, the military compiled internal data on Jewish groups as separate from other ethnic groups. This material was not released publicly. Because of the absence of similar data pertaining to other groups or to the army as a whole, the detailed information suffers from lack of context. Yet an awareness of the political climate that generated these data and an understanding of the dichotomy between the administration that commissioned the paperwork and the military that produced it permits one to examine it with a critical eye and to extract what is of value.

Generally, when collecting data, the military tended to disregard any distinctions between particular ethnic minorities or religious groups, singling out a specific ethnicity or faith only under direct order from the state administration or from the monarch himself.[47] It was the imperial administration's practice to

---

[44] See, for example, discussion of this theme in the Jewish press: *Russkii evrei*, no. 14 (1879): 502–504, 518; no. 2 (1880): 50–51; no. 17 (1880): 645–648; no. 2 (1881): 64–65; no. 8 (1881): 294–295; no. 9 (1881): 335–336; no. 10 (1881): 376–377; no. 18 (1881): 699–700; no. 25 (1881): 962–966; no. 38 (1881): 1492–1493, 1501–1503; no. 39 (1881): 1525–1527; no. 43 (1881): 1706–1707; and also in the Russian press: *Kievlianin*, no. 41 (1874): 2; no. 116 (1874): 3; no. 123 (1874): 112; no. 127 (1874): 1–2; no. 4 (1876): 1–2; no. 10 (1877): 1; no. 65 (1878): 1; no. 124 (1879): 1; no. 77 (1883): 2; no. 275 (1885): 2. The topic of draft dodging became so popular in the conservative Russian press that *Rassvet* described it as "a seasonal game" of conservative periodicals; see *Rassvet*, no. 30 (1880): 1165–1168. John Klier has undertaken meticulous analysis of the disputes concerning military statistics in the Russian and Russian Jewish periodicals. See Klier, *Imperial Russia's Jewish Question*, 332–349.

[45] The statistical committee of the Ministry of the Interior refused to heed the arguments and calculations of Jewish statisticians, who repeatedly indicated the committee's mistakes. See G. Sliozberg, *Baron G. O. Gintsburg. Ego zhizn' i deiatel'nost'* (Paris: Imp. Pascal, 1933), 113–116.

[46] See Mark Raeff, "Russia's Autocracy and Paradoxes of Modernization," in idem., *Political Ideas*, 116–125.

[47] The liberal military attitudes towards Jews were typical of War Minister Miliutin (1861–1881), whose term in the office essentially coincides with the period of Alexander II's reign (1855–1881). See, for example, a fundamental report prepared under the supervision of N. I. Obruchev on the situation in the Russian army in *Voenno-statisticheskii sbornik*, vol. 4, nos.1–2 (SPb.: Glavnyi Shtab, 1871).

request data regarding certain groups of soldiers either before or immediately after the introduction of a regulation explicitly concerning them. This occurred on the eve of the educational reform of Jewish society in the 1840s, during the implementation of the anti-Polish policies in the 1860s and 1870s, and before and after the introduction of segregationist measures against non-Russians in the 1880s and 1890s. Statistics had become an effective instrument of the state bureaucracy in its manipulation of minorities' rights and freedoms, whether these minorities were draftees or merely subjects of the state.[48]

Sometimes data were misinterpreted deliberately, to create a distorted picture of minority soldiers' moral qualities, whether they were Catholics, Muslims, or Jews.[49] The demand for sophisticated statistical reports increased after the 1874 military reforms; however, the imperial administration tended to misrepresent any military data that flew in the face of its agenda or expectations.[50] Closer to the end of the nineteenth century, and throughout World War I, the conflict between the state and the military over the lower-ranking Jewish soldiers (and some other non-Russians) intensified. If the crime rate in the army diverged from the view that "the worst element in the army is the aliens, and especially the Jews," the imperial administration preferred to disregard this reality altogether.[51] Often, it asked the military for data that could not be supported. At the height of the xenophobic postrevolutionary campaign, Deputy War Minister Polivanov commissioned the military high court to collect statistics that would demonstrate the prevalence of criminal behavior among Jewish soldiers. The court responded that it did not differentiate between Jews and others when considering the crime rate, while the Department of Mobilization argued that, "according to the available data, it is possible to obtain only rather approximated data on Jews in active service." After Polivanov received unsatisfactory data, testifying to the Jews' rather low crime rate, he commissioned a more detailed report on the punishment of Jewish

---

[48] For example, to boost the numbers of permanent Russian Orthodox residents in the Polish Kingdom and to downplay the number of Catholic Poles, state officials counted Russian soldiers temporarily billeted in the Polish Kingdom as permanent residents of these territories. See Theodore R. Weeks, *Nation and State in Late Imperial Russia: Nationalism and Russification on the Western Frontier, 1863–1914* (DeKalb: Northern Illinois University Press, 1996), 82–83.

[49] Russian statisticians monitored the crime rate after the introduction of the anti-alien laws, thus obtaining an entirely distorted picture of crime among the ethnic groups inhabiting Russian borderlands. For more detail, see Stephen Frank, *Crime, Cultural Conflict, and Justice in Rural Russia, 1856–1914* (Berkeley: University of California Press, 1999), 76–77.

[50] Thus, for example, when data was collected with reference to the crime rate among the Jewish lower ranks during the first Russian revolution, the commanders of the local brigades of the Saratov, Kazan, and Kharkov military districts responded that, during that period, "there were no" Jewish deserters. Yet it is not known whether any Jews in fact served in these regions during this time. See RGVIA, f. 400, op. 6, d. 960, ll. 36–45.

[51] A. Zolotarev, "Materialy," *Voennyi sbornik*, no. 6 (1889): 351. Anti-alien bias undermined the reports on Jewish soldiers by otherwise quite intelligent military statisticians such as Obruchev and Zolotarev, rendering them blind to the social and cultural aspects of Jewish life in the Pale of Settlement. On Obruchev's revolutionary illusions and his work in the ministry of Miliutin and Vannovskii, see Menning, *Bayonets before Bullets*, 17–20, 97–98.

soldiers; the military court department replied that such information "was not available."[52]

This volume proposes several ways to resolve the difficulties with military sources. Firstly, it compares reports generated simultaneously in different locales. Russia comprised a vast territory; regimental commanders were fallible human beings; and the absence of a modern means of communication prevented any homogenization of their responses to St. Petersburg. Consequently, the discrepancies between their reports offer useful insights into Jewish performance in the regiments. Secondly, this study balances the available military data against the bias manifested in the administration's inquiries, thus unraveling the questionnaires' and reports' ideological predisposition. Thirdly, wherever possible, this text compares internal military data on Jewish soldiers with existing data describing Jews in the Russian Empire. Finally, the reconstruction of the sociopolitical context considerably helps in interpreting the available data. For instance, in seeking to understand why the number of Jews reported to have received distinguished service decorations during World War I was half that of Christian soldiers, a historian should consider such factors as the belligerent 1915 xenophobic campaign in the Russian press, the expressed desire of the highest military figures to purge the army of Jews, the reluctance of some colonels to nominate Jews for an award, and the refusal of some commanders to acknowledge Jewish valor in front of the troops. The integration of statistics into the social, cultural, and political context is one of the principal contextualizing methods informing this study.

In examining Russian Jewish modernization, *Jews in the Russian Army* regards Jews as imperial subjects, uprooted from their shtetl environment and placed in the army. The communal context is replaced with a military one: Jews are part of the military enterprise. Only then does a comparison between the Jewish community in the Pale and the military experience of Jewish soldiers make sense. The voices of Jews, both adults and minors, find their way to the modern reader through thick layers of bureaucratic and military discourse. The voices reconstructed in this study challenge the ways in which historians and writers perceived Jewish soldiers in the tsarist army, Russian army commanders, and high-ranking personnel. This study discusses the Jewish soldier's army experience parallel to that of the Russian Orthodox or Catholic soldier, thus modifying and amplifying our understanding of the army, the tsar and his war ministers, and the relationship between the military and Russian public opinion. To recreate the Russian army context, this volume touches upon various aspects of Russian military history, integrating research by Dietrich Beyrau, John Bushnell, William Fuller, Elise Kimerling Wirtschafter, Eric Lohr, Bruce Menning, Matityahu Mintz, David Schimmelpenninck van der Oye, and David Alan Rich. If Jewish soldiers demonstrated qualities common to other members of the army, one may argue that Nicholas I's plan to effect their assimilation through the military succeeded, and that Jews became

[52] RGVIA, f. 400, op. 6, d. 960, ll. 1–2, 4, 15.

Russians. Conversely, if Jewish soldiers comported themselves like Jews in the Pale of Settlement, exhibiting differences vis-à-vis their Christian brethren, the argument of this book will be borne out: that Jewish soldiers in fact became Russian Jews, people of a dual self-awareness, a unique outcome of European Jewish modernization.

Jews in the Russian Army explores that uniqueness. It assesses the experience of Jewish soldiers according to the outcome of their service and incorporates memory and literary narratives solely as an addendum to the cultural history. The East European sociopolitical context assists in appreciating the nature of modernity: contemporary Russian Jewish public opinion soundly considered the Jews' military service an achievement of imperial modernization. Suffice it to say that, in the 1820s, the Jewish Committee argued against the conscription of Jews, whereas, on the eve of World War I, liberal Jewish public opinion vehemently opposed the exclusion of Jews from the army! Indeed, Jewish service in the Russian military emerges as a complex sociocultural process, which cannot be reduced to an exclusively military, political, or social perspective.

The Jewish encounter with the Russian military is a complex chapter in the history of imperial modernization. Social history methods of research are necessary, but alone are insufficient. *Jews in the Russian Army* employs a variety of methodologies and approaches, including microhistory, local history, quantitative history and statistical analysis, structural and cultural history, and case studies. Political history and the history of thought also are brought into play, with an emphasis upon the social ramifications of political and intellectual pursuits. It is hoped that consistent attention to sociocultural aspects of the military throughout this study will facilitate its methodological coherence.

This study offers a new perspective, for the first time utilizing hundreds of documents from various archives and collections in Israel, Poland, Ukraine, and Russia, and providing revealing glimpses into how Jews survived in the military. It compares and contrasts Jewish soldiers with their Christian counterparts in the military, rather than with their Jewish brethren in the Pale of Settlement or with their compatriots in European armies. It reveals the extent to which the border between the military and the society was blurred. The army emerges from this book as a *sui generis* society, a society in and of itself, with its own, very often problematic relations with the state apparatus and the tsardom. Just as Russian society at large had its own relations with its Jews in the Pale, the army had its own relations with the Jews in its ranks. *Jews in the Russian Army* advances a nuanced vision of the imperial Russian army, further elaborating the idea that "the armed forces were a microcosm of the state and society they served and protected."[53]

---

[53] See David McDonald, "The Military and Imperial Russian History," in David Schimmelpenninck van der Oye and Bruce Menning, eds., *Reforming the Tsar's Army: Military Innovation in Imperial Russia from Peter the Great to the Revolution* (Washington, D.C.: Woodrow Wilson Center Press; Cambridge: Cambridge University Press, 2003), 307–321.

I

The Empire Reforms, the Community Responds

The Russian imperial plan to reform the Jews dates back to the beginning of the nineteenth century. Although Alexander I himself did not actually implement the reform, he acknowledged the Jews' status quo in his 1804 statute and established two Jewish Committees, one in Warsaw and another in St. Petersburg, composed of mostly enlightened Polish and Russian bureaucrats, charging them to elaborate what he called the radical reform of the Jews.[1] The committees already had amassed most of the paperwork by December, 1825, when Alexander unexpectedly passed away, the Decembrists rebelled, Grand Duke Constantine resigned, and Nicholas I ascended the throne. Nicholas accepted the previously elaborated plans as a blueprint and implemented them in accordance with his own priorities. Thus, in terms of Jewish policies, there was a direct connection, rather than disruption, between him and his predecessor. Students of the Russian Empire now see a nuanced continuity in nineteenth-century Russian history, rather than clearly delineated periods such as the Alexandrine (1801–1825) and Nicholaevan (1825–1855), followed by Alexander II's Great Reforms (1855–1881) and Alexander III's Counterreform (1881–1894). In view of Alexander's plans, much of what has seemed the incomprehensible and arbitrary decision of Nicholas I to reform the Jews emerges as logical and continuous. Nonetheless, the nature of the reform, the environment informing Nicholas's priorities, and the reasons for the Jewish communal response require elaboration.

Radical Jewish Reform

In 1815, Napoleon's Duchy of Warsaw ceased to exist. By the decision of the Vienna Congress, the Kingdom of Poland became a constitutional monarchy in personal union with Russia. Alexander appointed his brother Constantine the viceroy of the Congress Poland making him eventually the commander in chief

---

[1] See Arthur Eisenbach, *Z Dziejów ludności żydowskiej w Polsce w XVIII i XIX wieku* (Warsaw: Państwowy Instytut Wydawniczy, 1983), 168–170.

of the Polish and Lithuanian troops. The reform of Jews in Poland began to move on a much faster pace than in Russia – although with some differences, first and foremost, regarding their conscription.

Following the recommendations of Alexander I, the Jewish Committee in Warsaw, apparently much more advanced in its reform proclivities than the one in St. Petersburg, suggested the establishment of state-run elementary schools and rabbinical institutions for teachers, as priorities for Jewish reform. The introduction of Jewish military service was a lesser consideration. The Polish War Commission (*Kommisja Rządowa Woyny*) argued that military service was both a duty and an honorable privilege for every Polish resident. Polish Jews deserved political rights; yet, to obtain them, they were required to serve in the army for ten years, and would not receive exemptions for marrying early. Only one rabbi and one cantor from each community were to be permitted exemptions of any kind. To prevent Jewish evasion of service, it was stipulated that a drafted Jew could be replaced only by another Jew. Nonetheless, the commission ruled against the immediate inclusion of Jews in the conscription pool. In the aftermath of Napoleon's invasion, the commission members believed, the Kingdom of Poland could not afford to conscript Jews. If Jews served in the army, they would become tax-exempt, causing the state treasury to lose about 700,000 złoty, which it could ill afford. Furthermore, in view of Poland's large Jewish population, the commission considered it too dangerous to provide Jews with arms. It is likely that the commission suspected the Jews of having joined the Poles against the Russians in the 1794 Kosciuszko Rebellion, and of having staunchly supported Napoleon during his stay in Poland.[2] It may have been speculated that the idea of Jewish army service was proposed by enlightened Warsaw Jews to foster Polish Jewish patriotism.[3] The negative ramifications of an immediate introduction of conscription in the newly established imperial borderland were only too evident. The committee decided to exempt Jews from military service and instead make Jewish communities in the kingdom pay a ransom of 600,000 złoty, while the Jewish community of Warsaw was to pay an additional 700,000 złoty. Some patriotic Jews protested, but the more cautious among the communal representatives at the Warsaw court, such as Avraam Blumenthal and Mayer Diamant from Krakow, Rabbi

---

[2] After the defense of Warsaw, Russian army general Alexei Ermolov wrote, in 1794, that even the Jews, presumably evil people, were able to fight: "In order to organize a modern army, one should look into the people's soul. Any people should be able to form an effective army. Praga [the Jewish suburb of Warsaw] was desperately defended by the Jewish battalion." See *Russkie liudi o evreiakh* (SPb.: A. M. Wolf, 1891), 34.

[3] Arthur Eisenbach, *Kwestia równouprawnienia Żydów w Królestwie Polskim* (Warsaw: Książka i Wiedza, 1972): 79, 80, 83, 84; on the reaction of Polish Jews to the introduction of the conscription of Jews in the Kingdom of Poland, see also Arthur Eisenbach, *The Emancipation of the Jews in Poland, 1780–1870*, ed. A. Polonsky (Oxford: Basil Blackwell in association with the Institute for Polish-Jewish Studies, 1991), 301–302. On the patriotism of Warsaw Jews and their fascination with the military, see Jacob Shatzky, *Di geshikhte fun yidn in Varshe* (New York: Yidisher Visnshaftlekher Institut (YIVO), 1947), 177–181.

Gizel Markusz from Płock, and Rabbi Berek from Lublin, signed the committee protocol. Alexander I approved the decision, and on April 19, 1817, ordered that Jews pay these sums rather than serve in the army.[4] As Jews in the Pale of Settlement similarly paid ransom and did not provide recruits, the homogeneity of the Jews' legal arrangement in both parts of the empire must have been satisfactory to Alexander.

Yet Jewish modernization was different in the Kingdom of Poland than elsewhere in the empire. Grand Duke Constantine, Nicholas I's elder brother, was more consistent than Alexander in his attitude toward Jewish reform. He began introducing elements of Jewish civil rights in the early 1820s. He cancelled the *kahals*, dismissing them as rudimentary, medieval bodies; he reinstated Polish Jews to city councils, and he introduced the *dozor bóżniczy* (synagogue steering committee), a state-controlled institution supervising Jewish communal activities.[5] These innovations prompted educational reform; the Jewish Committee in Warsaw suggested the establishment of rabbinical schools to train new rabbis, in the spirit of responsibility before "God, monarch, and people." In their 1825 report, the Jewish Committee members – including enlightened Polish Christians such as Ignacy Zaleski, Walerian Krasiński, Stefan Witwicki, Jan Iwaszkiewicz, Józef Kownacki, and Stanisław Hoge, the only convert among them – accorded greater importance to military duty, moving it from the twenty-sixth item in the reform undertakings to one of the five most urgent, second only to education. Their deliberations, conducted in French, were congruent with enlightened French rhetoric. The catchword *régénération*, often resonated at National Assembly meetings of the 1790s, also shaped the debates of the Warsaw Jewish Committee, although it did not appear in the report. Borrowing a page from the French model, the committee members asserted that military duty was a useful (*utile*) undertaking. In the army, they argued, the unmanageable, dirty, and hostile Jew would become "accustomed to keep order, cleanness, and comradeship." Any Jew who completed his term in the military departed once and for all "from the ills characteristic of his people"; he would not return to the idiosyncratic, self-isolating habits of his past. The army would teach the Jew a sense of honor, a love of the motherland (*l'amour de la patrie*), and respect for his fellow citizens (*concitoyenne*), thus effecting his civic, physical, and moral reform. Christians also perceived the utility of the Jewish draft: Jews became good soldiers, on equal footing with them. Indeed, the envisioned reform could succeed only on

---

[4] Among the twenty-eight paragraphs of the reform project, military duty is the twenty-sixth. See AGAD, zb. I Rada Stanu Królestwa Polskiego, sygn. 285 ("Rapporta z czynności Komitetu wyznaczonego do zaprowadzenia reformy Ludu Starozakonnego"), 53–73; AGAD, zb. I Rada Stanu Królestwa Polskiego, sygn. 387 ("Przepisy względem zasiągu do Woyska czyli Konskrypcja," 1816), ll. 2–3, 8, 18–19, 95–105; AGAD, zb. Kancelaria Senatora Nowosilcowa, sygn. 700 ("O, rekrutskoi povinnosti evreev, v Tsarstve Polskom obitaiuschikh"), 3–5, 10, 15–16; AGAD, zb. Sekretariat Stanu Królestwa Polskiego, sygn. 199, ll. 64–79. Also see RGIA, f. 1254, op. 1, d. 142.
[5] AGAD, zb. Kancelaria Senatora Nowosilcowa, sygn. 626, ll. 2, 9, 25–32, 70, 91.

the condition that Jewish and Christian soldiers received the same privileges. Ultimately, the committee members declared that Jews were capable of becoming good students in the army, "this genuine school of civilization and reform."[6]

The Imperial Jewish Committee in St. Petersburg followed suit. To design their own reform for Jews in the Pale of Settlement, the committee members, comprising Iakov Druzhinin, Petr Kaisarov, Maksim Fon-Fok, and Grigorii Kartashevskii, turned to their Warsaw colleagues, requesting that they share their plans and data. Their attached questionnaire demonstrated that St. Petersburg knew much less about the internal organization of Russian Jews than Warsaw did of the Jews in the Kingdom of Poland. The Warsaw officials sent elaborate answers, explaining why the elimination of the *kahal* and the introduction of Jewish state education were indispensable. However, Alexander did not apply the Polish reforms to his Jews in the Pale of Settlement. Unhappy with this discrepancy in state attitudes, Constantine insisted upon synchronizing Jewish reform in both parts of the empire. Otherwise, he asserted, Jews who opposed the reform could escape from one part of the empire to another, and could circumvent the benign new regulations. Constantine repeatedly contacted Alexander I before 1825, and Nicholas I thereafter, to persuade them to elaborate a single set of homogeneous measures designed to acculturate the Jews. Following his advice, on June 15, 1826, Nicholas asked Constantine to help establish contact between the two Jewish Committees and to unify their efforts. Yet, while members of the St. Petersburg Jewish Committee and their Polish colleagues were discussing the structure of the Jewish communities and the activities of Jewish sects (Hasidim, at first), Nicholas obtained the drafted reform and resolved to implement the proposed measures, starting with conscription.[7]

The ensuing discussion in St. Petersburg of the draft proposal yielded paradoxical results. Despite several efforts to make Jewish reform consistent throughout the empire, the imperial administration, following Nicholas' orders, announced the conscription of Jews in Russia but chose not to implement it in the Kingdom of Poland. Notwithstanding the efforts of the Jewish deputies acting behind the scenes, one person was responsible for single-handedly saving the Jews in the Polish Kingdom from conscription: Nikolai

---

[6] While the committee insisted upon the same regulations for both Jews and Christians in military service, they made two allowances: Jews served proportionately to their number in the general population, and completed a six-year term as opposed to ten years for Christians. For more detail, see AGAD, zb. Sekretariat Stanu Królestwa Polskiego, sygn. 199, ll. 71–71ob., 139–143ob., 146b–148ob. For an earlier version of this project, also originating with the chief of staff and characterized by the notion of radical moral reform of the Jews, see AGAD, Kancelaria Senatora Nowosilcowa, sygn. 700 ("O rekrutskoi povinnosti evreev, v Tsarstve Polskom obitaiushchikh"), ll. 50–76.

[7] AGAD, zb. Kancelaria Senatora Nowosilcowa, sygn. 938 ("Nastolnaia kniga," 1826), l. 373; ibid., sygn. 939 ("Nastolnaia kniga," 1827), l. 509; AGAD, zb. Sekretariat Stanu Królestwa Polskiego, sygn. 199, ll. 71–71ob., 139–1390b.

Nikolaevich Novosiltsev. A special envoy of the Russian tsars Alexander and Nicholas, with multiple functions and unfettered power, Secret Chancellor Novosiltsev was second in Poland only to Grand Duke Constantine. Novosiltsev was the senator and the head of his own chancellery; the organizer and primary inspiration of the civic and military secret police in the Kingdom of Poland, a member of various Polish legislative committees, and a mastermind of the viceroy's court.[8] Having been a member of the Jewish Committee, he was perhaps the preeminent court expert on Jewish matters. His reformist approach, sometimes buttressed, as it were, with considerable Jewish bribes, envisioned the establishment of full Jewish civil equality.[9] Although Constantine sometimes secretly monitored Novosiltsev's activities, in most cases he trusted him, and together they discussed every state project.[10] When, in April 1826, the commander-in-chief, in his "most humble report" to Constantine, suggested extending military service to the Jews, the latter found the idea useful because, he asserted, the Jewish people were harmful to Christian society. Yet, in order to avoid mismanagement of the draft and to properly determine whom to exempt, Constantine recommended that his Jewish Committee thoroughly consider the issue, and sent Novosiltsev the proposal regarding Jewish conscription obtained from the St. Petersburg Jewish Committee.[11]

Novosiltsev replied with a thoughtful, detailed, and devastating critique of the project. He cited a number of concerns, emphasizing the problems that later had surfaced with the first Jewish conscription in Russia. He pointed out that the project had confused communal, political, and geographical divisions. He predicted that such confusion would only provoke consternation among Jews, and arbitrariness in the behavior of local officials. He questioned the logistics of implementing the draft, since Jews did not have properly organized registers of births and deaths (i.e., metrical books) and so could not provide the military with accurate conscription lists. According to Novosiltsev, some stipulations made no sense whatsoever, such as the statute forbidding billeting the drafted Jews in Jewish neighborhoods. In most Polish towns, he reasoned, there were more Jews than Christians, but quartering Jews in the villages meant that they would starve, without access to kosher meat or cooking utensils. Novosiltsev also consulted Jewish statistics, noting that there were approximately fifteen thousand Jews in

---

[8] See Franciszka Ramotowska, "Kancelaria senatora Nowosilcowa," in *Archiwum Główne Akt Dawnych: Przewodnik po zasobie*. 2 vols. (Warsaw: DiG, 1998), 2:76–83.

[9] For more detail on Novosiltsev's proposals for Jewish reform, see John Klier, *Rossiia sobiraet svoikh evreev. Proiskhozhdenie evreiskogo voprosa v Rossii* (M., Jerusalem: Mosty Kultury and Gesharim, 2000), 273, 295, 299, 303–305.

[10] GARF, f. 728, op. 1, d. 2271, r. XX, t. 1 ("Materialy i cherty k biografii imperatora Nikolaia I i k istorii ego tsarstvovaniia. Zapiski stats-sekretaria barona Korfa"), l. 89ob. Among other things, Novosiltsev was responsible for drafting the constitutional charter for Russia as a whole. See David Saunders, *Russia in the Age of Reaction and Reform, 1801–1881* (London and New York: Longman, 1992), 71.

[11] AGAD, Kancelaria Senatora Nowosilcowa, sygn. 626 ("O evreiskikh kagalakh i shkolakh v Tsarstve Polskom," 1824–26), l. 263.

Poland available for conscription, in addition to about five thousand in Vilna. It was hardly feasible to control such numerous multitudes (*mnogochislennye skopishcha*). The sheer number of Jews and officials, and the failure to make the rules equally applicable to all (which he referred to as "arbitrariness"), could trigger riots that the local administration might be unable to control.

Consequently, Novosiltsev recommended rejecting the Jewish conscription project, and instead instituting a more uniform management of the Jews in Russia and Poland. Evidently, he tried obliquely to exert influence through Constantine upon the decisions rendered in St. Petersburg, juxtaposing his critique of the proposal of a Jewish draft with his suggestion to standardize the state regulations regarding Jews. Novosiltsev concluded that the project required the collection of far more data about the grassroots situation ("internal and inherent," as he put it); the authorities needed to know Jews better in order to reform them more effectively. The document did not accurately reflect the existing relations between the Jews and the authorities in the Kingdom of Poland; it did not match the care His Honor the Grand Duke extended to the Jewish people in his country, Novosiltsev claimed.[12] It is difficult to judge whether his report was the result of his skeptical rationalism, of Jewish intercession, or of both, but it worked: Constantine did not follow Nicholas's recommendations. His reluctance to extend conscription to Jews in Poland had serious repercussions. Nicholas introduced conscription in Poland only sixteen years later. By that time Constantine and Novosiltsev were no longer around. By the 1840s, Nicholas had suppressed the Polish rebellion of 1830–1831, abrogated the Polish constitution, and erased the vestiges of Polish independence. Now he thought integration of Polish Jews through the Russian army service would weaken Jewish–Polish bonds and strengthen Russian imperial policies in Russia's western borderland. He finally introduced the conscription of Polish Jews in 1843, in the wake of his full-fledged reform of East European Jews.[13] And yet, in 1827 Nicholas preferred not to argue with his brother, although in his own domain, he acted differently.

Nicholas's Priorities

In the winter of 1826, Nicholas had an entire set of proposed Jewish reforms. He reversed the sequence of the measures espoused by the two committees, however. First, he introduced conscription; next, he classified Jews according to their occupations (as useful or useless); thirdly, he cancelled the *kahal*; fourthly, he established state schools for Jewish children; and, lastly, he introduced rabbinic secondary schools. Initiating the Jewish draft in the late 1820s, Nicholas postponed the bulk of the reforms until the early 1840s. Although most historians have attributed this decision to his long-lasting romance with the army, in fact Nicholas's ostensibly shallow militarism had more profound roots.

[12] AGAD, zb. Kancelaria Senatora Nowosilcowa, sygn. 626, ll. 264–289.
[13] See Eisenbach, *Kwestia rownouprawnienia Żydow*, 79–84.

As a child, Grand Duke Nicholas (raised with his brother, Grand Duke Mikhail) preferred his toy soldiers to all other toys. As soon as he woke he would begin playing with his lead and porcelain soldiers, building toy fortifications and attacking the adversary's troops. Sometimes he planned battles and maneuvers, manipulating his colored, rectangular *fiches* (one inch by half an inch), variously imprinted with the words "infantry," "cavalry," and "artillery." Young Nicholas enjoyed wearing military clothing: in 1801, he owned sixteen uniforms (*mundirchik*) of the Izmailov cavalier guard regiment. He also had several dozen St. Andrew Silver Stars at his disposal: foil awards for his early military victories.[14] Although the widowed empress, Mariia Fedorovna, tried to distract the grand dukes from their military pursuits, the supervisors she hired for them only inflamed Nicholas's military imagination. General Matvei Lamsdorf, the head of the first cadet corps, was a rigid and cruel tutor who succeeded in instilling in the obstinate Nicholas a sense of discipline. Major General Akhverdov, whom Nicholas adored, taught him how to draw, and how to defend and to attack fortresses. Nicholas drew every day, demonstrating significant talent: he sketched soldiers, officers, uniforms, military maps, armaments, and engineering fortifications.[15] His military mania was irrepressible. In 1810, at the age of fourteen, he proudly proclaimed, "Best of all, I like the arsenal."[16] The Winter Palace records an incident in which, on the empress's orders, Akhverdov once assigned Nicholas an essay arguing that "The military is not the only service justifying the nobleman; there are other no less useful and honorable occupations." Nicholas spent an hour and a half considering the matter, and chose to write nothing in response to the proposed topic. Akhverdov was compelled to tell Nicholas what to write down and informed the empress about the incident.[17] Apparently it was the army alone that inspired Nicholas. While the empress did not allow Nicholas and Mikhail to visit the troops during the 1806–1807 military campaign (although they badly wanted to), Napoleon Bonaparte's burgeoning acclaim prompted her to invite

---

[14] For more detail, see GARF, f. 728, op. 1, ch. 1, d. 466 ("Graf M. A. Korf. Rozhdenie i detstvo imperatora Nikolaia I").

[15] Sometimes Nicholas's love of uniforms knew no bounds: when already in his twenties, he portrayed his wife clumsily dressed in a cavalier-guard's uniform. Nicholas's artistic talents have recently become public knowledge, but more has to be done to contextualize his caricatures and sketches. For Nicholas's etchings, aquarelles, and drawings, see GARF, f. 728, op. 1, d. 1314 ("Risunki velikogo kniazia Nikolaia Pavlovicha"), ll. 2, 4, 6. For the published version of some of his sketches, see *Urok risovania. Katalog vystavki* (SPb.: Petronius, 2006), l. VII.

[16] GARF, f. 728, op. 1, d. 722, t. 5 ("Uprazhnenia velikogo kniazia Nikolaia Pavlovicha v perevodakh i sochineniiakh na russkom iazyke, s otmetkami imperatritsy Marii Fedorovny," 1810), l. 13.

[17] GARF, f. 728, op. 1, ch. I, d. 466 ("Graf M. A. Korf, Rozhdenie i detstvo imperatora Nikolaia I"), l. 790b. See also Nicholas's moving notes to Akhverdov asking to forgive him for his obstinacy during the lessons, GARF, f. 728, op. 1, d. 709 (written between 1803 and 1805). This story also is retold, briefly, in N. K. Shilder, *Imperator Nikolai Pervyi, ego zhizn' i tsarstvovanie* (SPb.: A. S. Suvorin, 1903), 37.

two professional army instructors, General Opperman and Artillery Colonel Markevich, to instruct the grand dukes in the spirit of the epoch.[18] Under their supervision, Nicholas's early militarism acquired shape and meaning.

In his world history lessons, the teenage Nicholas found an idol to emulate: Peter the Great. Nicholas's essays did not portray Peter I as the Russian emperor who founded St. Petersburg, ordered the issue of the first Russian newspaper, established the first Russian museum of rarities, reformed the Duma, westernized Russian dress, or civilized the gentry. Instead, Nicholas was obsessed with Peter the Great as the venerable reformer of the army and navy. In his essays, he lavishly praised Peter's expansion of the ranks and of the conscription pool, and his establishment of the navy. He was enthralled with Peter's capacity to turn his "amusement" (*poteshnyi*) regiment composed of teenage soldiers into one of the core regiments of the budding Russian army. Apparently Nicholas nurtured a secret desire to emulate Peter, as he absorbed Opperman's accounts of military strategies and worked diligently, under Markevich, on military translations.[19] Nicholas cherished the pocket watch he had inherited from his distinguished predecessor, and like him, was intensely absorbed in the study of engineering and fortification. Almost in Peter's very words, Nicholas articulated his own love of the fatherland, his military patriotism and his belief in the necessity of a soldier's self-abnegation. Perhaps Peter's idiosyncratic admiration of the Prussian military prompted Nicholas to translate from German an account of the Seven-Year War and selections from the ethical tractates taught in the Prussian Military Academy.[20] Already an emperor, he was wont to repeat one of his forebear's favorite sayings: "I have no liking of lazybones."[21] When, in the early 1840s, Nicholas abandoned his luxurious apartments for a remote, ascetic room in a distant corner of the Winter Palace,

---

[18] GARF, f. 728, op. 1, f. 2271, r. I, ch. 1 ("Materialy i cherty k biografii imperatora Nikolaia I i k istorii ego tsarstvovaniia. Zapiski stats-sekretaria barona Korfa"), ll. 310b.–33, 38, 41–410b., 42, 46, 55, 75, 770b., 800b., 930b., 1060b.

[19] Nicholas studied types of war, army maneuvers, the theories of advance and attack, the structure and composition of Russian army regiments and of the Grande Armée, and how to expel Turkey from Europe. The latter was also a primary concern of Peter the Great. See GARF, f. 728, op. 1, d. 1039 ("Sobstvennoruchnye zapiski v. kn. Nikolaia Pavlovicha po chasti taktiki i strategii"), ll. 28–32, 33–56; GARF, f. 728, op. 1, d. 839 ("Uchebnye zapiski Nikolaia po fortifikatsii i strategii," 1810–1815), ll. 92–95, 182–185. Opperman praised Nicholas's phenomenal memory and his capacity to "ponder military issues with precision and clarity." See GARF, 728, op. 1, d. 921a ("Besedy s v. k. Nikolaem Pavlovichem po povodu izucheniia voennykh nauk. Raporty general-leitenanta Akhverdova i polkovnika Markevicha o zaniatiiakh velikikh kniazei Nikolaia i Mikhaila Pavlovichei po istorii i voennomu delu," 1816), l. 19.

[20] For Nicholas's translations, see GARF, f. 728, op. 1, d. 722 ("Uprazhneniia velikogo kniazia Nikolaia Pavlovicha v perevodakh i sochineniiakh na russkom iazyke, s otmetkami imperatritsy Marii Fedorovny," 1810–1811), t. 6. For reference to separate notebooks with Nicholas's translations, see GARF, f. 728, op. 1, d. 893 ("Sochineniia velikogo kniazia Nikolaia Pavlovicha po istorii, russkoi slovesnosti, istorii voin i dr.," 1812–1814), l. 133.

[21] "Ia do lenivkh ne okhotnik," see GARF, f. 728, op. 1, d. 2271, r. XX, t. 1 ("Materialy i cherty k biografii. Zapiski stats-sekretaria barona Korfa," 1826–1838), l. 10.

he took with him his colored porcelain soldiers, two canvases showing military parades, and a large portrait of Peter the Great.[22]

Having learned how to manage the state before he inherited the throne, Nicholas nonetheless concerned himself solely with military reform. Realizing that the army consumed a significant portion of the state budget, he offered a solution in his 1824 essay entitled "Thoughts on the transformation of the army in such a way that the expenses for it will be diminished, the effectiveness will be increased, and the standing troops will not be considerably cut."[23] This treatise envisaged the army as the primary state institution, which he himself planned to transfigure. He mocked those who asserted that the burden of the one-million-strong Russian army could crush the state of thirty-five million people. However, he agreed the Russian army had too many high-ranking and too few low-ranking officers. To address this problem, he suggested democratizing army management. He proposed to reduce the number of army generals per division by three and staff officers' positions per infantry regiment by two. The artillery, he declared, needed only one general per brigade. He planned to introduce elements of an entity elaborated forty years later by War Minister Dmitrii Miliutin: the officers' reserve pool. Nicholas argued that officers should step down from their positions but not from the service itself, thereby permitting the army to recall them in case of mobilization. Rather than wasting time on the daily training of soldiers, staff officers and lower-rank officers were required to study strategy and tactics, while senior soldiers trained the novices. Nicholas also proposed reducing the number of squadrons from seven to five per cavalry regiment, thus making regiments more mobile. By eliminating about 76,000 men and 30,000 horses in time of peace, he planned to save 34,894,000 rubles, for allocation to the army budget. Despite his penchant for uniforms and parading, in fact Nicholas was intent upon inculcating in his soldiers discipline and a familiarity with army regulations and the art of war. To this end, he commissioned Baron Korf to devise a plan for training the lower ranks (*nizhnie chiny*), which Nicholas subsequently approved as the outline for the garrison and the regimental service.[24]

Nicholas's reverence for Prussian order and militarism was only enhanced by his marriage to the princess of Prussia, which made Friedrich Wilhelm III his father-in-law. As a Russian historian observed, the "[m]arriage to a daughter of the King of Prussia in 1817 brought [Nicholas] into close contact with the European dynasty whose military traditions approximated most closely those of

---

[22] The military parade canvases belonged to the brush of Ladurner and Kruger. See GARF, f. 728, op. 1, d. 2271, r. XX, t. 3 ("Materially i cherty k biografii. Zapiski stats-sekretaria barona Korfa," 1839–1840), ll. 20–21.

[23] See GARF, f. 728, op.1, d. 1184 ("V. kn. Nikolai Pavlovich, Mnenie ob privedenii armii na takuiu nogu, chtoby ne umenshaia znachitelno nalichnogo chisla voiska umenshit izderzhki na soderzhanie ego i dat' sposob skorogo usileniia"), especially 19–200b.

[24] GARF, f. 728, op. 1, d. 2337 ("Ob obuchenii russkogo soldata"), 2–90b.

the Romanovs."[25] Beginning in the early 1820s, Friedrich regularly exchanged letters with Nicholas in German and French, the annotated publication of which is major scholarly desideratum. In his correspondence, Friedrich provided detailed descriptions of military parades, analyzed the Polish military and the structure of Polish troops, shared his ideas on the organizational and managerial aspects of the army, celebrated the grassroots friendship between Prussian and Russian soldiers, discussed the Ottoman Empire and its potential military threat, closely followed the news about Russian military innovations and subsequently the reports from the Russo-Turkish fronts, praised Nicholas's courageous army, and even exchanged military uniforms with Nicholas.[26] Perhaps Nicholas's upbringing and family connections also informed his acute sense of legalism. Whenever his subsequent advisers and petitioners asked him to consider the particulars of a case and to make an exception, Nicholas retorted, "The law must be uniform"; "No one is allowed to make exceptions to the law"; and, finally, "Stick to the letter of the law!"[27] The legalism, order, and discipline of Prussian military standards, among other political reasons, prompted Nicholas to reject the French version of *liberté* and *fraternité* which, as he argued in his essay "On Liberty," led to the destruction of the country's law and order.[28]

Nicholas had a visceral dislike of anything that did not conform to his vision of discipline, order, and obedience. Poles and Jews figured primarily among the residents of the empire whom Nicholas considered harmful, unruly, and disobedient, albeit not irreparable. He inherited his aversion toward Poles from his court nurse, Miss Lion, who repeatedly recited heartbreaking stories about the alleged cruelties of Kosciuszko troops in Warsaw in 1794, and the brilliant victory of the Russians under Field Marshal Suvorov.[29] Regarding the Jews, Nicholas penned in one of his very early essays about the various Russian ethnicities that "Yids are multiple in the provinces returned from Poland; they

[25] David Saunders, *Russia in the Age of Reaction and Reform, 1801–1881* (London and New York: Longman, 1992), 116. Cf. Wortman's statement that "Nicholas remained fully German in manner," see Richard Wortman, "National Narratives in the Representation of Nineteenth-Century Russian Monarchy," in Marsha Siefert, ed., *Extending the Borders of Russian History: Essays in Honor of Alfred Rieber* (Budapest and New York: Central European University Press, 2003), 54. Apparently the Prussian military also inspired Nicholas's vision of "human life only as [military] service." See N. K. Shilder, *Imperator Nikolai Pervyi, ego zhizn' i tsarstvovanie* (SPb.: A. S. Suvorin, 1903), 147.

[26] For Friedrich Wilhelm III's letters to Nicholas of 1821–1829, see GARF, f. 728, op. 1, d. 1019 ("Pis'ma korolia Prusskogo Fridrikha Vil'gel'ma III velikomu kniaziu (vposledstvii imperatoru) Nikolaiu Pavlovichu," 1816–1840), l. 26–260b., 28, 30–31, 42, 46, 47, 55–56, 79–80, 86–860b.

[27] See GARF, f. 728, op. 1, d. 2271, r. II, t. 1 ("Materialy i cherty k biografii imperatora Nikolaia I i k istorii ego tsarstvovania, pod red. M. A. Korfa"), l. 78; r. III, t. 1 ("Materialy i cherty k biografii"), l. 230b.; r. III, ch. 3 ("Materially i cherty k biografii"), ll. 24, 34, 39, 112.

[28] On Nicholas's attitude to revolutionary France, see GARF, f. 728, op. 1, d. 823, t. 4 ("Zaniatiia velikogo kniazia Nikolaia Pavlovicha. Istoria Frantsii (na frantsuzskom iazyke) s otmetkami imperatritsy Marii Fedorovny"), ll. 60–70; GARF, f. 728, op. 1, d. 893, t. 1 ("Sochinenia velikogo kniazia Nikolaia Pavlovicha po istorii, russkoi slovesnosti, istorii voin i dr.,"), ll. 65–66.

[29] GARF, f. 728, op. 1, d. 2271, r. I, ch. 1 ("Materially i cherty k biografii"), l. 180b.

live by trade and entrepreneurship (*promyshlennostiu*)."[30] Regarding their means of livelihood as manipulative and nonproductive, he thought Jews a suspicious and unscrupulous lot at best. His religious background reinforced this antipathy. Nicholas closely read his administration's explanatory notes outlining the reasons for not extending equal rights to Jews, as had been done in other countries. These notes asserted that the number of Jews in Russia did not permit such a measure, and that the Russian government and the Russian people were not as indifferent to issues of faith as were the Europeans. Beside this second explanation, Nicholas wrote in the margin, "Thank God," and underlined his words.[31]

Apparently, Nicholas could not countenance even the Old Hebrews. Although his teachers' daily notes generally commended his attention and diligence, a rare exception was an 1807 Old Testament lesson during which his behavior was noted as "not particularly attentive," and "not good."[32] Ultimately, Nicholas found both Poles and Jews useless to the empire in their present condition. While he traveled through Russia, he recorded in his travelogue what he heard from the court bureaucrats who followed him; yet, as his tutors mentioned, perhaps the only independent entry in his diary was that regarding Poles and Jews:

The Belorussian gentry, comprising predominantly rich Poles, showed no loyalty to Russia and, with the exception of several Vitebsk and Southern Mogilev lords, the rest proffered their oath of allegiance to Napoleon. The peasants, quite poor, pay heavy levy, and there is a complete destruction of peasants in these provinces. Yids are by and large the second masters here; they drain simple folk with their tricks. They epitomize everything here, they are merchants, and leasers, and inn-keepers, mill- and crossing-owners, artisans, etc., and they know how to oppress and deceive the simple folk, taking as collateral even the not-yet-sown summer wheat and the expected not-yet-sown crop. They are genuine blood-suckers, sticking to and exhausting completely these decaying provinces. Surprisingly, in 1812 they were remarkably loyal to us and even helped us, wherever they could, risking their lives.[33]

This observation is illuminating in several respects. Nicholas associates well-to-do Poles with entrepreneurial Jews (he uses the word *promysl* as "tricks," not "industriousness") and opposes them to the Russian Orthodox peasants.

[30] Although the word *promyshlennost* signified "industry" in nineteenth-century Russia, for Nicholas it suggested a middleman's manipulative way of earning money. For the entry in this Nicholaevan essay, see GARF, f. 728 op. 1, d. 722, t. 8 ("Ezhenedel'nye otchety velikogo kniazia Nikolaia Pavlovicha o svoikh zaniatiakh," 1810–1811), l. 38.

[31] For Nicholas's scattered comments on the draft regulations, see GARF, f. 728, op. 1, d. 2271, r. II, t. II ("Materialy i cherty k biografii. Gosudarstvennyi sovet," 1831–1840), ll. 43–44ob., 47, 62–63.

[32] The lesson was about Zerubavel and those Jews who remained in Babylon after they obtained permission to resettle in the Land of Israel. See GARF, f. 728, op. 1, d. 722 (Uprazhnenia velikogo kniazia Nikolaia Pavlovicha v sochineniakh i perevodakh ...," 1810–1811).

[33] Baron Korf considered this thought as entirely belonging to Nicholas; see GARF, f. 728, op. 1, d. 2271 r. I, ch. 1 ("Materialy i cherty k biografii"), l. 1180ob. Quote is from Shilder, *Imperator Nikolai Pervyi*, 68–69.

He emphasizes the political corruption of Poles and the economic corruption of Jews. He does not suggest any explanation for the Russian patriotism of Jews in the western provinces.

Thus, it was not merely his militarism that determined Nicholas's priorities. Once Grand Duke Nicholas became Nicholas I and swiftly suppressed the Decembrist revolt, he made Jews (and, immediately thereafter, Poles), those resourceful parasites, into subjects of his reformist zeal. He embarked upon a mission to transform his empire into a well-managed state based upon order, uniform legislation, and Prussian military standards. He did not subscribe to the view that the army, as the Warsaw Jewish Committee suggested, was a genuine school of civilization and reform. Yet he certainly regarded it as an excellent school of statehood in which to teach the unruly Jews the spirit of order, civic behavior, and obedience. As Andreas Kappeler advises, in the Russian empire, "The decisive elements of legitimization and organization were the ruler and the dynasty, the estate system of society, and the imperial mindset."[34] If this is so, then by the mid-1820s Jews had already become part of the estate system, and during the Napoleonic invasion, they had proved their loyalty to the ruler. They lacked only one legitimizing factor: the imperial mindset. And this was exactly with what Nicholas intended to confer upon them in the army. Now his Jewish Committee had to consider pros and cons of this measure and draft the proposal.

Final Deliberations

Several scholars have attempted reconstructing what was the Jewish Committee's agenda back in the mid-1820s; which proposals were discussed, and how the discussions proceeded. Yet they could only speculate on this matter, as the archive of the St. Petersburg Jewish Committee was lost in a fire in 1862, and with it the protocols of its meetings. However, in addition to Warsaw materials that shed light on the relations between the Russian and the Polish Jewish Committees, the archives preserved several *memorii* – memos, succinct reports of the daily meetings of the Jewish Committee regularly sent to the tsar. Several pages of these memos, albeit abrupt and generalized, provide fascinating insights into what the highest Russian officials thought about Jewish military service and how they arrived at the draft of the statute on Jewish conscription, which eventually was corrected, approved, and signed by Tsar Nicholas.

Two aspects were salient in the yearlong 1826 deliberations of the committee: the Jews' glorious reputation as warriors and the contemporary European attitudes toward their military service. Although Jews remained Jews on paper; Druzhinin, Fon-Fok, Kaisarov, and Kartashevskii considered Jewish

---

[34] Kappeler, "*Mazepintsy, Malorossy, Khokhly*: Ukrainians in the Ethnic Hierarchy of the Russian Empire," in Andreas Kappeler, Zenon E. Kohut, Frank E. Sysyn, and Mark Von Hagen, *Culture, Nation, and Identity: The Ukrainian-Russian Encounter (1600–1945)* (Edmonton and Toronto: Canadian Institute of Ukrainian Studies Press, 2003), 162–181, here 163.

military faculties in the spirit of the Age of Reason, treating Jews as Hebrews or Israelis, the people of the great biblical past. Names of the eighteenth-century European thinkers, to whom the committee notes randomly referred, also testified that the discussion followed the logic of the Enlightenment. The committee members heavily drew from the holy history of the ancient Hebrews. They emphasized that Jews not only conquered the biblical Palestine but also successfully defended it and extended its borders over the centuries. During the Babylonian bondage Jews temporarily lost their combatant qualities yet with the Maccabees they regained their military spirit. In the Ancient Middle East, Jewish warriors also served as soldiers and as military leaders beyond the borders of the Jewish state. In the post-biblical period they bravely defended Jerusalem and fought under – and against – the Romans. Western Christian countries persecuted Jews for their creed and hence Jews did not serve in the troops of medieval Europe, but they had a record of service in Muslim armies. Polish kings exempted Jews from the service and by the late eighteenth century Jews did not participate in military campaigns. However, Jews selflessly defended Praga, the Jewish district of Warsaw, in 1794. This military record, perhaps much more detailed in the lost proceedings than in the memos, signified that in the eyes of state officials Jews could fight, professionally and selflessly. Jews were no more inept, cowardly, and physically unfit dwellers of the empire's western borderland. Now it was the task of the government to help Jews regain this lost quality.

The committee meticulously studied the regulations on Jewish conscription in contemporary Europe and also looked into the early results of this measure. The committee members underscored that in France Jews served on a par with everybody else, enjoyed upward mobility, served as officers as early as in 1812, and were promoted even to the elite regiments. The committee carefully reviewed the laws on Jewish draft adopted in Austria in the 1780s and 1790s and noted that Prussia also introduced similar laws and that many Jews in Prussia volunteered their service. The European experience seemed to convince the Jewish Committee of the efficiency of conscription. Yet there were doubts, mostly connected to the purported incompatibility of army duties and the Jewish way of life. Jews, the committee underscored, were very attached to their creed. How could Jewish soldiers observe the Sabbath, where all work on that day was forbidden? And what would they do with their phylacteries, those small yet cumbersome leather boxes containing Jewish prayers, which every adult male Jew had to place on his hand and his head every morning? During the Holiday of Booths (*Sukkot*) they had to eat and drink under the green cover of branches, and over Passover they had to eat unleavened bread; this seemed to contradict the army's internal regulations. Moreover, drafting married Jews could economically ruin their families. And the inertia of the centuries-long exemption would make Jews consider conscription a burden to be circumvented, not a duty to be fulfilled.

Perhaps at that point the committee resorted to the opinion of Johann David Michaelis (1717–1791), a theologian, an outstanding Orientalist, biblical scholar, and Hebraist from the University of Göttingen; and, for more detailed discussion of the Jewish religious observance, to Tadeusz Czacki (1765–1813), Polish historian, reformist, and the minister of education well familiar with the Jewish rituals in his native Volhynia province. Michaelis was known among enlightened thinkers for his conservative stance on many issues of Jewish reform, particularly for his skepticism about Jewish military service. Paradoxically, the Jewish Committee members quoted him to support the idea of Jewish conscription, not to cast doubts about it. They drew heavily from Michaelis – who in turn used examples of King David and the Maccabees – to prove that Jews could fight over Shabbat as its laws were not applicable in wartime and that in general, the defense (unlike the offense) campaign nullified the rigorous religious observance. Likewise, the committee members referred to Czacki, who argued that some religious laws of Talmudic origin under certain circumstances could be canceled. Even such an authority as the Paris Sanhedrin had decided that Jews could be exempt from the rites of their creed while fulfilling their military duty. In practice, Prussian experience demonstrated that Jews had found ways to help their brethren observe the rites of creed in the army, as the rich German Jews had sent unleavened bread for Passover to their brethren on military service. The Russian army knew the precedents of conscripting non-Christians with similar needs: drafted Muslims fulfilled their military duty and observed their rites of creed – and even had a mullah assigned to the Tartar Uhlan regiment. Ultimately, the members of the committee seemed unanimous in their decision to apply the Talmudic *dina de malkuta dina* (the law of the country is the law for the Jew) regulation to army service, interpreting this statement far beyond its Talmudic usage for monetary matters. Jews should serve, concluded the committee, and one of their basic laws provided religious grounds for their acceptance of military duty.[35]

Sometime in 1826 the Jewish Committee shared its conclusions and concerns with a number of other state officials. Egor Kankrin, Nicholas I's minister of finance and one of the rare courtiers whose advice the tsar heeded, strongly supported the introduction of conscription. He maintained that the exemption of Jews from the draft had caused an illegal influx of the Jews from Austria into the Russian Empire and the only way to check it was to make Jews in Russia liable for military service. He also thought that those Jews who were afraid of conscription would work harder to attain a higher economic status and would not be harmful any longer to the treasury. The minister of people's education also agreed about the usefulness of Jewish conscription. Several unidentified ministers argued that Jews in Belorussia, perhaps the poorest ones, should be immediately sent into the army. On the basis of its deliberations and studies of various European laws regarding Jewish military service, the committee composed a proposal on Jewish conscription and dispatched it along with the memos to the tsar.

---

[35] RGIA, f. 560, op. 10, d. 180 ("Memorii zasedanii Komiteta, sostavlennnogo dlia prigotovleniia proekta novogo polozhenia o evreiakh za ianvar-dekabr 1826 g.," see CAHJP, HM2/9318.1), ll. 25–30.

Nicholas took a pencil and went over the memos, leaving multiple marginal notes. He liked the idea of the introduction of Jewish civil duty. He also noticed the importance of drafting Jews beyond the required quota as a punishment for their crimes and "for further success of their civil transformation." He marked four times the proposal to draft Jewish boys not younger than twelve as cantonists (see Chapter 3). He seemed to be nodding approvingly while reading about the necessity to exempt merchants, as the most trustworthy Jews, from the draft. He also agreed to have Jews registered under their Jewish, not similar Christian names. Finally Nicholas called for the definitive version of the statute to be put together.[36]

Objects of Reform

Before Nicholas's rule, nothing appeared to hinder the economic, social, and cultural stability of East European Jews at the end of the second decade of the nineteenth century and the start of the third. This was perhaps their most peaceful time, between the Partitions of Poland and the Great Reforms of Alexander II, when they found themselves between the vanishing Polish and the rising Russian power, in the midst of an administrative and managerial collapse. Polish projects for Jewish reform, designed during the Four-Year Sejm, vanished with the demise of the Polish state, and Russian projects had not yet crystallized. The plans of Nicholas's predecessor, Alexander I, to acculturate the Jews, including some of the far-reaching regulations of his 1804 statute, remained mostly on paper. Although Alexander I had some ambitious ideas on his agenda, upon which Nicholas I later capitalized, the former's appetite for reformation dissipated after the Napoleonic Wars, as he became immersed in mysticism and distanced himself from politics. The damage caused to the economy of the Pale of Settlement by the partitions and the Napoleonic invasion was soon repaired. Before 1825, the imperial administration confined its legislative activity regarding Jews to roughly three decrees annually. (Nicholas I would have as many as twenty.) The Russian government still favored Polish gentry in the western borderlands, endorsing the omnipotent Polish magnates who relied upon their indispensable Jewish middlemen. Approximately 900,000 to 1,200,000 Jews, whom Russia inherited from Poland, benefited from this magnate–Jew lease-holding relationship. Such ambiguous yet predominantly favorable relations with the Polish gentry were enjoyed until after the 1830–1831 Polish revolt,[37] when relations deteriorated.

---

[36] RGIA, f. 560, op. 10, d. 179 ("Predstavlennye gosudariu imperatoru zapiski evresikogo komiteta o khode ego del," 1826–27, see CAHJP, HM2/9318.2), ll. 15–16; RGIA, f. 560, op. 10, d. 181 ("Zapiski Gosudariu Imperatoru o zaniatiiakh evreiskogo komiteta," 1827, see CAHJP, HM2/9318.3), ll. 37–48.

[37] For an analysis of the relations between Jews and Polish magnates based upon the *arenda* system, see Murray J. Rosman, *The Lords' Jews: Magnate-Jewish Relations in the Polish-Lithuanian Commonwealth during the Eighteenth Century* (Cambridge, Mass: Harvard University Press and the Harvard Ukrainian Research Institute, 1990), 75–76, 106–142. To

In the late eighteenth and early nineteenth centuries, East European Jewish society was expanding territorially. Paul I sanctioned new urban Jewish settlements in Kamenets-Podolsk and Kurland province. In the 1810s to 1820s, Kiev was open to Jews; their proposed expulsion was deferred repeatedly, until the 1830s. The imperial administration supported the Jewish colonization of the southern regions of the empire, especially in Novorossiia and Taurida provinces, opening for them vast and rapidly developing regions. Between 1815 and 1825, the government went so far as to grant some Jews the privilege of distilling and selling alcohol in Russia's interior provinces, thus allowing some Jews to reside outside the Pale.[38] At the same time, Astrakhan and Caucasian provinces were still open for Jewish settlement; the government excluded these two provinces from the Pale only in the mid-1820s.

In the second decade of the nineteenth century, Jewish merchants predominated in the western borderlands of the empire: they were prominent in urban trade, controlled the westward grain and lumber traffic, and competed successfully with Christian wholesale merchants.[39] In Volhynia and Podol provinces, the numbers of trading Jews grew from 25 to 30 percent among all traders in the 1780s to 86 percent in 1818. At the biggest Polish fairs, 97 percent of all merchants were Jews from Lithuania and the Ukraine. Jews also were prevalent at the largest annual fairs in Balta, Berdichev, Dubno, and Uman. Inns and taverns in rural and urban areas were primarily Jewish. *Propinacja*, a lucrative right to distill and to sell alcohol, remained a Jewish occupation par excellence, engendering low prices and much competition. As in the eighteenth

illustrate the significance of Polish Jewish economic stability in the 1810s, suffice it to say that Polish landowners convinced the Russian imperial authorities to rescind their decision and to stop expelling Jews from rural areas. On expulsions, see I. Orshanskii, *Russkoe zakonodatel'stvo o evreiakh. Ocherki i issledovaniia* (SPb.: Landau, 1877), 275–279; the government canceled its attempt to banish Jews from the rural to urban areas before 1811, see *PSZ* I, 29: 22651; 30: 23424; the expulsion announced in 1825 was eventually deferred, and was not enforced until the 1830s; see *PSZ* II, 40: 30402.

[38] *PSZ* I, 24: 18132, the regime confirmed the right to settle in Kamenets-Podolsk in 1833, see *PSZ* II, 8: 5950; for Kurland, see *PSZ* I, 25: 18889; *PSZ* I, 25: 18336; enforced and expanded, *PSZ* I, 31: 24098; *PSZ* I, 30: 23132 paragraph 2; *PSZ* I, 31: 24185; I, 34: 27147. See also *PSZ* I, 36: 27794 (1819); enforced the same year, see *PSZ* I, 36: 27963. Jews immediately overruled a timid governmental attempt to limit the Jewish trade of liquor in the Chernigov and Poltava provinces, de facto substituting Jewish producers by hired Christian counterparts. The regime did not enforce its 1822 restrictions on liquor distilling in the Mogilev and Vitebsk provinces; besides, Jews easily circumvented them. See *PSZ* I, 38: 29079; *PSZ* I, 38: 29420.

[39] For the predominance of Jews in the grain trade, see Robert Jones, "Ukrainian Grain and Russian Market in the Late Eighteenth and Early Nineteenth Centuries," in I. S. Koropeckyj, *Ukrainian Economic History: Interpretative Essays* (Cambridge, Mass.: Harvard University Press for the Harvard Ukrainian Research Institute, 1991), 210–227; for the competition of Jews against Christian merchants, see the Senate discussion of a complaint of Polotsk Christians, *PSZ* I, 32: 25639; Jews dominated urban trade because Poles were not interested in urban settlement, see Piotr Wandycz, *The Price of Freedom: A History of East Central Europe from the Middle Ages to the Present* (London and New York: Routledge, 1992), 41–42, 70–72, 177–78.

century, Jews administered estates, mills, breweries. Some random Senate measures limiting illegal Jewish trade in Russia's interior testify to the attempts of Jewish merchants to conquer new markets.[40] The complaints of the *kahal* notwithstanding, the position of Jews in Russia during the last ten years of Alexander I's rule apparently was desirable from many perspectives. Unlike the 1880s, Jews sought to migrate to the Russian Empire, rather than westward, chiefly for economic advantage. The western and southwestern provinces of Russia experienced a significant influx (*vo mnozhestve*, to use the wording of the Senate) of Jewish migrants from Austria and Turkey. So many resorted to subterfuge to acquire legal permission and engage in trade that the government felt compelled to issue a prohibition on foreign Jews settling permanently (*vodvoriatsia na zhitel'stvo*) in Russia.[41] To suppress Jewish competition in trade, the authorities introduced a discriminatory tariff. Later in the 1830s, they made an attempt to suppress widespread Jewish smuggling by restricting new Jewish settlement within fifty miles of western border areas and vainly trying to resettle Jews who resided there.

The removal of Polish administration in the western provinces created a power vacuum that the Russian administration, both civil and military, slowly but steadily filled with a sophisticated infrastructure. In towns that retained their private Polish status (*shtetlakh* or *mestechki*) and in those that passed to state ownership (*kazennye goroda*), Jews accepted the legitimacy of the new urban administration and appealed to it for protection and privileges, which in most cases they obtained. To control unnecessary rumors among Jews and disseminate useful information about governmental plans, the imperial bureaucracy in St. Petersburg continued to rely upon the assistance of Jewish deputies, whose effective communal intercession the government ended half a year before the death of Alexander I. The reformist undertakings of the new, Nicholaevan, regime restricted the activities of the *kahal*, the traditional communal umbrella institution, and promoted the proliferation of grass roots, volunteer societies such as self-governing *havurot*, which functioned as religious brotherhoods and professional guilds and accordingly became the nucleus of a new social and economic structure.[42] These societies institutionalized

---

[40] *PSZ* I, 37: 28537; Ignacy Schiper, *Dzieje handlu żydowskiego na ziemiach polskich* (Warsaw: Nakładem Centrali Związku kupców w Warszawe, 1937): 375, 410–413, 424–427.

[41] *PSZ* I, 39: 30004; *PSZ* I, 40: 30436; I, 40: 30483. For the legal implications of these decisions, see I. Orshanskii, *Russkoe zakonodatel'stvo o evreiakh. Ocherki i issledovaniia* (SPb.: Landau, 1877), 31.

[42] Benzion Dinur, "The Origins of Hasidism and Its Social and Messianic Foundations," in Gershon Hundert, ed., *Essential Papers on Hasidism* (New York and London: New York University Press, 1991), 131–132. The development of voluntary communal institutions was part of the democratization of Jewish society at large rather than its demise and fragmentation, as Eli Lederhendler has argued. See his *The Road to Modern Jewish Politics* (New York and Oxford: Oxford University Press, 1989), 52, 68; on the horizontally oriented *havurot*, see Yohanan Petrovsky-Shtern, "Russian Legislation and Jewish Self-Governing Institutions: The Case of Kamenets-Podol'sk," *Jews in Russia and Eastern Europe*, vol. 56, no. 1 (Summer 2006): 107–130.

various aspects of Jewish tradition, fostered the establishment of Jewish artisans' groups as an alternative to the cumbersome, state-endorsed Christian guilds, and helped popularize important ideological messages such as Hasidic teachings.[43]

By the end of the second decade of the nineteenth century, ideological tensions and internal religious wars among East European Jews had waned. The late eighteenth-century hostility of rabbinical authorities toward pious Hasidim had softened, no longer resulting in open animosity, violence, and excommunication.[44] Staunch enemies, Hasidim and *mitnagdim* (their opponents) started talking to one another and seeking rapprochement, especially in view of Napoleon's invasion and his far-fetched reformist projects, and later as a response to the encroaching *Haskalah*, Jewish enlightenment. The intrinsic elements of Hasidism, such as piety, kabbalistic mysticism, religious enthusiasm, and spiritual revivalism, moved from relative obscurity to the very core of East European Jewish culture, winning over the vast majority of the Jewish population and establishing piety as the new paramount value of the traditional community.[45] In a number of locales, such as Vilna, Hasidim were elected as heads of the *kahal*, while R. Haim from Volozhin, the chief authority among the *mitnagdim* of the early nineteenth century, wrote endorsements for Hasidic books and allowed a Hasid employee to work as the town butcher. From a number of scattered communities in the central Ukraine (eastern Poland), Hasidism rapidly spread over the entire Ukraine, then moved westward and established courts in Lithuania, Belorussia, and central Poland. After several attempts to hinder the movement in the 1790s, the Russian authorities, beginning in 1804, adopted a neutral attitude toward Hasidim and legally endorsed their religious practices.[46] Russian persecutions of Hasidic masters (*tsadikim*), like the anti-Hasidic regulations of the Habsburg authorities, started later, in the mid-1830s and became particularly harsh only in the

---

[43] See paragraph 23 of the 1804 statute, *PSZ* I, 28: 21547; Moshe Kramer, "Leheker ha-melakhah ve-hevrot ba'alei-melakhah etsel yehudei Polin," *Zion*, no. 2 (1937): 312–319; On guilds and *havurot*, see Mark Wischnitzer, *History of Jewish Crafts and Guilds* (New York: Jonathan David Publishers, 1965), 274; Iu. Gessen, *Istoriia evreiskogo naroda v Rossii. Izdanie ispravlennoe* (M., Jerusalem: Gesharim, 1993), 2: 232–233; Yohanan Petrovsky-Shtern, "Hasidism, *Havurot* and the Jewish Street," *Jewish Social Studies*, vol. 10, no. 2 (2004): 20–54.

[44] See Sucher Ber Weinryb, *The Jews of Poland: A Social and Economic History of the Jewish Community in Poland from 1100 to 1800* (Philadelphia: The Jewish Publication Society of America, 1972), 285–302.

[45] Wolf Zeev Rabinowitsch, "Karlin Hassidism," in *Pinsk: The History of the Jews in Pinsk, 1506–1542* (Tel-Aviv: The Association of Jews of Pinsk in Israel, 1977): 37–39; Azriel Shokhat, "Ha-hanhagah be-kehilot rusia im bitul ha-kahal," *Zion*, no. 42 (1977): 143–147; Ze'ev Gries, *Sefer, sofer ve-sipur be-reshit ha-hasidut* (Hakibuts Hameiukhad Publishing House, 1992), 21; Shaul Stampfer, *Ha-yeshivah ha-litait be-hitva'atah* (Jerusalem: Merkaz Zalman Shazar, 1995), 33–36; Jerzy Tomaszewski, *Najnowsze Dzeje Żydow z Polsce w Zarysie* (Warsaw: PWN, 1993), 34–35.

[46] *PSZ* I, 28: 21,547 (ch. 5, par. 53).

mid-1860s.[47] Paradoxically, traditional Judaism appealed to some non-Jews, as well; at the beginning of the nineteenth century, hundreds of Christian families in the provinces of Tula, Orel, Saratov, and Voronezh, outside the Pale of Settlement, converted en masse to Judaism and called themselves the Ger sect – from the Hebrew *ger*, "proselyte." Another group became part of the Judaizing sect of Subbotniks, a phenomenon unheard of in Russian history since the suppression of the sixteenth-century Judaizers.[48]

The progressive reform of the Jewish people that already held sway in Western Europe fascinated some East European *maskilim*, the harbingers of the Jewish Enlightenment; yet these *maskilim* failed to create a medium for their ideas. Their desire to transcend tradition and to transport Jews out of the shtetl into the light of knowledge and civilization was expressed primarily through private correspondence between a few individuals. They did not represent any viable threat to traditional Jewish ways in the Pale of Settlement. In the 1830s and 1840s, a handful of progressive Jewish educators established a number of Jewish schools on the fringes of the Pale and across the border (in Riga, Odessa, Brody, and Tarnopol), yet their impact upon the Jewish community within the Pale was minimal. A new type of school emerged in the early 1820s, in Uman, but the community insisted upon its closure and its director defected, ending up teaching Semitic languages at Cambridge, in England. Jewish enlightened intellectuals, whom the community scornfully dubbed *berlinchikes*, were obliged to conceal the fact that they were reading books of secular character. The enlightened Jewish press, like Eisenbaum's Polish *Dostręgacz Nadwi-sliański* (Warsaw), had a very small circulation, while the Hebrew language *Minhat Bikurim* (Vilna), with a still smaller readership, appeared in 1834. The moderately reformist newspaper *Me'asef* had hardly any impact upon East European, progressive-minded Jews, who found it too radical. The individual treatises of the *maskilim*, with their detailed programs for Jewish reform such as Isaac Baer Levinsohn's *Teudah be-Yisrael* (1827), were little more than voices crying in the wilderness; they met with negative communal reaction.[49] While some *maskilim* recognized the necessity of convincing the imperial

---

[47] For an analysis of the anti-Hasidic persecutions in Galicia, see Rafael Mahler, *Hasidism and Jewish Enlightenment: Their Confrontation in Galicia and Poland in the First Half of the Nineteenth Century* (Philadelphia: The Jewish Publication Society of America, 1985), 74–76.

[48] Members of both sects were forcibly transferred to southern Armenia and southwestern Azerbaijan and the Altai regions late in the second decade of the nineteenth century. For more detail, see Valerii Dymshits, "Expedition to Azerbaijan," *East European Jewish Affairs*, vol. 30 no. 2 (2000): 37–52; Sergei Shtyrkov, "Strategia postroeniia gruppovoi identichnosti: obshchina sektantov-subbotnikov v stanitse Novoprivol'naia Stavropol'skogo kraia," in O. V. Belova, ed., *Svoi ili chuzhoi? Evrei i slaviane glazami drug druga* (M.: Dom evreiskoi knigi, 2003): 266–87; Aleksandr Lvov, "Subbotniki i evrei," *Paralleli*, no. 2–3 (2003), 401–412.

[49] Samuil Kraiz, "Batei-sefer ha-yehudiim be-safah ha-rusit be-rusia ha-tsarit" (Ph.D. diss., Hebrew University, 1994), 19–20; P. Marek, *Ocherki po istorii prosveshcheniia evreev v Rossii (dva vospitaniia)* (M.: Obshchestvo rasprostraneniia pravil'nykh svedenii o evreiakh i evreistve, 1909), 13; I. Zinberg, *Istoriia evreiskoi pechati v Rossii* (Petrograd: I. Fleitman, 1915), 21. Cf. the development of Haskalah in Germany, in full sway in the 1810s: David Sorkin, *The*

authorities to implement a full-fledged system of Jewish reform based upon the Enlightenment, it was only much later, in the 1830s and 1840s, that the *Haskalah* became "an ally of the regime of Nicholas or, if one prefers, an instrument in his hands."[50]

Communal Mobilization

Permeating the East European Jewish imagination as it did, religious piety also informed the Jewish communal response to conscription. Most Jews in pre-partitioned Poland perceived historical calamities through the prism of the rabbinic *be-anvonotenu ha-rabim*, "because of our great sins," a concept that had long been regarded as axiomatic wisdom. Whatever befell the Jews, they believed they fully deserved it because of their failure to repent and to return to God's precepts. The Almighty used the gentiles as a weapon to mete out his punishment to the Jews for their laxity in religious observance and their neglect of Torah learning. As a Hasidic legend has it – and documental evidence corroborates – Jews in the Pale of Settlement considered the forthcoming introduction of military duty as a *g'zeyre*, a calamity, or manifestation of divine rage. They believed that only righteous Jews, the Hasidic leaders and followers of the Ba'al Shem Tov (Israel ben Eliezer, ca. 1700–1760, the legendary founder of the movement, who also was known by his acronym, the Besht), were able to cancel the approaching calamity. Those who did not follow the Hasidic movement nonetheless believed that the miracle-working *tsadikim*, Hasidic masters, could avert national catastrophe by interceding before God. Upon hearing of the conscription edict, crowds of Jews flocked to Medzhibozh, the town where the Ba'al Shem Tov spent the last twenty years of his life, to see Avraham Yehoshua Heschel, the Apter Rebbe (who had served as the Rabbi of Apt, Polish Opatów). Knowing that the government was scheming to prohibit them from leasing postal stations, to banish them from villages, and to make them serve in the army, they appealed for a remedy to their situation. As if replicating the events of the Book of Esther, the Apter Rebbe sat on a high chair and imposed fasting and penitence on a number of Jewish communities, at least two of which, Bar and Berdichev, complied. He ordered the supplicants to reveal their hearts; if they prayed sincerely, they could succeed. The Apter Rebbe listened to their arguments, then announced his will as the will of God. He canceled both the ban on leasing the post offices and the expulsion of Jews from the villages, but not the draft; this was beyond his powers.

There is little doubt that Jews turned for help to Hasidic rabbis known for their supernatural abilities. However, this particular legend most likely emerged later, as authorities indeed deferred the first two plans but not the third

Transformation of German Jewry, 1780–1840 (New York and Oxford: Oxford University Press, 1987), 41–104.

[50] Emmanuel Etkes, *Rabbi Israel Salanter and the Mussar Movement: Seeking the Torah of Truth* (Philadelphia: The Jewish Publication Society of America, 1993), 140.

one. Documentary sources corroborate that, as early as the spring of 1826, Jewish communal leaders attempted to prevent the publication of the conscription law or to cancel its implementation. The informers of the gendarmes corps attested that Jewish communities imposed a fast upon themselves, organized public prayers at cemeteries, where they implored the souls of the righteous to intercede for them before God, blew the ram's horn, and called for repentance. According to other sources, Jews placed notes with their supplications addressed to the Almighty into the hands of the recently deceased, who would receive divine audience. Authorities unfamiliar with Jewish tradition misconstrued such practices; for five years afterward, the gendarme corps reported to the imperial administration that Jews composed special prayers to curse the emperor, and recited them on Mondays and Thursdays. The authorities finally realized that what was being described was the thousand-year-old penitential prayer (*tahanun*), and accordingly abandoned any attempt to read the matter politically. Yet they did fail to comprehend that there were reasons other than a pious worldview or the alleged Jewish proclivity for avoiding state duties that generated the Jewish overreaction to the introduction of the military draft.

The Russia of Nicholas I was unfamiliar with the concept of the public sphere in its late nineteenth-century sense. Imperial authorities discussed their plans behind closed doors, and Jews were bedeviled by rumors. The more secrecy was involved, the less credible was the news and the more crucial in the eyes of East European Jews the role of the deputies (*shtadlans*), those informal representatives who interceded with the government and state administration on the Jewish communities' behalf. During the first two years of Nicholas's rule, the deputies' position became even more critical, particularly when in 1825 the government dissolved the only St. Petersburg state institution of Jewish representatives, "the deputies of the Jewish communities." These were the Russian version of the Paris Grand Sanhedrin, created and later dismantled by Napoleon Bonaparte – although the Russian analog of the French institution had different objectives, methods of selection, and forms of operation. Once the rumors concerning the preparations for reform reached the Pale of Settlement, communal leaders took action, recognizing the pivotal role Nicholas assigned to conscription. In June 1826, the secret chancellery of His Excellency Grand Duke Constantine intercepted several letters indicating that Jews were well aware of the government's plans and sought to counter them. One of the letters addressed to the *kahal* in Brest-Litovsk bemoaned the forthcoming reform: Jewish hearts were sorrowful, hands weakened, tears poured from their eyes as the publication of the tsar's decree, this instrument of divine rage, approached. The letter decried "the decree of the crown, the authorities, and the ministers" scheming to destroy Jews through conscription, and interspersed rhetorical questions with practical appeals: "How powerful is the rage of the tsar who ordered to conscript us from the age of twenty! If he brings this to life, we will cease to exist and our name will vanish. Has anything similar happened to us before? Perhaps they may calm down when the tsar's courtiers and his ministers receive financial remuneration. Help us to save our lives!"[51]

This cry for help was one of many. Already in the early summer of 1826, groups of deputies emerged both in Russia and in the Kingdom of Poland to prevent the introduction of conscription. One of the most influential such groups enlisted David from Ochakov (called Ochakovskii), the purveyor for the Russian army and fleet; Yosef Leyb Kaminsky, a guild merchant from Berdichev; and Rabbi Moshe Varshaver from Warsaw. These and other deputies traversed the Pale, raising funds to bribe the ministers, to support the court Jews in the capital, and to grease the palms of the members of the Imperial Jewish Committee.

While Jewish deputies closely followed the negotiations over the planned reforms between the Jewish Committees in Warsaw and in St. Petersburg, the secret police closely monitored the deputies' activities. On January 7, 1827, the secret chancellery reported to Constantine that, according to rumors, Jews expected that Nicholas's order would enable them to enjoy all the privileges available to other inhabitants of the empire and that they would become susceptible to conscription. The Jews were unhappy with the prospect of conscription, continued the report, and therefore a delegation of *kahals* had arrived in Warsaw from Lithuania. They intended to submit a request to His Highest Excellency Grand Duke Constantine that he allow them to pay ransom, as before, rather than serve in the army. A detailed description of Jewish tactics was included: "Jewish rabbis arrive in Warsaw from the towns of Brest-Litovsk and Pinsk, to discuss with local *kahal* elders how to write the petition. And the *kahal* elder Shakhno promised to instruct them. After the discussion of how to compose a petition, they will write to Lithuanian *kahals*, calling their deputies to arrive here."[52]

The local governors in the Pale reported similar arrangements. Throughout the Pale, Jews contributed the obligatory fifteen silver coins per person, in addition to unspecified sums from wealthy Jews with which to bribe the officials, particularly the Jewish Committee members. Several spiritual and communal leaders joined the *kahal* representatives and the wealthy Jews. The Hasidic Rebbe Motl from Chernobyl used his charisma to raise roughly 80,000 rubles in the heavily Hasidic Volhynia, Podol, and Minsk provinces, while Rabbi Yitshak Ayzik Rappoport from Berdichev raised about 100,000 rubles in Poltava, Kremenchug, Nikolaev, and Kherson.[53] Attempts to revoke the draft mobilized the Jewish masses and created solidarity among them.

---

[51] AGAD, Kancelaria Senatora Nowosilcowa, sygn. 700 ("O rekrutskoi povinnosti evreev, v Tsarstve Polskom obitaiushchikh"), 35–38. Another letter, less clear and poorly translated, addressed the anonymous Jewish community, asking for thirty-five talers for the same purpose; see ibid., 41.

[52] AGAD, zb. Policja Tajna w. kn. Konstantego, sygn. 32 ("Zhurnal iskhodiaschikh bumag po tainoi kantselarii v. kn. Konstantina," 1827), l. 5.

[53] GARF, f. 109. First expedition, d. 196 ("O evreiskom ravvine evree Aizike, sobravshem s evreev den'gi dlia deputatov evreiskikh, nakhodiashchikhsia v Peterburge," 1828), l. 8–10, 15.

Having no idea whether the sums raised would produce the desired effect, Jews panicked. Imperial officials in St. Petersburg and Warsaw further contributed to the uncertainty. Constantine's staff in Warsaw requested a much lower payment for protection: they were satisfied with 5,000 gold rubles per person. Conversely, officials in St. Petersburg, particularly those in the Jewish Committee, stipulated much larger sums in exchange for favoring the Jewish agenda.[54] A month and a half after the publication of the law and the statute, several well-informed communal representatives continued to believe that the tsar would cancel the draft and that those already recruited would return home. Differences between Polish and Russian Jewish communal representatives exacerbated the confusion. By 1826–1827, about forty-eight affluent Jewish families had been granted permission to reside in Warsaw, which otherwise was closed to Jews. Jewish army purveyors, wealthy leaseholders, bankers, and guild merchants formed the nucleus of an upper-class Jewish community. These individuals were more deeply Europeanized than their brethren in St. Petersburg, greater in number, and better connected with the local administration.[55] St. Petersburg could not boast this kind of Jewish elite, and the illustrious first generation of Russian *maskilim* either did not reside in the capital or was Christianized. While there were acculturated Jews permanently residing in Warsaw able to influence Novosiltsev, apparently there was nobody in St. Petersburg capable of achieving such results.

Communal Reaction to Conscription

The Jews in the Pale of Settlement had good reason for their extraordinary communal activity: they perceived the forthcoming conscription as the beginning of radical reform. While hardly any of the Jewish deputies knew the full extent of Nicholas's plans and the implications of his "barrack enlightenment," they assiduously predicted and tried to counteract them. The military governor of Kiev province reported to Adjutant General Alexander Benkendorf, the head of the gendarmes corps, that Jewish reticence resulted from the package of reforms confronting them, including the introduction of obligatory civil education, the imposition of European clothing, the ban on certain economic activities, and the introduction of useful trades for the destitute.[56]

The Jewish Committee in St. Petersburg warned Minister of the Interior Vassili Lanskoi that Jews consider the conscription as the oppression of their

---

[54] GARF, f. 109. SA., op. 3, d. 2314 ("Zapiska o sredstvakh, k kotorym pribegaiut evrei s tsel'iu ukloneniia ot rekrutskogo nabora, 1827"), ll. 4–5ob.

[55] Eisenbach, *The Emancipation of the Jews in Poland,* 112–132.

[56] GARF, f. 109. First expedition, d. 330 ("O reaktsii rossiiskogo evreistva na vvedenie v deistvie rekrutskogo ustava 1827 goda, ob usiliiakh evreiskikh obshchin oblegchit' polozhenie evreiskikh kantonistov v Smolenske, Vitebske, Rige i dr.," 1827), ll. 40b.-5ob.

faith."[57] Perhaps Jews realized that they stood at the threshold of an aggressive and merciless experiment aimed at the radical transformation of their social and cultural life. Pious Jews were more apprehensive about the frightening changes to their status quo than they were about military service. The community as a whole viewed Jewish conscription, not without grounds, as the beginning of the end of traditional East European Jewry.

Conscription placed the traditional Jew in an institution regarded by Russian society as a penitentiary and by Jewish society as Russian Orthodox and alien.[58] Perhaps the religious implications of army service were the most frightening for the Jewish community. The regimental command neglected the Russian Orthodox rites on a day-to-day basis, but observed them rather strictly during festivals, the summer training season, and military campaigns.[59] Every Sunday, the lower ranks were required to participate in a church procession (*tserkovnyi parad*). During the regimental church service, Russian Orthodox priests ensured that all lower ranks repeated the creed (*Simvol very*) and the Our Father (*Otche nash*).[60] Before the ceremony, the priest read out loud and the lower ranks repeated several paragraphs from the conscript status regarding the fear of God, firmness of faith, and loyalty to the sovereign. Regimental priests arranged and supervised the three daily prayers that marked the soldier's daily schedule. Twice a day, the regimental buglers blew a special call followed by the drummers' signal and an order of the commander on duty, "To prayer," (*Na molitvu*) and "Hats off" (*Shapki doloi*). Like any other soldier, the Jewish private participated in these recitations and prayers, whenever they were conducted.[61] In the second half of the century, the army became increasingly religious, to the extent that

---

[57] RGVIA, f. 405, op. 2, d. 436 ("Raport evreiskogo komiteta ministru vnutrennikh del Vasiliiu Lanskomu," 1828), ll. 7.

[58] The fact that the army was a reservoir of outlaws, ranging from smugglers and rapists to Polish mutineers, increased its unattractiveness. Nicholas I introduced a number of regulations that replaced exile to Siberia with army service for vagabonds and criminals younger than twenty years of age, as well as for some Jews and sectarians. See A. Tavastshern, *Voenno-tiuremnye uchrezhdeniia*, SVM, XII, kn. I, ch. III (1911), 257–277; for the negative assessment of the pre-reform army in Russian society, see Elise Kimerling Wirtschafter, *From Serf to Russian Soldier* (Princeton, N.J.: Princeton University Press), 3.

[59] See, e.g., a description of Russian Orthodox services during the Russo-Turkish war in Anon., "Piat' mesiatsev na Shipke. Iz vospominanii ofitsera Podol'skogo pekhotnogo polka," *Voennyi sbornik*, no. 4 (1883): 298, and during the Russo-Japanese war in Mitrofan Serebrianskii, *Dnevnik polkovogo sviashchennika, sluzhashchego na Dal'nem Vostoke* (M.: Otchii Dom, 1996), 98–99, 136, and especially 162, 178 and 182. For the preliminary approach to this theme, see Hryhorij Fil', "Religion and the Russian Army in the XIXth Century," in J. G. Purves and D. A. West, eds., *War and Society in the Nineteenth-Century Russian Empire* (Toronto: New Review Books, 1972), 23–33.

[60] A. Zhelobovskii, *Upravlenie tserkovnym dukhovenstvom*, SVM, XIII, kn. 2, 62–63.

[61] On the other hand, because of the religious laxity of the military commanders, relations between them and the regimental priests were characterized by conflicts and tension. The priests repeatedly complained to the Holy Synod of the military command's negligence during training and campaigns. See N. Nevzorov, *Istoricheskii ocherk upravleniia dukhovenstvom voennogo vedomstva v Rossii* (SPb.: Tip. F. Eleonskogo, 1875), 66–67, 80–81.

the department of military clergy developed the concept of the army as a Christ-loving force (*khristoliubivoe voinstvo*).[62] By virtue of military discipline and daily routine, the Jewish soldier was exposed to the rites of Russian Christianity, which could not but affect his own *Weltanschauung*.

Traditional Jews in the Pale of Settlement assessed the army as they did themselves: strictly in religious terms. They greatly exaggerated the army's domineering Russian Orthodoxy. The looming conscription revived and breathed new meaning into the traditional concept of *pikuakh nefesh*, well known to every Jew in the Pale of Settlement. Ashkenazic Judaism understood *pikuakh nefesh* as a mortal threat, a situation that required effort to redeem a Jew from physical or spiritual death, bondage, violence, rape, or conversion from Judaism. In order to redeem a human life, a Jew may sacrifice everything, including Judaism's most sacred tenets. *Pikuakh nefesh dokhe Shabbat*, argues one of the main Jewish legal sources: "The necessity to redeem human life annuls [the obligation to observe the laws of] the Sabbath" (*Shulkhan Arukh. Orah hayim*, 92: 1). Reference to *pikuakh nefesh* appeared at least four times in a private letter written in 1828 by a Jewish merchant to Rabbi Yitshak Ayzik Rappoport in Berdichev. Intercepted by gendarmes and clumsily translated "from the Jewish to the Russian dialect" by a Berdichev-based public notary, the letter made no mention of conscription. It touched upon some vague news concerning the Jewish people, argued for the importance of philanthropic donations, expressed concerns about the author's son's residing in Berdichev, and made reference to some obscure certificate and a request to appear before the *kahal*. This letter could have as easily been written at the end of the eighteenth as at the beginning of the nineteenth century. Yet its recurrent references to the threat to, and the redemption of, the human being betrayed its main historical context: the impending draft, the fundraising for further bribing of state officials, and the necessity to provide the nearest relative with a valid certificate of registration in Berdichev, which granted exemption from military service in the home community. Evoking *pikuakh nefesh* helped to open the wallets of the affluent and induced artisans to donate their meager savings for the redemption of Jewish souls. Counteracting conscription became an expression of religious piety.

---

[62] In 1861, for instance, the Holy Synod authorized regimental Russian Orthodox chaplains and parish priests in the villages to start teaching religion to the troops, and ordered them to promote the spiritual education of the lower ranks. For more detail, see *Rukovodstvennye dlia pravoslavnogo dukhovenstva ukazy Sviateishego Pravitel'stvuiushchego Sinoda. 1721–1878* (M.: Tip. M. Lavrova, 1879), 339–340. One must take into consideration that early twentieth-century Russian military historians such as Kersnovskii made an attempt to read their nationalist and religious conceptualization of the army into the beginning of the nineteenth century, as if the "Christ-loving" concept had always been attached to the troops; see Kersnovskii, A. A., *Istoriia russkoi armii*. 6 vols. (Belgrade: Tsarskii vestnik, 1933–1938). For documents on the religious revival in the military, albeit without a critical approach to them, see A. Savinkin et al., eds., *Khristoliubivoe voinstvo: Pravoslavnaia traditsiia Russkoi Armii* (M.: Voennyi universitet, 1997), 109–119, 135–140, 143–155, 194–200, 275–296.

Most likely, the Sabbath sermons of the shtetl rabbis engendered both piety and action on the part of wealthy and influential Jews. In addition to saving Jewish souls, their attempts to counter conscription represented the duty to ransom prisoners, the performance of the commandment of *pidion shevuim* (ransoming Jews from the bondage). While Prussian and Austrian rabbis pronounced their sermons before units of Jewish soldiers and published them in small brochures for distribution among the congregants, the sermons of East European communal leaders of the 1820s never appeared in print. However, Jewish informers, semiliterate people with remarkable imagination, enable one to reconstruct some of these sermons and to demonstrate the centrality of concepts such as "redeeming a soul" and "ransoming prisoners" to the contemporary Jewish religious sensibility.

Once Nicholas had signed the statute on conscription, the most pragmatic of the Jewish deputies realized that a new epoch in the relations between the empire and the Jews had begun. Attempts to cancel the newly approved law were patently futile; the encounter between East European Jews and Russian modernity was imminent, and no effort should be spared to help Jewish communities meet the challenge and reduce their losses to a minimum. Not much is known about this group of deputies; it may have comprised several *kahal* representatives, self-appointed communal leaders, and relatives of Jewish draftees defending the interests of their brethren. Yet their unwritten task was crystal clear: to provide Jewish conscripts with basic conditions for Jewish observance in the army. And while the military was beating the timidity, clumsiness, sickness, and Yiddish out of its Jewish conscripts, substituting for these the ability to read the Russian regimental statute and to march in parades, Jewish deputies were bent upon making the service of Jewish soldiers as close to traditional life in the shtetl as possible.

Consider the denunciation against Rabbi Solman (or Salmon; there is an inconsistency in the documents) from the small town of Starye Zhagary, near Shadov. The police informer claimed that several Vilna rabbis arrived in the shtetl for the fall 1827 farewell meeting with Jewish conscripts. They provided the conscripts with pocket money and reassured them that the power of a certain Timos R. would not last long; all Jewish conscripts would be redeemed and would come home. The report cites certain of the rabbis' observations. Rabbi Solman appears to have compared Nicholas I to Titus (Titus Rufus, as Jewish sources refer to him in *Talmud Bavli*, Gittin 56a–57b), the Roman emperor who destroyed the Temple in Jerusalem in A.D. 70. Jewish memory connects his name with the beginning of the *galut*, the second exile. In Rabbi Solman's view, Nicholas I was a violent and cruel destroyer of the Jewish shrine, the Ashkenazic Jewish tradition. Observant Jewish conscripts were Nicholas's hapless captives. This denunciation brought the police to Rabbi Solman's house; he was suspected of an anti-governmental plot. The house search resulted in the discovery of several pages written in Hebrew, which an anonymous translator tried to present to the authorities as a dangerous composition based upon Kabbalah. Yet Rabbi Solman's notes scarcely leave any doubt as to their nature: they comprised a set of quotations for a Shabbat sermon, taking a listener from a Pentateuch verse to its reflection in the Prophets, to its interpretation in Rashi's commentary, to its discussion in the Talmud, to its legal implications in Shulkhan Arukh, and back to the biblical verse, now imbued with new meaning.

The confiscated text was the draft of a sermon on the ransoming of Jewish prisoners, constructed around Jeremiah 22:10: "Weep not for him who is dead, mourn not for him! Weep rather for him who is going away; never again will he see the land of his birth."[63] Rabbi Solman traced direct parallels between the conscription of Russian Jews and the destruction of the Temple, between parents who sent their children into the army and those insane mothers who boiled and ate their children during siege and famine, and between the conscripts and captives.[64] Then Rabbi Solman analyzed how the first-century rabbinic authority Yohanan ben Zakkai understood the verse from Jeremiah 15:2: "And it shall come to pass, when they say unto thee, whither shall we go forth? Then thou shalt tell them, Thus saith Jehovah: Such as are for death, to death; and such as are for the sword, to the sword; and such as are for the famine, to the famine; and such as are for captivity, to captivity." According to the Talmudic discussion (*Bava Bathra* 8b), argued Rabbi Solman, captivity was one of the most painful calamities, worse than famine or physical violence, since it affected both body and soul and prevented one from following the tradition of his people. Rabbi Solman drew a number of conclusions from his Talmudic insights. Firstly, he argued, if a person encountered an ethical dilemma and did not know whom to save, the one going to die or another one going into exile, it was preferable to save the exiled: that is to say, the conscripts. Secondly, those parents who voluntarily send their children into the army's bondage committed a crime worse than killing one's own offspring. Thirdly, he bemoaned that the time was out of joint, as there was no Jewish leader capable of protecting his people from the fatal events unfolding.[65]

The sermons of Rabbi David of Novardek (in Russian, Novogrudok, 1769–1837), one of the outstanding Jewish communal leaders of the early nineteenth century and the brother-in-law of Naphtali Tsevi Yehuda Berlin (the head of the renowned Volozhin rabbinical academy), were more sober and realistic. Rabbi David preached to Jewish conscripts in the early 1830s, teaching them stoicism, inspiring them with the wisdom of Ecclesiastes, and striving to reconcile them to circumstances that, he emphasized, even the Almighty was not able to change. Rabbi David called upon the Jewish soldiers to fulfill honestly their oath to the emperor, just as they fulfilled the oaths they made to God. He

---

[63] GARF, f. 109. First expedition, d. 383 ("Po obiavlenii sviashchennika Pavla Vladykina o sdelannom emu pokazanii matrosami iz evreev o sushchestvuiushchem budto by mezhdu evreiskimi ravvinami Solmanom i prochimi zagovore protiv imperatora," 1828), l. 22.

[64] See Deut. 28:53: "In the distress of the siege to which your enemy subjects you, you will eat the fruit of your womb, the flesh of your own sons and daughters whom the Lord, your God, has given you."

[65] GARF, f. 109. First expedition, d. 383, ll. 220b.-250b.

asserted that their impeccable service earned them the respect and benevolence of military authorities. Rabbi David compared Purim and Hannukah, two holidays signifying the Jews' victory over their enemies: in the Book of Esther, Haman schemed to destroy all the Jews physically, while Antiochus, in the Book of Maccabees, plotted the Jews' spiritual death. Rabbi David insisted that the Jews of the past survived as a result of their ability to maintain their faith under excruciating circumstances. He urged Jewish conscripts to view their army service as a test rather than as bondage, particularly since the tsar did not force conscripts to surrender their faith. In his two recorded sermons, Rabbi David addressed the themes of *anusim*, those who are forced to abandon Judaism, and *shevuim*, captives, but did so only in a polemical key. As though arguing against an invisible opponent (perhaps himself), Rabbi David attempted to reassure the conscripts that they remained free people, and that the laws of the imperial army did not cancel or supersede the laws of the Almighty. He refrained from wailing in public. His bitter complaints and despair he reserved for the sermon he delivered on the eve of the Day of Atonement. Standing in the synagogue before his congregation, he articulated his tragic conviction that the child-cantonists were indeed captives, and that there was no harsher suffering than to send them into slavery.[66]

Although it is difficult to extrapolate from the scant evidence available, one may cautiously assume that more rabbinic leaders regarded the draft as Rabbi Solman from Starye Zhagary did than as Rabbi David from Novardek did.[67] Apparently this was evident also to the members of the Jewish Committee in St. Petersburg, who stated in their report that "there are some Jews who understand their obligations before the state and accept their [military] duty with a due submissiveness; yet the majority, because of the novelty [of this duty] and the prejudice of faith, consider it an oppression of their people."[68]

Helping the slaves endure their hardships became a priority for the Jews in the Pale of Settlement. They tried to convince the military administration to endorse officially three privileges for Jewish conscripts: the celebration of Jewish holidays, the use of a separate kosher cooking pot, and the availability of rabbinic services. They flooded the military with oral supplications and written

---

[66] For the sermons of David from Novardek, see the publication by Yisroel Mendlowitz, "Gezerah hi mi-lifanai," in *Yeshurun: measef torani*, no. 12 (5763/2003): 695–726.

[67] Other oblique sources testify that not only the communal leaders but also the whole Russian population considered Jewish recruits as captives. Therefore, according to Haim Liberman, the Yiddish popular story book *Gedulot Yosef* (The Greatness of Joseph, 1794) enjoyed an enormous success in Russia, although not in Poland, and saw more than twenty editions after the 1820s. Among other things, the book tells the story of a miraculous apparition in which Rachel cries over her son Joseph while Joseph pleads with his mother to protect him and to redeem him from bondage. Liberman is quite right when he argues that the popularity of the book depended upon the conscription context. See Hayim Liberman, *Ohel Rakhe"l*. 3 vols. (New York: Empire Press, 1984), 3:5–6.

[68] Members of the Jewish Committee made this statement reacting to a proposal to consider the illegitimate sons of the Jews (like the illegitimate sons of the Christian soldiers) as belonging to the military. See RGVIA, f. 405, op. 2, d. 436, l. 8.

petitions. And while the confused military considered how to respond, Jewish deputies turned to a different strategy: grassroots negotiations. In the winter of 1828, they provided Jewish conscripts in the fortress of Krondshtadt with *matzah*, unleavened bread, and kosher Passover wine, to ensure that they could celebrate Passover.[69] Despite the prohibition against St. Petersburg Jews visiting Krondshtadt and meeting with the Jews of the local garrison, the official and nonofficial deputies were well aware of the situation that prevailed in the barracks. The Passover wine and *matzah* arrived, but local commanders refused to distribute them among the Jewish soldiers. Nor did the commanders allow the Jews to conduct the Passover liturgy, or to conduct the *seder* (ceremonial celebration of Passover) with the four glasses of wine prescribed by Jewish tradition. The commanders forced Jews to eat together with other soldiers, and permitted the *matzah* only as dessert. In Vitebsk, after numerous complaints by the local community, the brigade commander, Colonel Vokhin, allowed Jewish soldiers to have established prayer services, yet he rejected other pleas, such as separately cooked food for the Jewish soldiers and cantonists. He based this decision upon purely pragmatic considerations, although he admitted that there existed an unsolved contradiction between the Statute on Jewish Conscription and some sort of secret regulations – the contradiction that requires an explanation.[70]

Local commanders made odd references in their notes to the military authorities in St. Petersburg mentioning "the advantages of our religion" and sometimes "a secret regulation on the advantages of our faith."[71] Perhaps these alluded to a secret law, known to the heads of the army units, that does not appear among the military documents of Nicholas I's epoch. Historians of Russian Jewry have testified that such a regulation existed and that it targeted Jews.[72] However, it is most probable that this regulation targeted all drafted non-Russians (*inorodtsy*). Perhaps it urged army commanders to instruct soldiers of alien beliefs so that they would recognize the advantages of Russian Orthodoxy. Apparently, there was only an oblique connection between this unidentified document and the conscription of Jews. Even if one assumes that this secret regulation of Nicholas I referred exclusively to Jews, one could hardly accept the viewpoint of most historians, who considered conscription the beginning of the Russian government's anti-Jewish repressions, the start of an epoch of assimilation and state-sponsored antisemitism. On the contrary, if this document solely concerned the Jews who learned about the advantages of Russian Orthodoxy and subsequently joined the "official peoplehood" (which

---

[69] GARF, f. 109. First expedition, d. 330, ll. 16–20; ibid. ("Zapiska A. Kh. Benkendorfa k voennomu general-gubernatoru S.-Peterburga ot 12 marta 1828" ["Pis'mo Bunema, syna Aarona, Shlomo, syna Altera-Zeliga iz Vitebska ot 2 marta 1828 g."], "Raport nachal'nika 1-go otdelenia 3-go okruzhnogo korpusa zhandarmov A. Kh. Benkendorfu ot 20 marta 1828"), ll. 22–27.

[70] GARF, f. 109. First expedition, d. 330, ll. 19–21.

[71] GARF, f. 109. First expedition, d. 330, ll. 23.

[72] Michael Stanislawski, *Tsar Nicholas I*, 23.

only later appeared on the agenda of Nicholas I), it was part of the normative Russian absolutist discourse rather than anything else. From an enlightened vantage point, Russian Orthodoxy was better because it was the imperial religion; subscribing to it was a rational and pragmatic choice. The question, then, is not only how to interpret this secret regulation within the framework of imperial modernization, but rather how Jews reacted to it and how effectively the military implemented it. This is determined primarily by the interaction between the communities and the Jewish soldiers, and, secondly, by the relations between the Jewish communities and Russian imperial administration. The result of Nicholas's plan to unify the empire religiously was predicated upon the government's aggressive intentions and the Jewish communities' defensive efforts. Neither Nicholas's goals nor the petitions of the Jewish deputies filed with the military administration entirely met with success.

In 1828, the heads of the gendarme corps, the War Ministry's Department of Military Settlements, and the Ministry of the Interior's Department of Spiritual Affairs of the Foreign Creeds finally transferred multiple Jewish petitions and complaints to the St. Petersburg Jewish Committee. The committee met on June 1, 1829, to discuss the Jewish communities' petitions and their protests against the arbitrariness of the local garrison commanders. Committee members agreed with the explanations presented in the report of the commander of the Smolensk cantonist battalion, who stated that the special privileges granted to Jewish cantonists prevented them from succeeding in service, trade, and studies. Therefore, the committee members sided with the military, and concluded that questions of the Jewish soldiers' religious rights were the sole responsibility of local commanders.[73] As happened in other cases, the members' resolutions evinced their helplessness and confusion rather than their loyalty, since reports by the same commanders confirmed that a discrepancy existed between the statute and internal army rules, and that the military's treatment of Jewish cantonists contravened its own statute.

Unlike pleas to the Jewish Committee, Jewish petitions filed with the local military commanders and with the emperor were often effective. The parents of Jewish conscripts joined the communal deputies and raised their voices to protect their children. They wrote Nicholas the following petition, full of elevated language, submissive voice, and heartbreaking music:

Benevolent monarch! Look from your heights at this most humble petition of ours and of other parents of the little Jewish conscripts of the town of Vilna who fulfill their service in Riga. We beseech you only that our children would not be forbidden to observe the rites of their creed so that this observance would be a means to strengthen their hearts toward a more diligent continuation of their military service, and we do not protest that many parents of the above-mentioned conscripts who arrived for a brief sojourn to Riga were not allowed to see their children. Your Imperial Majesty, may you be so merciful as to announce your highest order which would allow the Jewish conscripts to observe their rites of creed without any hindrance and to attend synagogues

---

[73] GARF, f. 109. First expedition, d. 330, l. 38–380b.

for prayer, and in places where there were no synagogues, to gather for common liturgy in a corresponding place, and mercifully assign for them rabbis appointed by the Jewish communities, and do not force them to do work the religion forbids them on Saturdays and holidays.[74]

Jewish parents also turned to a number of cantonist battalion commanders with similar petitions, which the commanders dispatched to their military supervisors, accompanied by their own reports. For instance, the commander of the Smolensk cantonist battalion asked Major General Kern to issue a regulation concerning Jewish cantonists during Passover: he requested that this law acquiesce to the pleas of the Jewish communities, placing Jewish soldiers at a separate table and feed them with unleavened bread. Failing this, their petition should be rejected altogether, since, according to the letter of the internal statute on military service, the cantonists of Jewish faith had to study in classes, work in shops, and acquire military skills together with the Christians.[75] The bulk of petitions and complaints, the sudden increase of incoming and outgoing orders, the notes from local commanders, and the discrepancies between the gendarme corps and military administration caused ever-growing confusion among civil and military administrators. All these bodies asked that a supreme decision be rendered. Nicholas finally determined that Jews should be allowed to remain Jewish in the military. Once this was approved, Jewish communities concerned themselves not with their relatives in the army but rather with their own predicament as hostages of conscription duty.

Conscription Lists and Quotas

Novosiltsev had good reason to criticize the St. Petersburg conscription plan and to plead with Constantine to reject it. The 1827 draft precipitated the failure of uniform management among state bureaucrats, and caused consternation in the communities and bribery among communal elders. Irregularities in the keeping of metrical books, or registers, further added to the confusion. In 1827, conscription lists (*rekrutskie skazki*) for the Jewish population did not exist. Not until the mid-1830s did communities assemble them and present them to the military. Local authorities provided Jews with a conscription quota and then assigned to them the responsibility of deciding whom to draft. This determination was made logically. Jewish communities throughout the Pale were heavily in debt; sending out hard-working and reliable taxpayers between the ages of eighteen and twenty-five would cause a loss of communal income and a further sinking into debt. Additionally, the conscript's family, now bereft of a provider, would have to be counted among those needing financial relief. Conversely, sending minors into the army, as suggested by law, did not

---

[74] GARF, f. 109. First expedition, d. 330 ("Obrashchenie roditelei maloletnikh evreiskikh rekrutov iz Vil'ny k Nikolaiu I ot 18 maia 18, 1829"), l. 43.

[75] GARF, f. 109. First expedition, d. 330 ("Proshenie evreiskoi obshchiny Mogilevskoi gubernii," March, 1828), ll. 27–29.

undermine the community's economic stability. Nonetheless, it was in direct opposition to the ethical standards to which the community aspired. The *kahal* elders were forced to make a painful choice: either to preserve the community's economic stability and to compromise its ethical standards, or to retain their ethics and to destroy the community financially. Thus, Jewish societies had to choose between the immoral and the murderous. By default, the *kahal* elders resolved to maintain communal financial stability and to provide the army with those Jews whom they deemed least useful: the unmarried, unskilled, illiterate, unprotected, poor, and minors. In this category the *kahal* elders also included children from large and from poor families; orphans, bachelors, unruly adults, and those of dubious reputation or behavior or with an unacceptable way of thinking. The elders continuously revised their erratic lists, quite often rewriting them based solely upon a bribe or upon the absence thereof.[76] The Jewish communal decision did not differ from that of Russian Orthodox peasant communities, which sought to protect the householders, and provided the military with underage conscripts.

Whenever possible, Jewish *kahals* used conscription as a divinely sanctioned tool for the suppression of internal disturbances. Regular drafts allowed communal elders easily to get rid of individuals of dubious or scandalous behavior.[77] Threatening, capturing, and sending unwanted Jews to conscription centers became a sort of communal self-defense, which survived Nicholas I and lasted until the military reform of the 1870s. Perhaps, as Stanislawski argued, this was one of the reasons that shtetl Jews maintained their traditional worldview and successfully resisted what they considered the "harmful Enlightenment" until the very end of the nineteenth century. On the other hand, the Jewish youth of the 1860s–1870s had to resort to radical methods to escape the stagnant world of Jewish tradition and to join the realm of Russification and Enlightenment.

Although in 1834 Nicholas I replaced the twenty-five year service with a fifteen-year term, the shtetl Jew was as unwilling to fulfill his sacred duty as was the Russian Orthodox peasant. Like the peasants, Jews resorted to various gimmicks to escape the draft and, like the peasants, became the objects of harsh criticism and denunciation by local officials. According to the Ministry of the

---

[76] For nepotism and bribery among kahal officials see, for example, the case brought to the Iampol district court against elders Avrum Beker and Shloma Shkolnik: DAVO, f. 472, op. 1, d. 687 ("Delo po obvineniiu rekrutskikh starost vo vziatochnichestve", 1845–1848), ll. 51–52. On the other hand, bribes paid to *kahal* elders most probably ended up in the pockets of gendarmes and local bureaucrats. The elders seem to have been as poor as their brethren whom they tried to save from conscription. See, for example, the police inventory of one of the accused *kahal* elders: DAVO, f. 391, op. 1, d. 639 ("Delo po obvineniiu kagal'nogo m. Pikova Rozmarina Abrama v zloupotrebleniiakh po sluzhbe"), l. 23.

[77] See, for example, DAVO, f. 471 (Gaisinskii uezdnyi sud), op. 1, d. 6009 ("Delo po obvineniiu starosty Teplitskogo evreiskogo obschestva Reznika, ego pomoshchnika Shinklera, podatnogo starosty Rudogo i starshiny Kunitsa v podloge dokumentov i nepravil'nom naznachenii v rekruty chlena obschestva Shmuklera," 1864–1866), ll. 3–4.

Interior, the elders of the *kahal* protected their own relatives from conscription, they circumvented the law by hiring substitutes, and they manipulated the lists of their families so that somebody else's family was required to send their son to the army.[78] Some Jews, claimed the informers, bribed peasants, deserters, and vagrants, convincing them to accept the names of listed draftees, to join the troops as quota conscripts, and later to defect. One denunciation claimed that the introduction of Jewish conscription caused the spread of strange "finger epidemics among the Jewish people"; as soon as the recruit from a well-to-do family appeared on the conscription list, the local doctor arranged for an inflammation which required an immediate finger amputation – and the Jew fitting the physical requirements for the grenadiers had his name successfully removed from the conscription list.[79] There were other cases, too, in which communities tried to conscript those who should have been exempt because of illness or disability. In such cases, the novices ended up in court as self-mutilators. The court needed months of tedious interrogations, elaborate preparations, and medical examinations to prove the innocence of the disabled recruits and to return them to their communities. However, sometimes the interests of communal elders and local bureaucrats prevailed. Fulfilling the quota became paramount, and the sick novices remained in active service.[80]

Although the imperial administration insisted upon rigorous fulfillment of the conscription quota, provincial authorities did not approve of the harsh treatment of Jews. Consider, for example, a clash between the Kiev, Podol, and Volhynia province governor general and military officials, in which the former championed the Jewish cause. During the draft, Jews from several communities hid their children from conscription. The conscription clerks and Lieutenant Colonel Timkovskii then ordered that the heads of those Jewish families be chained and sent to the army, even though their number exceeded the quota. This intimidating measure produced an immediate result: the involved communities announced their readiness to send to the conscription center some seventy Jewish children who were ready to join the cantonist battalions. Timkovskii was inspired by his success. He contacted Count Bibikov, the governor general, asking him to endorse what Timkovskii touted as an effective measure: in case of absentees, adult Jewish householders should be drafted instead of the

[78] GARF, f. 109. First expedition, d. 335 ("Donesenie berdichevskogo zhitelia Aleksandra Iuzefovicha zhitomirskomu chinovniku 14 klassa Neimanu Eduardu," June 25, 1828 .), ll. 7–8.

[79] In some cases of self-mutilation in 1830–1840, the administration tried to protect semidisabled people (alleged self-mutilators) from communal conscript providers and recruiters who sought to fulfill the quota by providing unfit recruits. Cf. the case of the tailor Mordke Beingart, sick with epilepsy from childhood and sent to the army, in DAVO, f. 391, op. 1, d. 622 ("Delo po obvineniiu meshchanina Beingardta, obviniavshegosia v chlenovreditel'stve s tsel'iu ukloneniia ot rekrutskoi povinnosti," 1852–1853), ll. 10b., 6, 13, 14; the case of certain Shimil Brik sick with scurvy in DAVO, f. 391, op. 1, d. 627 ("Delo po obvineniiu Brika Shmilia v chlenovreditel'stve"), ll. 100b., 19.

[80] This is what happened to Aizik Gershkovich, ill with trachoma since childhood. See DAVO, f. 391, op. 1, d. 551 ("Delo po obvineniiu v uklonenii ot rekrutskoi povinnosti," 1844–1845), ll. 1–20.

absentee child conscripts. Bibikov sent requests to members of the gentry in his province and discovered that Baron Korf, in full compliance with the letter of the Statute on Conscription, had exempted from the draft all Jews working in factories. In turn, Major General Radishchev adamantly opposed Timkovskii, as it brought Jewish households to complete ruin. Bibikov, too, rejected the intimidating measure suggested by Lieutenant Colonel Timkovskii.[81]

The conscription system was an additional burden for the shtetl economy. Imperial officials asserted that Jewish mobility in the Pale resulted from the innate desire of perfidious Jews to evade the draft. They did their best to hamper the uncontrolled traffic of Jewish merchants.[82] Local police and governors attempted to control fully the movements of wholesalers and of petty-traders. In the first half of the 1830s, Jews needed a *kahal* certificate, a sort of a communal identification card, endorsing their travel through the Pale of Settlement. However, after 1836, the gendarmes ordered that Jewish merchants purchase the so-called placard passport (which cost twenty-five rubles); the certificate did not suffice.[83] This was an exorbitant sum. Only guild merchants could afford it, and restrictions further worsened the economic hardship. In addition to the continual increase in the number of conscripts, which the communities could not cover, their financial debts (*nalogovye nedoimki*) also were mounting. By the 1850s, conscription undermined not only the ethical foundations but also the economic wellbeing of Jewish society. At the end of the 1820s, the imperial administration repeatedly agreed to accept conscripts instead of tax arrears: one adult Jewish recruit for each 1,000 rubles and one child for 500 rubles debt. Yet Nicholas cancelled this practice, realizing that the *kahals* and provincial administration jumped at this opportunity and avoided direct payments to the treasury. Yet, in the 1850s, Kankrin was no longer around to argue, as he usually had done, against the unlimited expansion of the army at the expense of the state budget. Nicholas reintroduced this practice on the eve of and during the Crimean War, to further increase the number of active troops he needed in his campaign. Now Jews (and others) had to provide the army with a double and triple quota, sometimes 25 conscripts per 1,000 people. Nicholas agreed to accept one adult recruit for each 2,000 rubles in arrears; by 1853, this figure had dropped to 300 rubles. Simultaneously, he ordered that two Jewish children be accepted in lieu of one adult: it was not by chance that, in 1853, Jews sometimes represented a quarter of a cantonist battalion. To make things even more intimidating, in 1852 the administration introduced special draft exemption certificates: if a family member provided the army with a conscript whom he

[81] TsDIAU, f. 442, op. 152, d. 37 ("O narushenii evreiskimi obshchinami Podol'skoi gubernii pravil rekrutskogo nabora," 1843–1845), ll. 1–10b., 2, 5.

[82] TsDIAU, f. 442, op. 1, d. 2181 ("O zaprete evreiskim kahalam vydavat svidetel'stva na otluchku s mesta zhitel'stva," 1836).

[83] See the case of the semi-blind and physically disabled Iankel Itsko from Brailov and the urban dweller Kelner, DAVO, f. 391, op. 1, d. 558 ("Delo po obvineniiu v uklonenii ot rekrutskoi povinnosti," 1845), ll. 1–2, 17–170b.

hired, captured, bribed, forced, or blackmailed, he obtained an exemption from the forthcoming draft for his entire family.[84]

The communal elders, both Jews and non-Jews, went to great lengths to fulfill the quota. They severely restricted the mobility of rank-and-file members of the community who now could not leave their towns without informing the elders beforehand. The court cases mention Jewish absentees – small-scale artisans, shopkeepers, nonguild merchants who allegedly escaped the omnipotent elders and dared to request or to obtain an internal passport. Accusations against those Jews looking to earn extra rubles testify to the arbitrariness of both communal Jewish and imperial Russian authorities, rather than to the efforts of Jews to avoid military service. Despite the deficient system of justice in pre-reform Russia, the courts frequently managed to uncover the true motives for the accusations and helped to limit the autocracy of the communities. The state courts set free those falsely accused of absenteeism (*za ukloneniia*), as happened to Shimon Litman, who went to the communal elders seeking a passport and who was swiftly arrested and sent to the army to fulfill an additional quota; or as happened to Aron Bernshtein, who defected from the conscription center because he was not on the list.[85]

The fear of conscription fostered communal animosity. In some cases, communities resorted to extreme measures. In Ushitsa, for example, the community had an informer killed after he denounced to the state administration the alleged arbitrariness of the elders. In addition to some eighty people arrested, in Kiev province the authorities also arrested and imprisoned Israel Fridman, known as Israel from Ruzhin, the leader of the Hasidic community. They accused him of having signed the *psak* (rabbinic endorsement) to punish informers. In the Zaslav (Iziaslav) case, suspicion fell upon all Jews in the town: the authorities alleged that Jews had drowned the *kahal* elder for having put Hasidim at the top of his conscription list. In neither case did they manage to prove the guilt of Hasidim, but the fear and vengeance shaping the perception of conscription in Jewish society and triggering such an odious incident as the betrayal of an entire community, not to mention the murder of an informer, testify to the devastating impact of the draft system upon Jewish society at large.[86]

The Crimean War magnified all the ills of the conscription system because of the need to expand the army rapidly. The empire found itself under constraint and needed to expand the troops. The military announced the additional (*dopolnitel'nye*), intensive (*usilennye*), and punitive (*shtrafnye*) drafts: the cumbersome Russian troops could oppose mobile British and French troops

---

[84] Gessen, *Istoriia evreiskogo naroda v Rossii*, 65–66, 115–116.

[85] DAVO, f. 391, op. 1, d. 5 ("Delo po obvineniiu Litmana, Melmana i Avrumovicha v uklonenii ot rekrutskoi povinnosti," 1845), ll. 5–50b., 6, 10; DAVO, f. 473, op. 1, d. 752 ("Delo po obvineniiu rekruta Bernshteina," 1865), ll. 2–20b., 5–50b., 27–270b., 31.

[86] David Assaf, *The Regal Way: The Life and Times of Rabbi Israel of Ruzhin*, trans. David Louvish (Stanford, Calif.: Stanford University Press, 2002), 105–127; TsDIAU, f. 442, op. 1, d. 2110, ll. 2–4.

only as cannon fodder. To fulfill the increasing quota, between 1853 and 1856 Jewish communities resorted to the help of *khapers* (Yiddish for catchers), robust and merciless Jews who were paid experts in finding, kidnapping, and bringing to the conscription centers unprotected, undocumented, vagrant, and orphaned Jews – or simply unattended Jewish children. Enlightened and liberal-minded Jewish historians later blamed the Jewish communal administration, *kahal* elders, or *sborshchiks* (responsible for providing the army with the quota conscripts after 1844) and, ultimately, the entire Nicholaevan conscription system for the heartless treatment of their own people. Archival sources testify to the opposite: the hunt for conscripts was ubiquitous; rank-and-file shtetl Jews participated in it as desperately as the communal elders. A Jew from Mogilev-Podolsk behaved no better than a communally sponsored *khaper* when he spied his neighbors taking away their fifteen-year-old son and schemed to intercept him and to bring him to the conscription center instead of his own son.[87] The fear of the draft also split Jewish families; now they arranged for a speedy marriage of their eldest son and sent him as far from the conscription point as possible. At the same time, to fulfill the quota they maimed their youngest son and sent him to the army in the hope he would not be accepted.[88]

Conclusion

Nicholas I, with the help of his Jewish Committee, conceived of the conscription of Jews in the spirit of the European Enlightenment. Modernizing his state through a wide array of reforms, Nicholas planned to draft Jews into the empire, making them useful, loyal, and assimilated with the rest of the population. Nicholas started Jewish reform with conscription because he understood the reform as the extension of equal obligations, not equal rights. Unlike other exempt non-Russians, from the perspective of the regime Jews were privileged to fulfill their patriotic duty before the tsar and the fatherland. The regime had no intention whatsoever of divesting more than a million subjects of Judaism through the draft: this would have been an unfeasible task of enormous proportions and costs, too much for the Russian state budget. On the contrary, the Russian administration sought ways to make Jews into a productive constituency of the empire. In view of Nicholas's upbringing, there was a solid logic in his decision to start solving multiple economic and social problems in western Russian borderlands through this pragmatic solution: conscription.

The Jewish communal response to the unfolding reform had very little to do with the emperor's plans to unify the empire through the military. Hardly any strata of the Russian population responded differently. Jews and Russian Orthodox peasants shared the same attitude toward Nicholas's draft and

---

[87] DAVO, f. 475, op. 1, d. 324 ("Delo po obvineniiu Akselruda v uklonenii ot rekrutskoi povinnosti, 1856), ll. 2–11, 200b., 62.

[88] DAVO, f. 472, op. 1, d. 604 ("Delo po obvineniiu Leiby Tsukermana, Duvida Gatuke, Srulia Fishova i drugikh v ukryvatel'stve rekrut[ov]," 1856–1864), ll. 12–21.

shaped it in their imagination as a dirge.[89] Both Rabbi David from Novardek and Ukrainian poet Taras Shevchenko bemoaned the sacrifices their people, Jews and Ukrainians, offered up to Nicholas's insatiable monster, the army. Pious East European Jews perceived the conscripts as captives, the army as a prison, and the draft as an injustice. Saving a Jew from conscription was the equivalent of performing the religious deed of ransoming a prisoner. Even the proponents of Enlightenment who celebrated Jewish integration into Russian society grieved over the fate of Jewish sons, those minor Josephs sent into the austere exile of the military. The Jewish reaction came as no surprise: parents were appalled to find their children transformed into the toy soldiers of the Russian emperor. Their children should beautify the Passover seder at home; they should not observe Prussian military order in the Russian army. Moreover, Jews were not accorded anything in exchange for the sacrifice of their children: the community's financial burden was not eased; the social hierarchy was unchanged; the Pale of Settlement not only remained self-contained, but shrank; and many of their dear ones were hopelessly out of reach. The Jewish community was not impressed with the imperial social engineering project, since the imperial vision of utility sharply contradicted their sense of communal stability. Furthermore, the imperial administration failed to articulate convincingly the purpose of conscription to the Jewish communities; if Jews could not grasp the magnitude of the emperor's project, it was their problem. Notwithstanding his grandiose plans to emulate the reforms of Peter the Great and to homogenize society through the military, for Nicholas the Jews in the Pale were targets rather than products of the reform. Even with his zeal for order and unification, Nicholas never intended to have every Jew drafted into the army. In order to assess the results of his quest for imperial utility, one must turn to the Jewish soldiers' experience.

---

[89] See S. M. Ginzburg and P. S. Marek, *Yiddish Folksongs in Russia*, ed. Dov Noy (photo reproduction of the 1901 St. Petersburg edition) (Ramat Gan: Bar Ilan University, 1991), 283–302.

2

Militarizing the Jew, Judaizing the Military

On August 26, 1827, Nicholas I undertook a number of decisive steps to reorganize his empire. From 1824 to 1827, no tax levies were imposed, no draft was instituted to augment troop numbers, and no training was offered to new recruits. However, the escalating hostilities along the southern border and the prospect of an imminent clash with Turkey made Nicholas introduce mandatory conscription that would include segments of the population previously exempt from military service. Until then, a cumbersome system had differentiated between Russian Orthodox and non-Christian subjects, and between those who paid taxes and provided recruits and those who paid taxes but were not required to enlist. Other categories consisted of non-Orthodox Christians, Cossacks, and military settlers. Jews paid taxes but did not serve in the army. However, between 1827 and the early 1830s, Nicholas increased the number of taxpaying groups and incorporated them into the conscription pool. Against the advice of his Jewish Committee and of the acting war minister (*upravliaiushchii voennym ministerstvom*), he began his reforms with the Jews.

As is clear from its Byzantine title, "On obligating the Jews personally to perform the conscription duty, on the cancellation of the toll paid in its stead," the first of Nicholas's military edicts revoked the Jews' discretionary payment of 500 rubles per recruit in lieu of army service. The second, the Statute on the Conscription and Military Service of Jews, detailed, in several attachments, the duties of the civil administration, provincial authorities, and conscription officials with respect to Jewish conscripts. On the same day, Nicholas signed the decree "On the state-wide implementation of two conscripts for every 500 souls," accompanied by an explanatory addendum entitled "Instructions on the forthcoming conscription levy." He signed two further documents that day, one ordering the central and local authorities, particularly governors, to report monthly regarding the implementation of his orders, and the other announcing the uniforms required for the Senate and for the Ministry of Justice. Of the more than 870 orders that Nicholas signed in 1827 alone, one-quarter of them concerned army management. Using the *Polizeistaat* as a model, he sought to have the empire conform to his enlightened autocratic principles, and envisioned the army as a paragon of these values.[1]

The Statute on the Conscription and Military Service of Jews was couched in typical bureaucratic language, sprinkled with rationalist clichés. Yet it clearly asserted that Jews were obligated to fulfill their military duty equally with the rest of the taxpaying population and that military service would eventually make Jews productive. The Warsaw Jewish Committee's draft proposal, permeated as it was with the rhetoric of French emancipation, had similarly viewed conscription as an institution that unified various groups in their duty to the empire. Portraying Jews as a self-contained social and economic entity, the Russian administration believed that military experience would enable the Jews to improve themselves. This concept of *Verbesserung,* "improvement," commonly adopted by enlightened European monarchies of the era, had been propounded in the 1780s by the Prussian thinker Christian Wilhelm von Dohm. Skills acquired in the army, argued the statute along the same lines, would make the Jews useful members of the empire and would ensure their professional and financial success. In a curious manifestation of enlightened paternalism, the Russian regime assumed that Jews were backward and needed its imposed benevolence to effect their transformation.

While Nicholas's rejection of ransom money from Jews, despite the treasury's continuing deficit, recalled the earlier decisions of Napoleon and of Joseph II, other regulations fit specific circumstances in the western provinces. The statute forbade the Jewish *okhotnik,* a volunteer prepared to enlist in the stead of another on the conscription list. A further restriction prohibited Jewish communities from composing a shared list of draftees. Although small communities were permitted to join larger urban ones nearby, isolated districts had to send recruits independently. The administration required a Christian village to provide monetary compensation to a neighboring Jewish community that provided a recruit. The statute demanded that local authorities promptly conscript anyone who attempted to hide his relatives (*ukryvatel'*) or who mutilated himself in a bid to evade the draft (*chlenovreditel'*). Nicholas dealt with troublemakers by declaring, "Send them as over-quota recruits to the army" (*sdat' v rekruty bez zacheta*).[2] In addition to guild merchants, licensed artisans, and

---

[1] Dominic Lieven maintained that "[i]n the thirty years after 1825 Russia was ruled by a monarch of immense conscientiousness with a Petrine vision of universal service and whose sympathies lay in the minute regulation of society by the state." See his *Russia's Rulers under the Old Regime* (New Haven and London: Yale University Press, 1989), 23. For the concept of *Polizeistaat* and Russia's complex relationship to it, see Marc Raeff, *The Well-ordered Police State: Social and Institutional Change through Law in the Germanies and Russia, 1600–1800* (New Haven and London: Yale University Press, 1983), 181–187. I can hardly agree with the vision of Nicholas's reign as "a time of stagnation in both political and military spheres," see Brian Taylor, *Politics and the Russian Army: Civil-Military Relations, 1689–2000* (Cambridge: Cambridge University Press, 2003), 52–53.

[2] On various occasions, Nicholas ordered the conscription of unruly low-ranking members of the gentry, thieving or disobedient bureaucrats, rioting peasants, swindlers, vagrants, and Jews. His rule had its limits: he forbade sending those who had committed sacrilege to the army for

rabbinic leaders, Jews willing to study in Russian public schools, to work in factories, and to settle in agricultural colonies were deemed "useful Jews" and were exempt from conscription. Ordained rabbis also were spared, but heads of Hasidic communities (*tsadikim*) and professionals were not. Butchers (*shokh-tim*), preachers (*maggidim*), scribes (*sofrim*), and those who performed ritual circumcisions (*mohalim*) were required to serve in the army. Nicholas accorded less respect to Jewish communal infrastructure than did his colleague, Friedrich Wilhelm III of Prussia. Bureaucrats noted that, although Nicholas's regulations had a stated goal of homogenization, they marked Jews as a separate entity, therefore diminishing the army's modernizing impact upon this ethnic minority. As the head of the Main Staff reported to Baron Dibich, the laws governing Jewish conscription were "rules different from the general rules."[3]

The conscription of Jews necessitated new bureaucratic institutions. Enlistment points (*rekrutskie uchastki*) were established to compile lists and files of Jews. The elders of the *kahal* approved these lists, and dispatched the recruits promptly. Those younger than eighteen joined the army without having to swear an oath; those eighteen or older recited an oath over a Torah scroll before a group of communal representatives and state clerks. A magistrate, a lawyer, a rabbi or his deputy, and a prayer quorum of ten adult Jews were in attendance. The oath, determined after long consideration, was an amalgam of the military pledge and of the reinterpreted Talmudic law *dina de-malkuta dina* ("the law of the kingdom is the law for the Jew"), here extended to matters of civil law. This vow was recited in Hebrew, while the magistrate ensured an accurate reading by consulting a transliterated and translated text printed alongside it. The Jewish conscript promised to obey the Russian emperor's commands just as he obeyed the Torah's commandments; the emperor and the Torah were equally sacred. Jews now were bound by laws of military duty, state service, fealty to the emperor, and the country's fiscal laws. One of the regime's first documents designed to forge a dual self-awareness, this ruling signified a key shift in Jewish identity.

Although Nicholas considered the army a correcting and unifying institution, his vision of modernization was characterized by inequity. While recruits from other segments of the population were required to be eighteen to twenty-five years old, the age of Jewish conscripts ranged from twelve to twenty-five (to compare: in the Ottoman Empire the recruitment age in the 1820s was between fifteen and thirty); minors were sent to the cantonist battalions, and adults to the regular army. In contrast to the rigid physical requirements for adult Jewish recruits, virtually none existed for Jewish children; any would do. Perhaps this

punishment. See, for instance, GARF, f. 728, op. 1, d. 2271 ("Materialy i cherty k biografii imperatora Nikolaia I i k istorii ego tsarstvovania. Zapiski stats-sekretaria barona Korfa"), r. II, t. 1, ll. 95, 106–107; r. II, t. 2, l. 21, 69–690b.; r. II, ch. III, l. 30–300b.; r. XX, t. 2, l. 27–270b.; r. III, t. 1, l. 350b.; r. III, t. 1, ll. 780b-79.
[3] In Russian: "*sut' osobye ot obshchikh pravil pravila;*" see RGVIA, f. 405, op. 2, d. 436, l. 2.

was part of Nicholas's larger plan to reduce the "useless" population in the Pale and to eradicate those who served neither his financial nor his military purposes. Nicholas also decreed that all illegitimate offspring of Christian military settlers belonged to the Military Department and must be sent to the cantonist battalions. Jewish soldiers found themselves consigned to the same category; they essentially were serfs of the Department of Military Settlements.

Religious Rituals and Rights

Although the statute on Jewish conscription presupposed some religious accommodation for Jewish soldiers, initially army regulations made no provision for their needs. Military authorities resolved this contradiction by creating a special set of rules for what they called *nizhnii chin iz evreev*, "a private of the Jewish faith." While their rulings were not always consistent, they nonetheless crafted a formidable corpus of regulations and bylaws, canceled or reissued throughout the century, which outlasted the reign of Nicholas I and exerted significant influence upon the military.

The simple fact that Jewish privates, rather than immediately embracing Russian Orthodoxy, chose to persevere in their traditional ways presented a challenge to the largely Christian troops, unprepared for the influx of non-Christians. Even during the army's most aggressive missionary campaign, the number of baptized Jewish soldiers did not exceed one percent.[4] There were fewer baptized Jews to be found in the adult regiments than in the children's battalions. Taking into consideration the Jewish minors, the cantonists, submitted after 1840 to enforced conversions (see Chapter 3), attempts to Christianize Jews in the military yielded a maximum of 10,000 to 15,000 Jewish converts between 1827 and the 1870s; later this number diminished tenfold and became largely insignificant. Jewish deputies implored military commanders to abide by the rule of law; although the Russian military administration issued ex post facto a number of regulations permitting Jews to practice their faith, this benevolent gesture in fact resulted primarily from external and internal pressure.[5]

Nicholas's state bureaucracy attempted to accommodate Jewish customs. Consider, for example, the 1841 debate within the Department of Military Settlements concerning a request to establish an *eruv* in military settlers' districts containing a scattered Jewish population. Having presented to the Ministry of the Interior all the issue's pros and cons, including a discussion of the appropriate section of the Judaic legal codex *Shulkhan Arukh*, the department received a surprisingly sober recommendation from the Department of Spiritual Matters of Foreign Confessions: it should allow such measures

---

[4] RGVIA, f. 405, op. 5, d. 7370, ll. 108–109.
[5] This manifestation of the Russian bureaucratic omnipotence was typical of the legislation of the era, which was satirized in the famous "Note" of Konstantin Aksakov to Alexander II. See S. Ginsburg, *Minuvshee* (Pg.: Izd. avtora, 1923), 6.

privately, but should avoid "any formal decisions" in future cases. However, the War Ministry could not avoid regulating the Jewish soldiers' religious practices.[6] As directed in the 1827 statute, and as Stanislawski observed, Jews were to enjoy absolute religious freedom in the army.[7] However, the statute's fourteenth paragraph, providing for "freedom of conscience" for Jewish conscripts, proved problematic. While Jewish soldiers could legally perform their rituals, they were punished if their observance contravened army discipline. The same regulation that granted privileges and rights also could annul them.[8] This inconsistency in the 1827 statute engendered arbitrariness and misinterpretation.

In June 1829, a year and a half after the first conscription, the Inspector's Department of the War Ministry issued a circular regulating Jewish holiday observance. This directive allowed Jews to perform their religious rituals when free of military obligations, and instructed officers to accommodate such requests. It differentiated between holy days (*hagim*) and those regarded as half-holidays (*yomim tovim*), and adapted the army's training schedule accordingly. The circular recommended that Jews not be engaged in work on Saturdays or on the Day of Atonement. Half-holidays comprised *Rosh ha-shanah* (the Jewish New Year), *Sukkot* (the Festival of Booths), *Simkhat Torah* (marking the end of the Pentateuch's reading cycle), *Pesakh* (Passover), and *Shavuot* (Pentecost). When composing this policy, it is probable that the army consulted an enlightened Jew, to whom Judaism was a religion rather than an all-encompassing way of life. His explanations led to the coining of the Russian military's terms for the Jewish holidays: *simkhestoiru* (the Joy of Torah Festival), *sykois* (the Festival of Booths), *roshashunu* (New Year).[9]

The military exerted considerable effort to make Russian army practice compatible with Judaism's *halakhic* (legal) rules, thereby demonstrating the regime's willingness to accommodate Judaism as it drafted Jews. In spite of these rulings, the conflict between military law and Jewish rights persisted. The new regulation scrupulously distinguished between those activities allowed and prohibited to Jewish soldiers on major and minor holidays. During "half-holidays," Jews were exempt from certain types of labor, such as construction, factory work, handicrafts, writing, trading, and riding; however, they were not excused from kindling fires, slaughtering animals, cleaning uniforms and armaments, discharging weapons, or carrying munitions. Two hours of service per day were required on half-holidays, and commanders forbade Jews to celebrate any festivals not specified on the official list. While Jews thus were compelled to reshape their rituals, the military also revisited its operating principles, its religious bias, and its internal discipline.

---

[6] RGVIA, f. 405, op. 4, d. 3477, ll. 1–30b, 6.
[7] Stanislawski, *Tsar Nicholas I*, 21.
[8] This amendment may have been prepared by Novosiltsev, who was far more tolerant of Jews than was Nicholas I. See Gessen, *Istoriia*, 2: 34, n. 35.
[9] *PSZ* II, 4: 2949; *PSZ* II, 2: 1330, ch. XIV, par. 91 and *PSZ* II, 22: 20771.

Commanders were responsible for ensuring that their Jewish soldiers had a room in which to conduct religious services and a place to secure their ritual items. Since the troops were often in transit (barracks becoming ubiquitous only after the 1870s), the guardian of the regimental stores was in charge of the Jewish soldiers' prayer shawls, candles, wooden Decalogue, and sometimes the Torah scroll. If the troops were billeted near a Jewish community, commanders discharged their Jewish enlisted men for the holidays. Otherwise, they designated a room for the performance of their festive services.

The imperial bureaucracy continually adjusted its regulations regarding Jewish observance. On January 4, 1847, the Inspection Department distributed a calendar of Jewish holidays for the years ahead: Passover now was eight days long, entailed special arrangements, and imposed certain work restrictions during the first and last two days.[10] Jews were excused from labor on the Sabbath, although not from training exercises. At least in the military, Judaism appeared to have a good chance of becoming a state-protected religion.

Rabbis and the Army

Although Nicholas endorsed the Jewish recruits' retention of their religion in the army, he was not willing to empower Judaism. And despite the presence of Baltic Germans, who were predominantly Lutheran, in the highest military positions, Nicholas insisted that the empire's only official religion was Russian Orthodoxy. The existence of "chaplain rabbis" in the army, at the tsar's behest, illustrates the self-imposed limits of his efforts at modernization. A paragraph in the 1827 statute stipulated that, if there were more than three hundred Jews in a military unit whose service and behavior were satisfactory, and if there were no synagogue or rabbi in the vicinity, the soldiers could obtain a treasury-paid rabbi.[11] In addition, sick, wounded, and dying Jewish soldiers were entitled to have rabbis attend to them. They could attend to the Jews on military service as rabbis but not as chaplains. For instance, in December 1848, after the Russian suppression of the Hungarian uprising, the Minsk rabbi received from the army roughly one hundred rubles to address the spiritual needs (*dukhovnye treby*) of wounded Jewish privates who had been transferred to local military hospitals.[12]

---

[10] *PSZ*, II, 22: 20771. Sometimes legislative contradictions accorded Jews a privileged position, at least on paper. They were legally allowed twice as much rest as their Christian brethren, since they observed traditional Jewish festivals in addition to Christian and state holidays. This benefit, clearly an oversight by the military bureaucracy, remained in effect until December 1834, when the chief of the Central Naval Headquarters enforced the emperor's order to employ Jews in the navy during Christian holidays. It is not known when the infantry discovered and eliminated this anomaly. See *PSZ* II, 4: 3137; II, 7: 5855.

[11] *PSZ* II, 2: 1330 (issues 91 through 95).

[12] The order also facilitated the burial of Jewish soldiers in keeping with their tradition, including, at no cost, about twenty-one *arshin* (fifty feet, four inches) of fabric rather than a coffin, and two-and-a-half *arshin* (six feet) of fabric for the shroud. See *PSZ* II, 22: 21824.

On October 24, 1853, the tsar reversed his position, declaring in the Inspection Department's report that there should be "no state-paid rabbis in the army." Accordingly, he canceled Article 389 of the Code of Military Laws, which provided for such payment. A secret circular followed, informing corps commanders that the law was in effect only on paper. However, it remained in the Code of Laws, even reappearing in the 1859 version (as Article 385), until it was officially rescinded in March 1862.[13]

The War Ministry's departments implemented the emperor's decision in various ways. The navy, anticipating many of Alexander II's Great Reforms, was more tolerant than the army, and allowed rabbis to pay regular visits to Jewish sailors. When, in 1829, the rabbinate of Vilna asked the Ministry of the Interior to permit rabbis to visit Jewish cantonists, it received a resounding "No." But half a year earlier, in August 1828, the navy had approved a similar petition, consenting to have Il'ia Romm, from Mohilev or Shklov, provide liturgical services for Jewish sailors.[14] The Naval Department regularly informed its commanders of approaching Jewish holidays, so that "enlisted men of Jewish faith" (*nizhnie chiny iz evreev*) could enjoy a day off. It insisted that officers make arrangements for Jewish enlisted men to eat unleavened bread and special food during Passover. The navy also endorsed – and sponsored – prayer houses for its Muslims and Jews, one of which was in the Krondshtadt fortress. The Black Sea naval administration even succeeded in convincing Nicholas to allow Jewish sailors in Nikolaev and Sevastopol to keep their elderly parents with them, despite the tsar's express wish to banish Jews from these two towns. The navy was perhaps the only arm of the War Ministry to uphold the sanctity of the Sabbath. In response to an inquiry "whether it is possible to send Jews to do work in the Admiralty in case of urgent need," Vice Admiral Faddei Bellinsgauzen replied that the Sabbath was the Jews' holiest day, and that he could not assent to the request.[15]

The port administration, which reported to the Naval Department, did not bother to acquire special permission from the state. Relying upon the letter of the law, it allowed Jewish sailors to elect rabbis from their midst (men who had not undergone formal ordination), and ordered them to conduct services for Jews in naval hospitals. The navy consistently strove to meet Jewish needs,

[13] RGVIA, f. 1, op. 1, otd. 2, 2 st., d. 25376, l. 55; RGVIA, f. 400, op. 5, d. 16488, ll. 1–4.

[14] RGAVMF, f. 283, op. 1, d. 576, ll. 1, 2, 4, 7, 8–80b.

[15] RGAVMF, f. 283, op. 1, d. 1581 ("Po otnosheniiu Chernomorskoi khoziaistvennoi ekspeditsii," 1830), l. 10b.; d. 3242 ("O tom, chtoby nakhodiashchimsia v rabochikh ekipazhakh evreiam vo vremia Paskhi ne bylo zameshatel'stva po upotrebleniiu po svoim obriadam pishchi," 1834), l. 1; d. 3824 ("Ob izbranii iz sredy voennykh evreev rabbina"), l. 5; d. 6545 ("O naznachenii dlia voennosluzhashchikh morskogo vedomstva evreev rabbina [v Sankt-Peterburg]," 1847–1850 rr.), l. 6, 9; d. 7019 ("O postroenii v Krondshtadte novogo zdaniia dlia otpravleniia bogosluzheniia nizhnimi chinami magometanskogo i evreiskogo zakonov"), l. 1–10b.; RGAVMF, f. 410, op. 1, d. 389 ("O postanovlenii obshchikh pravil, na dozvolenie roditeliam evreev ostavatsia pri svoikh detiakh," 1837), ll. 1, 3–4; RGAVMF, f. 283, op. 1, d. 5499, l. 2.

unless Nicholas intervened – as occasionally happened. In 1837, when the Rabbi of Sevastopol became ill, the Naval Department asked the imperial administration for authorization to replace him with another capable candidate, who would administer to 1,117 Jewish enlisted men. Nicholas's vague response was "Postpone."[16] This veto was not viewed as setting a precedent; the Baltic Sea navy commanders continued to favor the rabbinic leadership and even to give rabbis special exams so that they could obtain one-third of a sergeant major's salary in return for their assistance. Naval commanders paid salary supplements to Jewish enlisted men who offered spiritual support to patients in navy hospitals, as they did for priests of other religions. However, the Naval Department's efforts did not always succeed; despite having requested an increase of 100 rubles in the salary of sailor Markus Vulfovich, who worked in the navy port unit, it could not secure the funds because the authorities rejected its petition.[17] It would be another twenty years before the War Ministry endorsed payments to rabbis in military hospitals.

After Nicholas's death, and before the 1874 reform, the War Ministry took concerted steps toward establishing an institute of military chaplains. In 1872, it had observed that soldiers of non-Russian (i.e., alien) creeds died in military hospitals without proper "observance of their spiritual rites" (*bez ispolneniia dukhovnykh treb*) and that this was no longer acceptable. On December 5, 1856, it decided to compensate mullahs and rabbis, covering their expenses on a two-horse carriage and providing them with a payment of sixty kopeks daily for personal needs. This gesture served as recognition of their help in administering the oath of loyalty and offering religious services to Muslim and Jewish soldiers. In May 1859, the war minister ordered that rabbis also receive compensation for ministering to the sick and dying Jewish patients in military hospitals. Beginning in 1859, Rabbi Ashkenazi attended Jewish soldiers at the Lublin Military Hospital, receiving an annual payment of 28.57 rubles from the army. When he died, in 1867 or 1868, local commanders arranged for his replacement. Yet it was only after lengthy discussion of the basis on which non-Orthodox clergy received reimbursement that the military resolved, in 1871, to pay rabbis and imams 28.57 rubles annually for every hospital they visited. At the same time, Russian Orthodox priests were being paid 36 rubles annually, plus 7.20 rubles for additional expenditures such as religious artifacts.[18]

---

[16] In Russian, "*Povremenit'*": literally, "no rush with that issue." See GRAVMF, f. 283, op. 1, d. 3026 ("Ob opredelenii k voennosluzhashchim v Sevastopole evreiam v ravviny meshchanina Moshku Razumnogo," 1837), ll. 10, 12, 16.

[17] RGAVMF, f. 283, op. 1, d. 6437 ("O tom, sleduet li unter-ofitserov iz evreev dopuskat' k ekzamenu na poluchenie imi odnoi treti praporshchich'ego zhalovaniia," 1847), l. 2; RGAVMF, f. 283, op. 1, d. 4812 ("O naznachenii ravvinu Sveaborgskogo porta Vulfovichu pribavochnogo zhalovaniia"), ll. 1–2, 8.

[18] RGVIA, f. 400, op. 2, d. 2061, ll. 2–20b., 5, 9; PSZ II, 30: 29904; PSZ II, 34: 34474; Archiwum Państwowe w Lublinie, № 136/1867–68, ll. 1–5; RGVIA, f. 400, op. 2, d. 1118, l. 206–2060b.

Yet rabbis never did become Russian Jewish chaplains. Despite radical changes in the army after Nicholas's death, the prevailing attitude toward non-Orthodox spiritual and communal leaders remained. Greek Catholic soldiers were now obliged to seek the services of a Russian Orthodox priest, not of a Roman Catholic one. The military also forbade Lutheran clergymen to conduct German services for Germans, Estonians, and Lithuanians, restricting them to services in Russian. As the War Ministry increasingly favored eastern ethnicities, such as the Muslims, its policies became less inclined toward ones like the Ukrainian Greek-Catholics, Poles, and Germans. These ethnic groups inhabiting western provinces of the empire found themselves suspected of potential disloyalty, bereft of military privileges, and submitted to an intensive Russification policy. In 1873, the ministry granted enlisted men functioning as imams in the army a number of important privileges, including permission to wear their national garb and exemption from shaving their beards. Rabbis found themselves in a less protected group.[19]

Soldiers' Synagogues

In the absence of properly ordained rabbis, Jewish soldiers themselves assumed religious leadership. Some acted as ad hoc rabbis when recruits took their oaths of induction. Others adopted the role of visiting rabbi in small Jewish communities, as did Avraam Katsman, a private in the naval dock workers' unit in Revel (Tallinn) who was elected as prayer-house warden (*gabai*) and spiritual guide by the local Jewish society.[20] In their newfound positions, these soldiers also interceded with military authorities to petition them to allow permanent houses of prayer. Consequently, dozens of soldiers' prayer and study houses (referred to, in military documents, as *soldatskie molel'ni* and *molitvennye shkoly*) sprang up in the Pale of Settlement and in the Russian interior from the mid-1830s. The local military command granted permission to establish soldiers' synagogues in areas including Sevastopol, Revel, Chardzhui, Kiev, Tomsk, Tiflis, and Irkutsk.[21] After the 1829 expulsion of Jews from Sevastopol, the town's synagogue and cemetery fell into the possession of Jewish soldiers who were billeted in the vicinity. Most of those soldiers perished during the Crimean War, and a bombardment of the town destroyed its synagogue. Then,

---

[19] RGVIA, f. 400, op. 2, d. 3592; RGVIA, f. 400, op. 2, d. 128, ll. 5–60b.; RGVIA, f. 400, op. 2, d. 2457.

[20] RGVIA, f. 400, op. 5, d. 2768, ll. 1–4.

[21] *Rassvet*, no. 46 (1861): 748–749; RGVIA, f. 400, op. 5, d. 2768, l. 4; RGVIA, f. 400, op. 15, d. 1711, l. 3; *Otchet dukhovnogo pravleniia tomskoi evreiskoi voenno-molitvennoi shkoly* (Tomsk, n.p., 1886); "Tiflisskaia voennaia sinagoga," *Ha-Karmel*, no. 34 (1862) (supplement). After a collective request by soldiers quartered in Kiev, a synagogue was approved and established in the Jewish section of Kiev, on Iaroslavskaia Street, Ploskii district, between two other synagogues, *Po'alei Tsedek* (Artisans) and *Gornostaipol* (Hasidic). For more details, see "Khodataistvo soldat-evreev o razreshenii im ustroit' otdel'no molel'niu," *Kievlianin*, no. 210 (1883).

ILLUSTRATION 1. Jewish soldiers' synagogue under restoration, Irkutsk, 1878–1879. Photograph taken December 2007. From the author's archive.

in 1859, about seventy-five retired soldiers and a group of merchants who had been permitted to resettle in the town were given permission to establish a new prayer house. It became the center of the community, remaining so until the late nineteenth century.[22] In Irkutsk, Jewish soldiers appear to have been favored over Jewish merchants who petitioned for the opening of a synagogue. The resulting edifice laid the foundation for the future Jewish community.[23]

The military's desire to address Jewish conscripts' needs may be demonstrated by an anecdote concerning the soldiers' synagogue in St. Petersburg, far beyond the Pale. In 1856, the barracks of the former sappers' training battalion, which had belonged to the Department of Military Settlements, were placed at the disposal of the War Ministry's Engineering Department. As the two departments negotiated details of the property transfer, the Engineering Department complained to the previous occupants that it could not take possession of the premises because a wing of the building still served as a prayer house for Jewish soldiers. The War Ministry learned that, in 1837, Major

[22] *Rassvet*, no. 46 (1861): 748–749.

[23] A. Garashchenko, "Kratkaia istoriia kamennogo zdaniia sinagogi v Irkutske," in *Sibirskii evreiskii sbornik* (Irkutsk: Arkom, 1992), 47–50.

TABLE 1. *The Attendance at the St. Petersburg Soldiers' Synagogue in 1856*

Army Units	Number of Jewish soldiers
Department of Military Settlements	12
Four military workers' companies	53
St. Petersburg artisans' unit	100
2nd Her Majesty's unit	8
Railroad workers	50
Police unit	40
Peter and Paul fortress and Engineers' palace	90
Judiciary Standards office and St. Petersburg battalion of military cantonists	30
Guard troops and other units	60
TOTAL	443

Source: RGVIA, f. 405, op. 7, d. 1176, l. 8.

General Krol had sanctioned the establishment of a synagogue there, which had been regularly attended ever since (Table 1).

Recognizing that they could not simply evict the Jewish conscripts, the Engineering Department compiled a list of congregation members. Most of the Jews in attendance were either artisans (153) or sentinels, including those stationed at the fortress and at the palace (more than 180). Others served as policemen (40), military settlement soldiers (12), and railroad workers (50). The presence of religiously observant Jews in the elite Her Imperial Majesty's Unit (8) and among the cantonists (30) must have surprised the authorities, particularly since elite units were not thought to admit religious aliens into their ranks. In any event, the War Ministry could not easily overlook the presence of 443 worshippers.

The transfer of the building's ownership did not mean the end of the Jewish prayer house. On the contrary, the War Ministry undertook to find them an alternative meeting place. The city barracks did not contain a suitable room, and a former factory for officers' uniforms was deemed inappropriate. Eventually, the Department of Military Settlements proposed a private residence. Gutkov, probably a St. Petersburg guild merchant, leased them a spacious apartment in his house. The military signed an annual rent contract in the amount of 300 rubles, and urged the landlord to maintain the stovepipes and toilet in good working order. The department inspector noted approximately 370 men in regular attendance at this new prayer house.[24] Clearly, in this case the military administration had assumed full financial and moral responsibility for the implementation of its regulations.

Thus, there is ample evidence that Jewish soldiers routinely practiced their religion. How did this work? Nicholas's support of religious freedom for adult

[24] RGVIA, f. 405, op. 6, d. 4545, ll. 120b., 15, 18–19, 22, 25.

Jews (although not for children) was fairly consistent. In May 1844, he responded to complaints about soldiers who spent time with local Jewish communities by proclaiming, "Nobody should prevent the Jewish ranks from enjoying the rights of their creed." He later recommended that commanders allow Jewish soldiers to attend prayer services regularly.[25] Of course, the extent to which Jews practiced their faith varied greatly, depending upon their origin and tenacity and upon the particular time, place, and commanding officer in question. These factors, rather than military or state policy, determined the outcome. The 1845 court case of Peisykh Shkablo serves as adequate illustration. On September 26 of that year, during the Jewish High Holidays service, Second Lieutenant Efremov entered a regimental workshop that was being used by drafted Jewish artisans as a prayer room, by permission of the regimental commander. Yelling and cursing them, Efremov ordered the Jews to abandon their service and to return to their duties. The soldiers, feeling entitled to the observance of their holiday, did not comply. Efremov then ordered twenty Christian carpenters under the command of Sergeant Tretiakov to eject the Jews from the workshop. The lieutenant blew out and broke the ritual candles, pulled the prayer shawls from the congregants' shoulders, knocked down the man conducting the prayer service, and shoved aside the Ark containing the Ten Commandments and probably a Torah scroll. As the carpenters expelled the worshippers, Efremov, stationed in the doorway, beat them. Both that day and on October 12, which also was a holiday, Efremov forced the Jews to work, in utter disregard of the exemption they had obtained. He announced repeatedly that he was "a killer of the Yids" and that he was going to eradicate their holidays and their laws. Shkablo, a drummer, was on leave on October 12 and so was not present at the roll call. After the holidays, it was his duty to return the religious articles to the Jewish regimental custodian and to restore the workroom to the regimental quartermaster's control. When he returned to the barracks, he witnessed Efremov flogging Private Meir Dynin for having been absent. Efremov then threatened to punish Shkablo as well. As Shkablo attempted to explain himself, Efremov kicked him in the face. Shkablo responded by tearing off one of Efremov's epaulets, running to the guardhouse, and surrendering to the commanders. When his case reached military court, Shkablo insisted upon having it transferred to Moscow. Elucidating his misconduct, Shkablo asserted that he had not returned Efremov's epaulet because, had he done so, his case might not have been heard. Recognizing Shkablo's sincere repentance and previous exemplary behavior, the court ordered him to twice run the gauntlet of 500 men, after which he was sent to a convicts' company of the engineer troops.[26]

[25] RGVIA, f. 405, op. 5, d. 8158, l. 50b., 80b.

[26] A. Liubavskii, *Russkie ugolovnye protsessy*, 4 vols. (SPb.: Obshchestvennaia pol'za, 1866), 4: 258–259. For a very different presentation of this case, consonant with the "lachrymose conception" of Jewish history, see M. Usov (M. L. Trivus), *Evrei v armii* (SPb.: Razum, 1911): 10.

Such an absence of legality in Russia's pre-reform army angered lawyer Liubavskii, who discovered and published this account in the 1860s. Jewish journalist Usov, who reprinted it in the 1910s, agreed with his assessment. A modern student of history might view this case differently; Efremov's violent treatment of enlisted men was the norm in that era.[27] The one thousand strokes meted out to Shkablo were considered light punishment, however repugnant this may be to modern sensibilities. Evidently, the head of the Judiciary Standards Department (*Auditoriatskii departament*) had sought a minor penalty.[28] Moreover, Jewish soldiers serving as craftsmen in a training regiment clearly had been accorded the right to practice Judaism. The regimental command had exempted them from work on holidays and had allotted them a room for their "authorized service," in full accord with legislation. The room resembled a synagogue in a shtetl, containing a Holy Ark, a pulpit, the Tablets of the Decalogue, candlesticks, and prayer shawls for worshippers. The regiment had appointed a Jewish custodian to safeguard the soldiers' ritual objects and to distribute them to the soldiers upon request. The soldiers disobeyed the order of a superior, believing that they were protected by legislation. Shkablo, aware of his legal rights, chose his own trial venue. Whereas the observance of Jewish rites in the regiment was typical, it was the court case that was unusual.[29]

Former Jewish soldiers, arrested, sentenced, stripped of their rank, and sent to military prison, retained the same privileges as their brethren serving in the regular army. Viktor Nikitin, a baptized Jewish cantonist, served in the Ministry of the Interior in the 1860s as an envoy on special assignment, inspecting military penitentiary institutions. He observed that Jewish prisoners, especially those held near Jewish communities, were treated decently. Those in the Brest-Litovsk military prison attended synagogue services and heard a rabbi's sermons afterward. Other military prisons, such as Bobruisk, had rooms specially allocated for the use of Jewish convicts. According to prison authorities, such policies had a beneficial impact upon the inmates' morale, enabling them to "more easily bear the burden of confinement."[30]

Crime among Jewish Soldiers

The justice system in Nicholas I's army was characterized by inefficiency and slowness.[31] Usually, a regimental commander meted out punitive measures in the form of informal physical violence (*mordobitie*) or formal corporal

---

[27] Kimerling Wirtschafter, *From Serf to Russian Soldier*, 101–109, 121, 131–2, 138, 142.

[28] A. Liubavskii, *Russkie ugolovnye protsessy*, 4: 257.

[29] This conclusion reflects the degree of freedom enjoyed by enlisted men before the 1874 reforms discussed in Kimerling Wirtschafter, *From Serf to Russian Soldier*, 123–124.

[30] V. N. Nikitin, *Byt voennykh arestantov v krepostiakh* (SPb.: Kolesov i Mikhin, 1873), 320 and 264.

[31] John Keep, "Justice for the Troops: A Comparative Study of Nicholas I's Russia and France under Louis-Philippe," *CMRS*, vol. 28, no. 1 (1987): 35–37; [Poruchik] Zubarev, "Nashi polkovye sudy," *Voennyi sbornik*, no. 5 (1892): 167–171; Keep, *Justice for the Troops*, 43–46.

punishment (*telesnoe nakazanie*). The troops' unruly behavior in the pre-reform army was common knowledge. As Prince Gorchakov, commander of the Siberian detached corps, reported, the soldiers' morale did not meet "the expectations of the government." Conscripts frequently "raised weapons against commanders." To cope with low discipline, Nicholas I recommended acting against offenders without publicity, subjecting those who were especially obstinate to three times a thousand rods, and not requiring officers to inform him of violations because distance rendered such communication impractical.[32]

And yet, despite petitions from corps commanders urging severity, Nicholas I consistently decreased the disciplinary measures for wrongdoers. In 1825, he replaced rods with lashes; in 1830, he abolished the branding of felons; in 1831, he banned punishments administered with the flat of a broadsword or with ramrods; and, three years later, he lowered the maximum number of men in a gauntlet from 6,000 to 3,000. While these changes did not represent reform, they established a basis for Alexander's restructuring of the military justice system. Nicholas I intended to amalgamate the articles of the army's criminal charter, an eclectic compilation from various sources (including clauses penned by Peter the Great and paragraphs from the French Field Charter), and to update the document without introducing any fundamental changes.[33] He established a commission expressly for this purpose. The 1854 version of the charter defined criminal offences in the army until it was superseded in the 1860s by Alexander II's major revisions to the penal code.

Jews, like other conscripts, appeared before a military court only after having committed a third or fourth crime. The punishment for the first two did not necessitate court involvement; local commanders simply dealt out punishment as they saw fit, without publicizing the incidents.[34] Only one-third of the offenses appeared in regimental books; crimes committed by enlisted men were recorded only after the head of the Judiciary Standards Department learned of them. Soldiers preferred "home" punishment, however harsh, to a judicial inquiry. Until the end of the 1850s, the majority of crimes consisted of draft dodging, embezzlement, fraud, and drunk and disorderly conduct, whereas military judiciary procedures primarily concerned serious crimes involving Russian, Kalmyk, Tartar, Uzbek, Kazakh (whom the administration later re-identified as Kirgiz), and Sart soldiers.[35] Between 1827 and 1860, Jews were guilty of few recorded crimes and were a disproportionate minority among

---

[32] RGVIA, f. 801, op. 64/5, st. 2, d. 5, ll. 3–5.

[33] Kimerling Wirtschafter, *From Serf to Russian Soldier*, 105–107; A. Tavastshern, *Voenno-tiuremnye uchrezhdeniia*. SVM, XXII, kn. I, ch. III (SPb.: [Voennoe ministerstvo], 1911), 257–258; V. Afanasiev, "Distsiplinarnye bataliony i roty," *Voennyi sbornik*, no. 7 (1890): 116–117; *Zhurnal Vysochaishe utverzhdennoi komissii dlia rassmotreniia proekta voinskogo ustava o nakazaniiakh* (SPb.: Gosudarstvennaia tipografiia, 1865), 6–7, 22.

[34] N. K. Imeretinskii, "Iz zapisok starogo preobrazhentsa," *Russkaia starina*, no. 77 (1893): 315–317; no. 58 (1893): 26–27.

[35] Compiled on the basis of the RGVIA inventories (*opisi*), f. 801, op. 32, 33/1, 33/3, 43, 64/5, 66, 67, 68, 69.

offenders. The most frequent charges brought against them were desertion and "theft of government property," since everything that a recruit wore or possessed when he left his regiment was considered stolen. For instance, on April 27, 1839, twenty-year-old Leizer Gershovich Kaganovich, a member of the Fifth battalion of the Novoingermanland infantry regiment, deserted his unit. He had previously been accused of fraud and vagrancy. When caught, he was sent to Novgorod. Escaping from the convoy, he exchanged his military overcoat for a coarse peasant's coat and became a vagabond. On June 27, he was arrested and delivered to the bailiff. The court sentenced Kaganovich to a 500-man gauntlet, twice, after which he was dispatched to a grenadier regiment.[36] Another offender, named Tovia Vainshtein, a private in a disabled soldiers' company (*invalidnaia rota*) in the Kishinev hospital, had served his country since the age of fifteen. He deserted on September 22, 1838, and was on the run for two months. He was apprehended in Tiraspol after robbing the home of Leiba Izmail'skii; he had broken into a chest and stolen between ten and fifty-three rubles. This was the third time that Vainshtein had tried to desert. On the first occasion, he was flogged; the second time, he received 500 lashes; the third time, a 500-man gauntlet, twice, and finally he was banished to a penal company.[37]

A comparison of punishments received by various ethnic groups indicates that the head of the Judiciary Standards Department did not single out Jews as deserving of worse treatment than other conscripts. Lutherans were dealt with in similar fashion. Moris Asman, a former laborer from Mitava, decided, in his fifth year of service, to desert the army. Recaptured in a flea market, he fought against arrest so violently that a corporal and five soldiers failed to subdue him. Although it was Asman's first attempt at desertion, he, like Kaganovich, was sentenced to a 500-man gauntlet, twice. However, no doubt because of his violent resistance, he was then sent to a penal company, while Kaganovich was not.[38]

There is no evidence that Jewish soldiers in the pre-reform army exhibited any unusual aggression, either toward officers or toward the dominant religion. Whereas there were numerous instances of sacrilege among Christian soldiers, the lone anti-Christian case involving a Jew was rather peculiar in nature. The head of the Judiciary Standards Department filed a lawsuit against thirty-four-year-old Leizer Freimovich, a private in the Fifth Siberian battalion, for the desecration of an icon of St. Mary. In April 1829, the *kahal* had sent Freimovich into the army as punishment for an attempted rape. During ten years of service, Freimovich had not received a single reprimand. On April, 24, 1839, he was standing guard at the Omsk Gates, close to the guardhouse. Restoration work was in progress, and laborers had moved an image of St. Mary to the sentry box for safekeeping. Without hesitation,

---

[36] RGVIA, f. 801, op. 66, 1 otd., 1 st., d. 28, ll. 1, 4–40b., 7.

[37] RGVIA, f. 801, op. 6, 1 otd., 2 st., d. 20, l. 1–2.

[38] RGVIA, f. 801, op. 67, 1 otd., 1 st., d. 16, ll. 1–2.

Freimovich punctured its eyes with a nail. Then he summoned two cantonists, Erakhtin and Perevalov, to show them that he had "screwed out" her eyes "so that she could not see far at night." For this transgression, Freimovich received a one-thousand-rod punishment three times over. He was expelled from the army and, after a period of convalescence, dispatched to a Siberian penal company.[39]

Sentences of 500- or even 1,000-man gauntlets were common.[40] Nevertheless, in an effort to escape this punishment, Jewish recruits sometimes expressed the wish to adopt Orthodox Christianity. For example, Meir Gotman served in the Eighty-seventh disabled soldiers' company in Kamenets-Podolsk. During his army service, he was charged with desertion, with forging documents, and with stealing public assets. To evade a sentence, Gotman announced his desire to enter the Orthodox Church. On April 1, 1841, he received Holy Communion, and formally became known as Maksim Semenovich Gorchakov. On May 28, he took a Christian vow, whereupon he was freed from the tribunal. His commanders exchanged letters in which they attempted to determine whether Meir was sincere in his desire to embrace Christianity; one of them spoke contemptuously of the opportunism evinced by Gotman's conversion.[41] Although the law explicitly freed those willing to convert to Christianity, local commanders opposed their men resorting to this device. In the fall of 1856, Abram Shteinshnaider, a private in the Forty-first disabled soldiers' company in the Second St. Petersburg Military Hospital, defected. One week later, he surrendered to the Gatchina police near St. Petersburg. His immediate commander wrote that, in February 1856, Shteinshnaider had expressed a wish to adopt the Russian Orthodox faith. Although he failed to join the Orthodox Church, he took up drinking as a means of avoiding his Jewish comrades, and finally deserted. Now known as Nikolai, Shteinshnaider succeeded in obtaining an exemption from punishment by rod and was transferred to the Inspectors' Department. His commanders considered this ruling a violation of both common sense and military honor.[42] They disliked Jews who converted to Christianity, especially those who they suspected were motivated by pragmatic reasons rather than by spiritual considerations. Perhaps this explains a certain grudging respect for Jewish enlisted men who practiced their own faith, and why the army endorsed the establishment of Jewish prayer groups: they deemed this measure a way of preserving discipline.

A Shtetl in the Army

When a regiment was billeted permanently in one place, a soldiers' synagogue was established; itinerant military units sometimes formed prayer groups or

[39] RGVIA, f. 801, op. 66, 1 otd., 1 st., d. 58, ll. 1–4.
[40] Keep, *Soldiers of the Tsar*, 167, n. 133.
[41] RGVIA, f. 801, op. 66, 1 otd., 2 st., d. 48, ll. 1, 5, 6–60b.
[42] RGVIA, f. 801, op. 67, 1 otd., 2 st., d. 2, ll. 1, 20b., 6.

even *havurot*, self-governing Jewish fraternities. In fact, many soldiers' synagogues had been founded as a result of the establishment of voluntary prayer groups, the creation of a self-governing society within the military unit, and the commissioning of a *pinkas*, a social register and community record.[43] Unfortunately, the dearth of documentary evidence precludes any detailed reconstruction of these Jewish soldiers' societies, with some significant exceptions, the case study of one of which is in order.

A story of a Jewish soldier's fraternity requires contextualization. The Russian imperial administration viewed the *kahal*, the self-governing Jewish umbrella organization, as a competitor that enjoyed unchallenged authority in the Jewish community. From late 1790 until 1844, when the *kahal* formally was abolished, the authorities sought to limit or to undermine its powers, favoring competing grassroots Jewish institutions such as the *havurot*. In the Pale of Settlement, these voluntary organizations performed various philanthropic, educational and religious functions critical to the operation of traditional society. Members of the *havurot* raised funds for communal needs, secured free loans, regulated the competition between Jews working in the same profession, organized groups for the study of basic Jewish texts, provided education and dowries for the poor and for orphans, accommodated travelers and alms-seekers, cared for the sick, buried their dead, and prayed together. While the proliferation of *havurot* in the nineteenth-century Pale of Settlement has not been subjected to serious study, the *havurot* that functioned in the army represent a singular parallel. Jews appear to have brought with them into the army not only their religious rites but also the shtetl's social framework. However, whereas a shtetl boasted numerous voluntary fraternities and institutions, there was only one such society per regiment, which assumed all the functions of the *havurot* in the Pale and strove to represent the entire Jewish community. The voluntary brotherhoods of the regimental Russian Orthodox churches were a similar phenomenon;[44] initially, the military endorsed both Christian and Jewish regimental confraternities.

An unreliable source claims that the first institution to provide relief for Jewish soldiers was established as the result of a Chabad-Lubavitch initiative. According to this account, Rabbi Menahem Mendel Schneersohn, the leader of the Lubavitch Hasidic movement, in 1827 sent messengers to the conscripts' assembly points. They attended to the recruits' spiritual needs, inspiring and encouraging them in the observance of Judaism, thus enabling them to

---

[43] The existence of minute books (*pinkasim*) and their function as regulators of these Jewish societies are described in Avraam Rekhtman, *Yiddishe etnografye un folklor* (Buenos Aires: YIVO, 1958), 195–241. For a discussion of *pinkasim* as a historical source, see Israel Halpern, *Yehudim ve-yahadut be-mizrakh eropa: Mekhkarim be-toldotehem* (Jerusalem: Magness Press, 1968), 313–332.

[44] See A. A. Zhelobovskii, *Upravlenie tserkvami i pravoslavnym dukhovenstvom voennogo vedomstva*, SVM, XIII, kn. 2, 53–54.

"resist the blandishments of conversion they would soon face."[45] The same source relates:

When the Cantonist Law was extended to Jews, consternation spread among the Jewish people. The Rabbi [Menahem Mendel] organized a special committee of three divisions. One was to devote itself to the communities, to assist them in lowering their quotas of conscripts. The second was to ransom conscripted children, by organizing a *Chevra T'chiyas Hamaisim* (Society of the Resurrected). The third division sent selected men to the Jewish assembly points, to comfort the children and to encourage them to be loyal to Judaism. This enormously responsible work entailed heavy expense and the grave danger of charges of sedition. Still, for twelve years (1827–1839), only those directly involved in the work were aware of these activities.[46]

No other source corroborates the existence of a Society of the Resurrected, too modern a title for early nineteenth-century Judaism. Nor does this society ever appear in references to self-governing Jewish institutions. Among some 350 extant East European minute books of the self-governing societies, there is no allusion to any such organization. Furthermore, the claim that Chabad-Lubavitch Hasidim were exclusively responsible for organizing self-governing societies of Jewish conscripts is misleading.

Jewish conscripts demonstrated a strong propensity for self-organization. Jewish law declared that a prayer quorum of ten Jews and a Torah scroll were sufficient to form a prayer society, in effect a mobile synagogue. On the eve of the Russo-Turkish War (1877–1878), the Jewish community of Biisk allowed 300 Jewish soldiers from the Viatka infantry regiment to borrow a Torah scroll from their synagogue; the regiment's commander sanctioned the soldiers' carrying the scroll with them to the Balkans.[47] In another case, Jewish soldiers billeted in Belostok (Białystok) established a quorum for worship in a local synagogue that later was transformed into a prayer society named the Route of the Righteous. In 1871, the society established its own *pinkas*, the Minutes of the Route of the Righteous Soldiers from Białystok. The society's stated goals were to strengthen its members' Jewish faith, to prevent quarrels among them, to visit their sick, to bury their dead, and to collect donations.[48] On the basis of

---

[45] Published in English in 1950, in the midst of American Judaism's rebirth, the volume by Yosef Yizhak Schneersohn presented the Chabad-Lubavitch Hasidic movement as the sole supporter of Russian Jewry during the dark age of Nicholas I, the era of conscription. While this work cannot entirely be disregarded, its obvious bias does not permit its acceptance at face value. Its descriptions of Chabad's clandestine activities, of the risks to which the movement exposed itself, and of the centrality of Chabad in Russian Jewish life are more applicable to the late 1920s, when Chabad assumed clandestine leadership of the Jews in the USSR. See Joseph Schneersohn, *The 'Tzemach Tzedek' and the Haskala Movement in Russia* (Brooklyn, N.Y.: Kehot, 1962), 9.

[46] Schneersohn, *Tzemach Tzedek*, 27.

[47] *Ha-Melits*, no. 17 (1878): 336.

[48] Abraham Herschberg, *Pinkos Bialystok*, 2 vols. (New York: gezelshaft fun der geshikhte fun Bialystok, 1949), 1:139.

a recently discovered Hebrew and Yiddish document, Michael Stanislawski reconstructed the history of the Psalms Society of Jewish soldiers in the Kopor'e regiment (*Koporskii polk*), which was active between 1864 and 1867. The society's regulations governed its members' moral obligations, attendance at daily prayers, elections, donations, fines, and the collection of money for the purchase of a Torah scroll.[49]

Among such Jewish voluntary institutions, the history of the Guardians of Faith Society of the Briansk regiment (*Hevrah shomrei emunah shel Brianski polk*) is particularly instructive.[50] The society was established in 1843, during the first conscription of Polish Jews under the reign of Tsar Nicholas I, and operated until 1893. It appeared in Belostok, and ceased its activities in Kremenchug, Ukraine. Rabbi Eliakum-Getsel Meir Podrabinek (who died in 1850) was the first to sign the minutes of the Guardians of Faith.[51] A prominent leader, Podrabinek became the head of the rabbinical court in Belostok in 1837. Well aware of the crucial role played by grass-roots movements, by 1843 he was an active supporter of the Jewish traditional confraternities. Between 1832 and 1849, he was a member of the Eternal Lamp Holy Society, a supervisor of the Book-restorers' Society, and a member of the Society of Tailors, a small communal prayer house. Simultaneously, he was a state-employed local censor of Jewish books.[52] In 1843, when newly recruited Jews from the Kingdom of Poland arrived at the Belostok conscription center, Rabbi Podrabinek offered them kosher food, and encouraged them to serve the tsar but not to abandon the creed of their forefathers.[53]

During the first twenty years of the society's existence, when the Briansk regiment traveled continually, Jewish soldiers routinely requested the help and endorsement of local Jewish leadership. They needed accommodation and arrangements for the Sabbath, as well as rabbinical letters of recommendation that would be kept in the minute book and shown to community leaders whom they expected to meet later in their travels. The minutes meticulously recorded rabbinic pleas inscribed in 1843, 1845, 1846, 1850, 1852, 1853,

---

[49] Michael Stanislawski, *Psalms for the Tsar: A Minute Book of a Psalms Society in the Russian Army* (New York: Yeshiva University, 1988). Stanislawski, following the inscription on the *pinkas'* title page, misidentified the military unit as the Saxon. In fact, it was His Majesty the King of Saxony's Fourth infantry Kopor'e regiment (or, *Koporskii polk*).

[50] Russian State Museum of Ethnography (St. Petersburg), Shlomo Ansky Collection, f. 2, op. 5, d. 52. My special thanks to the custodian of the collection, Liudmila Uritskaia, for inviting me to identify this manuscript and to use it for my research. For the full text of the Guardians of Faith Society, see Yohanan Petrovsky-Shtern, "Dual Identity Revisited: The Case of Russian Jewish Soldiers," an essay preface to the annotated publication of the "1843 Minute Book of the Guardians of Faith Society," *Jews in Russia and Eastern Europe*, no. 1 (2004), 130–144.

[51] *Pinkas Shomrei Emunah*, l. 4.

[52] Hershberg, *Pinkos Bialystok*, 1: 91, 93, 154, 165.

[53] Seven years after the society's establishment, Jews from the Briansk regiment retained contact with Rabbi Podrabinek. His subsequent death by drowning was noted in the minutes. *Pinkas Shomrei Emunah*, l. 54.

1854, 1855, 1857, and 1859. At least nineteen rabbis from Poland, Galicia, Ukraine, Bessarabiia, and Bukovina signed the minutes.[54] In 1853, Rabbi Meir Ha-Cohen Rappoport, the Rabbi of Korets, penned the following address:

> The people whose names appear in this notebook have gathered in the holy society and opened their hearts to righteousness. In order to strengthen the pillars of the world – Torah study, prayer, and good deeds – they established fixed bylaws and resolved to serve and to fulfill the will of our Creator. Accordingly, they also decided to observe the will and orders of our Tsar, let his glory be esteemed. The undersigned have asked me to sign their book and to testify to the righteousness of their acts. How wonderful it is to fulfill their request! May we assist them and support them in every matter, in any place they move to or settle, lest they should eat forbidden food. May they witness redemption! May they merit seeing Zion and Jerusalem rebuilt![55]

After 1882, the Thirty-fifth regiment settled in Kremenchug, and no further rabbinical inscriptions were made. During the society's last ten years, Dov Ber ben Liber, from Berdichev, who was trained as a traditional Jewish scribe, served as the keeper of the minutes, a position critical to the society's existence.[56]

The Guardians of Faith was a religious confraternity whose chief task was to assist its members in the performance of "each and every Commandment," thus ensuring the continued practice of Judaism. They espoused peacemaking and mutual respect. Daily prayers and observance of the Sabbath laws were mandatory. Their statutes enshrined the traditional aspects of the faith, concerning everything from the phylacteries to dietary laws. Society members visited their brethren in military hospitals, and arranged for Jewish burials with the corresponding seven days of mourning and prayer. Unlike most of its fellow societies in the Pale, the Guardians of Faith also regulated Jewish–gentile relations, specifically the relationship between Jewish soldiers and their commanding officers. The register stated that, when a society member was scheduled to stand guard or to work on the Sabbath or on a festival, wardens were responsible for beseeching his officer to release him from duty on his day of rest. Group solidarity was considered as important as military discipline; members were forbidden to betray a fellow Jew to an officer. If a society member lost or damaged his weapon, which frequently occurred in the pre-reform army, other members raised funds to save him from being disciplined for negligence. When a soldier was arrested and imprisoned, the society did its best to ransom him. Thus the society's members had to adapt their Judaic values to the requirements of the military. They could no longer assume they were Jews: they had routinely to negotiate the meanings of their Jewishness. Their focus upon the external society's interaction with the Russian army and the regimental commanders

---

[54] *Pinkas Shomrei Emunah*, ll. 8, 14–17. The last plea was written in 1882 by Israel Yakov Yabets, the Rabbi of Kremenchug.
[55] *Pinkas Shomrei Emunah*, l. 140b.
[56] *Pinkas Shomrei Emunah*, ll. 35, 47.

was the first indication of a profound transformation in the society members' self-perception.[57]

Although, to some extent, the Guardians of Faith mirrored the structure of the *havurot* in the Pale, they described their society in the register as *kahalenu* and *kahal*, "our community" or "our congregation," rather than as *havurenu*, "our society." They did not, in fact, represent the Jewish community at large, but served as a substitute for it, replacing all traditional *havurot*.[58] In addition to functioning as a prayer society, the Guardians of Faith engaged in vital activities such as redeeming the prisoners, visiting the sick, burying dead brethren, providing free loans, and interceding with the authorities.[59] Their bylaws sought to uphold all 613 Commandments.[60]

The society's *pinkas*, while not disclosing the age, military skills, rank, current occupation, or previous background of its constituents, detailed its membership's dynamics: There were twenty-eight active members in 1843; forty-nine in 1883; and forty-four in 1893. The Briansk regiment contained forty-two Jews in 1885, sixty-nine in 1886, thirteen in 1887, and thirty-two in 1889;[61] it is quite possible that most of them were society members. As soon as the Briansk regiment had settled into its newly built quarters in Kremenchug, the society displayed remarkable activity. For nearly a quarter of a century, its internal election results were meticulously recorded: in 1876, 1882, 1883, 1884, 1885, 1886, 1887, and 1893. Except for one in 1843, there had been no elections during the society's first twenty years of operation. Polish Jews held the leading positions, including that of society warden, and did not cede them until discharged into the reserves. Similarly, during the 1876 draft, newcomers retained their positions throughout the six years of their active service. After 1881, elections were held almost annually, and the leadership underwent regular change. Toward the end of its operation, there arose in the society a small yet influential group of Jews from Tulchin who secured leading posts,

---

[57] *Pinkas Shomrei Emunah*, l. 4–7.

[58] The principal idea embodied in the statutes paralleled the later religious advice of Rabbi Kagan (Rabbi Israel Meir Kagan Poupko) in his *halakhic* digest *Mahaneh Israel* (1881), which addressed the problems faced by observant Jews in the Russian army. See M. Yoshor, *The Life and Works of Rabbi Israel Meir Kagan of Radin* (New York: Mesora Publishers, 1997), 235–246. In this sense, the Shomrei Emunah Society can be compared with other multifunctional societies (*havurot murkavot*) that appeared among Polish Jewish artisans in the late eighteenth century. See Moshe Kramer, "Leheker ha-melakhah ve-hevrot ba'alei-melakhah etsel yehudei Polin," *Zion*, no. 2 (1937): 323–324.

[59] Cf. the traditional functions of voluntary Jewish societies in S. Baron, *The Jewish Community* (Philadelphia: Jewish Publication Society of America, 1942), 1: 348–374.

[60] This necessity of reinforcing the observance of the Commandments during army service is emphasized in *Ha-emek davar*, a mid-nineteenth-century Torah commentary by Tsevi Naftali Yehuda Berlin, whose disciples studied in the Volozhin yeshiva. See I. Hagar-Lau, *He-hayal ve-ha-hosen: Tsava u-milhamah be-ha-emek davar u-ve-meshekh hokhmah* (Jerusalem: Or Etzion, 1989), 99–108.

[61] RGVIA, f. 400, op. 5, d. 1023, l. 33.

promoting themselves to senior positions as the two first wardens and the first three electoral officers.[62]

In addition to its pragmatic, social, and religious functions, the Guardians of Faith Society also fulfilled a symbolic role for its members: its statutes reminded them of who they were. Thus, the values of traditional Judaism were preserved even when the society's members were unable to follow them. For fifty years, from 1843 to 1893, the regulations remained unaltered. The only innovation was the acquisition of a Torah scroll, which transformed the society into a self-sufficient prayer group and turned any room in which its members gathered for prayer into a synagogue. The minutes do not indicate any serious conflict, other than a case in which a soldier offended members by acting "non-Jewishly," possibly by converting to Christianity. The society erased his name from its list, banishing him from the ranks of the "Jewish military men, Guardians of Faith."[63]

His Majesty's Obedient Soldiers

Throughout the fifty years of its history, the Guardians of Faith Society comprised an essential part of the Briansk regiment to which it formally belonged. This regiment's illustrious history is detailed by Russian military sources.[64] The Thirty-fifth Briansk infantry regiment was founded in 1809, either by Alexander I during his military campaign in Galicia, or by Major General Gorbuntsov, as a musketeers' regiment on the Åland Islands (in the Baltic Sea) composed of garrisons from the islands of Åland and Gangut. In 1811, before the Napoleonic invasion, they renamed it an infantry regiment. Until 1814, it participated in Field Marshal Kutuzov's campaign against Napoleon. Upon its return, the regiment settled in Poltava, Ukraine. In the late 1860s, barracks were built for the regiment in Kremenchug, which then became known, until World War I, as the regiment's headquarters. By 1857, the regiment was listed as the Briansk Jäger regiment (*egerskii polk*); between 1857 and 1864, it was referred to as the Briansk infantry (*pekhotnyi polk*); after that, it was described as the Thirty-fifth regiment. The regiment fought in every military campaign. After the Crimean War, it was named after Adjutant General Prince Gorchakov,

---

[62] To a certain degree, the Guardians of Faith Society may be seen as a version of the *Landsmannschaftn* (*zemliachestva*) formed by groups of soldiers of the same provenance. Cf. John Bushnell, *Mutiny and Repression: Russian Soldiers in the Revolution of 1905–1906* (Bloomington: Indiana University Press, 1985), 18–19.

[63] *Pinkas Shomrei Emunah*, l. 44.

[64] M. Lyons, *The Russian Imperial Army: A Bibliography of Regimental Histories and Related Works* (Stanford, Calif.: Stanford University Press, 1968), 86–87; A. Kersnovskii, *Istoriia Russkoi Armii*, vol. 1, *Ot Narvy do Parizha* (Moscow, 1992), 206; *Pekhota. Spravochnaia Kniga Glavnoi Kvartiry* (St. Petersburg: n. p., 1913); V. Zvegintsev, *Khronologiia Russkoi Armii, 1700–1917*, vol. 2–3, (Paris: [Viraflay], 1961–1962), 46 (no. 615); Vasilkovskii, Grigorovich, *Pamiatka o stoletnei sluzhbe 35-go pekhotnogo Brianskogo General-Adiutanta Kniazia Gorchakova polka* (Kremenchug: n. p., 1909).

whose clear thinking and caution enabled him to save many troops and to avoid a greater disaster during the retreat near Sevastopol. In 1861, by the emperor's special order, the title "Prince Gorchakov Regiment" was ascribed to the Briansk regiment.

By its one-hundredth anniversary in 1909, the regiment had earned a reputation for bravery. Its campaigns delineated Russian geopolitics: Nicholas's attempts to become the gendarme of Europe; Alexander II's efforts to save his Slavic brothers, the Bulgarians, from the Turks; and the colonialist incursions of Nicholas II into the Far East. After effectively suppressing the 1830–1831 Polish insurrection, the regiment was awarded special military distinction "For the pacification of Poland." Following the Hungarian campaign, the first in which Jewish soldiers from the Guardians of Faith participated, the regiment was bestowed with silver trumpets inscribed "For the suppression of Hungary in 1849." In the early 1850s, the regiment acquired new percussion rifles, which were displayed at a parade ground near Warsaw and tested at a shooting show near Gomel. The Austrian and the Russian emperors both expressed great satisfaction with the troops' training. For their excellence, all Briansk regiment fighters were awarded one ruble each. Two years later, during the Crimean War, the regiment defended the empire's western borders before moving to Sevastopol, where it took part in that conflict's fiercest battles. The regiment suffered heavy casualties. During the defense of Sevastopol, it lost 3,287 men; only 1,460 able-bodied soldiers remained. For the heroic defense of Sevastopol, all the Briansk regiment soldiers were presented with two rubles each, and 122 soldiers, of whom some were Jews, received various distinctions.

After the Crimean War, the regiment was stationed in the Poltava and Kharkov provinces until the beginning of the 1870s, when it settled in Kremenchug. In 1863, it participated in the suppression of the Polish uprising and, in 1877–1878, it liberated Bulgaria from the Turks.[65] Jewish soldiers shared this victory with their Russian counterparts, participating in battles in the St. Nicholas and the Shipka Mountains. Several divisions operating in the Balkans included a considerable number of Jews. The Thirty-fifth division comprised two-thirds Russian and one-third Jewish soldiers. In the Sixteenth and the Thirtieth divisions, drafted in the Mogilev and Minsk provinces, where significant Jewish populations resided, Jews accounted for one-quarter of the ranks. In the midst of the Balkan campaign, commanders transferred three soldiers to the Briansk regiment from the Eletsk and Sevsk infantries, all of them Jews: Abraham Dubrovskii, Adolf Veiner, and Itska Fuks.[66] Could the men have requested this transfer, knowing of the Briansk company's Jewish

---

[65] See R. Leslie, *Reform and Insurrection in Russian Poland. 1856–1865* (London: Athlone Press, 1962), 232–251; S. Kieniewicz, *Powstanie Styczniowe* (Warsaw: Wydawnictwo Naukowe, 1972); Klier, *Imperial Russia's Jewish Question*, 392–395; Bruce Menning, *Bayonets before Bullets: The Imperial Russian Army, 1861–1914* (Bloomington: Indiana University Press, 1992), 51–86.

[66] RGVIA, Voenno-uchenyi arkhiv, d. 7964, l. 84.

Society? In any case, Jewish involvement in the victorious War for the Liberation of the Slavs is repeatedly mentioned by Russian memoirists and journalists. Jews such as Abram Kliakh, Samuil Brem, Naum Kolomiets, Moshka Umanskii, Isaak Rodzevich, and Moisei Masiuk were among those who stormed Plevna and captured Gali Osman Pasha, the head of the Turkish army.[67] On Shipka Mountain, the Briansk contingent saw almost 500 men killed or wounded; there is hardly a Russian military memoir that does not mention the heroism of this regiment in the face of grueling circumstances. When, in 1909, the company celebrated its one-hundredth anniversary, it received the Banner of St. George with an inscription "For Sevastopol in 1854–1855 and for Shipka in 1877."[68] The campaigns in which the regiment participated and the awards it received also reflected glory upon its Jewish soldiers, who had helped to earn the army unit its military fame.

Ten years after the last entry in the society's minutes, the regiment fought in the Russo-Japanese War. During this campaign, 124 Jewish soldiers of the Briansk infantry regiment were killed or wounded.[69] After the war, the regiment assisted the regime in suppressing unrest in the Poltava province during the 1905 Revolution. The regiment's one-hundredth anniversary coincided with the two-hundredth anniversary of the Battle of Poltava, in which Peter the Great defeated the Swedish troops. The Briansk regiment, renowned for its stalwart loyalty, protected Nicholas II during the festivities in Poltava. The minutes of the Guardians of Faith Society testify that the Jewish soldiers in the Briansk regiment did not miss a single military campaign, although they sometimes (as in Sevastopol and in Bulgaria) were too busy to seek rabbinic endorsement of their activities and to make entries in their register (Table 2).[70]

The Guardians of Faith Society represents a litmus test for emerging Russian Jewish loyalty and self-awareness. Society members referred to themselves as the *anshei hayil*, brave soldiers serving in a renowned Russian army regiment. The society's Hebrew register bore numerous regimental stamps and the Russian imperial insignia, as if it were an official Russian army document rather than one belonging to a private Jewish fraternity. At least on paper, the Guardians of Faith claimed that service to the Russian tsar was as important as service to the Almighty, and that a violation of the tsar's orders was tantamount to a transgression against the Torah. It is illuminating that the soldiers sought

---

[67] "Piat' mesiatsev na Shipke v 1877 godu. Iz vospominanii ofitsera Podol'skogo pekhotnogo polka," *Voennyi sbornik*, no. 6 (1883): 325; S. E. Korngold, "Russkiie evrei na voine 1877/78," *Russkii evrei*, no. 7 (1879): 227–230, no. 11 (1879): 384–387; A. E. Kaufman, "Evrei v russko-turetskoi voine 1878–1879 gg." *Evreiskaia starina*, no. 1 (1915): 56–72; no. 2 (1915): 176–182; S. Pozner, "Armiia v Rossii," *Evreiskaia entsiklopediia* (SPb.: Brokgauz-Efron, 1906), 3: 160–171, here 164.

[68] F. Isaichikov, "Brianskii polk na Shipke," *Brianskii Kraeved* no. 5 (Briansk, 1973): 175; Batsevich, Ruppenheit, *Ocherk voennyx deistvii, v kotorykh uchastvoval 35-yi pekhotnyi polk v kampanii 1877–1878 gg.* (Kharkov, 1886).

[69] Calculated after the data published in Usov, *Evrei v armii*, 112–114.

[70] See *Pinkas Shomrei Emunah*, ll. 2, 3, 8, 14–17, 46.

TABLE 2. *Localities Visited by the Jewish Soldiers'*
Guardians of Faith Society of the Prince Gorchakov
Briansk Thirty-fifth Infantry Regiment

Dates	Localities
1843	Białystok
1845	Sróck (32km SE of Lodz)
1845	Tiktin (Tykoczin, 26 km W of Byałystok)
1846	Ostrów (near Przemyśl, Białystok, or Lublin)
1846	Nowy Dvor (either Romania or Poland)
1846	Ilintsy (Biliniec, 50 km WNW of Czernowitz, Bukovina) or Linits (56 km E of Vinnitsa)
1850	Olkusz (32 km WNW Kraków)
1852	Kozelets (69 km NNE of Kiev)
1853	Korets (62 km E of Rovno)
1854	Kremenets (69 km SSW of Rovno)
1855	Kishinev (Bessarabiia)
1857	Hotin (45 km NE of Czernowitz)
1859	Luków (82 km NNW of Lublin)
1859	Kolevets (Kolowerta or Kolivets, Rovno district)
1859	Nezhin (94 km WSW of Konotop)
1882	Kremenchug (133 km WNW of Dnepropetrovsk)

Source: Russian State Museum of Ethnography, S. Ansky collection,
f. 2, op. 5, d. 52, ll. 2, 3, 8, 14–17, 46.

the society's support "lest [they] become lazy in serving [their] master, the tsar."
This seems to suggest that Jewish soldiers who resisted baptism and who
identified both with the Russian military and with traditional Jewish values
(they comprised an overwhelming majority in the pre-reform army) were the
first Russian and perhaps the first modern East European Jews to preserve their
Jewish self-awareness. Their dual identity was the result of an intensive social
interaction with and immersion in the dominant society. In a way, Jews in the
army underwent a process of acculturation similar to that of eighteenth-century
Anglo Jewry and unlike that of the first enlightened Russian Jews, who
converted to Christianity.[71]

The Pale beyond the Pale

Soldiers' prayer groups and synagogues established beyond the Pale of Jewish
Settlement subsequently blossomed into Jewish communities. At the beginning of
the twentieth century, the War Ministry decided to recognize religious institutions of "alien" faiths throughout the empire, primarily beyond the Pale. It
learned that Krondshtadt port had a prayer house with two rabbis, and that

---

[71] Cf. Todd Endelman, *The Jews of Britain, 1656 to 2000* (Berkeley, Calif.: University of
California Press, 2002), 41–78.

Arkhangelsk, Ialutorovsk, Petrozavodsk, Tobolsk, and Tumen each boasted a
Jewish prayer house. Belgorod, Dmitriev, Ekaterinburg, Kursk, Perm, Simbirsk,
and Tula, some of them thousands of miles beyond the Pale, each possessed two
synagogues. Jews also had established prayer houses and synagogues in Eniseisk,
Kamsk, Krasnoiarsk, Moscow, Nikolaev, Rzhev, St. Petersburg, Tomsk, Tver,
and Ufa.[72] These were relatively small congregations of 300–400 people each, in
most cases initiated by soldiers. For example, the military reported that, in
Blagoveshchensk, there were several Jewish families of retired soldiers who had
been drafted under the pre-reform conscription system.[73] Occasionally, the
names of streets on which prayer houses stood testified to their military origins:
in Tsarskoe selo, on the corner of Artillery Street, in Oranienbaum, in Military
Lane.[74] It is possible to extrapolate similar histories for other communities
that emerged over the length and breadth of the Russian Empire outside the
Pale. Local histories of Jewish settlements in the Russian interior, such as
Perm, Ekaterinburg, and Ufa, attest to the army's resettlement of Jews outside
the Pale.

The Jewish communities outside the Pale grew mostly due to the newly
retired soldiers being allowed to settle in places where they had served. In
Petrozavodsk, for example, in 1856 there were 214 men and 23 women of
Jewish faith. The retired soldiers returned to the Pale, married, and brought
their wives with them to settle beyond the Pale. Their professional activities
did not differ significantly from the occupational structure of their brethren in
the Pale. They worked as tailors, shoemakers, butchers, sausage-makers,
and smiths, yet the competition was significantly lower than in the Pale and, as
a result, their income was higher. Indeed, Russian, not Yiddish, was their
mother tongue.

A Jewish community appeared in Nizhnii Novgorod in the mid-nineteenth
century. Its members were cantonists from the city garrison and from the police
unit, NCOs, soldiers, military staff scribes, and musicians in the military band.
In 1859, some 300 Jewish enlisted men, mostly retired soldiers, and their
families lived in the city. Among them were twenty-one merchants, two home-
owners, one tailor, two carpenters, one bookbinder, five musicians, and one
soldier still on active duty. Jewish NCOs constituted one-quarter of all Jewish

---

[72] RGIA, f. 821, op. 10, d. 1118 ("Statistika o bogougodnykh zavedeniiakh dukhovenstva
inostrannykh ispovedanii," 1908–1909). ll. 14, 30, 32, 36, 38, 39, 42, 47, 49, 58, 72, 93, 95,
124. Among 300 Jews who settled in Ufa province in 1880–1881, 130 were retired Jewish
soldiers, members of their families, and cantonists' widows; see E. A. Shkurko, *Ocherki istorii
evreev Bashkortostana* (Ufa: n. p., 1999), 45–47. V. Iu. Gessen provides a detailed account of a
number of Jewish soldiers' prayer houses legally established in St. Petersburg between 1833 and
1867. They cemented the making of the traditional Jewish community in town, which consisted
predominantly of the observant Jewish soldiers and members of their families; see V. Iu.
Gessen, *K istorii Sankt-Peterburgskoi evreiskoi religioznoi obshchiny: ot pervykh evreev do XX
veka* (SPb.: Tema, 2000), 42–46, 150–154.

[73] RGIA, f. 821, op. 10, d. 1118, l. 97.

[74] RGIA, f. 821, op. 10, d. 1118, l. 126.

enlisted personnel in town. In 1877, among the seventy-eight residents of Nizhnii Novgorod, sixty-three were Jewish soldiers; fifteen were artisans or guild merchants. In 1846, there were three prayer houses in Nizhnii Novgorod: one on Nizhniaia Street, where Podisko, a retired soldier, acted as warden; one on Pochaininskaia Street, with Dolnik, an NCO, as warden; and one in the district of Oshara, where NCO Kui and merchant Aleshnikov served as wardens. Itska (Isaac) Podisko, a typical soldier, was born to an urban Jewish family in Rovno, in the Volhynia province. He was homeschooled and then inducted into state service from 1846 until 1867, first as a cantonist, and later as a soldier. Upon his retirement from the army, he worked in the ready-made clothes trade, and opened his own store in the Nizhnii market. He appears to have married Rebbeca Notena, from the Pale, and to have brought her to Nizhnii Novgorod. There they settled and raised two sons. Beginning in 1853, Podisko served as a rabbi, and the commander of the city garrison supported his appointment to the local civil administration. Podisko acted as a self-appointed rabbi and the warden of a soldiers' synagogue for twenty years. The warden of the newly established prayer group on Dvorianskaia Street, perhaps because he was more learned, then refused to acknowledge Podisko's authority.[75]

Retired Jewish soldiers who settled beyond the Pale sometimes became communal leaders. Small Jewish communities often requested that the Department of Spiritual Affairs of Foreign Confessions confirm the appointment of a retired Jewish soldier as a local rabbi. These individuals had not obtained *smikhah*, the legal certification of competence to fulfill rabbinic duties, nor had they passed corresponding exams in a rabbinic academy. Nevertheless, because of their traditional religious upbringing and their military experience, they met the requirements of the newly founded local communities as responsible, literate, and loyal citizens, on good terms with the military administration and knowledgeable in Jewish law. The army's commanders knew that Jewish societies were organized around their congregations, and that synagogue wardens registered such vital community statistics as marriages, births, deaths, and draft lists in their metrical books. Consequently, the military endorsed the appointment of Jewish soldiers, both retired and in active service, to positions of leadership in the community. In 1893, the governor of Orenburg petitioned the Ministry of the Interior to allow retired soldier Itshak Primak and Sergeant Major Nokhim Mednik to serve as rabbis. Instances in which the military prohibited Jewish enlisted men from forming a congregation were very rare, and usually easily explicable. For instance, when the governor of Irkutsk rejected a request that twenty-six Jewish soldiers in the Twelfth infantry

---

[75] V. Pudalov, "Iz istorii evreiskoi obshchiny Nizhnego Novgoroda v kontse XIX-nachale XX vv.," in Z. Kh. Liberzon, ed., *Evrei Nizhnego Novgoroda* (Nizhnii Novgorod: Dekom, 1993), 20–24.

Siberian brigade form a separate congregation, it was "because of their small number."[76] He was aware that a large local congregation already existed there.

Both in the Pale of Settlement and outside it, retired Jewish soldiers joined the lower middle class. The 1861 elections for a local rabbi provoked a scandal in Nikolaev (from which Nicholas I had banished Jews in 1834). Nearly a thousand Jewish families lived in the town, of which more than 950 were headed by Jewish reserve soldiers, artisans and town-dwellers, and forty by guild merchants. Under Nicholas I, Jewish soldiers' families had raised funds and built a synagogue. However, in the early 1860s, it was discovered that the congregation's only registered members were all merchants; it was their pre-rogative to appoint a rabbi, while the will of the overwhelming, unregistered majority could safely be dismissed. The retired soldiers complained to the Ministry of the Interior that, of one thousand families, only forty had been party to the decision, whereas "we, the poor class of Jews," were not allowed to participate, despite the fact that "we supported the synagogue by ourselves for twenty-five years."[77] Aleksandr Timashev, the minister of the interior, sup-ported the retired soldiers and ordered the governor to reconsider the mem-bership of the Jewish soldiers' families in the local community.[78]

Conclusion

In extending conscription to the Jews, Nicholas I synchronized the destinies of Jewish and Russians under the aegis of a shared duty before the state. Rather than relying upon culture, education, language, or civil rights (all "useless illusions," to use Nicholas's term), the tsar chose the army as the medium by which to integrate the two groups he saw as native Russians and alien Jews. In significant ways, the Russian military strove to accommodate this religious minority, furthering the enlightened policies of Catherine and Alexander I and radically departing from the anti-Judaic bias of the early modern Russian rulers such as Elizabeth (Elizaveta Petrovna, who ruled between 1749 and 1762). Although conflicts between local and state regulations were endemic, com-manders largely endorsed traditional Jewish observance in the belief that it enhanced military discipline.

The result of the combined efforts of the imperial authorities and the local military administration was a new Jew: Russian-speaking, militarily trained, loyal to the emperor, patriotic, and religiously observant. Jewish soldiers, as

---

[76] RGIA, f. 821, op. 8, d. 429 ("Evrei v Arkhangel'skoi gubernii"), ll. 3, 6–7; RGIA, f. 821, op. 8, d. 158 ("Evrei v Orenburgskoi gubernii"), ll. 1–2; RGIA, f. 821, op. 8, d. 179 ("Delo o vyborakh irkutskogo ravvina"), ll. 2, 3, 5, 7, 37.

[77] RGIA, f. 821, op. 8, d. 415, ll. 19–190b., 20–210b.

[78] This case is of particular interest both because the local provincial administration refused to implement the minister's decision, and because the Jewish merchants eventually resolved "to avoid accusations and calumnies in our big family of a thousand members and to inscribe the retired soldiers in the metrical books of the prayer societies, thus allowing them to participate in the elections." See RGIA, f. 821, op. 8, d. 415, l. 48.

most illustriously represented by the Briansk regiment, played a visible role in Russian military history. In turn, their army experience shaped their lives. Islands of the Pale of Jewish Settlement were created in Russia's interior. Nicholas I's integrating effort was a success: thousands of adults who fulfilled their sacred duty constituted the first large pool of modernized Russian Jews. To draft the Jews was a bold step: Nicholas's state-building and integrationist enthusiasm went farther than, for example, the rulers of the Ottoman Empire, who, throughout the nineteenth century, preferred to have their Christian and Jewish minority pay taxes rather than fulfill military duty.[79] However, Nicholas's enlightened rationalism clashed with his own vision of a Russian Orthodox empire. This collision jeopardized the entire Jewish modernization project and emphasized the limitations of his reform. These were particularly striking when viewed against the backdrop of the Habsburgs' Jewish soldiers, who could become officers by the second quarter of the nineteenth century, and who were not restricted from joining elitist regiments nor became objects of the missionary zeal of the monarch.

[79] Erik Jan Zürcher, "The Ottoman Conscription System, 1844–1914," *International Review of Social History*, no. 43 (1998): 437–449, here 446.

3

"Let the Children Come to Me"

Jewish Minors in the Cantonist Battalions

While Grand Duke Constantine and his retinue in the Kingdom of Poland sought to transform Jews primarily through elementary education, Emperor Nicholas I contended that the best educational establishment was the army. It rid visionaries of their unnecessary illusions, imparted useful skills to adults, and trained children to be obedient subjects. The pre-reform Russian army had its own educational program for minors, known as the cantonist schools. By 1827, when Russian supervisors for the first time brought Jewish children from the conscription points to cantonist battalions, military education for minors had already been in existence in Russia for over a hundred years.[1] In 1721, the innovative Peter I had instituted garrison schools for soldiers' children, each of which enrolled fifty students. Peter maintained that such children became the best trained and most reliable soldiers. In 1758, the Empress Elizaveta Petrovna passed a law altering the status of soldiers' male offspring: they were to be state serfs. Soldiers registered with the military department and dutifully sent their children to garrison schools. Pavel I designated these schools as military orphans' detachments (*voenno-sirotskie otdelenia*). Once they had arrived, the soldiers' children acquired new "parents": the army was their mother and the emperor their father. To describe these children Alexander I devised the term "cantonists" from the German word *Kanton*, an enlistment district. In 1824, the cantonist detachments officially became part of the War Ministry's Department of Military Settlements.

With his zeal for organization and management, Nicholas I reorganized the detachments into companies (of 250 children each), half-battalions (composed of two companies each), and battalions (consisting of 1,000 officers and men),

---

[1] For an analysis of the history of military and state legislation on the "soldiers' children" and the cantonists, see Elise Kimerling, " 'Soldiers' Children, 1719–1856: A Study of Social Engineering in Imperial Russia," *Forschungen zur Osteuropaischen Geschichte*, no. 30 (1982): 61–136; V. Shchepetil'nikov, *Glavnyi Shtab*, *SVM*, t. IV, ch. II, kn. 1, otd. 2, 3–302; M. Lalaev, *Istoricheskii ocherk voenno-uchebnykh zavedenii podvedomstvennykh Glavnomu upravleniiu. Ot osnovaniia v Rossii voennykh shkol do iskhoda pervogo dvadtsatipiatiletiia tsarstvovaniia gosudaria imperatora Aleksandra Nikolaevicha, 1700–1880* (SPb.: Tip. Stasiulevicha, 1880).

and incorporated each of these into five educational brigades.[2] Between 1827 and 1855, there were thirteen cantonist battalions, nine half-battalions and three separate companies, as well as various cantonists' units, schools of the carabineer regiments, and reserve mounted troops. Cantonist establishments dotted the Russian Empire: soldiers' children found themselves in places such as Arkhangelsk, Irkutsk, Kazan, Kiev, Krasnoiarsk, Omsk, Orenburg, Perm, St. Petersburg, Pskov, Revel, Saratov, Simbirsk, Smolensk, Tobolsk, Tomsk, Troitsk, Verkhneuralsk, Vitebsk, and Voronezh. In the late 1840s, there were more than a quarter of a million children from the ages of eight to eighteen serving in the battalions. During Nicholas I's reign, compulsory education in cantonist battalions was extended to include all children born to military settlers' families. In the main these were illegitimate children, born to soldiers' wives while the soldiers were serving elsewhere, but they also included children of army officers, children born to vagrants, children of impoverished noble families sent with their parents' consent; and street children and homeless orphans of the Polish Kingdom. In 1827, conscripted Jewish minors joined this list.[3]

Nicholas's Reform of Jewish Minors

Although Nicholas readily acquiesced in the practice of Judaism in the regular army, he planned to banish it, along with all other alien faiths, from the cantonist schools. His enlightened vision of the military, an invention that historians considered Russian, in fact had Prussian origins. The army would serve to unify the empire's multi-ethnic population, bringing Kazakhs (called Kirgiz by Russians at that time), Tartars, Uzbeks, Poles, Estonians, and Jews, among others, under the aegis of the majority culture. Since the empire needed useful subjects, and since Russian Orthodoxy was a useful belief, he reasoned, one should become Russian Orthodox to better serve the empire. For Nicholas, bringing non-Christians to Russian Orthodoxy fitted his program of integration. This supposed logic was in accordance with the mainstream of enlightened thought, which assumed the universality of what Chateaubriand called the genie of Christianity. Count Uvarov, the minister of education and an enlightened Russian bureaucrat, provided Nicholas with the formula "Russian orthodoxy, autocracy, nationality," inventively translating it from the German

---

[2] In a fully deployed battalion, there were up to 1,500 officers and men. Apart from the cantonists, the battalion was composed of one lieutenant colonel, two majors, six captains, one staff captain, five lieutenants, one first lieutenant, three sergeant majors, one tenth-class clerk to keep order, six teachers of the fourteenth rank, thirty-six corporals responsible for training in the classes, ten privates and one combat corporal teaching line drills. For more detail, see RGVIA, f. 405, op. 5, d. 3919, ll. 5–6, 7, 12.

[3] Keep, *Soldiers of the Tsar*, 202–204; Kimerling, "Soldiers' Children," 82–83, 125; Shchepetilnikov, *Glavnyi Shtab*, 5–10, 65, 75, 111–114, 166–167; *Voennaia entsiklopediia*, 11: 355–356; RGVIA, f. 1, op. 1, d. 29708, l. 4. Starting from 1832, the Russian army regularly drafted Polish children, too, resorting to brutal measures. See Wiesław Caban, *Służba rekrutów z Królestwa Polskiego w armii carskiej w latach 1831–1873* (Warsaw; DiG, 2001), 97–104.

state-making motto "God, Kaiser, and Fatherland." This formula implied that successful Russification was predicated upon Russian Orthodoxy; one was not a loyal subject unless one accepted the Eucharist à la Russe. While most European enlightened thinkers agreed that Jewish integration into the majority culture would sooner or later convert them into Christians, Nicholas chose to exercise his extreme penchant for control and to oversee this process. The best and most obvious way for a non-Russian to please the monarch and to benefit the empire was to become Russian.[4] This process Nicholas initiated with the military educational institutions, the cantonist schools.

The idea of converting Jews *in* the army occurred after, rather than before, the issuing of the 1827 law on conscription, and never became an attempt to Christianize them *through* the army. Military data from the 1820s and 1830s indicate that Nicholas did not fully formulate his policy toward Jewish conscripts. The ability to develop global strategy or far-reaching plans was not in his nature; the catastrophic defeat of his army in the Crimean War testified to his negligence in long-term planning.[5] Nonetheless, Nicholas I was fanatically dedicated to military discipline. He supervised all his projects with the diligence of a paranoid tactician; although he was not a strategist, tactics were his forte. He could not engineer a comprehensive campaign, but could administer the minutiae of army routine. Nicholas carefully monitored developments, reaching his conclusions after exhaustive inquiry.[6] His investigation into the 1825 Decembrist rebellion revealed his initial disappointment and hesitation, as well as his ability to analyze developments and to respond to them.

Most likely neither Nicholas nor his military bureaucrats were prepared for an influx of Jewish minors into the battalions. Initially there were no special policies in place to deal with them. Individual officers encouraged conversion as it homogenized the troops and made day-to-day running of the cantonist battalions more convenient. This spontaneous reaction of the army commanders to

---

[4] David Saunders, *Russia in the Age of Reaction and Reform, 1801–1881* (London and New York: Longman, 1992), 179, 182. Nicholas's attempts to baptize Jewish minors in the army comprised part of his project to convert members of other groups, including Muslims and Catholics, to Russian Orthodoxy. For more detail, see Andreas Kappeler, *The Russian Empire: A Multi-ethnic History*, trans. Alfred Clayton (Harlow and New York: Longman, 2001), 250–255.

[5] For a discussion of the possible impact of the defeat of Russian troops during the Crimean War and of the strange circumstances of Nicholas I's death, including his alleged suicide, see A. Presniakov, *Emperor Nicholas I of Russia. The Apogee of Autocracy, 1825–1855*, ed. and trans. Judith C. Zacek (Gulf Breeze, Fl.: Academic International Press, 1974), 78. For a more sober opinion on this issue that denies rumors of Nicholas's suicide, see Nicholas Riasanovsky, *Nicholas I and Official Nationality in Russia, 1825–1855* (Berkeley and Los Angeles: University of California Press, 1959), 34 n. 69.

[6] Nicholas I's military penchant is extensively discussed in Bruce Lincoln, *Nicholas I: Emperor and Autocrat of All the Russians* (Bloomington: Indiana University Press, 1978): 50–68; Riasanovsky, *Nicholas I*, 43; Keep, *Soldiers of the Tsar*, 315–317, 323–325; Stanislawski, *Tsar Nicholas I*, 14–15. For Nicholas I's astonishing attention to the details of everyday cantonist life and legislation, including his personal supervision of the implementation of minor orders, see V. Petrov, *Glavnoe upravlenie voenno-uchebnykh zavedenii. SVM*, t. X, ch. 2, 139.

the appearance of a substantial number of non-Christians among the troops triggered individual conversions which were reported up the chain of the command, and eventually to Nicholas, who demanded monthly reports on conversions. Some officers read Nicholas's requests as the highest approval of their missionary activities; they intensified conversions, and reported to Nicholas, who eventually concluded that the administration should implement the still incipient process of Christianization. In this respect, the fate of Jewish cantonists was similar to that of their peers in the army; Lutheran, Catholic, and Muslim children alike were encouraged to join Russian Orthodoxy, as well as those whom authorities considered pagans.[7] But Nicholas was no Russian Orthodox crusader: he saw conversion to Orthodoxy as a convenient vehicle serving integrationist purposes. Fifteen years after he had introduced Jewish conscription, Nicholas I resolved to convert Jewish cantonists "inductively."[8] Whether or not his handling of Jewish matters was progressive requires not only an analysis of Nicholas's viewpoint, as David Saunders suggests, but also an insight into the attitudes of all those involved.

Consider the 1827, 1828, and 1829 conscription, when altogether some 1,862 Jewish cantonists joined the ranks (Table 3). Of those, 125, or almost 7 percent, agreed to convert. If brutality on the part of the battalion instructors and sergeant majors had been a policy of the War Ministry, the number of converts would not have been so modest. Moreover, in the late 1820s, there was no plan to send the Jewish cantonists outside the Pale of Settlement, thus cutting their ties to local communities and expediting their conversion. Of the seven battalions of military cantonists operating in the 1820s, five were situated inside the Pale, while the rest were in the immediate vicinity of semi-legal areas of Jewish residence. The number of converted Jews appears to reflect the distance between the battalions and the Pale. The smallest number of converts was in the Kiev, Kherson, and Ekaterinoslav battalions.[9] Yet in the Pskov and Smolensk battalions, located outside the Pale, the number of Jews who converted to Christianity exceeded by tenfold those located within the Jewish Pale. In the Pskov, Smolensk, and Riga battalions, the proportion of converts reached 13 percent, 15 percent, and 11 percent respectively. The commander of the Vitebsk battalion, in which 26 percent were converts, either carelessly or deliberately considered a number of Lutheran and Catholic converts as Jewish converts, thus obtaining a higher percentage of Christianized Jews. By February 1829, several more Christianized soldiers had materialized: six in the Riga half-

---

[7] Regarding missionary activity among Muslims, Catholics, and members of the Uniate Church, see A. Zhelobovskii, *Upravlenie tserkvami i pravoslavnym dukhovenstvom voennogo ministerstva, SVM*, XIII, kn. 2, 13, 38, 54, 123.

[8] Nicholas I's "inductive" approach to solving problems, as opposed to the "deductive" thinking of Alexander I's administration, is proposed by David Ransel in his "Pre-Reform Russia, 1801–1855," in Gregory Freeze, ed., *Russia. A History* (Oxford and New York: Oxford University Press, 1997), 157–158.

[9] Kiev had been removed from the Jewish Pale as early as the 1830s, though, in its Ploskii and Lybedskii districts, Jews were permitted limited settlement.

TABLE 3. *The Number of Jewish Recruits Converted to Christianity by January 1829*

Battalions	Provinces Where the Draft Originated	Number of the Draft			Total Jews	Total Converts
		91 (1827)	92 (1828)	93 (1829)		
	Vitebsk	62	31	–		
Smolensk	Mogilev	150	5	–	248[a]	36 and 2[b]
	Lifland	1	–	–		
Riga	Kurland	6	9	–	412[c]	40 and 6[b]
	Vitebsk	97	130	169		
Vitebsk	Minsk	60	80	–	140	31 and 6[b]
Pskov	Grodno	59	76	–		
	Belostok	32	34	–	201[d]	12 and 10 and 4[b]
Kiev	Kiev	61	41	–		
	Chernigov	15	21	–	584[e]	1
	Volhynia	210	236	–		
Kherson	Kherson	4	13	8		
	Podol	179	62	6	272[f]	5
Ekateri-noslavsk	Ekaterino-slav	5	–	–	–	–
TOTAL		941	738	183	1862	125

[a] Data for Vitebsk and Mogilev provinces.
[b] In the original document, the figures in italics were later added with a pencil or a quill in addition to the basic index. Henceforth, the total number will be given.
[c] Data for Lifland, Kurland, and Vitebsk provinces.
[d] Grodno and Belostok provinces.
[e] Kiev, Chernigov, and Volhynia provinces.
[f] Kherson and Podol provinces.
Source: RGVIA, f. 405, op. 2, d. 1662, ll. 1–2.

battalion, two in Smolensk, and six in Vitebsk.[10] By this time, the number of baptized boys in the three battalions had reached 13 percent, 16 percent, and 30 percent respectively. With the exception of the Vitebsk battalion, the process of conversion proceeded slowly. Adjutant General Kleinmikhel, superintendent of the Military Settlements Department, received regular reports on the number of new converts, which showed no significant increases. Jews joined Christianity singly or in twos, perhaps yielding to mild exhortations. On June 10, 1829, Colonel Veimarn reported, "I have the honor to inform you that the Jewish cantonists from the Pskov half-battalion, Meir Sukenin and Itsko Rosental, became Christians as Petr Petrov and Aleksandr Petrov after their conversion to the Greek-Russian [i.e., Russian Orthodox] faith on the eighth day of the

[10] See the reports from these battalions in RGVIA, f. 405, op. 2, d. 1662, ll. 3, 4, 6.

month."[11] The military did not report, in the schools for minors, any mass conversions or campaigns to convert Jews.

Local commanders asserted that the fewer cantonists of alien creed there were in the battalions, the easier it was to control them. Regarding Russian Orthodoxy as superior to any other creed, they urged the Christianization of non-Russian Orthodox cantonists. They also baptized Jews. Yet neither in 1827 nor in 1828 did Nicholas specifically order the conversion of Jews. Battalion commanders included in their reports those who converted to Russian Orthodoxy from Judaism, in addition to those who converted from Lutheranism and Catholicism. For example, Count Kleinmikhel had requested information about the Jews alone, yet the reports described three men receiving the Eucharist in the Smolensk half-battalion, another man in the Revel battalion, and a further ten in the Pskov battalions; the last ten were former Lutherans who, certainly, had partaken of the Eucharist before converting. As the conversion policy became more imperative, anxious commanders juggled the statistics, to please Nicholas with exaggerated figures. Thus, the commanders of the Kiev battalion triumphantly reported that, out of 73 Jewish recruits, 136 (sic) had converted to Christianity! It is impossible to know with any certainty how many among those 136 "Russian Orthodox" converts were Jews, and how many were Lutherans or Catholics. However, Nicholas wrote in the margin of this report that each converted Jewish cantonist would receive twenty-five rubles, to give him a financial start. This instruction from the tsar became a new imperial order, thereby concluding the first stage of the missionary campaign.[12]

On July 18, 1829, Nicholas tried to expedite Jewish conversion. Upon reading a report submitted by the St. Petersburg battalion, he ordered the commanders, "Announce to the procurator general of the Synod that, in general, clergymen may operate in the military cantonists' battalions. The Jewish cantonists who have expressed their wish to adopt Russian Orthodoxy must be converted according to church rules, without future sanctions of the Church authorities." However, the Russian Orthodox clergy did not rush to make Jews into Russian Christians. Contrary to the argument of most Jewish historians, Russian clergymen did not conduct themselves like the fanatic Catholic clergymen in medieval Spain, who pressed Spanish Jews into Christianity; nor did they strive to outdo each other to earn the Order of St. Stanislav for their missionary activity. Considering the Jews not deserving of conversion, the clergy generally avoided such activism. Paradoxically, Nicholas's desire to bring Jews to Christianity was more enlightened than the clergy's reluctance to embrace them. Despite the unambiguous imperial order, the regimental and parish priests continually requested permission from the Synod. The church, in turn, seems not to have supported Nicholas's 1829 recommendation with any corresponding written order. Two months after having received Nicholas's

[11] RGVIA, f. 405, op. 2, d. 1662, l. 9.
[12] RGVIA, f. 405, op. 2, d. 1662, ll. 12–14, 36, 48; PSZ II, 4: 3052.

TABLE 4. *Jews in Military Cantonist Units, June 1839.*

Military Unit	Converted to Christianity (Jewish Converts)	Persisting in Their Creed (Jews)
St. Petersburg battalion	9	11
Pskov half-battalion	15	106
Revel battalion	6	88
Voronezh battalion	402	244
Saratov battalion	255	53
Simbirsk battalion	24	15
Kazan battalion	105	989
Perm battalion	136	132
Orenburg battalion	63	934
Troitsk battalion	111	163
Verkhneuralsk battalion	66	116
Omsk battalion	–	26
Tobolsk battalion	–	14
Tomsk battalion	–	7
Irkutsk battalion	–	9
Krasnoiarsk training companies	–	1
2nd training carabineer half-battalion	24	91
3rd training carabineer half-battalion	64	10
4th training carabineer half-battalion	114	10
TOTAL	1,394	3,019

Source: RGVIA, f. 405, op. 5, d. 3771, ll. 3–4.

circular, Stephan Slavskii, a regimental chaplain, wrote to the head of the Department of Military Settlements: "In relation to your order as of September 17, I have the honor to inform you that, regarding Jews willing to adopt Christianity, so far I have received no particular instruction from my superior [i.e., the chief chaplain of the army] regarding this issue."[13] He attached to his letter a note from an army official complaining of the bureaucracy's sluggishness: "The clergymen, they say, have no permission to baptize the Jews!" This complaint implies that the clergy did not require such permission for the conversion of Muslims, Lutherans, and Catholics. It was a long time before the Synod's machinery, the tsar, and the cumbersome military bureaucracy coordinated their efforts sufficiently to allow for action.

Ten years later, in 1839, Nicholas again commissioned Count Kleinmikhel to assess the general situation in the battalions (Table 4). Reports compiled by battalion commanders were summarized by Kleinmichel and then submitted to Nicholas. The resulting aggregate account indicated that, in mid-1839, there

[13] RGVIA, f. 405, op. 2, d. 1662, l. 24.

TABLE 5. *Information on the Number of Jewish Military Cantonists,* *August 1827–May 1840 (compiled by May 23, 1840)*

Total Number of Conscripts 1827–1840	Adopted Russian Orthodoxy	Persisting in Their Creed	Available by May 1, 1840	
			Christian Orthodox	Jewish
15,050	5,328	9,722	1,336	3,331

Source: RGVIA, f. 405, op. 5, d. 4468, ll. 1–3.

were 4,413 Jewish cantonists in the battalions. Over two-thirds of these, or 69 percent, "persisted in their creed," while converts constituted the remaining third. The distribution of the converts was very uneven. In the Pskov, Kazan, and Orenburg battalions, there were ten times more Jewish cantonists than converts. In the Perm battalion, the ratio was fifty-fifty. In the Voronezh battalion, converts outnumbered those who "stuck to their faith" by two to one, and in the Saratov battalion, by five to one. Driven into the most remote parts of the empire, Jewish cantonists in Siberian battalions demonstrated a remarkable determination to remain Jewish. The battalions in Omsk, Tobolsk, Irkutsk, and Krasnoiarsk had *no* converts from Judaism to Christianity.[14] The two-to-one ratio of Jewish cantonists to converts surprised Nicholas. Puzzled, he ordered a combined report on all Jewish cantonists from 1827, together with a complete report on Jewish graduates from the cantonist battalions. The resulting document detailed the first thirteen years of Jewish presence in the cantonist battalions, from the fall of 1827 to March, 1840 (Table 5).

Its contents did not diverge significantly from information gathered earlier. Of the 10,383 Jews who had passed through the cantonist battalions in the period between 1827 and 1840, 61.5 percent remained Jewish, while 38.5 percent converted.[15] Nicholas was not pleased with these results, but he determined to accept the converts as full-fledged Russians. An enlightened although biased rationalist, he noted in the margin of one report: "Those who have converted to Russian Orthodoxy should not be considered Jewish any more."[16] That is to say, Nicholas considered Christianization the end of the Jewish question. In practice, however, neither he nor his battalion commanders were bound by this order.

Nicholas the Baptist

In the early 1840s, Nicholas resolved to convert Jewish cantonists in order to homogenize the troops. Simultaneously, he embarked upon a broader policy of

[14] See RGVIA, f. 405, op. 5, d. 3771, ll. 3–4.
[15] See RGVIA, f. 405, op. 5, d. 4468, ll. 1–3.
[16] RGVIA, f. 405, op. 5, d. 3771, l. 14.

unification of the various Russian ethnic and religious groups. Thus, in 1839, he abolished the Uniate (Greek Catholic) Church, subjecting its entire faith community to Russian Orthodoxy. In the early 1840s, he also began transforming Jews into Russians far more aggressively. He launched educational reform, abolished the *kahal*, and ordered the draft of Jews in the Kingdom of Poland. On February 18, 1842, Nicholas "secretly and confidentially" ordered the conversion of Jews reduced to a formal procedure that required no special effort on the part of the battalion commanders. Lieutenant General Lev Perovskii, the minister of the interior, arranged that a circular be dispatched to all military districts; the police department was responsible for its distribution. The circular urged the commanders to collect data on Jews seeking baptism and conduct conversion as secretly as possible (*kak mozhno bezglasnee*). The circular demanded that Jews ready to convert provided recommendations obtained from Christians, the local chief of police or the town mayor and, wherever possible, from the local Russian Orthodox dean (*blagochinnyi*), and not from their Jewish fellows.[17] In practice, the new regulation sanctioned the involvement of the local military administration in the missionary campaign; battalion commanders obtained a carte blanche. Nicholas was intent upon attaining results.

In April 1843 the emperor decided to ascertain how well the army had implemented his recommendations for the simplified conversion of the Jews. The resulting report called into question previous accounts, according to which at least one-third of all Jewish cantonists had accepted Christianity. It now appeared that the number of converted Jews in the battalions was tiny: 5 percent in 1842, and 2 percent in 1843 (Table 6).

This suggested that, in defiance of Nicholas's orders, the army's missionary campaign had not intensified; on the contrary, it had been curtailed. Perhaps only at that point did Nicholas realize that his army, his clergy, and his state bureaucracy had not comprehended the importance of converting Jewish children. Evidently, in order to overcome the resistance of the Jewish cantonists, Nicholas first had to confront the inertia, obtuseness, and passivity of his own imperial administration. He realized that, without his constant supervision, the missionary campaign would come to naught: Jews would never become Russians. So he resorted to tougher tactics: he issued several unequivocal instructions, reinforced by regular reminders. He ordered that the battalion commanders submit to him, by the twenty-fifth day of each month, reports providing the numbers of newly converted Jews. This regulation, issued on June 26, 1843, and better known as the Number Three Order, read: "I require that the commanders of the training carabineer corps and the cantonist schools submit to the Military Settlements Department monthly lists on the number of men and Jewish cantonists who adopted Russian Orthodoxy; the lists are to include the name of the battalion, the number of enlisted personnel and of cantonists, the number of enlisted personnel and of cantonists converted." He

[17] RGVIA, f. 405, op. 6, d. 4545, l. 1.

TABLE 6. *Report from the Military Settlements Department on the Number of Jewish Converts to Russian Orthodoxy, 1842–1843*

Battalions	Number of Jewish Cantonists in 1842	Number of Those Converted to Russian Orthodoxy	Total Jewish Cantonists in 1843	Number of Those Converted to Russian Orthodoxy by April 1, 1843
Second Training Carabineer Corps	36	–	12	–
First Training Brigade				
Arkhangelsk	46	3	44	–
Pskov	122	–	104	–
Second Training Brigade				
Kiev	9	–	6	–
Revel	35	–	19	–
Kazan	1,868	24	1,789	63
Perm	774	150	656	27
Saratov	365	–	329	–
Simbirsk	123	6	95	–
Fourth Training Brigade				
Orenburg	1,171	–	1,073	–
Troitsk	116	–	83	–
Verkhneuralsk	85	–	65	–
Fifth Training Brigade				
Omsk	6	–	8	–
Tobolsk	15	–	19	–
Tomsk	20	1	28	–
Irkutsk	4	1	5	–
Krasnoiarsk	5	–	8	–
Voronezh	439	75	359	–
TOTAL	5,244	259	4,702	93

Source: RGVIA, f. 405, op. 5, d. 7370, ll. 6–60b., 7–70b.

also demanded data on the anticipated number of Jewish recruits in 1843, and ordered the replacement of some Russian Orthodox chaplains with "the best and most reliable" ones. Additionally, he commanded the chief chaplain of the army to issue a short set of instructions to regimental chaplains as to how to expedite the conversion of Jews.[18]

However, the task proved daunting. Most battalion commanders could not understand either the implications of the order or the reason to submit

[18] RGVIA, f. 405, op. 5, d. 7370, ll. 1–2, 6–60b., 7–70b, 8–9, 12, 17, 20–200b., 260b., 270b., 30–31.

annoying monthly reports. For approximately two years, the bulk of the reports sent to Nicholas contained variations on the phrase, "Our battalions have such-and-such number of Jews; none of them has adopted Christianity."[19] Nicholas was furious, and wrote, "Submit when additional data is obtained rather than reporting in part." (This inscription in pencil by the emperor appears on the combined report from the Military Settlements Department of June 24, 1843.) When several battalions failed to submit satisfactory reports, Nicholas ordered battalion commanders to report directly to the St. Petersburg department, bypassing the intermediary military commanders. In August 1843 he asked the Synod to expedite its work on the "exhortation for conversion." He ordered that eighty copies of his instruction be circulated in the battalions. In December, Nicholas related to Baron Korf the success of the Tobolsk battalion chaplain, who had converted forty-eight cantonists, adding that he would be very pleased if other clergymen followed that priest's example. Baron Korf immediately reformulated the emperor's desire into an explicit order and dispatched it to all cantonist schools. To encourage the priests, in early January 1844, Nicholas ordered an additional annual allocation of 57.14 rubles to each priest who converted a Jewish cantonist. At the end of January, he assigned two priests to each battalion, and one to each half-battalion. He began to monitor more closely the pace of conversion and to recalculate the data submitted to him. He was incensed when the consolidated returns from the department contained errors; he soon realized that the commanders had tallied the figures deliberately incorrectly, to present an all too glowing impression of the campaign's pace. With a pencil, he diligently corrected the report. In the Pskov battalion, only 17 Christianized, rather than 20; in the Kiev battalion, 4 rather than 5; in the Saratov battalion, 8 rather than 13, and so on, in the end yielding a total of 176 rather than 502. The message was crystal clear: the tsar saw through his incompetent bureaucrats. One can only imagine how the head of the department read Nicholas's corrections. To evade the emperor's rage, he rushed to circulate a new secret instruction to the department, emphasizing "the poor success" in the conversion of Jewish cantonists and the drastic need "to carry out the monarch's will."[20]

Beginning in the mid-1840s, the missionary campaign slowly proceeded, although conversion was quite haphazard. In some cases, the battalion commanders falsified the figures, adding the number of the newly converted to that of previous converts; others counted converted Muslims and Jews together. Some commanders attempted to convert the Jews en masse but, in large

---

[19] See, e.g., 96 pages of such formal replies and empty lists until December 1843: RGVIA, f. 405, op. 5, d. 7371. Sometimes the battalion commanders preferred to report regularly on the number of Jews in the battalions as if their composition might have changed under circumstances other than graduation and new enrollment. Other commanders reported that there were no Jews in their units. See RGVIA, f. 405, op. 5, d. 7371, ll. 1–13, 61, 141.

[20] RGVIA, f. 405, op. 5, d. 7370 (Po predpisaniiu voennogo ministra, o predstavleniiu gosudariu imperatoru ezhemesiachno vedomostei o evreiakh, sostoiashchikh v zavedeniiakh voennykh kantonistov ..." 1843/44), l. 34–35, 37–38, 47–48, 52, 63–63ob., 72ob., 82.

battalions, the results were meager.[21] Especially disappointing was the situation among former cantonists in the training regiments; in 1843, only four out of 456 men converted, that is, fewer than 1 percent. During the same period, 199 out of 3,472 cantonists converted (6 percent). The only successful cantonist unit was the Voronezh battalion, where Colonel Romanus, rather than the local chaplain, took credit for the conversion of some 500 students; this was most likely an exaggerated number, however. His accomplishment earned approval: circulars distributed by the Military Settlements Department urged others to emulate Romanus's efforts. Consequently, by the late 1840s, an increasing number of battalion commanders – although not local priests – resorted to mass conversions of Jews. To force the cantonists into Christianity, some commanders apparently employed physical abuse.[22] Nicholas began to receive positive reports, indicating a rapidly accelerating pace of conversion. On March 11, 1849, he signed a circular warning against excessive zeal. He recommended abstaining from coercive measures, as these contradicted the spirit of Christian teaching. Exhortation of the cantonists should be conducted only under the supervision of the local commanders, he stipulated; young and inexperienced NCOs should not meet with groups of cantonists. In their desire to achieve immediate results, opined Nicholas, the NCOs could be transported by excessive zeal, producing converts who were shaky and weak in their faith.[23]

Some scholars have argued that this latest circular did not prevent extreme measures designed to convert Jews, and that its objective was not to dilute the campaign.[24] In their view, the directive encouraged aggressive missionary activity, and was merely a manifestation of Nicholas I's sanctimony and hypocrisy. However, there was no need for Nicholas to be careful in his declarations; no liberal press or public expression of opinion existed during his rule. Nor was the general public sentiment at all sensitive to Jewish

[21] For example, in 1843 some 945 Christian neophytes appeared in the Voronezh battalion. The Novgorod, Pskov, Arkhangelsk, and Tobolsk battalions contributed only 73, 53, 98, and 48 converts respectively. In the Orenburg and Kazan, there were only one or two converts. See the reports from these battalions in RGVIA, f. 405, op. 5, d. 7370, ll. 108–109.

[22] In 1852, 49 young men under the age of eighteen from Rovno, Podol province, joined the cantonist battalions. Fifteen of them were Jews. Shortly after their arrival, 11 converted to Christianity. Some of them ended up in the hospital, but three maintained their Jewishness until 1859. One youth, identified as Nakhman Korman, seems to have paid with his life for the desire to remain Jewish. For more detail, see RGVIA, f. 324, op. 1, d. 1318, ll. 1390b.-140.

[23] Perhaps upon the suggestion of Reverend Kutnevich, the chief army chaplain, this circular did not appear in the Legal Code. We were unable to locate it in PSZ from 1848 through 1851. In any case, the existence of such a circular is puzzling; few 1848 reports describe more than a modest or moderate pace of missionary success. Thus, in January of 1848, 9 out of 10, 2 out of 56, and 10 out of 10 Jewish cantonists of the Pskov, Verkhneuralsk, and Saratov battalions, respectively, adopted Christianity. At the same time, 323 cantonists of the Moscow artisans' command, and 85, 27, 56, 59 of the First, Second, Third and Fourth training carabineer corps, respectively, remained steadfast in their faith; only two Jewish cantonists were converted in all of January. RGVIA, f. 405, op. 5, d. 10987, ll. 2, 5, 30, 43, 45, 52, 54, 56.

[24] Ginsburg, *Historishe verk*, 354–369; Stanislawski, *Tsar Nicholas I and the Jews*, 23.

issues. The circular of March 11, 1849, evinced Nicholas's concern for the depth and strength of the converts' Christian beliefs, rather than for their sheer numbers.

Resistance to Conversion

Despite Nicholas's determination to convert Jewish cantonists en masse, the missionary campaign encountered insurmountable difficulties. Firstly, some battalion commanders considered the campaign incompatible with the spirit of the military, if not altogether repugnant, and so participated only very reluctantly. When the campaign acquired momentum in the early 1850s, there were 5,991 Jewish cantonists in the battalions; 4,565 of them (comprising three-quarters) converted. This figure may be attributed primarily to the tremendous pace of conversion in the Kazan battalion: 10 percent monthly, if the reports are to believed. Yet, in the Second carabineer corps, in the Revel, Smolensk, Omsk, Pskov, Tobolsk, and Astrakhan battalions, each numbering 100 to 500 Jewish cantonists, fewer than 10 percent of the total number adopted Christianity.[25] This clearly indicates the military's passive resistance to Nicholas's campaign.

Another stumbling block to mass conversion was the Holy Synod's aversion to the most zealous of the local missionaries. In the early 1850s, Colonel Dessimon, the commander of the Kiev battalion, ordered Father Efim Remizov, whom he considered an expert on Hebrew and on debates with Jews, to convert his Jewish cantonists. Remizov conducted a number of conversions, summarizing his experience in a pamphlet entitled *The Message of a Christian to the Jews on the True Faith*. Composed of sixteen articles, this work was intended "to cool the Jews' superstitious devotion to groundless talmudic commentaries." It upheld the truth of the blood libel (asserting that "it is normal for a Jew to kill a *goy* on the eve of the Passover and to suck his blood"), and described the "malicious vindictiveness and brutality of the Jews in relation to all peoples of the world." According to Remizov, his work merited approbation from the Synod and state-sponsored publication. He believed his reasoning to be convincing, clear, and comprehensible. (Remizov used the Russian for St. Thomas Aquinas's famous *veritas, caritas, claritas*.) Colonel Dessimon enthusiastically supported the immediate publication of this volume and its circulation among Jewish cantonists. The chief procurator of the Synod

---

[25] RGVIA, f. 405, op. 5, d. 18024, ll. 50b., 90b., 11, 17, 230b. The monetary awards irregularly requested by the commanders of the battalions from the Military Settlements Department and from the Treasury reveal the sporadic nature of the missionary campaign. Thus, in 1837, in the First, Third and Fourth training carabineer corps, the Revel and Simbirsk battalions only Christianized one or two Jews each. Meanwhile, in the Saratov, Voronezh, and Perm battalions, there were between nineteen and thirty-six converts. In 1843, in the Pskov and Simbirsk battalions, the Second training carabineer corps applied for one or two monetary awards each. During the same period, the commanders of the Perm and Kazan battalions applied for twenty-seven and thirty-five monetary bonuses, respectively. See RGVIA, f. 405, op. 5, d. 1761, ll. 1, 7, 16, 21; f. 405, op. 5, d. 6953, ll. 4–60b., 7–100b., 120b., 13, 160b.-17, 180b.

carefully studied the text, discussed it in a meeting at the St. Petersburg Theological Academy, and subsequently reported to the war minister that the church
did not regard the manuscript as useful to Jewish cantonists; it was not at all
convincing, clear, and comprehensible.[26]

Apart from the sluggishness of the military authorities, there were several
other reasons for the campaign's ultimate failure. A sense of community and
mutual responsibility prevailed among Jews in the army, particularly between
the soldiers and the cantonists. The military commanders could not always
isolate Jewish children from Jewish adults serving in the same locations. When
the commander of the Third training brigade in Saratov attempted to persuade
four cantonists, Gofman, Berenshtein, Rubak, and Lisenberg, to adopt Christianity, his plans came to naught because of the efforts of Froim Furman. An
adult Jewish shoemaker in noncombatant service in the Saratov garrison, he
discouraged the children from converting. The angry commander immediately
demanded Furman's removal from the garrison, along with that of two other
Jewish recruits, Shpitsman and Broverman, who were tailors for the cantonists;
in this way, "nothing of the kind could happen again."[27] Lieutenant Colonel
Voidenov, the commander of the Kazan battalion, lodged similar complaints
with the Military Settlements Department. On June 6, 1845, he apologized in
his report for the small number of converts under his command, emphasizing
that "the unconverted Jews, who are obstinate in their unwillingness to adopt
Russian Orthodoxy, strongly influence the junior cantonists by their example,
spending their daytime in the workshops and secretly persuading the latter to
stay firm against the Christian religion. This is why persuasion has had no
success." There were roughly 1,500 Jewish cantonists in his battalion. Unless
these twenty troublesome shoemakers and tailors (who, according to him, were
"rather good artisans") were removed from the battalion, there was no hope
of persuading Jewish children to convert. At Colonel Voidenov's request,
two months later the military administration transferred eighteen of the men
elsewhere.[28]

There also were external communal contacts. In locations close to the Jewish
Pale, the cantonists established links with local Jews. The commander of the
Revel battalion complained to the department that the efforts of Father
Golubtsev to convert Jewish cantonists were fruitless because Lieutenant
General Patkul allowed Jews to attend religious services "in the *kahal*" (i.e., in
the Jewish community) where the rabbi "admonished the Jews against con-
verting."[29] Even when sent far from the Pale, cantonists rarely were entirely
isolated. Sometimes they obtained permission to visit their hometowns for a

---

[26] RGVIA, f. 405, op. 5, d. 17973, ll. 2–20b., 5, 10–120b.

[27] RGVIA, f. 405, op. 5, d. 6953, ll. 31–32.

[28] RGVIA, f. 405, op. 5, d. 8413, l. 1–10b.

[29] The commander tried to prohibit the cantonists from observing Jewish holidays; he refused
them permission to go home and confined them to their barracks. Nicholas disapproved: "The
measure is untimely. Let them go to synagogue as they are used to." For his reply of May 31,
1844, see RGVIA, f. 405, op. 5, d. 8158, ll. 1–50b.

short leave.[30] Many of them received support from their parents, and regular pocket money sent from home was of more importance than the significant one-time bonus promised for conversion that often failed to materialize. Major Iakubovskii, the commander of the Novgorod battalion, lamented to the department that all his efforts to convert Jewish children were worthless: "The major stumbling block, as I have learned from Jews, is that by adopting Russian Orthodoxy, they are deprived of any financial support from their parents forever. This is the reason why they remain firm."[31]

Internal Transformation

Notwithstanding the military's mixed success in converting Jews, Jewish children underwent a radical transformation in the battalions. How did Jewish minors between twelve and eighteen years of age, and sometimes much younger, withstand the pressure exerted upon them? How did the experience affect them? To answer this query, it is useful to trace the cantonists' movements between the conscription points and their battalions. To reach their assigned military posts, Jewish minors had to travel hundreds of miles. Their supervisors, the accompanying officers (*partionnye ofitsery*) personally responsible for the recruits, hired wagons for them and allowed their parents to accompany them. It is unfair to follow the Jewish literary sources in accusing the accompanying officers of neglecting their duties and of being indifferent toward the Jewish cantonists. On the contrary: it was the accompanying officers who complained to the commanders of the intolerable living conditions during their journey and who requested that changes be made. These officers adhered to a strict schedule and route to the conscripts' assigned posts, and submitted detailed reports concerning their progress. If an accompanying officer was reproached for the high mortality rate among the conscripts, this would seriously jeopardize his career.

However, the officers did not have inns to lodge in on their way, they had limited funds for food, and they could not provide the children with medical assistance. By the time the young recruits reached their battalions, many of them suffered from common diseases.[32] In 1831, more than 70 of the 100 Jewish children who entered the Vitebsk battalion were ill. A total of 65 suffered from mange (in Russian, *parsha*) and scabies (in Russian, *chesotka*); 1 from epilepsy and scrofula; and 4 from eye inflammation. Only 23 recruits, about one-quarter of the conscripts, were healthy. At the end of the same year, 103 cantonists from Mogilev province arrived at the Smolensk battalion; 54 were ill: 17 with mange

---

[30] Thus, for example, in 1859 four Jewish cantonists – Movsha Ulanovskii, Iankel Klein, Aizek Shtarbel', and Zusia Dyshon – were on leave from the Smolensk cantonist battalion. See RGVIA, f. 324, op. 1, d. 458, l. 9.

[31] RGVIA, f. 405, op. 5, d. 2670, l. 37.

[32] For more detail on the reports of the accompanying officers, see RGVIA, f. 405, op. 5, d. 4662, ll. 3, 18, 40, 67–68, 77–80, 120–126.

and 34 with scabies. Out of the 133 recruits from Volhynia province enrolled in the Iaroslavl battalion, 20 had mange and 54 scabies. Among 156 cantonists who arrived at the Pskov battalion from Belostok (Białystok) and Grodno provinces, only 13 were healthy. Of those who were sick, 11 children from Belostok and 6 from Grodno suffered from herpes (in Russian, *lishai*); 19 from Belostok and 6 from Grodno, from a mild scabies; 43 from Belostok and 19 from Grodno had severe scabies; 1 from Belostok and 5 from Grodno had mild mange; 19 from Belostok and 3 from Grodno had severe mange; 2 recruits from Belostok had venereal scabies. Among 54 recruits in the Smolensk battalion, 4 suffered from mange and 15 from scabies. The situation was better in the Southwest (Ukrainian) districts than in Lithuania and Poland; out of 76 children from the Kamenets-Podolsk district arriving at the Nizhnii Novgorod battalion, only 3 were sent to hospital. Of the 38 who joined the Voronezh battalion from Kiev province, only 1 was hospitalized.

The poor health of the Jewish conscripts shocked the battalion commanders. Hoping to train their new cantonists, they found themselves obliged first to cure them. Protests to the Military Settlements Department followed. The commanders demanded the establishment of more stringent physical requirements and improved conditions for the transfer of conscripts. They needed healthy students, not sick ghosts.[33] Yet, over the course of ten years from the inception of the draft, the situation remained unchanged. Both the Jewish communal organizations and the military conscription points rejected the idea of increasing the physical requirements for conscripts. The former may have feared that it jeopardized the *kahal*'s ability to meet the quota, while the latter were simply unwilling to accept any decrease in the number of conscripts. The commanders continued to report to St. Petersburg about the medical conditions in the Jewish community, but to no avail.[34] However, they knew that Jews were not the only sick recruits: poor health was endemic among the other cantonists. Official reports include numerous grievances about the sanitary situation in the battalions. An inspector of the Simbirsk battalion reported, "The cantonists' uniform is very good, the combat training is impressive, the economic situation is rather good, the beds and mattresses look excellent," but, nevertheless "the number of sick cantonists is significant."[35] In 1840, after persistent

[33] For example, in 1835, a group of Jewish children arrived in the Vitebsk battalion from the Vitebsk and Mogilev districts. The battalion commander, Colonel Koltovskii, protested to the department, writing that, out of the 198 Jewish children, only 9 satisfied the medical requirements, whereas the rest suffered from scabies, mange, and scab, as well as other illnesses or disabilities. See RGVIA, f. 405, op. 5, d. 1723, ll. 1–3, 80b.

[34] See RGVIA, f. 405, op. 5, d. 7015, l. 33. When some insignificant numbers of cantonists managed to prove that they had been ill before being drafted, the commission sent them home. The scanty data available show that there were as many Jews as Christians among them. See RGVIA, f. 405, op. 5, d. 10152, ll. 3–30b., 4–5, 10–100b.

[35] This report addresses cantonists in general, not only Jews. See RGVIA, f. 405, op. 2, d. 4619, l. 42. Other reports indicate that the numbers of sick cantonists among non-Jews were relatively the same as among Jews: about 70 percent. On May 19, 1831, the commander of the Second training carabineer corps wrote to the War Ministry: "Out of 207 who arrived at the

complaints, the Military Settlements Department approved having a medical officer examine each group of newly arrived recruits at the conscription point, to determine who was unfit for service.[36] Yet the department suggested no improvements in the sanitary conditions of the quarters or of the battalions themselves.

The cantonists received barbarous treatment. Army medical assistants (*fel'dshery*) prescribed castor oil for trachoma, fever, and diarrhea! They also practiced collective healing methods. According to a cantonist of Prussian Polish origin, senior soldiers led children to the bathhouse and smeared them with chicken droppings, sulfur, and tar. Then they beat them with rods to drive them to the upper shelf of a steam bath, from which the children were not permitted to descend until the disease had abated.[37] This primitive treatment made its way – with steam bath, rods, and children falling from upper shelves – into Jewish historical memory, where it acquired a new ideological rationale. Ultimately, it surfaced in Jewish historiography in the form of "tortures" the commanders employed to persuade Jewish cantonists to convert.[38]

In the mid-1850s, when cantonist schools were transferred to the auspices of the Military Schools Department, the sanitary conditions in the battalions improved. Now the battalion commanders more often sent recruits to the reserve because of illness or unfitness, a practice that subsequently became customary.[39] Consider the Saratov cantonists' battalion, which comprised eight companies, with 1,611 cantonists altogether. Of these, 506 lived in apartments in Smolensk and 886 in villages. In July of 1858, 32 cantonists were ill: 19 with trachoma, 3 with epilepsy, 2 with diarrhea, stomach ulcer, and venereal disease, and 1 with typhus or yellow fever. Four died in July: 3 Orthodox Christians and 1 Jew.[40] If one includes the deceased men, the percentage of sick cantonists in the battalion was 2.2 percent, much lower than twenty years before.

corps, 121 arrived with severe scabies; 23 with chronic mange on the head; 3 are sick with inflammation of the eye; 1 cantonist has an ulcer of the scrotum (*iazva moshonki*), and 1 has a fever." See RGVIA, f. 405, op. 2, d. 4738, l. 30b. Christian cantonists, as well as Jews, complained of poor living conditions. In 1831, 8 cantonists were sent to the St. Petersburg hospital suffering from scabies, which, as it later was determined, they had contracted from the landlords of their quarters. An order was issued prohibiting the billeting of cantonists in such quarters. However, this order remained on paper, since nobody bothered with an inspection of the quarters. See RGVIA, f. 405, op. 2, d. 4551, l. 5–50b.

36   RGVIA, f. 405, op. 5, d. 1723, ll. 34–41.

37   M. A. Krechmer, "Vospominaniia," *Istoricheskii vestnik*, no. 31 (1888): 652.

38   Cf.: P. Ia. Levenson, "Zakoldovannyi. Byl," *Voskhod*, no. 7 (1884): 38–39.

39   On October 6, 1856, a group of Jewish cantonists from Kiev province (whose number is not disclosed in the document) arrived at the Saratov battalion, 6 of them having various disabilities: one of them was missing a finger; another suffered from cramp in his elbow joint and discharge from his ears. The battalion commander informed the inspection department of the unsatisfactory new recruits, declaring that they had been enrolled "against the recruitment rules." The department ordered a reexamination of the ailing conscripts. Consequently, only one of them was sent to receive treatment, while Haim Podol'skii, suffering from epilepsy, was sent home. See RGVIA, f. 324, op. 1, d. 1256, ll. 1, 4, 8, 48.

40   RGVIA, f. 324, op. 1, d. 453, ll. 7, 140b., 340b.

There was little point in countering with hard figures the notorious observation of Alexander Hertzen that Jewish cantonists "die off like flies."[41] The
pre-reform military never collected statistics indicating the mortality rate. Quite
the contrary: they concealed the available figures by all possible means. A
Russian military historian claimed that the number of patients in military
hospitals was manipulated, to obscure the mortality rate among the cantonists.[42] On the basis of the inadequate data available, it is impossible to arrive at
a reasonable conclusion.[43] The aggregate data for 1827–1840 provides material on the mortality rate among those who remained Jewish and among those
who converted. The only way to gauge the death rate is to interpret the number
of Jewish converts to Christianity in the battalions as bona fide Christians and
to compare that with those who remained true to their Jewish faith. If Jews and
Christians were treated differently, as most Jewish historians assumed, this
would be reflected in the mortality rate. Yet this method yields an almost
identical mortality rate for both groups. For the Christians, 4.8 percent (out of
3,992 Christians, 192 died); for the Jews, 5.5 (out of 6,391 Jews, 350 died).[44]
On the basis of this case study, one may arrive at the tentative conclusion
that the Jewish mortality rate was no different from that of any other group of
cantonists.[45]

Jews stoically endured their tenure in the battalions, and successfully finished
their terms in the cantonist schools. When seventeen- and eighteen-year-old
cantonists graduated and joined the troops, they were as fit for combat service
as were their Christian colleagues, if not more so. Consider the 1838 distribution of the cantonists to the regular troops from ten different cantonist
battalions and units throughout Russia: 65 percent of Jewish graduates were fit
for combat service, compared to 63 percent of Christian cantonists. The Jews
provided 123 cantonists under the age of eighteen who were suitable for service;
this represented 33 percent of their total population. At the same time, the
Christians provided only 197 recruits, which constituted 20 percent of their

[41] As cited in Stanislawski, *Tsar Nicholas I and the Jews*, 27; Keep, *Soldiers of the Tsar*, 330.

[42] "The groups of disabled and weak men in the units for disabled soldiers (*invalidnye komandy,
gopsital'nye komandy*) served as an inexhaustible reservoir for a supply of the sick to the
hospital when the latter needed additional patients to match the number of the deceased" ; N. I.
Kulbin, *Sanitarnaia obstanovka voisk*, SVM, t. VIII, ch. 2, 169.

[43] Thus, for example, we learn from the 1838 report of the Kazan battalion commander that,
among the graduates, three had died: one Christian and two Jews. The same year, a Jewish
cantonist died, in the Troitsk battalion. In the Perm battalion, which had a fair number of Jews,
none of the four who died in 1839 were Jewish. For scattered reports, see RGVIA, f. 405, op. 5,
d. 2703, ll. 90, 185–188.

[44] RGVIA, f. 405, op. 5, d. 4463, ll. 1–3.

[45] The death of Nicholas I made possible the publication of the military journal *Voennyi sbornik*,
and hence some military statistics. Only then did it become clear how the cantonists affected
the army's mortality rate. It was reported that, in 1851, the mortality rate was 1:27, whereas, in
1858, it dropped to 1:51. The direct influence of the dissolution of the cantonist system upon
these figures can be correctly assessed if one takes into account the obvious impact of the
Crimean War (1854–1856). See *Voennyi sbornik*, no. 3 (1861): 3.

total number of graduates. With regard to physical fitness, seventeen-year-old Jews surpassed their Christian fellows; there were 1.5 times more Jewish graduates of that age suitable for combat service than there were Christians. Finally, there were slightly fewer Jews than Christians unfit for service: 0.80 percent compared to 0.92 percent.[46] These results of the graduating Jewish cantonists constitute perhaps the best proof that Jewish children survived the cantonist battalions and entered the troops as vigorous individuals, fit for army service.

Jewish Children among Their Fellow Soldiers: Training, Skills, and Discipline

Initially, Jewish minors were as little prepared for study and service in the cantonist battalions as were their Christian counterparts. Furthermore, upon joining the army, Jewish children generally demonstrated less ability than their peers, the soldiers' children. Unlike those children and the offspring of the military settlers, Jewish minors found themselves on equal footing with yet another group utterly unprepared for the military: boys from the Kingdom of Poland. Like Jewish minors, Polish children became cantonists as a result of their communities' attempts to offset a shortage of adult conscripts. The percentage of Polish boys of eleven, nine, and even eight years of age in the battalions was the same as that of Jewish children. The commanders forced Polish boys into Russian Orthodoxy, just as they did Jews. Poor sanitary conditions during the journey to their assigned service post, and the consequent high rate of illness, were equally a feature of the Polish experience. Perhaps following the forcibly baptized Jewish cantonists who rebelled against their imposed identities, after 1855 some Poles also confessed their collective deviation from Russian Orthodoxy.[47]

In addition to combat fitness, two other characteristics distinguished Jewish cantonists: they had more discipline and a lower crime rate than their Christian counterparts. This is clear from the aggregated 1853 report of desertions among enlisted men and cantonists. There were 43 desertions among Christian

---

[46] See RGVIA, f. 405, op. 5, d. 2703, ll. 10–11, 14–15, 17–43; RGVIA, f. 405, op. 5, d. 2703, ll. 128–139, 154, 185–188, 193; RGVIA, f. 405, op. 5, d. 2703, ll. 131–153; RGVIA, f. 405, op. 5, d. 2705, ll. 47–66; RGVIA, f. 405, op. 5, d. 2707, ll. 3–9; RGVIA, f. 405, op. 5, d. 2707, ll. 72–76; RGVIA, f. 405, op. 5, d. 2707, ll. 98–99; RGVIA, f. 405, op. 5, d. 2701, ll. 1–49; RGVIA, f. 405, op. 5, d. 2701, ll. 83–115; RGVIA, f. 405, op. 5, d. 2701, ll. 141–194. For the aggregated table comprising data from these files, see Yohanan Petrovsky-Shtern, *Evrei v russkoi armii*, 145.

[47] See the report of the officer accompanying the cantonists of the 1829 draft, mainly Poles, through the Taurida province, RGVIA, f. 405, op. 2, d. 2892, l. 70; the detailed report on a group of 71 Polish boys who arrived at the Kiev military cantonist battalion in 1843 from the Zamosc and Novogeorgievka garrisons, RGVIA, f. 405, op. 5, d. 7015, ll. 130b.-35; the file of 11 Poles of the Iaroslavl garrison battalion on their retreat from Russian Orthodoxy (Rachinskii, Katepshych, Iuzvek, etc.), RGVIA, f. 801, op. 17, d. 39.

soldiers; none among the Jews; 5 among Christian cantonists; and 1 among Jewish cantonists. The majority of Christian soldiers who deserted were former cantonists, while the only Jewish cantonist registered as having disappeared over this period in fact was on leave in a village near Iaroslavl. To fully appreciate the low, if not negligible, rate of Jewish desertion, one should take into consideration that, in 1853, Nicholas announced mass levies throughout the empire and began a new military campaign that later escalated into the Crimean War.

The most common crime in the cantonist battalions was theft.[48] Poor and strictly rationed meals, and a ban on taking bread from the canteens, forced the cantonists to supplement their meager rations by whatever means they could. As a rule, battalion commanders did not charge cantonists with food theft, and filed no cases against them; they even sheltered those who were guilty. Theft was regarded as a necessary means of survival, rather than a matter for a military court's consideration. Cantonists preyed on military settlers and on peasants trading at the Sunday markets; skill in stealing without being caught earned one the respect of others. Cantonists competed to steal a roll, a meat pie, or a sweet wheat loaf. The only known case of theft by a Jewish cantonist concerned a bet between Alexander II and General Treshkin at the 1856 maneuvers near Uman. Treshkin bragged that his cantonists could steal anything from anybody, whereupon Alexander assured his general that the cantonists would not be able to steal anything from him. During the maneuvers, Cantonist Khodulevich, a Mogilev Jew known throughout the division for his manual dexterity, managed to steal a watch from Alexander's pocket. The astonished Alexander rewarded him with a twenty-five-ruble prize.[49]

Jews who graduated from the cantonist battalions exhibited characteristics similar to those of their Christian peers. They had been taught not only how to march in military parades and to respond to a bayonet attack, but also were instructed in reading, writing, arithmetic, fractions, grammar, geometry, military sciences, military statutes, and drawing. The commanders distinguished between eighteen-year-old cantonists and those who were younger, grouping them into various categories: highly trained for army service, poorly trained for army service, fit for noncombat service, and entirely unfit for army service. In 1838, ten years after the first draft, Jews comprised 371 of 1,349, or 26 percent of the cantonist battalions' graduates. The number of unconverted Jews among well-trained cantonists was twice as high as the number of those who converted to Christianity.[50] The majority of the cantonists (73 percent) were poorly

---

[48] Nikitin, "Mnogostradal'nye. Ocherk byta kantonistov," in *Otechestvennye zapiski*, no. 9 (1871): 90–91; Kretchmer, "Vospominaniia," *Istoricheskii vestnik*, no. 32 (1888): 136; Fedorov, "Igrushechnaia armiia," *Istoricheskii vestnik*, vol. 78, no. 10 (1899): 157–158.

[49] The Russian memoirist who witnessed this event was no lover of Jews, yet he tells this story with sympathy, if not hidden admiration. See Fedorov, "Igrushechnaia armiia," *Istoricheskii vestnik*, vol. 78, no. 11 (1899): 565–566.

[50] Among the well-trained graduates that year were Haim Girshovich Kramenitskii, from the Vasilkov district, who was drafted into the cantonist facility in the Ninety-second levy; Vigder

trained.[51] Among Christian graduates dispatched the following year to eight different army units, the highly trained accounted for 29 percent, the poorly trained for 63 percent; and those untrained for combat service 8 percent.[52] Thus, the percentage of poorly trained soldiers was not specifically a Jewish phenomenon; with respect to their educational success, they were no different from their Christian peers.[53] Nor did the military differentiate between the cantonists according to their faith. Christians and Jews continued their army service in the same military units: the training division of the Fourth infantry corps; the Second training carabineer regiment; town garrisons; and also as engine drivers (*mashinisty*) and stokers (*istopniki*) of the government's steamships.[54] In 1839, poorly trained Jews from the Pskov battalion, as well as Christian cantonists, went into the First carabineer training regiment and into the reserve division of the infantry; both Jews and Christians unfit for combat service obtained jobs at the Warsaw field hospital.[55] Thus, in the first decade of their service, Jewish minors had much in common with converts and Christian cantonists. Nonetheless, it should be noted that Jewish cantonists in the battalions acquired greater skills than did their brothers-in-arms. While the service reports of most cantonist-soldiers' children indicated "No special skills," most of the Jews had learned some craft: eighty-three who served at the headquarters of the Fifth infantry division were tinsmiths, roofers, tailors, shoemakers, or blacksmiths.[56]

(Avigdor) Geliovich Skop, from the Oszmiany district, drafted into the Ninety-eighth levy; and Iankel Yoselevich Kots, from the Vilkomir district, drafted into the Ninety-eighth levy. See RGVIA, f. 405, op. 5, d. 2703, ll. 12–13.

[51] Such a large number of Jews among the poorly trained cantonists probably can be explained by the fact that almost all of them were taken into the Ninety-eighth levy, i.e., in 1836; thus, they remained in the battalions only for two years. The specific age category and ethnic origin of the recruits cannot be ascertained. One may find among them Jewish children from the Oszmiany, Suwałki, Vilna, Rossien, Teliszew, Białystok, Minsk, and Druja *kahals*, as well as from the small Olyka *kahal*. See RGVIA, f. 405, op. 5, d. 2703, ll. 17–26. In 1839, poorly trained cantonists also comprised the majority among both Jews and Christians in the Perm battalion: seventy Christians and fifteen Jews were poorly trained, as compared to the forty-eight Christians and one Jew who were highly trained. See RGVIA, f. 405, op. 5, d. 2703, ll. 185–188.

[52] Compiled from reports of the particular battalions, from the tables indicated in RGVIA, f. 405, op. 5, d. 2706, ll. 1–212.

[53] Even in those battalions famous for their brutal treatment of Jewish cantonists, the number of poorly trained Jews was equal to that of converts and Christians. Among the 1857 graduates from the Kiev battalion, there was not a single well-trained cantonist, although among poorly trained cantonists and those fit for line service, there were forty-seven Christians, fifty-three converts, and fifty-three Jews. See RGVIA, f. 324, op. 1, d. 413, ll. 131–205.

[54] RGVIA, f. 405, op. 5, d. 2701, l. 1910b; RGVIA, f. 405, op. 5, d. 2707, ll. 530b.-54.

[55] RGVIA, f. 405, op. 5, d. 2704, ll. 177, 185.

[56] These cantonists graduated from the Voronezh battalions and joined the regular army in 1858. See RGVIA, f. 405, op. 1, d. 413, ll. 545, 546–549, 556, 560. For memoir evidence, see Nikitin, "Mnogostradal'nye," *Otechstvennye zapiski*, no. 9 (1871): 90–91; Krechmer, "Vospominaniia," *Istoricheskii vestnik*, no. 32 (1888): 136; Fedorov, "Igrushechnaia armiia," *Istoricheskii vestnik*, vol. 78, no. 10 (1899): 157–158.

Despite their initial difficulty with Jewish minors entering the cantonist battalions, the commanders seem to have been satisfied with the results of the Jews' education by the time they were dispersed among the regular troops. Very few complaints of poor training or of physical disabilities were made by supervising commanders or by the regimental staff responsible for accepting the graduates.[57] Furthermore, many army commanders rejected as baseless the attempts by civil authorities to criticize Jews for their inadequacy as soldiers and to isolate them from the general cantonist population. A report from the Saratov battalion commander furnishes a startling example: in 1839, he appealed, in an official report, to Count Kleinmikhel regarding rumors circulating in Saratov and the nearby towns of Volsk and Kuznetsk of fires allegedly started by Jews. The local residents had requested the removal of all Jewish cantonists and their transfer to another location, claiming that Jews had repeatedly been seen loitering around the sites of the fires. The commander of the Saratov battalion conducted an investigation. He reported that the total number of cantonists was 1,281, including 255 converted Jews and 53 who had not converted; 59 Jewish cantonists lived together in the barracks. The commander attached to his report a multi-colored plan of cantonist accommodation in Saratov, and concluded that the army commanders should categorically "deny the rumors" and "reject the absurd claims" against the Jewish cantonists.[58] Gertsel Tsam, well familiar with the literary image of the Jewish cantonist such as Grogorii Bogrov's Ierukhim, and himself a stalwart religious Jew and a former cantonist, wrote: "Bogrov vividly depicted the horrors which the Jewish cantonists had to go through. But I cannot say the same about the Tomsk cantonists. We were treated on a par with the Christians. And the only difference was that that the Christian cantonists were allowed to spend holidays with their relatives and friends whereas Jews were not allowed."[59]

[57] Consider the request of Colonel Gulevich, the commander of the Third training carabineer regiment. In his report, Gulevich asked that his regiment not be sent cantonists "of slack, dull and poor physique." He attached a list naming 144 men whom he already had received and who were, he asserted, unfit for combat service; it contained no Jews. See the set of reports in RGVIA, f. 405, op. 5, d. 2705, ll. 6–23. In another complaint of the same sort (of "dullness and incapacity"), no Jews are found among the 30 cantonists of the St. Petersburg battalion. See RGVIA, f. 324, op. 1, d. 413, l. 2.

[58] RGVIA, f. 405, op. 5, d. 3771, ll. 1, 2, 6, 90b. When, twenty years later in Saratov (for the first time in Russia since the reform, and for the first time outside the Jewish Pale), Jewish soldiers were accused of ritual murder, the newspaper of the War Ministry, *Russkii invalid*, sided with the Jewish soldiers. See Klier, *Imperial Russia's Jewish Question, 1855–1881* (Cambridge: Cambridge University Press, 1995), 419–420.

[59] For Ierukhim, see Grigorii Bogrov, *Zapiski evreia*. 3 vols. (Odessa: Sherman, 1912–1913), 1: 67–70; 2: 15–137; 3: 146–238; for Tsam's autobiographical essay, see "Kapitan G. Ia. Tsam," *Voina i evrei*, no. 7 (1914–1915): 7–11, here 7.

Jews of Mosaic Faith versus Jews of Christian Faith

How did the experience of those soldiers who, as the military reported, "persisted in their creed" differ from that of the Jewish converts? What did these converts acquire in addition to the twenty-five rubles officially awarded them? Between 1827 and 1838, more Jewish cantonists than converts joined the regular troops (1,548 vs. 1,245), and more Jews than converts joined rifle battalions (77 vs. 23). More Jews obtained sinecure positions with noncombatant units such as the musical sub-units and corps headquarters (15 vs. 7). The monopoly of Jewish cantonists in the Black Sea Fleet and the absence of converts there (180 vs. 0) can be explained by Nicholas's prejudice: He thought that Jews were cowards in need of re-education in the most demanding service, the navy.[60] Jews were demonstrably more diligent than converts; twice as many of them obtained positions in the reserved cavalry troops headquarters (94 vs. 43). Similarly, there was a prevalence of Jews in the interior guard (228 vs. 88 converts), perhaps because these troops ordinarily comprised those whom the military considered less desirable.[61] There were ten times more Jews among military settlers (1,778 vs. 153), which suggests that perhaps the commanders enlisted the settlers' help in reeducating Jews according to Russian Orthodoxy. Among nonmilitary artisans, Jews were less well represented (227 vs. 326), and among medical orderlies, artisans, and munitions artisans, there were only a few more converted than unconverted Jews. Converted cantonists were permitted to work in the armories (*oruzheinye zavody*), although this was a rather dubious privilege, since the labor conditions there were notoriously harsh.[62] The financial advantages of conversion were hardly alluring; apparently the cantonists were well aware that mid-level authorities embezzled the monies owed to the former, and quite often the twenty-five-ruble bonus did not reach its intended recipient. Furthermore, the cantonists who converted to Christianity outside the cantonist battalions, whether they were Muslims, Catholics, or Jews, did not receive their bonuses even when the omnipotent Count Kleinmikhel petitioned on their behalf. The military administration replied that only soldiers' children and cantonists, rather than regular army soldiers, received the reward for conversion.[63]

Conversion did not necessarily entail an improvement in one's military position; the ratio of highly trained converts to highly trained Jews was virtually equal. Nor did converted Jews constitute a special group in terms of talent, learning ability, or distinguished career. In 1858, both Jews and converted Jews from the Voronezh cantonist battalion joined the internal guard troops. The

---

[60] See Riasanovsky, *Nicholas I*, 232 n. 93, and also *Glavnyi shtab. Komplektovanie voisk v tsarstvovanie Nikolaia I* (SPb.: Glavnyi shtab, 1902), 11.

[61] *Voennaia entsiklopediia*, 6: 442–446.

[62] The department ordered that groups of converted cantonists be dispatched to the Sestroretsk and Izhevsk munitions factories. See RGVIA, f. 405, op. 5, d. 1692, l. 60b.; f. 405, op. 5, t. II, d. 6096.

[63] RGVIA, f. 405, op. 5, d. 2670, l. 37.

baptized soldier Altemberg and the Jewish Milshtein both were sent to the Kargapolsk dragoon regiment. Although artisan skills distinguished the converts and Jewish cantonists from the rest of the men, conversion conferred no real advantage. For example, in November 1857, out of twenty-eight persons assigned to service the court carriages, the army removed ten: two coach upholsterers who were converted Jews, six Jewish saddlers, and two Jewish wheelwrights. The reason was the same for all: neither Jews nor converts could serve as carriage artisans. That the converts were treated the same as Jews was especially disappointing to their local commanders. Major General Baron Seddeler praised the converts as intelligent and diligent soldiers, lamenting that they were not accorded a chance to fully employ their abilities; they were not permitted to become cartographers, artillerists, or field engineers, a discrimination which he felt was "against the teaching of the Gospel."[64]

Despite Nicholas's order to consider Jewish converts to Russian Orthodoxy as non-Jews, the state and military administration mistrusted them and in many cases clustered them with Jews rather than with Christians. Furthermore, in 1848, Nicholas forbade Jewish converts to change their surnames. A Jewish cantonist could become Fedor, Vassilii, or Afanasii, but remained Vaisberg, Rosenvasser, or Grinboim. It is doubtful that Nicholas tried to impress upon Jews the advantage of a new Christian soul attached to an old Jewish family name. More likely, while his radical reform of the Jews followed enlightened policies, his mistreatment of converts counteracted it. The state control of Jews did not imply their immediate parity with the Russian Orthodox; nothing seemed capable of purifying their primordial sin, their Jewish origin. Jewish converts did not become a new Russian subculture: the regime's integrationist efforts were seriously limited. Some Jews in the Russian army became Russians religiously and culturally, yet they still remained Jews for the authorities, albeit baptized Jews. And converted cantonists missed no opportunity to protest against Nicholas's version of the Enlightenment.

Mutiny of the New Christians

In 1856, newly converted cantonists caused serious disruption in the Department of Military Settlements; by the 1860s, the resulting destabilization had acquired alarming proportions. The death of Nicholas and the first decrees of Alexander II, who canceled the conscription system and the draft of minors, created an impression among the cantonists that they finally had entered a new era of justice and legality. Possibly they assumed that the tsar whose coronation coincided with the end of the dreadful Crimean War would be better than his bellicose predecessor. Alexander had refused to accept the child offerings brought onto the altar of the fatherland; perhaps he could help them reestablish

---

[64] RGVIA, f. 405, op. 1, d. 413, ll. 545, 546–549, 556, 560; RGVIA, f. 405, op. 5, d. 2701, l. 59; RGVIA, f. 405, op. 5, d. 16468, l. 162; RGVIA, f. 405, op. 5, d. 6953, ll. 155–1560b.

justice. This hope spurred some cantonists into action. In November 1856, Alexander II sojourned in Kiev, where he inspected the troops. During the inspection, three converted cantonists handed him a petition, complaining that they had been forcibly baptized. Alexander II ordered the military governor general of Kiev "to investigate and report." The governor general opined that the petition was absurd, that the insolent petitioners had not followed proper procedure, and that they should be sent to a monastery. "It would be better to send them to Eastern Siberia," retorted Alexander.[65]

Against the backdrop of later events, this incident was minor. The authorities simply silenced it, as they did a second occurrence: that same year, the commander of the First rifle battalion reported that five cantonists serving as artisans in St. Petersburg, who were Jewish converts to Christianity, had repudiated their baptism and expressed the wish to return to their former faith. In response to a request from the military administration, the commander of the artisans' company clarified: "I am entrusted with the command of artisans, composed of five hundred men of Jewish faith who work under free foremen. There is no possibility of looking after five converts; it would be better to send them to a cantonist school." The administration removed the five troublemakers from the artisans' company. To explain the cantonists' outrageous actions, the commanders advanced a formula that had appeared throughout Nicholas's reign, even in the reports of those who had repented joining the Decembrists. The cantonist who wished to return to Judaism did so "out of [his] own foolishness" (*po sobstvennoi gluposti*). The commanders dictated to cantonists, and compelled them to sign, an explanatory note asserting the formulaic "out of my own foolishness." Three of the converts agreed to remain Christians, but two, Varlaam Banshchik and Varlaam Noga, obstinately resisted. The Holy Synod intervened, offering to send them to a monastery and to keep them there "unless they atone." The military agreed, and dispatched the boys to the Iuriev monastery.[66] But the resulting scandal within the department steadily grew.

In late 1856, Accompanying Officer Usov, an ensign of the first Arkhangelsk garrison battalion, brought a group of cantonists to the Sixth army corps and reported to his commanders that forty-one converted Jewish cantonists refused to practice Christianity. Three of them, Iudovich, Lezerovich, and Meerovich, continued to observe Jewish rites. The staff of the internal guards' corps requested the converts' service records and established an investigation commission. In the meanwhile, another fifty-one converted Jews declared their unwillingness to remain Russian Orthodox. These were joined by another sixteen. To confront the increasing numbers, Staff Officer Sokolov, responsible for the investigation, resolved to interrogate not only the cantonists and their commanders, but also their godfathers. The commission brought from Kronstadt two Jewish sailors, Feifert and Fidler, who had served earlier in the Arkhangelsk battalion. The sailors confirmed that the battalion commanders

[65] RGVIA, f. 324, op. 1, d. 117, l. 85.
[66] RGVIA, f. 324, op. 1, d. 22, ll. 58, 65–76.

had forced the cantonists to learn Russian Orthodox prayers, had punished them for failure to comply (although the documents provide no detail), and had warned them to practice Christianity if they hoped to avoid further punishment. The cantonists confirmed that they had practiced Christianity only under duress, and on the condition that, after their graduation from the battalion, they would return to Judaism. They hid their religious books and ritual artifacts, planning to retrieve them upon their transfer to the regular army. Despite the evidence, the commission ruled that the former Jews were lying, and the battalion commanders, good Christians who affirmed that the cantonists had converted voluntarily, were right. The commission rebuked the mutineers, and was careful to add to their secret report, in self-justification, that the commanders had "applied only mild measures of warning and instruction" to influence the cantonists to adopt Christianity.[67] To save face, the Department of Military Settlements preferred to investigate such cases independently rather than to go to military court, where the entire War Ministry would hear of the affair. However, it became increasingly difficult to conceal such incidents, particularly since Jews were not the only ones to rebel.[68]

On December 12, 1858, 161 men, including 37 Christians of Jewish origin, arrived in Moscow from the Kiev cantonist battalion. Among them there were Aleksandr Beletskii, Afanasii Gliksberg, Vasilii Moos, Nestor Tsuker, Andrei Dreiker, Kirilo Iakubovich, Gerasim Finkelshtein, Fedot Boim, Vasilii Gokhman, and Timofei Ezerskii, all cantonists with Russian Orthodox first names and Jewish surnames. The thirty-seven converts immediately assumed their former Jewish first names, declaring that they had not accepted Christianity and did not recognize the Russian Orthodox creed. The furious Colonel Dessimon, the commander of the Kiev battalion, immediately dispatched a report to the Department of Military Settlements, demanding the arrest of the cantonists and the application of the full rigor of the law.[69] The Moscow investigation commission determined that the cantonists had adopted Christianity between 1853 and 1855; in 1854, many of them had studied with Father Remizov, Dessimon's protégé. Others cantonists maintained that they had been small children when the commanders compelled them to join the Orthodox Church. It was discovered that none of the thirty-seven wore a breast cross, while Serapion

---

[67] RGVIA, f. 405, op. 9, d. 3354, ll. 1, 3, 5; RGVIA, f. 405, op. 9, d. 3143, ll. 4, 17, 230b.-24, 270b ; RGVIA, f. 405, op. 9, d. 3143, l. 270b.

[68] To a certain extent, the collective religious revolt by Jewish children was a microcosm of the protests against forcible baptism and of the deviations from Russian Orthodoxy among the representatives of various ethnic groups during Nicholas I's reign. For Nikifor Semionov's and Ivan Brodiaga's deviation from Russian Orthodoxy in 1852, see, RGVIA, f. 801, op. 67, otd. 1, st. 1, sv. 284, d. 79; for Moris Asman, who also broke away from Russian Orthodoxy in 1852, see RGVIA, f. 801, op. 67, otd. 1, st. 1, sv. 281, d. 16; for Aburunov, a Cossack, who abandoned Russian Orthodoxy in favor of the *dukhobory* sect, RGVIA, f. 801, op. 69/10, d. 9. In matters of religious disobedience, the Poles most closely resembled the Jews. For the case of seven Polish recruits of the Iaroslavl garrison battalion forced into Russian Orthodoxy from Catholicism who returned to Catholic practices, see RGVIA, op. 69/10, d. 39.

[69] RGVIA, f. 324, op. 1, d. 117, ll. 2–30b.

Smarkatenko, yet another rebel cantonist, had "a Jewish *lapserdak*" (i.e., a *tallit katan*, a four-cornered undershirt with fringed corners) and "Jewish books," which he used to pray with his comrades. Although the commanders confiscated all religious artifacts, they seemed uncertain as to how to deal with the offenders.

During individual interrogation, the cantonists behaved like true conspirators. Afanasii, alias Pinkhes, Gliksberg maintained that he knew nothing about his godfather, that he had never attended a single confession, had never attended Remizov's classes, had never received a monetary award for conversion, and had no idea why, in written reports, he was addressed by a Russian name. Timofei, or Moshka, Ezerskii claimed that he had never adopted Christianity, had not received communion, and had never attended church services. He freely practiced Judaism in the battalion, and had even been allowed to go home for the Jewish holidays. Frustrated, the investigators turned to provocative questions, bluntly demanding of Vasilii, originally Leiser, Moos, "Do you observe Jewish law? Did you receive any money at church after baptism? Have you ever met an adult Jewish soldier who asked you to reject Christianity?" Vasilii Moos parried, "I practiced Judaism secretly; on Jewish holidays, neither I nor any other cantonists could go anywhere; I met no soldier on the road … And as to money: yes, some unknown person near the church gave out fifty kopecks to us 'for [shoe] brushes and shoe-polish.'" After many hours of confrontation, interrogation, intimidation, and threats, twenty-five men, including Afanasii Gliksberg, Timofei Ezerskii, Vasilii Moos, and Fedot Boim, repented and confessed. The commanders submitted their purportedly original baptismal certificates along with testimonies from the priests in Kiev that the cantonists had received communion. Perhaps frightened by the official appearance of the certificates (brand new, and almost identical, as if a meticulous regimental scribe had created them the previous day), the cantonists signed a statement confirming that they were Orthodox Christians. Their statements testified that they were "not serious" about breaking away from Russian Orthodoxy and that their conversion was voluntary. Even afterwards, twelve men continued to resist. The school's administration decided to hush the matter up, and continually warned the rebels that they could find themselves in the Siberian battalions "so that in the army they may reflect upon their wrongdoing and come to repent."[70]

However, it was no longer possible to prevent the mass abandonment of Russian Orthodoxy. In Odessa, in the late fall of 1858, 119 cantonists joined the regiments of the Fifth army corps. Of these, forty-four Jewish converts submitted a complaint: the commanders had blackmailed them into baptism "without any preliminary explanation of the beliefs."[71] As this was the third attempt at a mass retreat from Russian Orthodoxy in two-and-a-half years, the department predictably overreacted. The resulting case provides exhaustive information regarding the cantonists' forcible conversion, and corroborates

---

[70] RGVIA, f. 324, op. 1, d. 117, ll. 69–69ob., 70–71, 90.
[71] RGVIA, f. 324, op. 1, d. 22, l. 10b.

some of the descriptions of mistreatment of Jewish children that appear in a much exaggerated form in memoirs and literature.

This time, the investigation was more thorough. The commission made a dedicated attempt to hold the commanders of the Kiev cantonist battalions responsible, and the accused were more frank. Aleksandr Khune, a poorly educated, sixteen-year-old Jew, stated that senior cantonist Mostak persuaded him, at the age of twelve, to adopt Christianity by threatening to beat him and to deny him food if he refused to comply. Ivan Novikov testified that senior cantonist Svintovskii allegedly beat him with a stick. He became ill and spent time in hospital; upon his return to the battalion, Svintovskii beat him once again. Novikov claimed that he had not disclosed these incidents earlier because "the cantonists always beat those who tell about forcible conversion to Russian Orthodoxy." Cantonist Milshtein, probably a baptized Jew, beat cantonist Vikentii Damskii on his hands for a period of two weeks, in an effort to persuade him to accept Christianity. At the end of this time, Sergeant Major Antonov announced, "Whoever does not want to adopt Christianity, step forward." Damskii did. Antonov purportedly slapped him in the face and declared, "Now wait, you rascal." The next day, Damskii was forcibly "Christianized." Evsei Veitsman, a soldier, asserted, in turn, that Captain Borodin informed Sergeant Major Antonov, "By tomorrow, everybody must wish to adopt Christianity." They started beating Veitsman and several other boys on their hands and the soles of their feet with a bar. After two days, they took the cantonists to a nearby Orthodox church and baptized them, without bothering to teach the hapless converts any of the prayers. Evsei Groiskop reported that a senior soldier pierced his fingers with a needle and burned his feet with a hot tin plate. Then they took him to a local parish church, where the priest poured water on him. Groiskop saw neither his godfather nor his godmother, and argued that they were absent during the ceremony. Averkii Zhiroka, a converted cantonist, tried to complain about the commanders' brutality, but was not allowed out of the barracks; meanwhile, his beatings only intensified.[72]

The department commission summoned the high-ranking officers involved, Colonel Dessimon and Major General Bazilevskii, and questioned them uneasily: Did the battalion commanders follow the policies regarding admonition? Did they baptize cantonists within the first week of their stay in the battalion? Why had Zheleznov, Groiskop, and Novikov been sent to the battalion hospital? The battalion doctor, Lukin, denied that the cantonists were mutilated upon arrival, and claimed that they all had a fever. Major General Bazilevskii rejected the evidence of the cantonists as "the result of a conspiracy that typified the devious Jews." Colonel Dessimon declared that all the cantonists' evidence was an invention, and that none of them had converted under pressure. The commander of the Second training command volunteered that, during his inspections of the battalions, none of the cantonists had complained and, in general, that he had never "heard anything of the kind." Lieutenant

---

[72] RGVIA, f. 324, op. 1, d. 22, ll. 250b., 29, 460b.

Borodin tried to be candid, acknowledging that "senior cantonists took it upon themselves to persuade Jews to adopt Russian Orthodoxy. Many willingly agreed, because converted cantonists labeled Jews in the battalion as "Yids."[73]

The commanders failed to apprehend that another epoch had arrived; the commission members were interested in justice. They determined that Groiskop could not have recovered from fever in the course of a single week (from July 10 to 18, 1854), as the battalion officers asserted; therefore, Dr. Lukin must have lied, apparently because he had been instructed to do so by Major General Bazilevskii. Thus, Bazilevskii had lied too. If this was the case, it was Colonel Dessimon who had initiated the deception. The commission concluded that the soldiers' evidence was reliable. Following the commission's recommendations, the department adopted several resolutions, two of them unprecedented in army practice: Major General Bazilevskii received a strong warning, and Colonel Dessimon a severe reprimand, for he had interrogated neither the lower ranks nor the cantonists. The department decided that, once it had reinvented itself as the Department of Military Schools, Dessimon was not to be offered a position. The case was sent to the Kiev governor general for further investigation. The commission honored Nicholas's 1849 circular enjoining authorities to refrain from violence in their attempts to convert Jews. The war minister signed a Special Circular, no. 2400, and sent it to the Synod, which, on December 18, 1858, duly enforced the ban on involuntary baptism of Jewish cantonists.[74] All forty-four cantonists who had submitted complaints announced that they wished to remain Orthodox Christians.[75]

This outcome merits examination, particularly since similar cases occurred until the end of the 1850s. The formerly Jewish and later Christian cantonists Petr Tsigelman, Mitrofan Davydovich, Pavel Reisvasser, Ivan Rolnitskii, Pavel Frankshuler, Assei Finkelshtein, Iakov Sar, Kuzma Isovich, and others, all of whom had been baptized between 1853 and 1855, succeeded in convincing the commission of the truth of their testimony. The commission issued a bold statement, deploring the treatment to which Jews were subjected in the army: "We discovered that, while converting Jews, generally they did not properly observe the corresponding rules and did not always persuade and exhort them with due diligence."[76] Nonetheless, *all cantonists* – except two, sent to a monastery – agreed to remain Russian Orthodox. Certainly, among those who converted under duress there were some who were happy with their new status and who truly wished to remain Orthodox Christians. Other soldiers may have been intimidated into remaining Russian Orthodox by threats of being sent to remote parts of the empire if they rebelled.

---

[73] RGVIA, f. 324, op. 1, d. 22, ll. 5, 15, 91.

[74] See *Rukovodstvennye dlia pravoslavnogo dukhovenstva ukazy Sviateishego Pravitel'-stvuiushchego Sinoda. 1721–1878* (M.: M. Lavrov, 1879), 344–346.

[75] RGVIA, f. 324, op. 1, d. 22, ll. 95ob., 100ob.

[76] The 1859 case involved a group of one hundred men from the Kiev cantonist battalions, thirty-two of whom were converts, who declared that they had adopted Christianity under duress. See RGVIA, f. 324, op. 1, d. 1108, ll. 2–20b., 60b., 110b.

These religious rebellions could only have succeeded had they received publicity. Unfortunately, the commission members had unequivocal instructions not to wash the army's dirty linen in public. Consequently, the proceedings were conducted secretly. In the late 1850s, Alexander II's Great Reforms had just begun to take shape; no mention of such cases was leaked to the press, either in the 1860s or later. Moreover, the jury stipulated in Alexander's judicial reforms was years away, and it was precisely this instrument that the cantonists would have needed to employ to help them. Thirdly, Nicholas's 1850 Criminal Code (*ulozhenie o nakazaniiakh*), still in effect, classified apostasy from Russian Orthodoxy as one of the most heinous of crimes. Baptism was one of the seven sacraments; it could be nullified only under extraordinary circumstances. Hence, reconversion of Russian Orthodox converts to their original faith – Judaism, Catholicism, or Islam – was an apostasy, and subject to prosecution by the state.

New Christians who returned to their previous beliefs forfeited their civil rights, their property, and the right to appeal. The Criminal Code provided for a routine sentence of eight to ten years hard labor. Those deviating from Russian Orthodoxy were "sent [by the authorities] to spiritual leaders for admonition and instruction."[77] The law did not allow any possibility for escape, forcing former Russian sectarians, Jews, Catholics, and Muslims alike to return to the state's official creed.[78] All of these reasons serve to explain why so few cantonists obstinately persisted in renouncing the new faith foisted upon them. Thus, Vladimir (David) Samson from Vilna province, while in the Pskov battalion, declared on December 12, 1860, that he had reverted to "the creed of his parents" because of violence on the part of the instructors in the First training carabineer corps in which he had served. Father Zakharii Obraztsov tried to admonish Samson, but to no avail. The priest contended that Samson knew neither the Jewish language nor Jewish law; the significant number of Jews in his unit had compelled him to make his claim. The newly minted Department of Military Schools ordered Samson to "stop his contacts with other Jews," and later exiled him, with other young apostates, to a line battalion in East Siberia. There the authorities were "to admonish him to repent during his period of service."[79] A year later, Noga and Banshchikov, who had been the first to complain, repented their rebellion from their seclusion in the Iuriev monastery, and were released. They were sent to serve in the Novgorod cantonist battalion.

---

[77] Articles 190 and 191. See *Ulozheniia o nakazaniiakh ugolovnykh i ispravitel'nykh* (SPb.: E. I. V. Kantseliariia, 1845): 43–47.

[78] Consider the case of the baptized Tartars (Muslims), who deviated in the early 1830s from Christianity and re-adopted Islam. The commanders separated them from other Muslims and placed them under the strict supervision of local priests, who were responsible for returning them to Russian Orthodoxy. See *Rukovodstvennye dlia pravoslavnogo dukhovenstva ukazy*, 339–340.

[79] RGVIA, f. 324, op. 1, d. 151, ll. 1, 11.

Russian Christians of Judaic Faith: Individual Fates

The Christianity of the converts from Judaism was uncertain. Sometimes former cantonists, Russified and apparently good Christians, with Russian names and Christian spouses, announced their rejection of Christianity years after leaving the battalions, and returned to Judaism. The radical 1864 reform of the Russian judicial system set the stage for new attempts by former cantonists to reestablish their ancestral faith. While the military heard some of these cases, most ended up in the civil courts. In 1867, Korabelnikov, an assistant doctor at the Hassav-Iurt military hospital, returned to Judaism and urged his wife, Alexandra, and his children to follow suit. Korabelnikov had been a Christian for more than twenty years; he claimed to have been forcibly converted in the Voronezh cantonist battalion, in 1843. His wife, an Old Believer, confessed during her interrogation that her husband had informed her before they married that he was a Jewish convert and that, sooner or later, he would return to Judaism. Five years after their marriage, the Korabelnikovs moved to Aleksandrovsk, a Cossack village, where the Subbotnik sect resided. Alexandra had attended the Subbotniks' assemblies and had been exposed to their beliefs, which helped her afterwards to adopt Judaism. The Korabelnikovs instructed their children – Fekla, aged sixteen, and Semen, a twelve-year-old – in Jewish law, although, fearful of discovery and prosecution, they had their children baptized. The children knew they were Christians, but never attended church. They could read and write Yiddish, and proclaimed during their interrogation that Jewish law would never change. It was the Korabelnikovs' refusal to baptize their third child that had exposed them to scandal.[80]

To compensate for their delay in reporting the case, local commanders were extraordinarily punitive: they deprived Korabelnikov of the bronze medal he had earned for his role in the Crimean War, divested him of his civil rights, and sentenced him to eight years of hard labor. His wife petitioned military headquarters on her husband's behalf, portraying him as a loyal soldier with a blameless service record, who had twice been wounded in battles in the Caucasus. The military court's decision reflected the state's new liberal proclivities: "Korabelnikov should not be punished nor deprived of his rights and advantages, but sent to live in a distant district of Russia." However, the army's decision differed: it resolved to "exclude him from the military medical department; dismiss him from the service; issue an imperial order; but refrain from mentioning its subsequent confirmation and the reasons of his dismissal." In other words, the intent was to deprive him of his rank and of the right to his profession as a military doctor. At the same time, the army was embarrassed to disclose to Korabelnikov the true reason for his dismissal, perhaps also fearing a legal appeal and the resulting publicity. In the end, the military sent the family

---

[80] RGVIA, f. 400, op. 15, d. 232, ll. 3–7, 13–130b., 14–140b., 15.

to Kharkov province, rather than Irkutsk, paid Korabelnikov's pension, and did not bar him from medical practice.[81]

The fate of those cantonists who dared to return to Judaism after their assignment to reserve duty was no better than the fate of the Jewish boys baptized under duress whom the commanders transferred to the army. The former were embittered by their impression of civil inequality and sense of helplessness. For example, in 1871, the military considered a denunciation against Shmuilo Rozenfrukt, who, after his seventeen-year term in the Kiev cantonist battalion and later in the army, settled in Moscow, and attempted to establish contact with his Jewish relatives in Radom province. According to military documents he was Gavrila Rozenfrukt, a convert from Judaism, whereas he claimed he was Shmuilo (Yiddish for Samuel), a Jew. The military, exasperated with such cases, sent his file to the Department of Foreign Creeds in the Ministry of the Interior, which accused Rozenfrukt of "relapsing to Judaism." The outcome of his case (completed four years later) was similar to that of Meier Goldshtein, also from Radom province and from the Kiev cantonist battalion. From 1858, Goldshtein served in the Second division as the Christian Nikolai Goldshtein. He was caught performing Jewish religious rites and was dispatched to a monastery as punishment. Even after enduring four years of the monastic life, Goldshtein persevered in his desire to remain a Jew. He retired, settled in Kurland province, worked as a shoemaker, and plied the War Ministry with his unusual petition: to return his name to him. "Instead of a well-merited award for immaculate service, I retire from the army bereft of my real name, given to me according to Jewish law. I petition to return to me my name and not to consider myself a Christian." At the request of the Main Staff, the Ministry of the Interior replied that Goldshtein should be sued for having relapsed from Christianity, while "the spiritual authorities should exhort the legally apostate Christians in the true faith." Goldshtein found himself under strict police and church surveillance. His persistence was to no avail; the Ministry of the Interior treated his petitions as "not deserving of approval."[82]

Local Jewish communities and, more importantly, local Russian authorities were far more responsive than the Ministry of the Interior. According to the report of the Kiev, Volhynia, and Podol governor general, the entire Jewish population of the town of Zaslav (Iziaslav, Volhynia province) supported the apostasy of Ivan Shpigel, who had been sent into a battalion in 1852, at the age of nine, and had been Christianized against his will. Prompted by the local police chief, Father Davidovich tried to exhort Shpigel to convert, but encountered firm resistance. Assistant district attorney Tomsky regarded the suggested punishment of exile to Tobolsk, in Siberia, as foolishness. He recommended that the authorities allow Shpigel to remain in his place of residence and to "profess Judaism publicly." The authorities did not share this view. They considered Shpigel's interrogation in the presence of a local priest a "confession." Since

---

[81] RGVIA, f. 400, op. 15, d. 232, ll. 170b., 190b.
[82] RGIA, f. 821, op. 8, d. 201, ll. 1–20b., 9–10; RGIA, f. 821, op. 8, d. 202, ll. 4, 9, 11, 12, 17.

Shpigel had confessed, he was a Christian, who therefore should be brought back to the right path. They sent him far away from his community, to Kostroma province, under police surveillance, and canceled this surveillance only when Ivan Semenovich Shpigel submitted a written statement promising not to return to Judaism again. This promise he broke after 1905.[83]

Shpigel was one of many former cantonists of dual identity, legally registered as Christians but identifying themselves as Jews. A similar calamity befell retired soldier Nikolai (Hirsh) Ryzhkov. He became a Christian in 1851, in the Novgorod battalion, then served in the Ingermanland infantry regiment, and after retirement found himself in court for apostasy. A regimental scribe, Epelman, baptized in 1851 in the Kungursk battalion, also persisted in his desire to return to Judaism. He was secluded in a monastery, from which he fled, and appeared before the military demanding a public trial. The former cantonist Arie Morgenshtern, who also was baptized, tried to return to Judaism in order to marry a Jewess named Rachel. In a bid to regain his Jewish status, he rejected the promotion he had earned as a Christian soldier. The army imprisoned him for eight months and then sent him to the clerical authorities for reeducation. Semen (Zukher) Klias, arrested in 1869, fared not much better. Baptized while a cantonist, he served in the Third East Siberian battalion, returned to his home community in Zholkva (Żółkiew), regained his Jewish status, and even married a Jewess, Faige Meizner; at that point, he was arrested and sent to the dean of the Helm church to be persuaded back to "the true faith." When persuasion did not work, his case was transferred to the court-room.[84] Baptized Jewish cantonists believed in the power of publicity, law and, since Nicholas's death, a new military justice. However, having integrated its Jewish cantonists, the Russian army suppressed any manifestations of the dual Judeo Christian identity, elsewhere in Europe synonymous with modernization.

And yet, the regime was not homogenous, the bureaucracy and the police were fallible, and some successful attempts to return to Judaism (although hardly numerous) did occur. For example, in 1880, the court acquitted the former Jewish cantonist Movsha Aizenberg, accused of passport forgery. Aizenberg was baptized at the age of eleven.[85] After he retired, he commissioned a bogus passport that registered him as a Jew, in order to marry a Jewish girl. Moisei Volondarskii (Mikhail Ivanov), a resident of Tomsk, baptized against his will in 1847 in the Omsk cantonist battalion, in 1896 successfully petitioned the authorities to grant him the right to return to Judaism.[86] The family archive of Larry Benowitz, of Boston, yields another story: as a twelve-year-old, his great-grandfather was drafted into the Russian army and

---

[83] RGIA, f. 821, op. 8, d. 200, l. 7, 44. Despite this statement, Shpigel considered himself a Jew throughout his life. See M. Shpigel, "Iz zapisok kantonista," *Evreiskaia starina*, no. 1 (1911): 249–259.

[84] RGIA, f. 821, op. 8, d. 198, ll. 1–40b.; RGIA, f. 821, op. 8, d. 197, l. 1, 30b., 12; Archiwum Państwowe w Liublinie, f. 109, d. 1869, ll. 1–2.

[85] *Russkii evrei*, no. 4 (1880): 137–38.

[86] CAHJP, HM 2/777.5. For the original, see RGIA, f. 821, op. 8, d. 209, l. 2–20b.

made a Christian. He completed his military service, and after retirement settled in the Russian interior with his Christian wife. Only his worn-out *tallit* (prayer shawl), which he somehow had preserved, and a note with his parents' address, sewn into his clothes, reminded him of his origins. Eventually he rediscovered his *tallit* and told his wife of his desire to return to Lithuania. She followed him, and in Mariampol adopted Judaism, becoming Haya Sarah, a name often found among converts to Judaism.[87] According to this undocumented family legend, the Benowitzes knew no persecution.

The former Jewish cantonists were productive individuals possessed of great physical strength, will, and conviction. Regardless of their military and religious experience, cantonists uniformly expressed a profound commitment to the Jewish people.[88] It is worth noting that these same characteristics distinguished those who remained converts, such as Volf Nakhlas (Aleksandr Alekseev).[89] Some baptized cantonists, like Victor Nikitin, a special envoy in the Ministry of the Interior, succeeded in pursuing a career in the imperial administration.[90] However, claims that high-ranking Russian officers, such as Vassilii Geiman or Konstantin Gershelman, were former Jewish cantonists are

[87] Rosa Uriash, oral communication. Larry Benowitz to Yohanan Petrovsky-Shtern, private correspondence, May 2002, author's archive.

[88] See I. Itskovich, "Vospominaniia arkhangelskogo kantonista," *Evreiskaia starina*, no. 1 (1912): 54–65; M. Merimzon, "Rasskaz starogo soldata," *Evreiskaia starina*, no. 3 (1912): 290–301; no. 4 (1912): 406–422; no. 6 (1913): 86–95; no. 11 (1913): 221–232; M. Shpigel, "Iz zapisok kantonista," *Evreiskaia starina*, no. 1 (1911): 249–259. See also the case of Movsha Aizenberg, *Russkii evrei*, no. 4 (1880): 137–138. An affluent former cantonist of Jewish descent transformed himself into a forerunner of Russian industrialism and a genuine protector of former Jewish soldiers; see P. Ia. Levenson, "Zakoldovannyi. Byl," *Voskhod*, no. 7 (1884): 15–41.

[89] Nakhlas was born to a wealthy Hasidic family and received a traditional education. He later was captured by *khapers* (*kahal*-commissioned kidnappers) and sent to the Volsk cantonist battalion in Saratov province, where he was baptized. In his new-minted identity as Aleksandr Alekseev, he became an ardent missionary. Nonetheless, he ably refuted the blood-libel accusations brought against Jewish soldiers in the Saratov case. See A. Alekseev, "Byvshii voennyi uchitel iz evreev. O evreiskikh bratstvakh 'khevres.'" *Dukhovnaia beseda*, no. 17, 18, 19, 22, 23, 24, 25 (1860); Sh. Tsitron, *Me-ahorei ha-pargod. Momrim, bogdim, mitkakhshim.* 2 vols. (Vilna: Tsevi Mats, 1923), 1:219–223.

[90] The son of an obscure Jewish soldier, Nikitin was a cantonist in the Fourth training carabineer regiment in Nizhnii Novgorod, and later served as a regimental clerk. In 1857, he was promoted to the rank of an NCO. See A. Reitblat, "Nikitin Viktor Nikitich," in *Russkie pisateli, 1800–1917* (M.: Entsiklopediia, 1989), 4:305–306. Nikitin's conventional military career and his rapid civil advancement indicate that, by 1857, he must have been Christian; when, subsequently, he became a journalist, he was regarded as a Russian Christian author. See, for instance, Yehuda Slutsky, *Ha-itonut ha-yehudit-rusit ba-meah ha-19* (Jerusalem: Mosad Bialik, 1970), 147. Nikitin's memoirs begin with his baptism; later he wrote an extensive account of the life in the cantonist battalions. See N. V. Nikitin, "Mnogostradalnye: Ocherki byta kantonistov," *Otechestvennye zapiski*, no. 8 (1871): 351–396; no. 9 (1871): 69–120; no. 10 (1871): 407–440; idem., "Vek prozhit' – ne pole pereiti," in *Evreiskaia biblioteka*, no. 3 (1873): 164–214.

not supported by evidence.[91] General Grulev, sometimes mentioned among the baptized Jews in the Russian army, presents a more tricky case: he had never been a cantonist, was a Jew before embarking upon a military career, and became a Christian specifically in order to acquire an officer's rank. Identifying himself as Russian Orthodox, he successfully moved upward in the army and eventually was appointed the deputy Main Staff. Grulev retired early in the second decade of the twentieth century, and twenty years later, having emigrated, published his famous book *The Notes of a Jewish General*, outwitting his readers: he was never a Jew in the army and was not a military man when he bequeathed the income from the sale of his memoir to the Israeli Fund, a major sponsor of Jewish settlement in Palestine.[92]

Until the 1905 Russian Revolution, the administration punished former cantonists for their desire to return to Judaism with imprisonment, police surveillance, exile, and seclusion in a monastery. Only after the Ministry of the Interior's Special Circular no. 4624, published on August 18, 1905, did the regime cease persecuting those who converted from Russian Orthodoxy to Judaism (or to any other faith). And, for the first time, authorities inscribed "deserves approval" on the petitions of seventy-year-old cantonists wishing to regain their Judaic faith.[93]

The Fall of the Cantonist Institutions

Despite the express desire of the newly enthroned Alexander II to cancel the draft of minors, it took the military some fifteen years finally to dismantle the cantonist institutions. In 1859, the war minister ordered that battalions be transformed into military schools. Russian cantonists and those who had converted to Russian Orthodoxy and were firm in their faith (*utverdivshiesia v onoi*)

---

[91] Brusilov incorrectly portrays Lieutenant General Vasilii Aleksandrovich Geiman (1823–1878), the commander of the Twentieth division in the Caucasus during the Russian-Turkish campaign, as a Jew. See A. A. Brusilov, *Moi vospominaniia* (M.: Voennoe izdatelstvo Minoborony SSSR, 1963): 31. Regarding Geiman, see also S. Iu. Witte, *Vospominaniia*, 3 vols. (M.: Sotsial'no-ekonomicheskaia literatura, 1960), 1: 53. Concerning Konstantin Ivanovich and Fedor Konstantinovich Gershelman, sometimes wrongly identified as Jews, see G. B. Sliozberg, *Baron G. O. Gintsburg: ego zhizn i deiatelnost* (Paris , 1933): 69–70; regarding their antisemitism, see V. N. Lamsdorf, *Dnevnik. 1891–1892*, ed. by F. Rotshtein (M., L.: Academia, 1934), 105, 111, 372–373; *Dnevnik gosudarstvennogo sekretaria A. A. Polovtsova* (M.: Nauka, 1966), 372; Anon., "Iz martirologa Moskovskoi obshchiny," *Evreiskaia starina*, no. 4 (1909): 175–177; S. Dubnov, "*Furor judophobicus* v posledniie gody tsarstvovaniia Aleksandra III, 1890–1894," *Evreiskaia starina*, no. 10 (1918): 27–59; S. S. Vermel, *Moskovskoe izgnanie (1891–1892)* (M.: 1924); P. A. Zaionchkovskii, *Rossiiskoe samoderzhavie v kontse XIX stoletiia (politicheskaia reaktsiia 80-kh-nachala 90-kh godov)* (M.: Mysl, 1970), 136–137.

[92] See M. Grulev, *Zapiski generala-evreia*. Paris: Izd. avtora, 1930.

[93] Jews petitioned the Ministry of the Interior to explain the meaning of its circular: see, for example, petitions of Aizenberg, from Arkhangelsk, and Linetskii, from Simferopol, in RGIA, f. 821, op. 8, d. 209, ll. 95–96, 100–1000b., 122–1220b.

continued their training, becoming students at the military schools.[94] Handicapped, badly trained, and Jewish cantonists were sent home until they attained
the age of twenty; they then returned and continued their service in the regular
army.[95] This, at least, was Alexander II's new law. The reality proved more
complex.

Jews in the Pale of Settlement welcomed the emerging Russian rule of law.
They were eager for the return of their children for two years or more, and
inundated the Department of Military Schools with requests for their sons'
discharge. The sheer volume of these applications suggests that Jewish parents
requested the return of *all* cantonists, both Jews and converts, even though the
military forbade Jews to care for their baptized children.[96] Yet the authorities
spared no effort in ensuring that the Jewish cantonists remained in the military.
The parents' requests, movingly simple and clear, contained competent references to the law, but usually encountered the formal bureaucratic reply: "Your
son cannot be discharged, as no law exists for this."[97] Since the law demonstrably did exist, and complaints predictably ensued, the military quickly
redistributed the Jewish cantonists. Anxious to find some excuse for their
reluctance to uphold the letter of the law, the Department of Military Schools
assigned the Jews to artisans' units (*masterovye komandy*) and forced them to
sign labor contracts with the foremen.[98] Because artisans' apprentices were
accorded a different status, and a distinct set of laws regulated their discharge,
this tactic meant that Jewish cantonists remained subjects of a military machine
unwilling to release them.

The department's 1859 report demonstrated that the military employed the
rule of law to exclude Jews from the newly established rules, rather than to
include them. Its author, Adjutant General Sukhozanet, stated that there were

---

[94] Military schools for 10,000 pupils were established in St. Petersburg, Moscow, Pskov,
Iaroslavl, Nizhnii Novgorod, Kiev, Kazan (800 pupils in each of those), Voronezh, Chuguev
(400 pupils), Arkhangelsk, Smolensk, Voznesensk, Perm, Saratov, Simbirsk, Omsk, Tobolsk,
Irkutsk (250 pupils in each), Astrakhan, Tomsk (150 pupils in each). See "Po upravleniu
uchilishch voennogo vedomstva," *Voennyi sbornik*, no. 8 (1862), 100–105; "K istorii voenno-
uchebnoi reformy imperatora Aleksandra II," *Russkaia starina*, no. 54 (1887), 707–709.

[95] *PSZ* II, 31: 30877; this regulation was enforced in December 1856, December 1857, and
itemized in April 1858. See *PSZ* II, 31: 31313, 32572 and 33162. As a result of the reform of
the cantonist battalions, some 378,000 children were reported to be "returned to their previous
status," that is, discharged from the army. See "Obshchii obzor preobrazovanii vooruzhennykh
sil Rossii s 1856–1860 g.," *Voennyi sbornik*, no. 1 (1861): 8.

[96] The August 1856 regulation stated: "People of the Jewish creed are forbidden from petitioning
for the return of their sons or relatives who served as cantonists and adopted Christianity." See
RGVIA, f. 1, op. 1, d. 29933, l. 6. This regulation became a state law. See *PSZ* II, 31: 30877,
article 27, regulation 6. Gregory Freeze suggested, in conversation, that the desire to go home
could be one of the reasons for cantonists to reject baptism.

[97] See, e.g. RGVIA, f. 324, op. 1, d. 651, l. 2.

[98] The economic factor was certainly a consideration; the income generated by the work of some
579 apprentices who remained in the commands in 1860 yielded 9,263 rubles to the military.
On the commands of artisans, see more detail "Masterovye komandy voennogo vedomstva,"
Voennyi sbornik, no. 8 (1862): 104–105.

as many as 1,200 Jewish children serving as apprentices in the artisans' units.[99] His justification for the department's bypassing the law was particularly specious. "The Jewish cantonists," he wrote, "are recruits who were conscripted (*rekruty po naboram*). Thus, they do not fall under the law of December 25, 1856, on the dismissal of soldiers' children." Certainly, Jewish cantonists were not soldiers' children automatically co-opted into the army, but recruits. However, the no. 144 order of 1859 clarified that the military was obligated to provide junior cantonists with a ticket and to discharge them; this implied *all* cantonists, not just soldiers' children.[100] Nevertheless, Sukhozanet's argument was clear enough: the new laws had nothing to do with the Jews. Khornes Rubin, the father of cantonist Beniamin Rubin, described his son's poor health and petitioned the department to release him until he reached manhood. The military doctor conducting the examination of Jewish cantonists wrote: "Beniamin ... has a squint in the left eye, and is short and sickly. It would benefit his health to return him to his parents for the improvement of his health. If he reaches manhood (sic – *esli dostignet sovershennoletiia*), he could meet the physical requirements for the artisans' command." Local commanders decided differently: "Do not let the Jew go home; hand him over to the artisans' command; tell his parents that those under contract are not covered by the order." Iosif Brodianskii also sent a petition requesting that his son be returned to him; like many others, his plea elicited no reaction.[101] In this manner, the parents of Jewish recruits were mistaken twice: once when, in 1827, they thought their offspring were leaving Judaism forever; and again in 1859, when they expected that their sons would be returned.

When the War Ministry began introducing military reform, cantonists still continued to exist as a separate stratum.[102] On September 25, 1868, some ten years after the official closure of the cantonist institutions, the chief of His Imperial Majesty's personal escort reported to the War Ministry that the cadre of the escort was composed of cantonists, both Jews and converts. He queried whether the cantonists were to serve for twelve years after having reached the age of eighteen (as soldiers' children had), or whether they were subject to different regulations. After the dissolution of the battalions, army commanders acted at their own discretion: some returned Jewish cantonists to their parents; others registered them with the military, granting them the right to retire after twelve years, while still others enrolled them in military schools with the right to retire after six years. Dmitrii Miliutin, the new war minister, addressed a note to

---

[99] It is important to mention that this group of Jewish apprentices comprised more than half of all the cantonists who learned handicrafts in Moscow. See [Ofitsial'nyi otdel] "Masterovye komandy voennogo vedomstva," *Voennyi sbornik*, no. 8 (1862): 104–105.

[100] The law mentioned Jewish cantonists in particular as the recipients of this regulation. See *PSZ* II, 34: 34727.

[101] RGVIA, f. 324, op. 1, d. 651, ll. 8, 49–490b., 80.

[102] See, e.g., regulations concerning their status in the military in the 1860s: *PSZ* II, 42: 44470 and 44506.

the main military codification committee: "Make the service of Jewish cantonists conform to the general rules."[103]

Miliutin's note triggered a two-year discussion of legal niceties. Finally, on
September 24, 1871, the military council made a final decision, placing Jewish
cantonists on the same footing as soldier's children, and granting them equal
rights regarding army service and transfer to the reserve. The council explained
that, in view of the recent tendency of Russian legislation to equate Jews' rights
with those of other nationalities, and in view of the recognized ability of the
Jews to fulfill many noncombatant and other functions for the Military
Department, including exceptional cases when they were appointed to high
posts, it had been decided to acknowledge their rights. Thus, they were permitted to rise to officer or civilian rank and, in general, to foster their further
career development. The council also stated that the issue of upward mobility
was of special importance and should be discussed separately.[104] In 1871, the
military legally acknowledged what already had become evident when the first
cantonists graduated from the battalions: that a Jewish cantonist, despite the
restrictive laws and orders imposed upon him, was equal in terms of army
service to his Christian peer.[105]

Conclusion

With the exception of the Ottoman Empire, which recruited fifteen-year old
peasant children, and Russia, which conscripted soldiers' children, there was no
army in nineteenth-century Europe that drafted minors. Neither Nicholas nor
his military administration intended to flood the cantonist battalions with
Jewish children. The number of teenagers selected by the Jewish communities
and sent to the army – sometimes 50 percent of the levy – took the Russian
military by surprise. The commanders read the prescription to train Jews in the
battalions on a par with the Christians as the order to assimilate Jewish children
with the rest of the cantonists.

Initially Jewish minors were less fit for service than their Russian Orthodox
peers, who spoke Russian and grew in a rural environment. The Jewish children
spoke Yiddish and were raised in small towns; however, they demonstrated an
amazing adaptability. By the end of their term in the battalions they scored
grades similar to those of their Christian peers. Jewish cantonists performed
decently in training and drills, they acquired useful skills as artisans, and
compared with their Christian peers demonstrated higher results in discipline
and hygiene. When the commanders transferred them to the regiments, they
were robust, well-trained, cunning, and tough Russian soldiers of Jewish
creed, no longer sickly Jewish minors in ill-fitting trench coats. Their ability to
resist or reject enforced Christianization proved their strong Russian Jewish

---

[103] RGVIA, f. 1, op. 1, d. 27547, ll. 1–2; RGVIA, f. 1, op. 1, d. 29933, l. 20.
[104] RGVIA, f. 1, op. 1, d. 29708, l. 24.
[105] *Sobranie uzakonenii i rasporiazhenii Pravitel'stva za 1871 god*, nos. 792 and 1119.

self-identification, their resolve and stamina, their belief in the ultimate justice of the Russian authorities, and their attachment to their Judaic origins.

The missionary campaign in the army, going bottom to top, involved children of other creeds, encountered various difficulties, and was also highly uneven. It could not change the successful integrationist outcome of the conscription of Jewish children. Nicholas I's mission to Christianize the Jewish cantonists seems to have been a clumsy and unnecessary move to expedite the integration of Jewish minors and make them useful servants of His Majesty. It brought more consternation, pain, and trauma than positive results. Furthermore, the missionary efforts did not change the fate of the New Christians, baptized or not, for Jewish children served on a par with their Russian Orthodox peers and continued to serve in the same regiments. Privileges acquired by the converts from Judaism were hardly palpable. Eventually even the military recognized that the missionary campaign was unnecessary and that the cantonist institutions on their own were a sufficient tool to turn Jewish children into worthy Russian soldiers. While the military abolished the cantonist schools and continued to elaborate a major reform of the army, thousands of anonymous Jewish cantonists had become an important lever in the on-going debate on Jewish equality. The question now was how to Judaize the military reform, extending to Jews not only their equal duties before the state but also equal rights and privileges in the army.

4

Universal Draft and the Singular Jews

Although the War Ministry helped accelerate the state's reform, it was slow to redesign the army. It took Alexander II half a year to release the surviving Decembrists, six years to emancipate the peasantry, nine to modify the court system and to introduce a jury, fifteen to establish self-governing urban institutions, and nearly twenty years finally to reform the military. This restructuring began long before the 1874 introduction of the law on universal liability to conscription. From the early 1860s, War Minister Dmitrii Miliutin engineered reforms to enhance the army's professionalism, to recast its cumbersome organizational structure, and to improve the disbursement of arms and supplies to the troops.[1] Immediately after the suppression of the Polish uprising of 1863–1864, Miliutin started to implement his long-cherished plan: to reduce the number of troops and to create strategic reserves. He calculated that this would achieve two goals: decrease individual lengths of service, and enable rapid army expansion in time of mobilization. Critically analyzing the Russian army's tactics in the Crimean War, he proposed replacing the bulky military corps with a more mobile system of military districts. From the mid-1860s – and with particular intensity after the 1870–1871 Franco-Prussian War – the imperial administration agreed to a gradual transformation of the army.[2]

[1] See Beyrau, *Militär und Gesellschaft*, 254–276; Menning, *Bayonets before Bullets*, 11–21; Miller, *Dmitrii Miliutin*, 67–87; Zaionchkovskii, *Voennye reformy*, 68–135. Modern studies of Miliutin's reforms present variations on the first fundamental article on this theme, published anonymously and approved by Miliutin. See Anon., "Dmitrii Alekseevich Miliutin vo vremia upravleniia ego voennym ministerstvom, 1861–1881 gg.," *Russkaia starina*, no. 49 (1886): 240–256. An American-based Russian military historian suggested an innovative interpretation of Miliutin's plans, arguing that Miliutin's "overriding ambition was to build an imperial army that resembled a national army"; see Robert F. Baumann, "Universal Service Reform: Conception to Implementation, 1873–1883," in David Schimmelpenninck van der Oye and Bruce Menning, eds., *Reforming the Tsar's Army: Military Innovation in Imperial Russian from Peter the Great to the Revolution* (Washington, D.C., and Cambridge: Woodrow Wilson Center and Cambridge University Press, 2004), 11–33, here 13.

[2] In a sense, Miliutin continued implementing the military reforms designed by Nicholas I, albeit more effectively and consistently. See Geyer, *Russian Imperialism*, 19–21; Kipp, "Grand Duke

After the 1861 abolition of serfdom, views of the soldier's function altered considerably. The army needed a soldier able to fight. The Crimean catastrophe had demonstrated the advantage of troop mobility and of local control. Additionally, Miliutin emphasized the supreme importance of literacy, especially in the lower ranks, in order to foster a thinking soldier. He also planned to improve the very poor professional training of the soldiers. He ordered that the construction of barracks be expedited; in early 1860, almost half the army still resided in temporary quarters.[3] The war minister replaced the commissariat and the provision departments with a quartermaster bureau, significantly diminishing the potential for embezzlement and corruption among the top military administration.[4] On his initiative, the army ended the humiliating practice of shaving the heads of recruits (*brit' lob*) and then marching them off to the regiments as if they were prisoners. The military eventually acquired the view that the army was not a penal institution to which delinquents were banished. Ultimately, the War Ministry emerged as one of the key catalysts of Alexander II's glasnost; the monthly *Voennyi sbornik* offered up the most sensitive military and social issues for professional discussion, while the daily War Ministry newspaper *Russkii invalid* became, under Miliutin's direction, the pan-Russian herald of progress and reform.[5] All of these changes furnished the foundation for Miliutin's major proposal: universal liability to military service (*vsesoslovnaia voinskaia povinnost'*). This order was proclaimed in the new 1874 statute on military duty. A modern army required new relationships between the military and society at large. The idea was to place all social, ethnic, and religious strata of Russian society on equal footing, all engaged in the sacred duty of defending the empire. Thus, Miliutin adopted one of Alexander II's chief reforms, perhaps more ambitious than his transformation of the peasantry. The question is whether Miliutin's modernization plan accorded Jews the same treatment as it did other ethnic groups.

Equal but Different

To craft the 1874 statute, the War Ministry established a Special Commission on the Improvement of Military Service in the Russian Empire and the Polish Kingdom. Doctor of Philosophy Iosif Zeiberling, Professor Daniil Khvolson (Chwolson) and Baron Goratsii Gintsburg (Horace Guenzburg), all experts on the Jewish question and de facto representatives of Jewish communal interests,

---

Konstantin Nikolaevich," 232–239; Menning, *Bayonets before Bullets*, 30–33; Zaionchkovskii, *Voennye reformy*, 136–180.

[3] For petitions of the top military command regarding the regimental barracks, see RGVIA, f. 970, op. 1, d. 975, l. 232–232ob.

[4] Beyrau, *Militär und Gesellschaft*, 310–313; Keep, *Soldiers of the Tsar*, 355; Miller, *Dmitrii Miliutin*, 54–57.

[5] For a systematic in-depth analysis of the role of *Russkii invalid* in Miliutin's reformist program, see E. Willis Brooks, "The Russian Military Press in the Reform Era," in Schimmelpenninck van der Oye and Menning, eds., *Reforming the Tsar's Army*, 107–135.

joined the commission and were granted voting privileges.[6] The meetings swiftly devolved into heated debates over Russian modernization. Conservative, aristocratic members asserted that Russian society was not prepared for universal liability to military service; nor were the state's Jews. The liberal, democratic camp believed the opposite. Within governmental circles, this conflict flared into open animosity between the pro-reform War Ministry and the more conservative Ministry of the Interior: or, to be more exact, between War Minister Dmitrii Miliutin on the one hand, and Minister of the Interior Alexander Timashev and the chief of the gendarmes, Count Petr Shuvalov, on the other.[7] Indeed, the divide was manifest throughout Russian society. Some members of the Special Commission advocated complete legal parity for Jews, especially regarding call-up and service. Others deemed it impossible to grant Jews equal rights, either in the draft or in the service, unless the imperial administration reached a decision with respect to Jewish civic status.

The army became the first Russian state institution to decide in favor of Jewish emancipation. The commission had been considering whether to promote Jews to the rank of officer, a question that engendered frenzied arguments.[8] Earlier, the Jewish Committee, a remnant of Nicholas I's reign, had attempted to convince Alexander II to grant lower-ranking Jewish soldiers certain service benefits, such as promotion. In 1858, the Jewish Committee submitted to the emperor's chancellery detailed information about the number of Jewish officers in the French army, hoping that the French model for military reform would result in the introduction of equal rights for Russian Jews. Alexander agreed to allow Jews to become noncommissioned officers, but his administration resolutely resisted extending this parity to officer's rank. An officer's career might conceivably be rewarded by having nobility conferred upon him; why ennoble members of a potentially dangerous ethnic group that did not enjoy civil equality? However, the members of the Special Commission thought differently: if conscription was universal, the privileges granted to those in active service should also be universal. The commission members conceded that Jews with a higher education could, in certain circumstances, obtain an officer's rank. The liberal members of the commission prevailed, garnering twenty-five votes on the issue. From then on, Jews in the army had legal

---

[6] John Klier mentioned Iakov Brafman among the members of the commission, but I did not find any confirmation of this. See Klier, *Imperial Russia's Jewish Question*, 335. Cf. Zaionchkovskii, *Voennye reformy*, 307–308.

[7] The conflict between the War Ministry and the Ministry of the Interior remained a characteristic feature of Russia's officialdom. The temporary 1868 victory of Shuvalov over Miliutin marked the end of the daily newspaper *Russkii invalid* as a mouthpiece of the War Ministry's political liberalism; from then on, the newspaper functioned only as a professional military publication. Miliutin's victory in 1874, however, resulted in the honorary exile of Shuvalov to an ambassadorial position in London. See Richard G. Weeks, "Peter Andreevich Shuvalov: Russian Statesman," (Ph.D. diss., University of Minnesota, 1977), 66, 88–91.

[8] For more detail, see Klier, *Imperial Russia's Jewish Question*, 336–337; Miller, *Dmitrii Miliutin*, 220–221; Zaionchkovskii, *Voennye reformy*, 309.

equality, as was the case in France, Italy, and Austria, although not in Prussia. According to the new law, Jews could volunteer, pass officer's examinations, and join military schools to train for a professional army career. Certainly it appeared as though this aspect of Alexander II's Great Reforms had been realized, so that the army truly embodied Jewish emancipation.

Nevertheless, the Ministry of the Interior considered call-up its own prerogative rather than the army's, and subscribed to a very different opinion of Jewish soldiers. The ministry believed that Jews did their utmost to evade the draft and that their military performance was inferior to that of their peers. Moreover, they held that Jews were selfish, cunning, and deceitful. They proposed a number of restrictive amendments to address this troublesome group. Eleven commission members, representing a minority, voted against these amendments as contradicting the reformist spirit of the universal service statute. In the final ballot, as John Klier has described, the vote cast by Count Geiden, the commission's chairman, was decisive; Geiden firmly opposed Jewish equality, whether in pubic life or in the army. Consequently, the commission adopted measures singling out Jews. Miliutin did not interfere with this decision. His position on ethnic minorities in the army, and on Russian policy regarding them as a whole (especially Poles and Baltic Germans), testifies to the limits of his liberalism. His attitude toward Jews reveals him to be a military technocrat, a moderate reformer, and a conservative with respect to ethnic issues.[9] In his continual disputes with the Ministry of the Interior, he managed to enact those reforms he considered crucial, but he conceded on less important issues, including those touching upon Jewish equality. By the end of his ministerial term, Miliutin's position was decidedly ambiguous: while he believed in Jewish equality in principle, his secret orders concerning Jews in military service anticipated the notorious circulars of his successor, Petr Vannovskii.[10] This inconsistency afforded Miliutin's opponents significant leverage. Now the Ministry of the Interior could monitor the Jewish draft independently of that of other ethnic minorities and could present the data to argue its case to the excessively liberal War Ministry.

Published on January 1, 1874, the statute made the vast majority of the country's male population liable to military service. Soldiers served six years in

[9] Miliutin and his supporters held a moderate centrist position that seems liberal only vis-à-vis the opponents of Alexander's reforms, such as the ultraconservative General Fadeev and Prince Bariatinskii. For more detail, see Beyrau, *Militär und Gesellschaft*, 279–284; Bruce Lincoln, *The Great Reforms*, 155–156; Menning, *Bayonets before Bullets*, 50, 96; Miller, *Miliutin*, 201–206, 229–230; Zaionchkovskii, *Voennye reformy*, 289–293.

[10] For example, in April 1880, the commanders of the Warsaw military district asked Miliutin for his opinion of Jewish medical interns serving in fortresses. Miliutin answered, "It is desirable not to post Jewish doctors in fortresses; but it is necessary to inform the appropriate commanders in strict confidence and not to make announcements." See RGVIA, f. 400, op. 5, d. 479, ll. 1–3. For a brief critical analysis of the inconsistencies in Miliutin's segregationist stance on ethnic minority issues in the army and especially in the officer corps, see Baumann, "Universal Service Reform," 23–24.

the standing army and nine in the reserves, except in Siberia, where seven years were required in active service and three in the reserves. The statute established three preferential categories (i.e., exemptions) for sons who were their families' breadwinners. University, grammar school, and high school graduates served from six months to eighteen months. Ordained priests of all Christian faiths received exemptions, but rabbis and imams did not. Mennonites, Czech settlers, railway officers, guild industrialists, and merchants also were exempt. The statute permitted Jewish volunteers (*vol'noopredeliaiushchiesia*) to pass examinations for the officers' ranks, but members of the Jewish lower ranks were not given promotions either to officers' ranks or to noncommissioned officers' ranks. The new statute preserved elements of Nicholas's 1827 regulations, basing the draft upon the recruit's place of registration rather than of his residence. Considering the mobility of the Jewish population, this stipulation created insurmountable problems.[11] Tens of thousands of migrants, mostly Jews, who had moved from Lithuania to the Polish Kingdom or to the southeastern provinces in the 1860s–1880s to escape the famine and to find work were the first to run afoul of this requirement. Moreover, Jews were regarded as a separate group; whereas priests or imams provided birth records to the draft centers, the clerks at the Ministry of the Interior did not trust the rabbis to do so, and so compiled their own lists of Jewish recruits. Unfamiliar with Jewish nomenclature, the clerks considered Moshka, Moyshe, and Moisei, a single individual variously listed in different places, as three separate people; similarly, Yitshak Ayzik was understood to be either Yitshak or Ayzik, each of whom had to serve. If a Menahem Nahum died and the books registered the deceased as Nahum, Menahem nonetheless had to present himself before the draft commission. As a result of such basic administrative errors, an extraordinary number of Jews already in active service, still residing in the Pale, or deceased were listed as draft dodgers.

The imperial administration included in the statute other amendments that served to undermine its universal intent. Another 1874 order of the Ministry of the Interior allowed newly accepted draftees a temporary discharge, after which they traveled to their military district centers on their own; but this provision was not available to Jewish recruits.[12] While Christian and Muslim novices traveled independently to their regiments, the military moved the allegedly treacherous Jews collectively to their destinations. To combat the purported draft dodging by Jews, a supplement to the statute ordered a special census of the entire Jewish male population. Four months after the statute's publication, all Jews, regardless of their social status or personal reputations, were prohibited from serving on the draft committees. While the law indicated that Jews served equally with everyone else, their experience of the draft was different.[13]

---

[11] *Ustav o voinskoi povinnosti*, 28 (paragraph 17), 51 (paragraph 56), 54 (paragraph 62), 93 (paragraph 106), 236 (amendment 9, paragraph 1).

[12] *Ustav o voinskoi povinnosti*, 122 (paragraph 155, reference).

[13] The Senate and the War Ministry granted the draft commissions "the unrestricted right" to question the authenticity of documents concerning Jewish marital status. *Rasporiazheniia*

Thus, one of the most liberal documents of Russian modernization, the Statute on Universal Liability to Military Service, created a legislative basis for subsequent restrictive anti-Jewish regulations.

The external pressure and the court intrigues of the Ministry of the Interior after the statute's publication impelled the War Ministry to further circumscribe the magnitude of the reforms. The War Ministry issued a special order restricting to 3 percent the number of Jewish volunteers permitted to apply for promotion to officer rank. The following year, it barred Jews entirely from enrolling in military schools.[14] Consequently, between 1874 and 1917, a total of 9 Jews gained promotion to army officer rank.[15] Only one, Gertzel Tsam, became an officer in recognition of his personal qualities.

The fact that Tsam was the sole exception demonstrates the contradiction between the army's universal principles and its implementation of them; in practice, Jews were excluded from the higher ranks. Born around 1844, Gertsel Iankelevich Tsam (who signed the 1907 soldiers' synagogue record book as Tsvi-Herts ben Yehuda Yankev Tsam) lived with his widowed mother and his four brothers in Gorengrod, a small shtetl near Rovno. In the autumn of 1852, when he was eight or nine years old, he was seized by two army "catchers" from the nearby Olyka *kahal* and brought to the conscription point in Rovno. From there, he was dispatched to Zhitomir and then to Tomsk, in Siberia. Along with 200 other Jewish boys, he served in the cantonist battalion under the auspices of an intimidating senior Jewish cantonist named Shulman. Despite pressure from an Orthodox priest that resulted in the conversion of roughly half of the Jewish cantonists, Tsam retained his faith. He joined the regular troops in 1858, by which time he was so weak that he could barely hold a rifle. Consequently, in violation of existing prohibitions, he was promoted to the position of battalion scribe. In 1870, he passed an exam qualifying him as a low-ranking military clerk.

Pravitel'stvuiushchego Senata, no. 1398, February 18, 1893. The decision casting doubts on Jewish integrity and patriotism led to the description of the 1874 statute as a "fatal crisis" in the history of the relationship between the Jews and the Russian army. See *Voina i evrei*, 40.

[14] David Raskin, "Evrei v sostave rossiiskogo ofitserskogo korpusa v XIX-nachale XX veka," in D. Eliashevich, ed., *Evrei v Rossii: Istoriia i kultura. Sbornik nauchnykh trudov* (SPb.: Peterburgskii evreiskii universitet, 1998), 171.

[15] This number does not include Jewish doctors who obtained officer's shoulder-straps for service excellence, but who were regarded as civil rather than military clerks and so never were considered as army officers. In archival photographs, they may appear as Russian Jewish army officers. See, e.g., the case of Grigorii Goldberg (b. 1853), a Jew who, in 1894, served in the Second Rostov grenadier regiment as a junior doctor, received three high distinctions (St. Stanislav orders of second and third rank and a St. Anna Order) and a bronze medal. According to the table of ranks, he served as a court counselor (*nadvornyi sovetnik*) and wore a civil clerk's uniform, but had no military rank (private archive of the author, courtesy Professor Michael Buckland, Berkeley).

ILLUSTRATION 2. Gertsel Iankelevich Tsam, a former kidnapped Jew, a cantonist in Omsk battalion, the only Jewish combat officer in the Russian army, promoted to captain after retirement; ca. 1900. From the archives of the YIVO Institute, the papers of Saul Ginsberg Collection, RG 1121.

After the 1874 introduction of universal military service, Tsam applied for promotion to the officers' ranks. However, the Omsk district commander rejected his application, asserting that Jews who remained Jewish were not eligible to become officers. Tsam's wife responded by filing a formal complaint with Miliutin. The war minister ruled that if Tsam could pass the required exams and if his commanders found his ethical qualities satisfactory, his appeal would be considered by the tsar himself. Tsam obtained very high scores and again applied for promotion. After due consideration, the Main Staff grudgingly granted him the lowest officer's rank of ensign, stipulating that all the officers in the Tomsk battalion must agree to accept him as their fellow-in-arms. To the Main Staff's astonishment, General Narskii and the district officers agreed unanimously. Thus Tsam obtained his first officer's shoulder-straps. By his own admission, nobody in the officers' corps mistreated him because he was a Jew. Quite the contrary: his district commander repeatedly promoted him. Tsam had acquired the rank of staff captain when War Minister Vannovskii ordered him transferred, in order to test his skills as a line battalion commander. Tsam assumed the command of a low-ranking unit, retrained it and attained excellent results. His immediate commanders supported his application for the post of a captain, but the Main Staff did not deign to reply to his repeated requests; Tsam never was officially appointed a battalion commander. Retiring in 1893, after thirty-five years of service, he was accorded the rank of retired captain only ten years later.[16]

Unlike Tsam, the other eight Jews, sons of the most prominent Jewish bankers, obtained the rank because of their family status. Alfred and Aleksandr Gintsburg, the sons of Baron Gintsburg, enlisted as reserve second lieutenants in the Seventeenth Volhynia dragoon regiment. Certainly, neither son intended to devote himself to military service. However, the war minister and the tsar personally decided upon these promotions, while at the same time determining that they should not create a precedent. The decision against promoting Jews to officers' ranks was made in the wake of a xenophobic campaign against all lower ranks of non-Russian-Orthodox soldiers. On November 16, 1892, Circular Letter no. 49761 forbade the representatives of "harmful sects," such as the Molokans, the Dukhobory, the Iconoclasts, the 'Judaizers,' the Skoptsy, etcetera, to be granted the rank of corporal or to serve in a training capacity. On February 21, 1897, Vannovskii, in Circular Letter no. 1782, ordered that all Dukhobory and other sectarians be sent to Yakutia for their entire terms of service. On June 22, 1906, the Main Staff's Circular Letter no. 42761 stipulated that all possible measures be taken to protect the troops from the influx of males of "alien creed."[17]

Draft Dodging: A Russian Jewish Crime

The orders limiting Jewish access to military schools should be understood in the context of a major campaign to combat Jewish draft evasion. As a result of Alexander's reforms, previously unavailable military data could now be misinterpreted at will and used as a tool against the Jews. The Ministry of the Interior exploited the accusation of Jewish draft dodging contained in the statute as a springboard for its counterreform political campaign. While pursuing a broad conservative agenda, it employed erroneous conscription data to argue that Jewish emancipation was out of the question. The evasion of the draft, claimed the ministry's spokesmen, demonstrated that Jews did not possess the same integrity, patriotism, and sense of duty as did other Russians. Calculating Jewish draft dodging served the agendas of various groups across the political spectrum.

The Ministry of the Interior furnished impressive statistics, claiming that, in 1875, the Russian Orthodox population was obliged to compensate for a deficit of 4,000 recruits because of Jewish noncompliance. Jews provided 64 draftees fewer than anticipated in Podol province, 320 fewer in Bessarabiia, 247 fewer in Volhynia, 178 fewer in Kiev, 169 fewer in Kovno (Kowno), and 151 fewer in

[16] *Voina i evrei*, no. 7 (1915): 8–11.
[17] See RGVIA, f. 400, op. 5, d. 1153, ll. 1–2, 5, 155–156.

Suvalki (Suwałki). The Ministry of the Interior cited both physical incapacity and draft evasion as reasons for the shortage, and blamed doctors for disqualifying too many Jewish recruits.[18] It explained the rate of absenteeism (especially in the province of Mogilev, where 17 percent had evaded the draft by improperly registering) by arguing that the crafty Jews had registered in military districts outside their places of residence or in districts where army selections already had taken place. Others, most likely Hasidim, escaped to Austria and the Kingdom of Poland.[19] "We noticed ubiquitous draft dodging among members of this nationality right at the outset of the call-up," asserted the report, which was filed by staunch opponents of Miliutin.[20] In response, Miliutin ordered an immediate search for Jewish deserters, and even called for a special commission on draft evasion. However, since Jews were not the only alleged dodgers, he did not implement any radical measures.[21] Perhaps because draft evasion declined, by 1876 accounting for the loss of only 1,918 recruits, which represented a decrease of slightly more than 50 percent, he did not accede to the Ministry of the Interior's calls for action.

Meanwhile, the police continued to accuse the military of laxity in its treatment of Jews and to bombard Miliutin with new data. The Ministry of the Interior's assessments now mentioned proportions rather than figures, arguing that the conscription shortfall among the Jewish population was as high as 49 percent in Russia and 47 percent in the Polish Kingdom. The Balkan war succeeded in arousing Jewish patriotism, so that, in 1878, the draft shortage in Russia and in the Polish Kingdom fell to 33 percent and 30 percent, respectively. Apparently the situation gradually improved, according to the Ministry of the Interior; in 1880, some 9,268 Jews appeared before the draft commissions after the call-up, resulting in a shortage of only 2,983 men, representing 24 percent. More detailed figures appeared to corroborate the general ones: in Minsk province, the draft shortage in 1876 was 16.5 percent; in 1877, 27 percent; and in 1878, only 4 percent.[22] Confronted with these figures,

---

[18] On December 4, 1877, the Ministry of the Interior reported to Count Geiden that, in the Tomashov (Tomaszów) military district of Lublin province, not a single Jew was recognized as fit for military service, and that the doctors' unreasonably high standards for recruits' physical fitness were responsible for the draft shortage. See RGVIA, f. 400, op. 14, otd. 5, st. 1, d. 15147, l. 79.

[19] According to reports, in the border shtetls of Gusiatin and Sandomir (Sandomierz), about a thousand young Jews of draft age were half-starving and were subject to the influence of "inured, fanatical old men" (most likely *tsadikim*) who were hindering any attempt to dispatch them to military service.

[20] RGVIA, f. 400, op. 14, otd. 5, st. 1, d. 15147, l. 20b., 30b., 4–40b., 9.

[21] The fear of compulsory military duty and attempts at draft dodging, including the maiming of children, were not peculiar to Russian Jews. On the contrary, Jews lagged in this respect behind other ethnic groups, including Russians. In prereform Russia, local authorities reported that, upon hearing news of a call-up for military duty, entire village populations ran away; those who did not manage to hide deserted their troops at the first available opportunity. See RGVIA, f. 481, d. 18027, l. 11.

[22] See RGVIA, f. 400, op. 14, otd. 5, st. 1, d. 15147.

Miliutin finally charged the specially organized Commission on Jewish Draft Evasion with elaborating stringent measures against dodgers. This was another victory for the xenophobic Ministry of the Interior over the liberal-minded military. The commission assembled on September 22, 1879, to consider how to "explore measures to enforce strict Jewish compliance with the draft procedure." Its members included the deputy minister of the interior, a ministry office clerk, the manager of the Zemstvo Committee (a department of the Ministry of the Interior) and only two professionals from other governmental offices: the director of the Central Statistical Department, and the aide to the chief of the Main Staff. Never questioning the data collection techniques or the figures obtained, this commission began with the premise that Jews evaded the draft more than any other group, and submitted several proposals to resolve the problem. Upon reaching the age of seventeen, each Jewish male would receive a registration certificate from the municipality. Every Jew was required to complete his military duty in the same locality as the conscription center at which he was registered, rather than in the one nearest his place of residence. (This innovation was likely to cause even larger draft losses.) The commission also threatened to extend the draft age of Jews up to twenty-eight, and to suspend Jewish eligibility for the officers' ranks.[23]

The governors general of the western provinces called for still harsher measures. The Suvalki governor suggested limiting the right of Jewish movement within the Pale, while Bessarabiia, Vitebsk and Grodno provinces' governors wished to make Jewish communities collectively responsible for any evasions of the draft. The Ministry of the Interior approved most of the commission's recommendations and circulated them to the provinces. Accordingly, in late 1880 and early 1881, the procedure for issuing registration certificates became increasingly complex. The certificates now had to include detailed physical descriptions of Jewish registrants, including hair and eye color, and birthmarks. In addition, the ministry encouraged the reexamination of handicapped Jews, while local police were to award fifty rubles to anyone who captured a Jew hiding or attempting to avoid enlistment. Draft dodgers were fined 500 rubles, an exorbitant sum. Draft centers were instructed to enroll not only those fit for service, but also those Jews whose chests technically were too small to allow them to pass the medical examination. In 1881, after receiving reports from the provincial commanders of Kurland, Tomsk, and Warsaw provinces, the commission added new limitations, forbidding Jews to transfer from one draft district to another. The commission revoked the Jews' right to replace conscripts with their brothers, removed the exemption for guardianship of disabled parents, and effectively eliminated the physical requirements for Jewish recruits.[24]

---

[23] RGVIA, f. 400, op. 14, otd. 5, st. 1, d. 15703, ll. 198–201, 288.
[24] RGVIA, f. 400, op. 14, otd. 5, st. 1, d. 15147, ll. 199–201, 374, 386, 388.

Jewish Response to Universal Military Duty

Although internal military reports present a confusing picture of the Jewish draft, the available data sheds considerable light on Jewish responses to the reformed army. Draft districts reported the number of Jews (and only Jews; all other ethnic groups were ignored) registered for the draft, the number selected by lot, the number who reported for duty, and, lastly, the ratio of those who reported for duty to the number on the draft rolls. That is, the draft reports consistently compared the entire draft pool with the number drafted, rather than the number drafted with the number of those selected by lottery. The accusations that Jews consistently evaded the draft had so convinced the military statisticians that they persevered in this error. An examination of the ratio of non-Jewish conscripts who arrived at the draft offices to their numbers in the books should have sufficed to contextualize Jewish draft dodging (by no means a nonexistent phenomenon). Had the percentage of Jews in a particular province or military district been contrasted with the percentage of those who reported to the draft offices, the conclusions drawn about Jewish participation in the draft would have been different.

The results of the 1882 draft in Volhynia province are instructive (Table 7). Zhitomir had 928 Jews on the draft roll, 137 of whom were selected by lottery. A total of 145 men appeared at the call-up: that is to say, 106 percent of the selected number. Yet the military diligently compared those at the call-up with

TABLE 7. *Data on Jewish Recruits from Volhynia Province in 1882*

Localities	Registered	Selected by Lottery	Responded to the Call	% of the Registered	% of the Selected*
Zhitomir	928	137	145	15.63	105.8*
Novograd-Vol.	747	135	135	18.08	100*
Zaslav	495	108	108	21.82	100*
Ostrog	407	76	76	18.67	100*
Rovno	627	124	127	22.55	102.4*
Ovruch	494	86	86	17.41	100*
Luck	505	98	98	19.41	100*
Vladimir-Vol.	624	99	99	15.86	100*
Kovel	581	68	67	11.53	99*
S.-Konstantinov	436	92	91	20.88	99*
Dubna	378	57	83	21.09	145.6*
Kremenets	510	69	69	13.53	100*
TOTAL*	6,732*	1,149*	1,184*	17.59*	103*

Note: *My calculations: figures do not appear in the War Ministry reports.

Source: RGVIA, f. 400, op. 5, d. 957, ll. 4–5. Hereafter I retain discrepancies and inconsistencies in the numbers provided by the Ministry of the Interior and the War Ministry.

TABLE 8. *Data on Jewish Recruits from Podol Province in 1882*

Localities	Registered	Selected by Lottery	Responded to the Call	% of the Registered	% of the Selected*
Kamenets	528	116	115	21.78	99.1*
Proskurov	487	91	91	18.68	100*
Letichev	401	85	85	21.19	100*
Litin	431	68	68	15.78	100*
Vinnitsa	483	57	57	11.80	100*
Braslav	557	97	97	17.43	100*
Gaisin	597	87	86	14.41	98.8*
Olgopol	682	114	114	16.72	100*
Balta	862	182	182	21.11	100*
Iampol	554	70	69	12.45	98.5*
Mogilev	513	62	62	12.09	100*
Novo-Uglitsk	482	66	66	13.69	100*
TOTAL*	6,577*	979*	977*	14.85*	99.8*

Note: *My calculations: figures do not appear in the War Ministry reports.
Source: RGVIA, f. 400, op. 5, d. 957, ll. 8–9.

those registered and inscribed, resulting in a figure of 16 percent who responded. Novograd-Volynsk had 747 Jews; the lottery selected 135 of them for military duty. Although the entire 135 appeared at the draft office, the military recorded a different figure: 18 percent, the remaining 82 percent being draft dodgers. There were 378 Jews fit for service in the books of Dubna's Jewish community; the 1882 lottery selected 57 of them, but 83 arrived at the draft center, that is, 146 percent of those obliged to present themselves. In Volhynia province, two towns, Staro-Konstantinov and Kovel, gave 99 percent, while the other Jewish communities contributed 100 percent, with 1,184 draftees in total, or 104 percent of those selected. In Podol province, 979 were selected, and 977 presented themselves. The aggregate data for the 1882 draft in the three provinces of Volhynia, Podol, and Kiev yielded the same results: 20,844 Jews were on the books; of those, 3,138 were selected by lot, and 3,194 were drafted; there were 3,237 in all, including substitutes (for Volhynia, see Table 8; for Kiev, see Table 9). Excluding substitutes, Jews provided the army with 102 percent of the required recruits. The 1888 conscription drive was similar. In Kherson, Bessarabia, Vitebsk, Mogilev, and Minsk provinces, there were 21,271 Jews on the registration rolls. The lottery selected 3,174 of them for the service, of whom 2,982 appeared, providing 94 percent of the required recruits (Table 10).[25] This 6 percent deficit is hardly the 20, 30, or even 80 percent posited by the Ministry

[25] RGVIA, f. 400, op. 5, d. 957, ll. 4–5, 8–9, 11–12.

TABLE 9. *Data on Jewish Recruits from Kiev Province in 1882*

Localities	Registered	Selected by Lottery	Responded to the Call	% of the Registered	% of the Selected*
Kiev	804	80	78	9.7	97.5*
Radomysl	705	101	107	15.18	105.9*
Berdichev	532	113	113	21.5	100*
Lipovets	489	85	85	17.38	100*
Uman	757	105	104	13.74	99*
Zvenigorod	626	78	77	12.31	99*
Cherkassy	651	87	86	13.21	98.8*
Chigirin	550	72	88	16	122.2*
Kanev	602	65	64	10.33	98.4*
Tarashcha	563	68	68	12.07	100*
Skvira	566	60	67	11.83	111.6*
Vasilkov	690	96	96	13.91	100*
TOTAL*	7,535*	1,010*	1,033*	13.7*	102.2*

Note: *My calculations: figures do not appear in the War Ministry reports.
Source: RGVIA, f. 400, op. 5, d. 957, ll. 4–5.

TABLE 10. *Comparative 1888 Data on Jewish Recruits from Five Provinces in the Jewish Pale*

Provinces	Registered	Selected by Lottery	Responded to the Call	% of the Registered	% of the Selected*
Kherson	4919	502	506	10.29	100.8*
Bessarabiia	3674	370	365	9.93	98.6*
Minsk	5455	1133	939	18.21	87.6*
Mogilev	4097	752	760	18.55	101.06*
Vitebsk	3576	417	358	10.01	75.9*
TOTAL*	21,721*	3,174*	2,982*	13.7	93.9*

Note: *My calculations: figures do not appear in the War Ministry reports.
Source: RGVIA, f. 400, op. 5 , d. 957 , ll. 11–12.

of the Interior. The relevant figures support the view of Jews as a compliant ethnic minority.[26]

Furthermore, Jews were overrepresented in the army as urban dwellers. The urban population in the empire contributed approximately 10 percent of the

---

[26] According to internal military statistics, Romanians, Lithuanians, and Poles were the principal draft dodgers, while, from a geographical point of view, Moscow and Petersburg provinces held the lead. Thus, Jews did not constitute the majority of offenders from an ethnic or geographical viewpoint. See Zolotarev, "Materialy," *Voennyi sbornik*, no. 5 (1889): 139–140.

TABLE II. *Ratio of Drafted Jews to the Drafted Urban Population of the Empire, 1903–1908*

Years	Total Call up	Number of Urban Dwellers among the Draftees	% of the Total Number of the Draft	Jews	% of Jews among the Selected Urban Residents
1903	314,796	34,358	10.9	17,849	52.0
1904	– *	–	–	–	–
1905	443,969	44,035	9.9	16,721	38.0
1906	445,455	48,175	10.8	18,966	39.4
1907	440,542	45,270	10.3	17,828	39.4
1908	– *	45,882	–	18,108	39.2

Note: *Data missing.
Source: *Voina i evrei*, 244.

draftees, about 45,000 of the 450,000.[27] Unruly urban dwellers were more likely to dodge the draft than were the peasants. Jews, essentially an urban population, constituted about 40 percent of those 45,000; thus, in absolute figures, they were four times more active in the draft than was the entire Russian urban population (Table 11).

Local military commanders who interacted directly with Jews confirmed that the latter sent their required quota of recruits. In fact, on December 10, 1885, the head of the Kharkov military district responded to the War Ministry's query about Jews in the infantry regiments of the Ninth and Tenth army corps by complaining that there were "too many Jews in the troops." He provided the following data: in the Fifth division of the military district, 10 percent of the soldiers were Jewish; in the Ninth division, 12 percent; in the Thirty-first division 11 percent; and in the Thirty-sixth division, 10 percent. After soldiers from the 1881 and part of the 1882 drafts were dispatched to the reserves, he remarked, the number of Jewish soldiers "became even greater." In the Kozlov infantry regiment, with 1,479 enlisted men, there were 267 Jews, 18 percent of the cadre. The commander of the military district requested that the Main Staff take drastic measures: "Due to the great percentage of Jews amongst the enlisted personnel in the military district infantry units under my command, I find it necessary to ask you to consider whether it is possible to reduce the number of Jews directed to my district when distributing new recruits?" The Main Staff ignored this request, on the theory that the percentage of Jews in the military must be insufficient. On May 4, 1886, the commander of the Kharkov military district received a formal reply: "Owing to the recently adopted severe governmental measures to prevent draft dodging among the

[27] *Voina i evrei*, 244.

Jews, it is impossible to expect in the future any reduction in the number of Jewish recruits subject to the draft; consequently, in the army, the Jews will inevitably always be present in a more or less significant percentage."[28]

For the imperial officials, the alleged Jewish underrepresentation in the army was an indisputable fact. The military annually dispatched a circular letter that included an inquiry into the ratio of drafted Jews to the district quota of Jewish conscripts.[29] This comparison disregarded the draft shortfall in every other ethnic group, holding only the Jews responsible for what was, after all, a universal phenomenon. Accordingly, argues a Russian military historian, "the consequences of this vicious circle undermined both the position of the Jews in the army and the principle of universal service."[30] Jews entered the epoch of Alexander III's counterreforms as brazen draft dodgers and bad patriots who deserved no civil or military privileges. It is not surprising that, on the eve of World War I, the statistics on Jewish draft dodging had become a major political issue.[31]

"Fit for Service"

During both the pre-reform and reform periods, there were two grades of fitness for military service: combat fitness (*goden k stroevoi sluzhbe*) and noncombatant fitness (*goden k nestroevoi sluzhbe*). Throughout the nineteenth century, in an attempt to fulfill its own self-imposed quota, the military drafted the ill and the disabled into special noncombatant units.[32] Draft offices accepted recruits suffering from mange, herpes, eczema, scabies, aural discharge, first-degree scurvy, and syphilis as fit for combat service. To noncombatant posts they drafted recruits with bowel dysfunction, certain hearing defects, and limb impairment.[33] There was no uniformity in attitude toward the sick recruits: one draft office accepted even recruits with recognized illnesses, while others rejected those whom they deemed unfit. The noncombatant recruits eventually found themselves in army hospitals, where army doctors petitioned for their discharge.

---

[28] RGVIA, f. 400, op. 5, d. 794, ll. 1–10b., 4.

[29] See, for example, circular letters of 1889: RGVIA, f. 400, op. 5, d. 1022, ll. 5, 7, 13, 14; RGVIA, f. 400, op. 5, d. 1023, l. 7; circular letters of 1900: RGVIA, f. 400, op. 5, d. 1643, ll. 17, 22, 27; the same, for 1902: RGVIA, f. 400, op. 5, d. 1712, ll. 13, 16, 22, 25.

[30] Baumann, "Universal Service Reform," 30.

[31] See, for example, comparative data on draft dodging by both Christians and Jews from the Berdichev and Odessa regions during the 1914 draft: RGVIA, f. 400, op. 19, d. 105, ll. 93–105.

[32] For lists of the diseases with which draftees were accepted to line service and to noncombatant service, see *Ustav o voinskoi povinnosti, so vsemi dopolneniiami i raz'iasneniiami, posledovavshimi so vremeni obnarodovaniia ego* (SPb.: Gogenfelden, 1875), 218–225 (app. 7, registers A, B, V).

[33] A. Radetskii, "Zametka k statiam 'Nesposobnye k sluzhbe novobrantsy,'" *Voennyi sbornik*, no. 11 (1885): 110–112.

The military reassured itself that Jews unfit for combat service were over-represented in the noncombatant units. The western provinces, with their dense urban and Jewish populations, yielded twice as many unfit recruits as did the empire's interior provinces. In the 1880s, out of every 100 recruits in the Polish Kingdom, the military commissions discharged and sent home 43 physically impaired men, whereas in European Russia they sent back only 22. Most disabled recruits came from the Baltic provinces, the Polish Kingdom, and the southwest: that is, from more urbanized regions, which were densely populated by Jews. The smallest number of disabled servicemen was in Astrakhan, Don, Dagestan, and Stavropol provinces, largely nonurban regions beyond the Pale.

The statistics for deferment of military service mirrored those for inductions. As a rule, 75 percent of all deferments were attributed to poor physique, and 25 percent to various forms of illness. More than 27 percent of all draftees in Kalish (Kalisz) province deferred service, 30 percent in Warsaw, 31 percent in Sedlets (Siedlce), 31 percent in Suvalki (Suwałki), 32 percent in Petrokov (Piotrków), 33 percent in Polotsk (Połock), 37 percent in Radom, 39 percent in Keltsy (Kielce), and 44 percent in Lublin. But Zabaikalie, Dagestan, Samara, Saratov, and Tomsk provinces yielded only between 9 and 12 percent unfit recruits. Based upon these data, Zolotarev, the highest military statistics authority, concluded that the Jews and the Poles were the worst groups in terms of recruitment, whereas Russians, especially Great Russians (not Belorussians or Ukrainians) were the best. The military statisticians demonstrated a unique blindness to the social aspects of this issue. Clearly, the least fit groups were not the Poles and the Jews, but the representatives of the most urbanized territories of the empire, where an industrial revolution was taking place. And yet, while the urban population in the western borderlands yielded a large percentage of unfit recruits, the empire's two capitals, with their 0.5 percent Jewish population, produced a no less significant number. In 1878, the St. Petersburg military district registered 9 percent of all draftees as unfit for combatant service.[34] During the 1882 call-up, the Moscow military district released roughly 69 percent of all recruits because of physical disabilities.[35] Obviously, the problem was socioeconomic, not ethnic. And the Russian capitals provided a higher percentage of men unfit for service than did urban clusters in the Pale, with their rampant poverty and overcrowding.

Despite the army's assertion of their inferiority, Jews hardly differed physically from other recruits. The War Ministry relied upon the reports of officers with little or no medical knowledge, who repeatedly remarked upon the Jewish recruit's narrow chest, small stature, and disproportionately long trunk. A Jew's average lung volume was 1.626 cubic liters, whereas a Karaite's was 1.645, and the Russians, Lithuanians, Belorussians, and Ukrainians had volumes of 1.657, 1.659, 1.668 and 1.670, respectively. A narrow chest, argued

---

[34] See Zolotarev, "Materialy po voennoi statistike Rossii," *Voennyi sbornik*, no. 2 (1888): 336; no. 6 (1889): 340, 358.
[35] *Voina i evrei*, 97–100.

the officers, was symptomatic of the Jews' poor physical condition, and was one of the main reasons for the assumption that Jewish soldiers were unfit for line service (it was not accidental that numerous complaints by the biased military also mentioned the Polish lower ranks as short in stature and physically ill-prepared). Military doctors and professional anthropologists knew that the primary indicator of physical development was not chest volume itself, but the ratio of the chest volume to half of the individual's height. For Polish Jews, this parameter exceeded the norm by thirty-six millimeters; for Jews in north-western districts of the Pale of Settlement, this excess was twenty-five milli-meters; in Kuban, it was nineteen millimeters; in Dagestan, twelve millimeters; and, in Kutaisi, ten millimeters.[36]

Trachoma was considered one of the most widespread and dangerous dis-eases in the army, especially among ethnic minorities and, above all, among the Jews. Regardless of their background, recruits suffering from trachoma served in the so-called eye troops (*glaznye komandy*), where the disease was endemic. Its high incidence caused despair among military doctors, who feared that reserve soldiers would lose their sight. These doctors took resolute measures against drafting trachoma-stricken men. They claimed that, "contrary to sci-entific and theoretical arguments," the army lost nothing in refusing to draft the sick, even in the case of "aliens such as the Poles, the Tartars, and the Jews." In fact, Jewish soldiers demonstrably did not suffer disproportionately from trachoma; whereas trachoma damage would hinder one's marksmanship, Jews were among the best sharpshooters in the infantry regiments. Among all Jewish servicemen, 25 percent were sharpshooters of the first rank, 38 of the second rank, and 21 percent of the third rank. Among Russian soldiers, the first, second, and third ranks of sharpshooters comprised respectively 23 percent, 35 percent, and 28 percent. Therefore, there is no reason to claim that Jews particularly suffered from trachoma.[37]

While the draft commission's xenophobic bias colored the reports on the Jewish recruits' health, postdraft data spoke clearly in favor of the Jews. The military reported the greatest number of sick solders as coming from the St. Petersburg, Kazan, and Omsk military districts; the lowest number from the Kharkov, Odessa, Vilna, Warsaw, and Kiev districts. The highest rates of illness were from the St. Petersburg, Turkestan, and especially the Caucasus districts. The highest death rates were in the Caucasus, Turkestan, and West Siberian military districts, the lowest in the Kharkov and Odessa districts. Thus, in the Pale, where the greatest number of Jewish soldiers resided, the sickness and death rates were significantly lower than in the districts outside the Jewish Pale. Additionally, the lowest death rate and rate of sickness occurred in the artillery,

---

[36] *Voina i evrei*, 81–87, 103–104; Usov, *Evrei v armii*, 43–45; RGVIA, f. 400, op. 2, d. 525, l. 13.

[37] A. Zhikharev, "Zametki uezdnogo voinskogo nachal'nika," *Voennyi sbornik*, no. 9 (1890): 129–135, 130–132; D. Stakovich, "K voprosu o prieme trakhomotoznykh novobrantsev v voiska," *Voennyi sbornik*, no. 9 (1891): 116–117; *Voina i evrei*, 116, citing [no initials] Tarasov, *Chto predstavliaet soboi russkaia armiia v strelkovom otnoshenii* (SPb.: n. p., 1911), 19.

which, before the 1890s, had a quite high percentage of Jews. In the army as a whole, the death rate among Jewish soldiers was, in fact, the lowest. Between 1886 and 1895, Russian Orthodox men constituted 75 percent of the sick draftees, and 74 percent of those who died. Roman Catholics constituted 8 percent of the ill, whereas the usual death rate of Roman Catholics in the troops reached 14 percent. Among Protestants and Muslims, the proportion of dead also exceeded the number of ill: sick Protestants constituted less than 5 percent, while those who died constituted almost 5 percent. Similarly, there were 3 percent of sick Muslims, and 4 percent who died. Only for the Jewish soldiers was the death rate half the rate of sickness, or less: Jews comprised 6 percent of all ill soldiers, but only 2 percent of the deceased.[38]

Thus, in the reform epoch, Jews as a group did not have a higher rate of sickness than the rest of the troops. Perhaps the contrast between the high degree of illness among Jewish recruits and their low death rate in the army demonstrates that they were less fit before their induction, but more fit once drafted. Jews displayed certain stamina and a greater ability to survive under army conditions. Oddly, many were materially better situated in the underfed and undersupplied army than they had been in the starving Pale of Jewish Settlement shtetl. While some Jews – as well as Russians – sought and found ways to simulate illnesses that would qualify them from exemption (the discussion of this issue follows), the stereotype of Jews as obstinate self-mutilators and sickly soldiers does not hold water. Military data reject it as biased and false.

The Jewish Soldier's Budget

As will be explained in more detail in Chapters 5 and 6, in the last quarter of the nineteenth century the living standards of most Jews in the Pale rapidly declined. The gulf between the categories of drafted Jews steadily grew wider. Some Jewish soldiers receiving support from their families and local communities had more money than their comrades-in-arms, including those of other ethnic minorities, whereas other Jews, perhaps the majority, lacked any such support and were much poorer than their peers.

The years spent in military service struck a severe economic blow to most Jews from the Pale who had been engaged in retail trade or small-scale crafts. They lost their businesses, could not regain their standing vis-à-vis the competition upon their return, and found themselves in desperate circumstances. Jewish communities were well aware of this situation and attempted to provide Jewish draftees with some funds, ensuring both that they presented themselves to the draft offices, and that they used the money to start up a business upon the conclusion of their military careers. Crown rabbis reported that, with the approach of conscription, the two principal issues facing their communities

---

[38] Zolotarev, "Materialy," *Voennyi sbornik*, no. 6 (1889): 328–29; "Otchet o deiatel'nosti voennogo ministerstva," *Voennyi sbornik*, no. 9 (1878): 58–59; *Voina i evrei*, 112–113.

were how to "avoid the shortage" and how to "raise funds." M. Khandros of Vladimir-Volynskii traced a direct parallel between the absence of any enlistment shortfall in his district and the ability of the Jewish community to collect 9,000 rubles, representing a 300-ruble cash donation to each draftee. In 1880, as a financial incentive, the community of Eishishok (Ejszyszki), in the Lida district, collected nearly 150 rubles for each Jewish recruit. In the same year, the communities of Nikolaev, Ufa, Vilna, and Krasilov also raised as much as 150 rubles per recruit, while Dubossary and Tiraspol amassed between 50 and 100 rubles for each Jewish soldier. In 1882, the Balta community collected 2,500 rubles for thirty-one Jewish recruits (i.e., up to 80 rubles for each), and secured 100 percent of their target number of draftees. The Jewish community resorted to the same tactic in Voronovo (Vilna province) and Vysoko-Litovsk, obtaining up to 200 rubles for each recruit. In 1881, the Berdichev community tried to avoid an enrollment shortfall by collecting 25 rubles from each tax-paying household and by appealing to synagogue-goers to raise the minimum of 200 rubles per draftee.[39] Although the Russian Jewish press was quick to report such campaigns, the communities capable of assisting their recruits in this fashion comprised not more than one tenth of the Pale of Settlement; Jewish recruits from smaller and poorer localities seem not to have had any such support. Most likely, the Jewish soldier's wellbeing differed only slightly from that of the typical Russian Orthodox soldier.

All members of the Russian army's lower ranks dressed and repaired their clothes and equipment from their personal resources. In terms of design and quality, the governmental supplies equipped a soldier poorly for the conditions he confronted in European Russia or in Siberia. He generally either sold or exchanged parts of the uniform provided by the military (*kazennye materialy*), usually for a pittance; this amount he used to clothe himself and to obtain better supplies.[40] The provisions department provided the obligatory two pairs of high boots only on the eve of military campaigns. In peacetime, a soldier was given the material for boots and was responsible for their manufacture, while the army deducted a substantial sum from his provisions allowance (*amunichnye den'gi*).[41] This situation remained unchanged until after the 1905 Russian Revolution, when considerable improvements were introduced.[42] The few

---

[39] *Russkii evrei*, no. 1 (1881): 54–55; *Rassvet*, no. 34 (1880): 1338–1339; no. 15 (1879): 570; *Russkii evrei*, no. 52 (1882): 1933; no. 47 (1881): 1855; no. 45 (1881): 1755.

[40] P. Agapiev, "Mundirnaia odezhda v polkovom khoziaistve," *Voennyi sbornik*, no. 5 (1891): 168–183.

[41] (Kapitan) Levshinovskii, "O sberezhenii nog nizhnikh chinov, o portiankakh i sapogakh," *Voennyi sbornik*, no. 6 (1891): 351–368.

[42] Nokhum Blokh, a recruit from the Berdichev district, arrived at the regimental headquarters in 1908 and obtained the standard kit: three shirts, three pairs of underwear, three handkerchiefs, two pairs of boots, two towels, two sheets, six pillowcases to make into a mattress, one blanket, and one tie. See RGVIA, f. 2649, uncatalogued (*listovoi*), d. 116, order (*prikaz*), no. 10. Interestingly, Blokh received this kit a year after the War Ministry had made a decision to improve the soldiers' provisions, following the 1905 Revolution.

available documents concerning monetary transactions in the regiments indicate that most of the money transfers were between Jews, which implies that Jewish soldiers had much closer ties to their distant relatives than did Christians. Despite general Jewish impoverishment at the turn of the century, the amount of Jewish help given to their brethren was more substantial than that of Christians to their kin. Nonetheless, most Jewish soldiers received nothing.[43]

Jewish soldiers were as poor and as dependent upon the meager personal budget as were the regular Russian soldiers.[44] A soldier in an infantry regiment consumed a quarter pound of *makhorka* (an inferior tobacco) for 6 kopecks per week, i.e., 2.88 rubles annually; two boxes of matches per week, about 98 kopecks annually; sewing materials to make a pair of boots for 4.50 rubles and 70 kopecks for labor; tar and blubber oil, necessary for blackening, shoe polish, and cleaning materials, 1.84 rubles annually; a pair of foot bindings (*portianki*, worn instead of socks), 15 kopecks a pair, and not fewer than three pairs, or 45 kopecks annually; shirts and underwear, 1.05 rubles; soap for washing and laundry, 3 kopecks per week, 1.56 rubles annually; baths (except for regular washing in a public bath covered by the military) twice a month, 3 kopecks per month, 36 kopecks annually; stationery for the 25 percent of soldiers in a company who were deemed literate, 10 kopecks per month, 1.20 rubles annually. Tea was one of the principal treats for a soldier, though the quartermaster not infrequently stole it, as he did the cheap, subsidized vodka. The price in the regimental shop for a pack of tea and three pieces of sugar was 2 kopecks. A half-company paid 40 kopecks per month, or 4.80 rubles annually, if it could afford such a luxury. In addition, soldiers had to purchase the following items each week: bread rolls for 3 kopecks, 1.56 rubles annually; and cucumbers, radish, meat and onions for 6 kopecks per week, 3.12 rubles annually. A soldier usually spent about two rubles per year on gifts for women.[45]

---

[43] Consider the data available for the Thirty-fifth Briansk regiment, in which some Jewish soldiers were much better supported financially than their Christian fellows. Between April and May 1908, eight soldiers received money transfers. Five were Jews. The three non-Jewish soldiers received little more than one ruble altogether. The Jews received sums almost ten times higher: Samuil Zaits, three rubles; Daniil Mashtaler, one ruble forty kopeks; Avraam Kacher, three rubles; Kopel Krasovsky, three rubles; and Avraam Shvarztukh, three rubles. See RGVIA, f. 2649 uncatalogued (*listovoi*), d. 116, order (*prikaz*) no. 124. The Briansk regiment had 200 or more Jewish soldiers in its ranks at that time who did not receive any money. This estimate is based upon the fact that the Briansk regiment lost 123 Jewish soldiers, who were wounded or killed during the Russo-Japanese War; see Usov, *Evrei v armii*, 112–114.

[44] For the poor state of the soldiers' kit, see F. Nikolaev, "Issledovaniie soldatskikh sukon," *Voenno-meditsinskii zhurnal*, vol. 114, no. 8 (1872): 183–200; (Kapitan) Levshinovskii, "O sberezhenii nog nizhnikh chinov, o portiankakh i sapogakh," *Voennyi sbornik*, no. 6 (1891): 368; A. Rediger, *Istoriia moei zhizni: Vospominaniia voennogo ministra*, 2 vols. (M.: Kanon-Press, Kuchkovo pole, 1999), 1:430–431. For the cases of Jewish soldiers of various regiments who suffered frostbite because of their low-quality footwear, see RGVIA, f. 400, op. 15, d. 3521, l. 98.

[45] These calculations are made upon the basis of a forty-eight-week period. See Captain Lossovskii, "Zametka ob usloviiakh pitaniia," *Voennyi sbornik*, no. 7 (1887): 92–95.

Thus, a soldier's typical minimum budget came to just about twenty rubles per year, whereas his salary was a little bit more than two rubles. "In terms of its financial status the army was little more than a beggar," argued War Minister Rediger. He cited specific financial harships among the causes that fostered mutinies in the troops during 1905–1907: "His salary [the soldier's] was ridiculously scanty: the lower rank in the army got two rubles and ten kopeks per year! The linen and footwear were of such a low quality that the lower ranks sold them dirt-cheap and instead bought things for themselves; money allotted for stitching the boots was minuscule; the soldiers had to pay an additional two rubles from their own pocket."[46] It was only in 1909 that the War Ministry managed to increase the sums allotted for the stitching of the soldiers' boots from 35 kopeks to 2.50 rubles per year.

To alleviate financial hardship, a special January 1847 regulation exempted Jewish soldiers from paying the heavy burden of the obligatory kosher meat tax (*korobka*). This enabled them to purchase meat at a cost 25 percent less than its price to civilians. An individual was entitled to purchase one pound of tax-free kosher meat per day, and a soldier's family, two pounds.[47] The military enforced this law in March 1859, confirming that Jewish soldiers did not have to pay the kosher meat tax.[48] However, in practice, this applied only to the wholesale supply of kosher meat to the army. As a rule, expenditure on meat and dairy products by Jews exceeded the equivalent expenses of other enlisted men. In order to meet expenses, soldiers in general and Jewish soldiers in particular were compelled to seek every opportunity to make money. They joined the *artel*, a traditional self-governing association in the military allowing soldiers to earn extra money and stock some vegetables for winter (especially cabbage).[49] As an *artel* member, a soldier could earn from five to fifteen rubles annually, about ten rubles on average. Such independent earnings varied from 18.5 kopecks to as much as 29 kopecks per day.[50] From the sale of surplus bread and flour, a soldier could earn about 4.80 rubles. By selling the unsatisfactory cloth received from the state, he obtained another ruble per year. On average, money transfers from his family or from a bank amounted to five to ten rubles annually (600–700 rubles for each company per annum).[51] Ideally, the

---

[46] See A. Rediger, *Istoriia moei zhizni: Vospominaniia voennogo ministra*, 2 vols. (M.: Kanon-Press, Kuchkovo pole, 1999), 1: 475–476, 478.

[47] *PSZ II*, 22: 20856.

[48] *PSZ II*, 34: 34037.

[49] For more detail, see John Bushnell, "The Russian Soldiers' Artel, 1700–1900: A History and Interpretation," in Roger Bartlett, ed., *Land Commune and Peasant Community in Russia: Communal Forms in Imperial and Early Soviet Society* (Basingstoke: Macmillan, in association with the School of Slavonic and East European Studies, University of London, 1989), 376–394.

[50] RGVIA, f. 400, op. 2, d. 275, l. 11.

[51] [Captain] Lossovskii advances a more conservative figure of five rubles, whereas [Colonel] Agapiev's figure is five to ten rubles per soldier annually. See Lossovskii, "Zametka ob usloviiakh pitaniia," 95–96; Agapiev, "Mundirnaia odezhda," *Voennyi sbornik*, no. 5 (1891): 73.

soldier should cover his own budget entirely. Nevertheless, the annual deficit presumably was at least ten to fifteen rubles, and even higher for a Jewish soldier.

A number of factors contributed to this situation. Firstly, money earned from side ventures did not travel directly from an employer's pocket to the soldier's pocket. Monetary disputes between members of the lower ranks and junior officers were a frequent occurrence.[52] The soldier generally received less than his true earnings. Moreover, part of his money went toward the company's communal fund. The cost of a meal depended upon the season and upon the troop's location: in the winter, food was far more expensive than in the summer, while bread in the central and northern provinces always was three to four times more costly than in the south.[53] A considerable part of the Jewish soldier's earnings went toward the common pool. He did not receive cash to meet his specific need for kosher food, and support from home was not always sufficient to alleviate his poverty.[54] Any soldier who regularly received money from home immediately attracted a crowd of friends, drunks, and other hangers-on wishing to enjoy themselves at another's expense.[55] Jewish soldiers, according to a literary source, were no exception.[56] The rank-and-file Jews and non-Jews, most likely, shared economic poverty and one and the same company pot. Surprisingly, military court documents reflect no economic tensions between them. It seems that the army created a much better melting pot for various ethnic groups than civilian society, seized with an explosive economic tension between Jews and Russian Orthodox.

Judiciary Reform and Jewish Offenders

The ongoing Russian judiciary reform and a fundamental revision of disciplinary measures engendered significant changes in the military penal code.[57] In 1867, acting upon Miliutin's advice, Alexander II approved a draft proposal, which presupposed the establishment of permanent courts in the army units, under the supervision of a military procurator. It was no longer the prerogative of army commanders to assign punishment to soldiers; accused men had the right to a legal advocate. Professional lawyers with specialized training were to

[52] Kimerling, *From Serf to Russian Soldier*, 80–81.
[53] Robert Jones, "Ukrainian Grain and the Russian Market in the Late Eighteenth and Early Nineteenth Centuries," in I. S. Koropeckyj, ed., *Ukrainian Economic History. Interpretative Essays* (Cambridge, Mass.: Harvard University Press for Harvard Ukrainian Research Institute): 210–227.
[54] Anon., "Zametki po povodu uchebnykh sborov zapasnykh nizhnikh chinov v 1888 godu," *Voennyi sbornik*, no. 4 (1888): 298–321; Luganin, "Zametki po povodu uchebnykh sborov zapasnykh nizhnikh chinov v 1887 godu," no. *Voennyi sbornik*, no. 5 (1888): 131–169.
[55] Kn. Imeretinskii, "Iz zapisok starogo preobrazhentsa," *Russkaia starina*, no. 587 (1893): 33.
[56] Bogrov, *Zapiski evreia*, 3: 234–235.
[57] *Zhurnal komissii*, 13, 154–155; Lincoln, *The Great Reforms*, 105–117.

occupy posts in the justice offices.[58] These reforms exerted a lasting effect upon the army's crime rate.

In the late 1880s, Jewish soldiers were implicated only in minor crimes and violations, and did not appear among the population of major offenders. Among Jewish petty criminals were such soldiers as Iuda Savolinskii, caught selling forged tickets for a market show (*bilety v balagany*), or the worker Moshka Segal, who used his foreign passport to speculate on gold coins.[59] Nor did Jews figure in military courts among the frequent offenders. Indirect statistical data concerning army discipline indicates a remarkably low crime rate among Jewish enlisted men. In 1871, military penal institutions contained 6,314 Russian Orthodox convicts, 308 Catholics, 216 Protestants, 103 Muslims, 79 Jews, 25 Old Believers (*raskol'niki*), 4 pagans, 3 members of the *edinovertsy* sect (Old Believers who accepted the Russian Orthodox liturgy), and two Greek Catholics (Uniates) – a total of 7,054.[60] Thus, Jews constituted 1 percent of convicts, 50 percent less than their proportion in the army at that time.[61] This figure is even lower if one includes the lower Jewish ranks drafted before 1871 and still in active service.[62]

Later, deteriorating attitudes toward Jews in the empire, a wave of pogroms in 1881–1883, and repressive anti-Jewish regulations provoked a disproportionate rise in the crime rate among Jews in the Pale: in 1888, they constituted 8.6 percent of all convicts.[63] Likewise, an increase occurred in the number of convicted Jewish soldiers in the punitive battalions, which eventually reached 8.8 percent, twice the percentage of Jews in the army at that time.[64] And yet, Jews were underrepresented among the most typical offenders. Between 1860 and 1890, most crimes committed by the lower ranks involved larceny, fraud, desertion, disrespect toward officers, insubordination, and neglect and loss of state equipment and assets.[65] There were no Jewish perpetrators of serious crimes.[66] Jewish soldiers either mutilated themselves or deserted. In some cases,

---

[58] Zubarev, "Nashi polkovye sudy," *Voennyi sbornik*, no. 5 (1892): 172–190.

[59] RGVIA, f. 324, op. 1, d. 127, 139.

[60] *Voennyi sbornik*, no. 8 (1873): 35.

[61] In 1871, 2,045 Jews from the Polish Kingdom and 1,090 Jews from the rest of the empire, making 3,035 in all. In 1871, the total number of drafted men reached 147,710. Thus, the Jews comprised 2.1 percent of the 1871 recruits. See *Voennyi sbornik*, no. 11 (1872): 167–169.

[62] Regarding the number of Jewish soldiers in the penal companies, the ratio remains consistent over the years, reflecting a lower percentage. See reports of the Chief Military Prison Committee in *Voennyi sbornik*, no. 4 (1874): 154–155; no. 12 (1874): 210–211; no. 12 (1878): 285–286; no. 10 (1880): 139–140; no. 9 (1882): 76–78; no. 10 (1883): 140–141.

[63] Frank, *Crime*, 76.

[64] *Voennyi sbornik*, no. 11 (1885): 84–85.

[65] See, e.g., "Obshchee obozrenie prestupnosti po voennomu departamentu," *Voennyi sbornik*, no. 8 (1873): 104–105; *Voennyi sbornik*, no. 7 (1881): 34–36.

[66] Among the crimes committed by Jewish soldiers, there are two cases of murder, the only ones in the entire thirty-year period, and thorough study of both cases compels one to doubt the fairness of the charges and the sentence. See RGVIA, f. 801, op. 43, 2 otd., 1 st., sv. 99, d. 77, l. 3–3ob., and RGVIA, f. 801, op. 31, 3 otd., 2 st., sv. 815, d. 58, ll. 2–5, 13–13ob., 94ob.-95ob. The robbing of a fish seller named Koncheva by a private of the Kherson modular

the mutilations were deliberate; in others, the convictions were the results of a prejudice towards the accused. For instance, Shimon Oirik, of the Fifty-third Volhynia regiment, convicted of mutilating himself, received one year in a penal company. His excellent service record did not help him. The court refused to consider Oirik's petition to admit the testimony of the local doctor, who was aware of Oirik's disability. Gersh Volf Shraf, of the 154th Derbent regiment, supposedly inflicted a wound upon himself with ammonium chloride in order to escape the service, and received one-and-a-half years in a penal company. The court rejected Shraf's claim that he suffered from regular headaches and ear problems and needed the remedy for treatment. The court accused Jewish soldier Itska Sokol of attempted mutilation for having helped someone else obtain a medical discharge.[67]

Desertion and the "pilfering of crown assets" (stealing and selling the uniform) remained among the most common offences in the reformed Russian army, committed by non-Jews and Jews alike. Gabriel Shenkman, of the Forty-seventh Ukrainian regiment, deserted in 1876; he was caught in 1884 and sentenced to ten months in a discipline battalion. Avrum Grunfest, of the 123rd Kozlov infantry regiment, was on the run from January 1883 until March 1885, when he was apprehended and sentenced to eight months in a discipline battalion. Leiba Dorfman, of the Sixty-sixth Butyrsk infantry regiment, received one-and-a half years in a punitive battalion for desertion and the theft of state possessions (a second hand overcoat, a worn pair of pants, a belt with a badge and a knife bayonet, which he wore when running away).[68]

In contrast to the Jewish civilians who participated with the Poles in the 1863 Polish uprising, the overwhelming majority of Jewish soldiers remained loyal subjects "of the Emperor and the Fatherland."[69] The military courts heard numerous cases of Jews in the Kingdom of Poland, mainly merchants and petty bourgeois, who sympathized with or assisted in the Polish rebellion. The military court file, entitled "On those indicted and charged for their involvement in the Polish rebellion of 1863–1864," contains the names both of Polish homesteaders (*odnodvortsy*) and of Jews; Jews accounted for 9 percent of the arrested. Most of the suspects were released, while some were tried in civil courts. Two privates from an infantry regiment, Leib Korsh and Srul Kosoi,

---

command, Iankel Kupershtein, also does not fit with the typical crimes committed by the military. Kupershtein saw Koncheva pay for vodka and beer in an inn, attacked her, stole fifteen rubles in silver, and disappeared into the courtyard of a Jewish brothel. Kupershtein, who had served three years in the military, and was married and literate, could not prove his alibi and received six years' forced labor. See RGVIA, f. 801, op. 31, 3 otd., 2 st., sv. 837, d. 30, ll. 160b.-190b.

[67] RGVIA, f. 801, op. 43, 2 otd., 3 st., sv. 105, d. 119, ll. 2–20b., 11–12; d. 116, ll. 20b., 6, 14; op. 43, 2 otd., 2 st., sv. 114, d. 111, ll. 2, 170b.

[68] RGVIA, f. 801, op. 43, 2 otd., 1 st., sv. 100, d. 130, ll. 2–12; op. 43, 2 otd., 2 st., sv. 113, d. 23, ll. 1–9; op. 43, 2 otd., 1 st., sv. 100, d. 140, ll. 1, 30b.-4, 9.

[69] On Jewish–Polish relations on the eve of and during the rebellion, see Magdalena Opalski and Israel Bartal, *Poles and Jews: A Failed Brotherhood* (Hanover and London: Brandeis University Press, 1992), 38–57, 84–85.

found themselves in prison in the Kiev military district, although the charges against them never were clear. Some Jews cooperated with the Russian army, military authorities, and police. In August 1863, a resident of Krivoe Ozero named Goldfarb denounced Anishevskii, a landowner from the Balta district, of having been involved in the rebellion. Aron Finkelshtein notified the commander of the Zaslav (Iziaslav) military police administration that the aristocracy in the village of Gorovichi had not surrendered its weapons.[70] Except in the case of two arrests, it was impossible to ascertain any support for the Polish rebels on the part of the Jewish soldiers; the concern of the Russian authorities was proven unfounded.

In the late 1870s and 1880s, the office of the war minister compiled data twice each month concerning the troops about to depart on leave. The "most humble reports" (*vsepoddaneishie doklady*) detailing army incidents were submitted to the emperor. These included data on suicides, desertions, manslaughter cases, accidental and deliberate injuries and wounds, cases of blasphemy, insolence, escapes from arrest, violence, infringements of discipline while serving guard duty, theft of state assets, mutilation, hooliganism, honorable actions, and punitive expeditions at the request of the local civil authorities. The aggregated report divulged no information on the creed of the offenders or their victims. Yet the accused appeared in court with their full records, and the military added incident files for future reference. Therefore, it is possible to obtain an estimated crime rate among the lower Jewish ranks. The early 1880s, with their pogroms against the Jews, the rise of aggressive Russian nationalism, the toughening of the army's xenophobia, and the beginning of mass Jewish emigration, represented a critical period.[71]

What crimes did Jewish soldiers commit between January and August 1882, and between March and July 1884? Benzion Koganskii, of the Sixty-seventh Tarutino regiment, injured his own arm while on guard; the court classified this as self-mutilation, although even military commanders raised doubts about it. Moisei Bergman, of the Mozhaisk regiment, accidentally discharged his gun and

---

[70] RGVIA, f. 1759, op. 8, d. 701, ll. 10, 11, 22, 23, 50, 97, 98; d. 693, ll. 12, 69, 497; d. 655, ll. 10b.-20b.

[71] Based upon reports submitted from January to August, 1882: RGVIA, f. 400, op. 15, d. 744 (for the second half of January 1882), ll. 63–730b.; d. 745 (for the first half of February 1882), ll. 58–66; d. 746 (for the second half of February 1882), ll. 81–920b.; d. 747 (for the first half of March 1882), ll. 71–79; d. 748 (for the second half of March 1882); d. 749 (for the first half of April 1882), ll. 40–49; d. 751 (for the first half of May 1882), ll. 65–750b.; d. 752 (for the second half of May 1882), ll. 71–820b.; d. 753 (for the first half of June 1882); d. 754 (for the second half of June 1882), ll. 83–95; d. 755 for the first half of July 1882), ll. 34–44; d. 756 (for the second half of July 1882), ll. 85–101; d. 757 (for the first half of August 1882); d. 758 (for the second half of August 1882); and also from March to July 1884: RGVIA, f. 400, op. 15, d. 840 (for the first half of March 1884), ll. 83–93 ob.; d. 841 (for the first half of April 1884), ll. 56–63; d. 842 (for the second half of April 1884), ll. 79–91; d. 843 for the first half of May 1884), ll. 50–59; d. 844 (for the second half of May 1884); d. 845 (for the first half of June 1884), ll. 73–85; d. 846 (for the second half of June 1884), ll. 99–119; d. 847 (for the first half of July 1884), ll. 70–83; d. 848 (for the second half of July 1884), ll. 65–780b.

wounded Private Fedorenko. On guard at the Bobruisk prison, Jewish Private Isakov shot at a prison window from which seven jailed Jews were throwing stones at him, killing one and wounding another. In Zabludov (Zabłudów), Faivus Murnik, a young soldier of the Sixty-first Vladimir regiment, escaped a morning training session, hid in a Jewish home, resisted attempts to arrest him, and surrendered only to an armed detachment sent for him.[72] Except for special punitive expeditions aimed at suppressing anti-Jewish violence, these were the only incidents specifically citing Jews, with the exception of one murder considered a display of honorable vigilance while on guard and therefore excluded from the aggregate report.[73] During the same period, the following crimes were reported among the army's non-Jewish population: 59 murders, 115 suicides, 7 cases of sacrilege (pillage of churches), 64 cases of accidental wounding or manslaughter, 24 cases of destruction of state assets, 14 cases of infringement of discipline while on guard duty, and 23 cases of insolent statements against the sovereign. Jews were not implicated in any of these.

The low crime rate among Jewish soldiers reflected the low crime rate in the Jewish Pale as a whole. Most of the 1882 draftees under arrest or judicial inquiry came from St. Petersburg, Vologda, Estland, Lifland, and Arkhangelsk provinces (between 4 and 14 out of 1,000 men), and also from the provinces of Western Siberia, Zauralie, and Northern Caucasus. The lowest numbers were in the western, northwestern, and southwestern provinces: that is, throughout the entire Pale of Jewish Settlement.[74] Some legal cases involving Jewish soldiers found their way into the press, chiefly in the column "Selected Decisions of the Supreme Military Court" of the monthly *Voennyi sbornik*. They reveal a similar picture of crime among Jewish soldiers. Between 1873 and 1888, out of 30 crimes involving Jewish men, 8 entailed absence without leave,[75] 7 were

[72] RGVIA, f. 400, op. 15, d. 752, l. 76; d. 848, l. 28–29; d. 839, ll. 60b., 32; d. 837, ll. 410b., 560b.-57.

[73] Reports of incidents in the troops offer a comprehensive perspective of the troops' participation in preventing the murder of Jews during 1881–1884. Approximately one quarter of all punitive troop expeditions were designed to prevent anti-Jewish upheavals. However, this matter merits separate consideration. As a whole, the archival materials regarding the army's involvement in preventing mass murder confirm the hypothesis of Michael Aronson that, in 1881–1883, Russian troops had no direct part in the murders. See Michael Aronson, *Troubled Waters*, 57–59.

[74] A. M. Zolotarev, "Materialy po voennoi statistike Rossii," *Voennyis sbornik*, no. 6 (1889): 344–346.

[75] Zisel Khidekel, of the Novyi Torzhok regiment, was charged with unauthorized absence, drunkenness, and offences against a corporal; see *Voennyi sbornik*, no. 9 (1873): 45–46. Similar verdicts were received by Daniil Til'man, of the 121st Penza regiment; see *Voennyi sbornik*, no. 9 (1883): 75–76; Gersh Gershon, a gunner of the Ninth artillery brigade; see *Voennyi sbornik*, no. 10 (1882): 232–233; Borukh Prasol, of the 129th Bessarabiia regiment; see *Voennyi sbornik*, no. 1 (1885): 54–55; Shaia Beznos, of the 126th reserve infantry battalion; see *Voennyi sbornik*, no. 10 (1886): 204–205; recruit Shlema Skul'skii; see *Voennyi sbornik*, no. 2 (1887): 204–205; Srul Sirkis, of the 133rd Simferopol regiment; see *Voennyi sbornik*, no. 6 (1889): 176–180; no. 5 (1889): 66–67. The gunner Eduard Krulikovskii, of the Ninth artillery brigade, left the barracks without authorization and stole a Jewish passport and coat; see *Voennyi sbornik*, no. 11 (1885): 88.

cases of larceny,[76] 4 were of disobedience,[77] 4 were attempts at dodging the draft,[78] 3 were alleged mutilations,[79] 2 concerned unauthorized relations between the lower ranks and their peers, and 2 constituted military offences.[80] To the credit of the appeals commission, it upheld the decisions of the local military court only in 11 of the 31 cases. Twenty verdicts were reconsidered, and either canceled for a lack of *corpus delicti* or sent to another court for a new hearing. Among the proven offences, Jewish soldiers entered into unauthorized relations within the ranks.[81] For example, Kalinik Gornik, Iankel Mild and Maksim Mefodiev, of the Sixty-fifth Tiflis regiment, escorted Georgian prisoners, allowed them to rest, drank vodka with them, and did not shoot when their prisoners ran away.[82] Mendel Kunin, of the Tenth Malorossiisk grenadier regiment, drank tea with a Russian Orthodox prisoner and released him from

---

[76] Moshka Tokatsynskii, Zelman Filipek, and Leiba Lipolatskii, privates in the Seventy-seventh Tenginsk regiment, stole military uniforms; see *Voennyi sbornik*, no. 9 (1873): 56–57; a corporal of the Twenty-second reserve personnel battalion, Iosel Shnapir, embezzled public assets and offended his commanders; see *Voennyi sbornik*, no. 11 (1882): 88–91. Abram Blank, of the 156th Elisavetinsk regiment, stole a watch; see *Voennyi sbornik*, no. 5 (1885): 83–84; civilian Portnoi, Lieutenant Colonel Perkov, Lieutenant Kaplinskii and Lieutenant Slonovskii allegedly attempted to sell stolen public cloth; see *Voennyi sbornik*, no. 3 (1888): 54–57; Berko Miller, Iokhan El'man, Shlema Fuks, Meier Dymont, and Vol'f Shikhman, privates of the Eighty-first Apsheron infantry regiment, tried to steal and sell gunpowder; see *Voennyi sbornik*, no. 1 (1888): 47–50; Mendel Natanson, of the 107th Troitsk infantry regiment, attempted to steal soldiers' shirts; see *Voennyi sbornik*, no. 6 (1889): 183–184.

[77] Faivel Madenberg, a junior laboratory assistant in the St. Petersburg military district, forgot to salute his commander; see *Voennyi sbornik*, no. 10 (1874): 150–151; Gershka Freiveld, of the Forty-sixth Dnieper regiment, disobeyed his commanders; see *Voennyi sbornik*, no. 7 (1883): 79–81; Khaim Blokh, the veterinary doctor's assistant of the Thirty-eighth artillery brigade, refused to show respect to an attendant; see *Voennyi sbornik*, no. 5 (1888): 26–30.

[78] For recruits Avrum Breselman, Avrum Soifer, and townsman Volf Fishman, see *Voennyi sbornik*, no. 9 (1882): 130–133; Osip Strudniarzh and Iankel Grier, of the 128th Caspian, did not register in time for the draft lists; see *Voennyi sbornik*, no. 8 (1885): 177–178; Private Abram Itska Lozovadovskii of the 125th Kursk regiment failed to appear at the draft commission examination; see *Voennyi sbornik*, no. 8 (1880): 208–209; Iankel Fisher, of the Forty-first Selegin regiment, also failed to appear at the examination; see *Voennyi sbornik*, no. 8 (1885): 181–182.

[79] For Uter Khaim Gutman and Shlema Duvid-Shmul Reznik, of the local command of the Seventy-sixth Kuban regiment, see *Voennyi sbornik*, no. 12 (1880): 194–195; for Aron Vishnevetskii, of the 126th Rylsk regiment; see *Voennyi sbornik*, no. 12 (1886): 182–183; for Mania-Srul Cherny, a private of the Iakutsk regiment, see *Voennyi sbornik*, no. 9 (1885): 93–94.

[80] Itska Tepletskii fell asleep while on duty; see *Voennyi sbornik*, no. 5 (1888): 46–47; senior clerk (corporal) Gersh Spivak and junior clerk Meyer Fishberg, of the 156th Elisavetinsk regiment, in response to the refusal of the regiment commander to allow some Jewish soldiers leave for holidays, composed false applications for their brethren; see *Voennyi sbornik*, no. 12 (1883): 181–182.

[81] The punishment of convicts sentenced to the penal (military correctional) companies entailed a command "to keep unconditional silence" during the day. For more details concerning prisoners' punishments, see Afanasiaev, "Distsiplinarnye bataliony," *Voennyi sbornik*, no. 7 (1890): 118–120.

[82] *Voennyi sbornik*, no. 7 (1874): 33–35.

the lockup so he could meet his girlfriend in the city.[83] An unnamed Jewish soldier helped his uneducated Christian fellows in a penal battalion to understand the basics of Christianity.[84] These examples obliquely confirm the complexity of interethnic relations in the Russian army and the existence of solidarity between soldiers of different creeds.

Defending Mother Russia

Like other members of Russian society, Jews perceived Alexander's Great Reforms as the beginning of their emancipation. In the 1860s, these developments wrought profound changes in the Pale of Settlement. Some Jews, particularly certified artisans, now could settle permanently outside the Pale. Those seeking integration into Russian society enrolled as university students. A trilingual Jewish press (Hebrew, Yiddish, and Russian) was slowly reaching into the most insular of shtetls. Jewish lawyers and doctors, newly minted graduates of prestigious Russian universities, with offices in St. Petersburg and Odessa, composed the nucleus of a Russian Jewish intelligentsia. The introduction of Jewish civic equality and the dismantling of the Pale could offer exhilarating possibilities, which even traditional Jews sought. A newfound Jewish allegiance to the Russian motherland became the best argument for the long-anticipated Jewish emancipation; for the first time in the nineteenth century, the Jewish soldier realized how profoundly his combat conduct and his military spirit influenced the fate of his brethren. At the same time, communal leaders in the Pale discovered that their attitude toward the Russian army and toward Jewish enlistment affected Russian society's attitude toward the Jews. Previously a minor theme in the writings of a handful of Russian *maskilim*, Russian patriotism emerged as a Jewish communal priority.

In the first years of Alexander II's reign, Russian Jews realized that conscription did not eliminate their sympathy for the military cause; repudiating the army would imply indifference to the fate of countless Jewish brethren in active service. The Crimean War had sharpened Jewish political sensibilities. As memoirs testify, while some Jews looked for ways to protect their sons from the impending draft, Jewish children marched with wooden guns as troops passed through their towns toward Sevastopol. In the wake of the war, a Jew in Kovel calculated the military outcome of the Crimean conflict using kabbalistic numerology. During the campaign, Jewish contractors and merchants in the Pale provided horse fodder to the Russian army. State officials differentiated between Jews and "self-seeking merchants," testifying that the former offered "bargains most advantageous to the treasury."[85] After the war, hundreds of

---

[83] *Voennyi sbornik*, no. 5 (1889): 83–84.

[84] Peter Brock and John L. Keep, eds., *Life in a Penal Battalion of the Imperial Russian Army: The Tolstoyan N. T. Iziumchenko's Story* (York: William Sessions, 2001), 38–39.

[85] Jewish merchants, if they belonged to a guild, were allowed to participate in tenders for supplying the army. See RGVIA, f. 1, op. 1, otd. 1, st. 2, d. 25376, l. 1–10b. For Meerovich and

Jewish soldiers, including former cantonists, received bronze medals and other memorabilia (but not the orders ordinarily accompanying them) in recognition of their heroic behavior during the defense of Sevastopol. Soon after the Crimean War, Main Staff Colonel Petr Lebedev, the editor of the War Ministry daily *Russkii invalid*, praised Jewish soldiers' patriotic fervor. He maintained that nobody should rebuke Jews as there were dozens of thousands of them in the Russian army. They fulfilled their duty serving the tsar and the motherland "honestly and faithfully." Lebedev emphasized that the "strongholds of the long-suffering Sevastopol" were covered not only by Russian blood but also by the blood of Jewish soldiers.[86]

One outcome of this encounter between Russians and Jews was that Jewish communal leaders and the harbingers of the *Haskalah* rushed to demonstrate publicly their regard for Russian statehood and for the Russian army. The fledgling Russian Jewish periodical *Rassvet* proclaimed that the prevailing political environment inspired Jews to fulfill their military duty voluntarily and wholeheartedly, together with the entire Russian people. Sholem Abramovits (Mendele Moykher Sforim), known as the grandfather of Yiddish literature, wrote extensively about Russian Jewish patriotism, in an attempt to shape a new Jewish perception. He also translated the 1874 statute into Yiddish, thus making it available to thousands. The famous *maskil* Moshe Leib Lilienblum, in his enlightened zeal, absolved the military administration of inconsistency in its dealings with Jews, chastised the Jewish community for deficits in the draft, demanded an end to their time-honored practice of bribing doctors, and called upon every conscripted Jew to serve with pride. The editor of the Hebrew *Ha-Magid* was among the first to acknowledge the connection between the execution of military duty and the implementation of Jewish civil equality, urging Russian Jews to serve in the army in order to merit emancipation, like their brethren in Galicia. To foster enlightened Jewish self-awareness, *maskilim* from Vilna were reported to have volunteered their services to the army, so that they could teach Jewish soldiers to read and write Hebrew.[87] Many residents in the Pale of Settlement became vitally interested in Russian geopolitics. Jews read in Russian newspapers and discussed with their Yiddish-speaking brethren the latest accounts of the Balkan military campaign.[88] Overcome with patriotic

other Jewish purveyors for the Russian army, see RGVIA, f. 801, op. 68, 1 otd., 2 st., d. 1861, ll. 201–2020b, 3390b.

[86] *Russkii invalid*, no. 39 (1858).

[87] R. K., "Rekrutstvo," *Rassvet* 40 (1861): 639–641; *Ha-Melits*, no. 6 (1878): 110–118; no. 15 (1878): 284–285; no. 4 (1878): 77–79; *Ha-Magid*, no. 7 (1881): 51–52; 12 (1881): 93–94; no. 3 (1881): 21.

[88] See, for instance, the description of a Jew who read articles from the Russian official *Severnaia Pchela* and explained the significance of the military campaign to Jews in Griazinsk for small amounts of cash: Lev Levanda, *Ispoved' del'tsa: roman v dvukh chastiakh* (SPb.: Tuzov, 1880), 20, 28–29. For a similar description of a group of shtetl Jews divided into pro-Russian and pro-Turkish camps during the Balkan war who publicly debated military and political issues, see S. Ansky's "Mendel Turk" in his *The Dybbuk and Other Writings*, ed. David G. Roskies (New York: Schocken, 1991), 93–117.

fervor, Khaim Fuks, from Kherson, wrote to Alexander II requesting permission to enroll in a military high school; although this privilege was not granted to unbaptized Jews, he received not only permission but also state sponsorship.[89] Whereas the *maskilim* were in the forefront of a new Russian–Jewish rapprochement, the traditional communal leadership, as will be shown later, also supported manifestations of the Russian Jewish patriotism.

In the 1860s, a group of Jews resolved to raise funds for the erection of a monument to five hundred Jewish soldiers who had perished near Sevastopol, declaring that the victims were not merely Jews, but Russian Jews. Designed by François Vernet, the monument was completed in 1864. It featured biblical lines written in Hebrew and an inscription affirming that these Jews had died "for the fatherland" (*za otechestvo*). Lest there be any ambiguity, the words "during the defense of Sevastopol" were added. The Russian liberal press, which had its origins in the early years of Alexander II's rule, eloquently praised Jewish patriotism.[90]

The Jews' commendable military performance gradually transformed Russian attitudes toward them. Leo Tolstoy, who served in the army during the Crimean War, noticed Jewish soldiers "with curly hair" among the cantonists and, in his *Sevastopol Stories*, mentioned their fearless conduct during the cannonade.[91]

Liberal-minded Russian officials collaborating with the military were among the first to stress the significance of growing Russian Jewish allegiance and the importance of recognizing Jews as genuine patriots. After the Crimean War, Count Stroganoff petitioned the war minister to award six Jewish doctors for their service. There had been eleven doctors serving in Sevastopol, he explained: some of them, including doctors Kamoen and Link, received a St. Stanislav Order of the second rank, while doctors Frenkel and Shneider were given the same order of the third rank. Yet six Jewish doctors – Bertelzon, Margulis, Drei, Rozen, Pinsker, and Shorshtein – received only gifts of 143 rubles each. Stroganoff was shocked to discover how uneven the distribution of awards was. Jewish doctors, he argued, worked twenty-four hours ceaselessly, some for payment and some for free, but all with a singular self-abnegation in their determination to save lives. Shorshtein had also attended the Russian army officers, free of charge. Stroganoff maintained that the Jewish faith should not present any obstacle to the deserved awards, "particularly since the law does not prevent Jewish doctors from serving the state and does not forbid awarding them high military distinctions given also to Muslims. Stingy (*skudnye*) awards are not compatible with the reputation of the government." The chancellery of the war minister responded that, albeit there was no prohibition against awarding Jews for their military service, no one had ever done so. Stroganoff

[89] *Ha-Melits*, no. 11 (1979): 226.
[90] *Russkie liudi o evreiakh* (SPb.: A.M. Wolf, 1891), 34, 39, 191.
[91] See L. N. Tolstoy, *Polnoe sobrante sochinenii*. Pod red. V. G. Chertkova (M.: Gosizdat, 1932), 4: 109–110.

ILLUSTRATION 3. A monument to 500 Jewish soldiers who perished defending Sevastopol during the Crimean War in 1855. Sevastopol Jewish Military Cemetery, architect François Vernet, 1864; reconstructed in 2004. Hebrew inscriptions on the façade from Psalms 84:8 and 116:16. From the author's archive.

was the first to demand equal treatment of Jews with respect to awards. The chancellery was able to prove the doctors' selfless heroism and offered them conciliatory gestures, but Stroganoff persisted in his efforts to convince the war minister that the "Jews manifested brilliant examples of selflessness and self-sacrifice." Finally, all six doctors received a St. Stanislav Order of the third rank, thereby becoming the first Jews ever to be awarded Russian state orders.[92]

The 1877–1878 war in the Balkans, known in contemporary Russia as the War for the Liberation of the Slavs (*voina za osvobozhdenie slavian*), was the first campaign fought by the reformed Russian army. Several participating divisions had a significant number of Jews in their lower ranks. The Thirty-fifth division was composed of two-thirds Russian Orthodox and as much as one-third Jewish soldiers. The Thirteenth and the Sixteenth divisions, drafted in Minsk and Mogilev provinces, which possessed significant Jewish populations, were one-quarter Jewish in their composition. Although reports from the front appeared in the midst of a vociferous campaign against Jewish purveyors to the military (which will be discussed in the next chapter), both Russian and Jewish journalists highlighted positive examples of the Jewish soldiers' performance. Whatever antisemitic prejudices they had had earlier, whatever suspicions about the bravery of Jewish soldiers they may have had, they had been markedly, if not entirely, assuaged by what they saw during the war. As if disagreeing with the commonly held view of Jewish cowardice, a Russian officer wrote of the Jews in the Grodnensk regiment: "There were plenty of Jews in one of the regiments that participated recently in the battle against the Turks. And so? The Jews fought bravely and even desperately."[93] Aleksei Kuropatkin, a combat officer, major general, future war minister and commander in chief in the Russo-Japanese War, shared this opinion. Recollecting his battlefield experience during the Balkan campaign, he boldly claimed that the ethnic minority groups in the army had demonstrated courageous behavior in Bulgaria: "The majority of the Tatars and the Jews were capable and will continue to be capable of fighting and perishing as heroically as the rest of the Russian soldiers." Thus the combat commanders, who saw Jews in the battle, formed a sort of a Jewish lobby in the army.

Some Jewish soldiers received the St. George Cross, the highest combat award given to members of the lower ranks. Leibush Fenberg, an artillerist, caught a bouncing cannon ball that had fallen onto his battery, flung it away, and saved the battery. Grand Duke Nicholas conferred an award upon Finkelstein, from the Skobelev detachment. Five Jewish names appeared next to the names of Russian soldiers on the internal walls of the Plevna Memorial Chapel in Moscow; these Jewish soldiers, Abram Kliakh, Samuil Brem, Naum Kolomiets, Moshka Umansky, Isaac Rodzevich, and Moisei Masiuk, were among those who stormed Plevna and captured Gali Osman Pasha, the head of the Turkish army. Like the Crimean War, the war in the Balkans brought

[92] RGVIA, f. 1, op.1, d. 23774ll. 1–4.
[93] See *Golos*, no. 229 (1877).

Jewish doctors to the front. Despite their being promoted to the rank of military doctor before the war and banished from that rank afterward, Jewish medical personnel in the late 1870s still enjoyed enthusiastic acceptance in the army.[94] Future Russian Jewish medical celebrities such as Vykhodtsev, Grosman, Shkliaver, Shapiro, Rabinovich, and Zeitlin began their careers at regimental hospitals during the Balkan campaign, and received for their contributions special acknowledgment "for excellence in fight against the Turks."[95]

To persuade their Russian readers that Jews were Russia's patriots, Jewish journalists told and retold the accounts of Jewish heroism on the Balkan front. In spite of the absence of statistics concerning awards presented to Jewish soldiers, the Jewish press furnished some reports. Its political agenda permitted anecdotal, unproven, and unreliable evidence, but testified nonetheless to a consistent attempt on the part of Russian Jews to ignite patriotic fervor among its readership. Some of these stories are more impressive than reliable. For instance, Major G. reported that a company of the Sixteenth division was crossing the Selchen Pass when it encountered a Turkish unit five times its size. Retreat seemed the most practical strategy, but a steep vertical drop behind their position effectively eliminated any possibility of escape. Suddenly, seven or eight Jewish soldiers rushed toward the Turks. Shouting, "Roll the Turk!" each of them grabbed two Turkish soldiers and jumped with them off the precipice. Other soldiers followed their example. Stunned by this fanatically valiant deed, the Turks fled. After the battle, calculations disclosed that sixty-seven Turks ended up in the abyss, as did twenty-six Russian soldiers, among them nineteen Jews.

Other stories seem entirely apocryphal. For example, the following report appears to have been based upon a century-old myth repeatedly recycled in both Europe and America. General P., in command of a Russian division, related how the Russian troops attacked Turkish trenches near Gorny Dubniak. The Turks desperately defended themselves, forcing the Russians to retreat. In the midst of the confusion, a group of Jewish soldiers advanced and, shouting, "Shema, Israel (Hear, O Israel)," resumed the offensive. The column of Russians immediately picked up the strange cry and, echoing it, rushed headlong into the Turkish trenches, vanquishing the enemy. Another such story is of similarly dubious value. After an unsuccessful battle near Plevna, a Russian army unit, one-fifth of which was Jewish, was ordered to capture the Turkish position at night. The detachment moved through a field strewn with enemy corpses. The Turks allowed the detachment to advance to a distance of fifty steps, and then opened fire almost at point-blank range. As the detachment began its panicked retreat, a Jewish noncommissioned officer picked up a discarded fez from the ground, held it out to a Russian officer, and cried out, "Your honor, put it on; shout Allah!" In a moment, all the Russian soldiers

---

[94] *Evreiskaia starina*, no. 2 (1915): 176–182.
[95] Usov, *Evrei v armii*, 65.

ILLUSTRATION 4. The Plevna Memorial Chapel, dedicated to the grenadiers who perished near Plevna during Russo-Turkish War, 1878–1879; architect V. Shervud, 1887. The interior of the chapel has bronze plaques with names of 18 officers and 542 soldiers, including 6 Jewish soldiers who helped capture Osman Pasha. From the author's archive.

were disguised in Turkish fezzes, taken from the corpses. Shouting out "Allah," they caused bafflement among the Turkish artillery, stormed the trenches, and eventually captured the Turkish positions. Perhaps these tales testified to an emerging Russian Jewish self-awareness. Yet they also represented important objectives: Prescriptive rather than descriptive, they displayed the heroism to which Jews aspired and encouraged Russians to view Jews more favorably. At any rate, they pointed to the desire of Jews in Russia to be considered the Russian Jews – integrated, loyal, patriotic, and Russified culturally and politically.

Judaizing the Military

Once the army had succeeded in militarizing the Jew, Jewish society attempted to return the favor: to Judaize the military. While it was relatively simple to impress upon Russian Jews the indispensability of their conscription to their newly accorded role in society, conveying to the army the cultural aspects of the Jewish soldier's identity proved somewhat more challenging. Both traditional and enlightened leaders naively rushed to praise the new conditions of service delineated in the 1874 statute, ignoring its shortcomings. In a dramatic reversal, army experience was suddenly regarded as beneficial to the Jew. Rabbis argued that military service now permitted a soldier to retain his traditional ways and to eat kosher food; he was even discharged for the holidays. *Maskilim* maintained that simply fulfilling one's sacred duty as a soldier took precedence over obtaining an army promotion or remaining faithful to one's traditional customs.[96] Obligations, they claimed, were more significant than rights.

The Balkan war further intensified the contacts between Jews and the military. Several crown and spiritual rabbis greeted Russian troops and praised the Jewish soldiers going to fight for the great Slavic cause.[97] Other communal leaders, like Crown Rabbi Lev Binshtok, organized a *kiddush* (blessing of the wine) ceremony for the Russian army, providing wine and bread rolls for a regiment returning from the Balkan campaign, and prompting laudatory speeches by the regimental commanders about the loyalty of Jewish soldiers.[98]

Jewish conscripts found themselves cast as mediators in the encounter between the army and the community. To prove their allegiance to the tsar, Jewish communities throughout the Pale chose to commemorate important Russian calendar dates, particularly those celebrating military campaigns or

---

[96] *Ha-Melits*, no. 1 (1878): 18; no. 19 (1878): 359–360.

[97] Salomon Mandelkern, *Slovo, proiznesennoe v odesskoi glavnoi sinagoge po povodu perekhoda russkikh voisk cherez Dunai* (Odessa: n. p., 1877); "Rech ravvina Mandelkerna k opolchentsam-evreiam," *Novorossiiskii telegraph*, no. 742 (1877); L. Kleinberg, *Rechi, proiznesennye v vilenskoi sinagoge v dni prochteniia Vysochaishego manifesta ot 12 aprelia 1877 g., prazdnovaniia vziatia Plevny 2 dekabria 1877 g. i 25 fevralia 1878 g. po povodu radostnoi vesti o preliminarnom traktate* (Vilna: n. p., 1878).

[98] See the report of the Kursk regiment (under the command of General Alexander Galer), returning from the Balkan front, *Ha-Melits*, no. 14 (1878): 269–270.

crucial events in the emperor's life. In 1878, upon the initiative of the Biisk Jewish community, the commander of the Viatka regiment allowed his 300 Jewish soldiers to take a Torah scroll with them to the Balkans. The same commander, accompanied by the town magistrate officials, regimental officers, and the chief of local police, participated in the ceremonial return of the scroll to the Biisk prayer house upon the conclusion of the campaign.[99] In 1879, immediately after an unsuccessful attempt on the life of Alexander II, a guild merchant, Ioffe, suggested honoring the day of the emperor's miraculous redemption. To this end, he commissioned and donated Torah scrolls to the Jewish soldiers of the Fifty-first Lithuania regiment, quartered in Sevastopol. On August 30, 1879, some five hundred Jewish soldiers carrying the newly written scrolls marched through the streets of Sevastopol, with the Belostok regimental orchestra and high-ranking military and city officials following behind. While announcing in the Jewish prayer house the donation of the scrolls to the regiment, Ioffe stipulated that the Jewish soldiers of the Lithuania regiment read them both on the obligatory days of Torah reading and during thanksgiving services marking the emperor's salvation (Karakozov's attempt on the emperor's life was on April 4, 1864; Sokolov's attempt was on April 2, 1879.)[100]

The Torah dedication ceremony accomplished several objectives. Principally, it demonstrated that Jews were loyal subjects of the empire who shared the political ideals and social values of Russian society. It employed Jewish soldiers as tacit intercessors on behalf of Russian Jews, while upholding the interests of Jewish soldiers in the eyes of the military administration. Local civil and military officials were favorably impressed by such community-sponsored festivals, which assisted in dissipating long-held anti-Jewish bias. Additionally, it is likely that the community wished to remind soldiers of their origins and obligations. The distinction between assimilation, which presupposed surrendering their traditional sensibilities, and integration was made clear: while engaged in service to the Russian emperor, Jewish soldiers also fulfilled the 613th Commandment, the collective writing of the parchment scroll of the Pentateuch.[101]

Between 1870 and 1890, Jewish communities helped soldiers establish prayer houses, interceded on behalf of conscripts wishing to observe Jewish holidays, arranged Passover festivities in the soldiers' canteens, greeted Russian troops at welcome and farewell ceremonies, and donated Torah scrolls to the regiments. Pragmatic military officials understood the importance of communal outreach in establishing good relations with the Jewish enlisted men. At the Skobelev military camp in Nesvizh, Colonel Annushkin agreed to a communal Passover celebration in his Fortieth artillery brigade.[102] Colonel Makeev, of the Fifty-ninth Lublin infantry, approved the participation of his Jewish soldiers in

[99] *Ha-Melits*, no. 17 (1878): 336.
[100] *Russkii evrei*, no. 5 (1979): 153–154.
[101] See Simcha Cohen, *The 613th Commandment: An Analysis of the Mitzvah to Write a Sefer Torah* (Northvale, N. J.: Jason Aronson, 1994).
[102] RGVIA, f. 400, op. 15, d. 3521, l. 164–164ob.

the *haknasat torah* (the Pentateuch scroll consecration festivities). Similar celebrations occurred in the Lithuania regiment in Simferopol, in the Molo- dechensk regiment in Vilna, and in the regiments quartered in Chardzhui and Rogachev.[103] The involvement of the local administration transformed these events into a Jewish Russian military symbiosis. In Rogachev, the commander of the regiment, the district police officer, his deputy, and the commander of the town garrison attended a Torah scroll dedication in which some 140 Jewish soldiers of the 159th Guriisk infantry commemorated the recovery of their "adored emperor," Nicholas II.[104] In Serpets (Sierpc), Colonel Korbut, in command of the Forty-eighth Ukrainian imperial dragoons regiment, permitted Jewish soldiers to raise funds to commission a Torah scroll, and then arranged the ceremony, which he described to the War Ministry:

> Curious about a ritual I had never observed, I went to the local synagogue together with several officers and the head of the district police. All the elders and the Rabbi met us there, and offered us honorable and specially prepared places. The festivities started with the Rabbi's prayer for the emperor, followed by the national anthem. Then the Rabbi gave a fiery patriotic speech about the kindness and the mercy of the emperor and the tolerance of Russian Orthodoxy. Afterwards, they started to write the afore- mentioned Torah. The Rabbi approached each of us, asked us to hold the feather and, behold, a letter appeared on the parchment. Having satiated our curiosity, we left the synagogue, but, condescending to the petition of the honorable old Rabbi, we entered his apartment to enjoy his hospitality. The aforementioned Torah is a lengthy scroll of parchment on which the whole Pentateuch is written. The entire work represents a remarkable example of calligraphy and will be finished in five to eight months. Our Jews consider the above mentioned private visit to the synagogue an extraordinary event. It provided them with a strong and pleasing impression.[105]

The visit also made a strong and pleasing impression upon Colonel Korbut, who had supported his Jewish soldiers in their endeavor. He treated them as loyal servants of the empire and refused to segregate them. He continually reassured the authorities of the wisdom of his actions, believing they would benefit the military as a whole. The military, as will be explained later, chose not to heed his arguments or those of like-minded army commanders. After the Balkan war, the army's conservative tendencies came into play and the move- ment toward reform was suppressed.

Conclusion

The military reform of the 1870s presupposed that universal equality with regard to military privileges would follow universal liability to military service – for everybody, Jews included. The representatives of Russian Jewry fighting for

---

[103] RGVIA, f. 400, op. 15, d. 1711, ll. 3, 16, 18.
[104] RGVIA, f. 400, op. 15, d. 2053, l. 1.
[105] RGVIA, f. 400, op. 15, d. 1711, l. 7.

Jewish rights expected to obtain de jure equality for Jewish soldiers in recognition of their de facto integration into the Russian state through the military.

In contrast with Nicholas I's conscription system, this reform considerably changed Jewish attitudes to the army in a positive way. While some Jews dodged the draft, by and large Jews responded to the call-up better than most of the Russian urban dwellers. Most Jewish novices were fit for the service, were better disciplined than non-Jews, and demonstrated excellent performance during the Crimean and the Balkan military campaigns. The accusations of Jewish draft dodging should be regarded as a fabrication of unimaginative Judeophobes. By the 1880s, Jewish soldiers were thoroughly integrated with the Russian military and represented everything we call today modern: they firmly established themselves as dual-identity Russian Jews; they were patriots and loyalists; they believed in Mother Russia, and were ready to spill their Jewish blood for her. They shared with their Christian brethren such things as language, food, clothes, daily obligations and daily routine, training and combat experience, economic hardships and material values, and perhaps concerns and hopes. Judaism became for Jewish soldiers simply a religion rather than a way of life. They celebrated their Russian Jewish identity and sought to be accepted as Russian Jews. Some officers tried to accommodate them, endorsed their public religious festivities, and joined Jewish soldiers in the celebration of their militarized form of Russian Judaism.

Jewish soldiers fully deserved equal privileges granted elsewhere to Jews fulfilling their sacred duty before the state. The United States Army, for example, had several lieutenant colonels and majors of Jewish origin, let alone lieutenants, as early as the 1820s. Once the Civil War broke out, Jews fought as soldiers and as mid-rank officers on both sides of the divide. Judaism was also at this time legalized in the U.S. military. In the early 1860s, President Lincoln established the institute of military chaplains and rabbis were allowed to serve as religious leaders remunerated by the state. By the 1880s, Austrian and Italian armies also had Jewish majors, colonels, and even generals.

Unlike these countries, nineteenth-century Russia and Prussia had *one* Jewish combat officer each in the troops, and even their corresponding promotions in the military were considered an anomaly not to be repeated. Rabbis were not legitimized as chaplains in the Russian military. Eventually the War Ministry ruled against extending equal privileges to Jews, emphasizing their singular status within the troops. The counterreform of the 1880s thwarted most of Miliutin's liberal objectives. While Jewish soldiers claimed the Russian military as their own, the Russian military disowned Judaism in disgust.

5

The Russian Army's Jewish Question

The era of Alexander II gave rise not only to liberal but also to conservative tendencies dormant in Russian society. The clamorous counterreformist press, increasing state chauvinism and xenophobia, and concomitant persecutions of ethnic minorities began in the midst of reforms and fully manifested themselves under Alexander III (1881–1894). The nascent conservative trend fostered the imperial perception of the Jews as a harmful, even parasitic ethnic group that had brought upon itself the pogroms of the early 1880s. After Alexander II's assassination the regime rejected Minister of the Interior Loris-Melikov's opinion that the Pale should be abolished. The empire's approach toward Jewish society gradually evolved from one of selective integration to one of integral segregation, urged by statesmen of the previous regime, such as Timashev and Shuvalov. Minister of the Interior Ignatiev's provisional regulations, known as the 1882 May Laws, restricted Jewish settlement in rural areas and eventually reclassified many small shtetls as villages, the measure that made Jews leave their places of residence, now illegal, and move to towns and cities. The May Laws effected the coercive urbanization of Jews, who had allegedly been making the Russian peasants drunk, and were the government's response to the first large-scale pogroms in nineteenth-century Russia.

Other regulations of the late nineteenth century, such as the introduction of the state monopoly on distilling and selling of alcohol, swiftly resulted in the impoverishment of Jews in the Pale; they increasingly turned proletarian, became radicalized and joined socialist parties, aligned themselves with burgeoning Jewish nationalism, or emigrated. For those who continued to serve the tsar and the fatherland, the counterreform coup of Alexander III altered the conditions of military service. Attempts to segregate Jewish soldiers began with military reform, gained momentum in the wake of the Balkan war, and culminated in the anti-Jewish regulations introduced by the War Ministry in the 1880s. While Europe, especially Germany, experienced the rapid spread of a new political phenomenon known as racial antisemitism, the roots of Russian anti-Jewish sensibilities palpable in the late 1870s–early 1880s were quite different.

The Alleged Jewish Conspiracy against the Army

Russian historians have identified the 1877–1878 Russo-Turkish War as a turning point, after which anti-Jewish prejudice became a significant presence in Russia.[1] Reasons include Benjamin Disraeli's successful attempt to limit Russian gains at the 1878 Berlin Congress, the crystallization of postwar Russian imperial chauvinism and nationalism, and the new regime's counter-reform. Yet historians have overlooked the internal causes of such radical change. Perhaps nothing triggered the dramatic increase in anti-Jewish sensibility, particularly within the military, so much as the activities of the Partnership (*Tovarishchestvo*) of Greger, Gorvits, and Kogan and of its associate, Varshavskii; together, they were the monopolist purveyors to the Russian army during the Balkan war. Russian society perceived their case as a litmus test for Jewish modernization, for the Jewish encounter with the military, and for Jewish loyalty and patriotism. The actions of the Partnership during the 1877–1878 military campaign created the impression that Jews had embezzled the army funds at the expense of the Russian soldiers who languished, frostbitten and hungry, in the Balkan Mountains.

At the height of the Balkan campaign, the Partnership found itself confronting accusations of "unscrupulousness and speculation."[2] Miliutin called Varshavskii, who was responsible for the transport of supplies to the army, "the Jewish crook."[3] By the end of the conflict, the Russian press across the political spectrum referred to the Partnership as a classic example of the sinister Jewish influence upon the campaign. The view that the Partnership scorned the army it had undertaken to feed became the stock-in-trade of Russian antisemitic literature.[4] The scrupulous Simon Dubnow also joined those condemning the Partnership, calling its members "scum," and pleading that Russian society differentiate between the Jewish nouveaux riches and Russian Jews in general.[5] The condemnatory evaluation of the Partnership's activity reemerged in Soviet historical narratives, which argued that Greger, Gorvits, and Kogan reaped a profit at the expense of the starving army.[6] It is worth examining why the relations between the government and the Partnership ended so badly and

---

[1] Kritikus [Simon Dubnow], "Literaturnaia letopis," *Voskhod*, vol. 9, no. 1 (January 1891): 24–41; Klier, *Imperial Russia's Jewish Question*, 392; Beyrau, *Militär und Gesellschaft*, 428–429.

[2] S. Iu. Witte, *Vospominaniia* (M.: Izd. sotsialno-ekonomicheskoi literatury, 1960), 1: 316–317.

[3] *Dnevnik D. A. Miliutina*, ed. P. A. Zaionchkovskii (M.: Gosudarstvennaia Biblioteka im. Lenina, 1949), 2:179.

[4] See, for example, V. I. Nemirovich-Danchenko, *God voiny* (SPb.: Soikin, n. d.), 1: 124, 148–158, 184–190; A. S. Shmakov. *Svoboda i evrei* (M.: Gorodskaia tipografiia, 1906), 26–27, 504; V. V. Krestovskii. *Sobranie sochinenii* (SPb.: Obshchestvennaia pol'za, 1899), 8:217–287.

[5] Kritikus [Simon Dubnow], "Literaturnaia letopis," 39.

[6] L. G. Beskrovnyi, *Russkaia armiia i flot v XIX veke* (M.: Nauka, 1973), 471; idem., Beskrovnyi, *Russkoe voennoe iskusstvo XIX veka* (M.: Nauka, 1974), 317. John Klier also accepted this view; see his *Imperial Russia's Jewish Question*, 392–393; cf. the assessment of the Partnership's activities in Beyrau, *Militär und Gesellschaft*, 423–429.

provided Russian conservatives with an ostensible reason to reject Russian-Jewish rapprochement.[7]

The Partnership was predominantly Jewish. Two high-ranking Russian officials owned shares in it: 55 percent belonged to Gorvits, Greger, and Nepokoichitskii (the latter headed the army headquarters of Grand Duke Nikolai Nikolaevich, the Balkan corps' commander in chief), while Kogan, Liubarskii, and Arenson owned the remaining 45 percent.[8] In 1877, the Partnership, created for this purpose, was the only single contractor willing to undertake the daunting task of supplying an entire army fighting far beyond Russia's borders. Before the Great Reforms, the military Commissariat and the Provisions Department (*proviantskii departament*) routinely managed all deliveries to the army. The Provisions Department proved incompetent, and many troops starved during the 1828–1830 Turkish and 1830–1831 Polish campaigns.[9] When the Commissariat managed the transport of food supplies to the army in Sevastopol in 1853–55, embezzlement was the normal practice, and soldiers ate "rotten biscuits with mould and worms."[10] Even though Miliutin had reorganized the Provisions Department into the Chief Commissariat Administration, the new ministerial subdivision was not able independently to coordinate food delivery to the troops.

Although the army had had previous dealings with Jewish purveyors, this Partnership was a new phenomenon. The inept Commissariat compelled the War Ministry to assign to contractors the supply of provisions to the army in the field. In both early modern and modern Europe, Jewish merchants frequently acted as purveyors.[11] The Russian military also occasionally outsourced the supply of provisions for troops to Jewish contractors, particularly because so much of the army was garrisoned in the Pale.[12] On the eve of the Balkan campaign, the Main Staff contracted with the Partnership to provision the army, and signed another contract with Varshavskii, a guild merchant, who supplied and managed the transport carts. While the Partnership officially involved four or five major Jewish purveyors, in fact it engaged the assistance of

---

[7] To evaluate the situation, see the sixteen voluminous files in RGVIA, f. 485, op. 1, d. 354 ("Materialy o prodovol'stvennom i furazhnom snabzhenii voisk i ob organizatsii intendantskoi sluzhby"); d. 355–368 ("O sledstvii i sude nad ofitserami i chinovnikami, otvetstvennymi za snabzhenie voisk v posledniuiu voinu"); d. 371 ("Otchety i spravochnye materialy o snabzhenii voisk").

[8] RGVIA, f. 485, d. 355, l. 8ob.

[9] Because of the poor organization of food supplies to the troops during the Turkish war of 1828–1830, plague, scurvy, and fever occurred, as a result of which more than 22,429 men died. See *Glavnoe voenno-meditsinskoe upravlenie*, in SVM, t. VIII, 3: 50.

[10] Poor food quality caused an epidemic of gastrointestinal diseases: 43 percent of the 7,027 troops suffering from diarrhea died. See SVM, t. VIII, 4: 33–45.

[11] Jonathan Israel, *European Jews in the Era of Mercantilism, 1550–1750* (Oxford: Clarendon Press, 1989), 129–132; Maurycy Horn, *Powinności wojenne Żydow w Rzeczypospolitej w XVI i XVII wieku* (Warsaw: Państwowe Wydawnictwo Naukowe, 1978), 29–43.

[12] RGVIA, f. 1, op. 1, otd. 1, st. 2, d. 25376, l. 1–10b; RGVIA, f. 801, op. 68, 1 otd., 2 st., d. 1861, ll. 201–2020b.

hundreds of agents, middlemen, wagon-drivers, other contractors and sales-men, most of whom were Jews.

The contractors did their utmost to feed the army. If soldiers in previous campaigns had considered bread a luxury, and rusks (*sukhari*) their daily food, this time bread was the norm, and rusks the exception. However, the Part-nership encountered certain insurmountable difficulties, such as the poor quality of hay in Rumania, where the Russian cavalry blamed the "rotten hay" on Jewish purveyors. When the army entered Bulgaria, relations between the military Commissariat and the Partnership deteriorated. The civil commander in chief, Prince Cherkasskii, unilaterally decided that the Commissariat itself was capable of providing the army with available local resources, and seized possession of large quantities of food that the Partnership had obtained for the troops. St. Petersburg's repeated intercessions eventually secured the release and delivery of the supplies. From then on, the Partnership was obliged to pay Russian military officials huge duties in exchange for the privilege of shipping food to the Russian army.[13]

In violation of the contract, the Partnership found itself obligated to function as an intermediary not only between the food producers and the troops, but also between the troops and the Russian military hierarchy, bribing them in return for the support of various military subdivisions. However, when the roads became impassable for tens of thousands of Varshavskii's carts, the military forbade the use of its transport to assist the Partnership, and Varshavskii's desperate efforts to obtain help fell upon deaf ears.[14] Furthermore, army offi-cials forbade the transport of food in carts, which effectively suspended further deliveries to the troops fighting in Bulgaria. Against all odds, the Partnership struggled to fulfill "what the military administration failed to perform."[15] Contradictory accounts emerged of the Partnership's efforts, especially when supplying soldiers serving under difficult climatic, geographical, and military conditions.[16] General Zotov, who had heard of the "notorious Partnership," recalled the troops' continuous complaints about its disorganization. He blamed both the army and the Partnership, complaining that "we had two Commis-sariats: one was official, the ministerial; the other belonged to the Yids."[17] Military officials accused not only the Partnership, but the Commissariat as

---

[13] *Ocherk deiatel'nosti Tovarishchestva Greger, Gorvits i Kogan po prodovol'stviu deistvuiushchei armii v Vostochnuiu voinu 1877–1878 godov* (Bucharest: n. p., 1878), 40–41, 43, 60, 67, 75, 82.

[14] The military, in turn, rebuked Varshavskii, claiming that "[I]t is not possible in any way to facilitate the consignments of the civil commissariat, and the passage of vehicles with oats should be suspended until a safer time." See *Vol'nonaiemnyi intendantskii transport v Turetskuiu voinu 1877–1878 gg.* (Bucharest: n. p., 1878); see especially "Prilozenie," 16, 123.

[15] *Ocherk deiatel'nosti Tovarishchestva*, 86.

[16] For more detail on the provision of supplies to the troops in Bulgaria, see S. Sobolev, "Russko-Turetskaia voina v Bolgarii," *Russkaia starina*, vol. 54, no. 6 (1887): 764–765; vol. 55, no. 8 (1887): 342–343.

[17] Despite its bias, Zotov's memoir in many respects corroborated the complaints of Greger and his colleagues. See [P. Zotov], "Zapiski generala ot infanterii P. Zotova. Voina za nezavisimost' slavian 1877–1878," *Russkaia starina*, no. 49 (1886): 220; 50 (1886): 436–437.

a whole. The head of the Military Commissariat, Arens, either was unwilling or unable to cooperate with the Partnership; when the campaign was fully underway, he departed for Odessa.[18] The Partnership complained, with reason, that the military Commissariat, numbering six thousand men, had vanished the moment the campaign started.[19]

The inadequate provision of supplies to the troops and the clashes between contractors were symptomatic of a larger problem. Swift service by the Partnership would have signified Jewish readiness to support the War for the Liberation of the Slavs, to abandon allegedly self-serving financial practices, and to prove the Jews' wholehearted patriotism. The Partnership's performance would determine whether Jews indeed could become Russians. These were high stakes, as both the Partnership and its opponents were aware. The Russian press closely monitored the conflict between the Partnership and the military. In its reports about the subsequent lawsuit, several important newspapers resolutely supported the Partnership.[20] They noted that the commander in chief considered Jewish businessmen to be reliable, while the army Commissariat did not. Commissions established to supervise the Partnership's actions discovered no embezzlement; in view of the price fluctuations in Rumania and Bulgaria, it was absurd to blame the Partnership for unstable purchase prices. The allegations of spying similarly were proved groundless. Furthermore, the troops crossed the border on April 12, 1877, while the contract was signed on April 16; yet the Partnership had provided supplies to the troops from the first day of the campaign.

Nonetheless, the governmental and military officials were not favorably disposed toward the Partnership. In September 1878, Staff Officer Totleben presented Alexander II with a report "On the procedure for settling accounts with the Greger, Gorvits, and Kogan Partnership, which provisioned the troops and army hospitals."[21] As a result of this paper's severe criticism of the services rendered by the Partnership to the Russian troops, the emperor ordered a formal and thorough investigation of the Partnership's and the Commissariat's activity. A commission was established, whose investigative results seemed preordained: payments to the Partnership were suspended indefinitely.[22]

The army hit upon an easy way to defend its honor. It proclaimed that the Partnership was Jewish; that Jews were notoriously unscrupulous in their dealings with non-Jews; and that the Partnership solely sought financial gain, and was indifferent to the plight of the Russian soldier. This sufficed to explain

---

[18] The Odessa military commandment requested that charges be brought against Arens for obstruction and for exceeding his authority. See RGVIA, f. 485, d. 355, l. 13. Cf. references to Arens as "an impeccably honest person" in the encyclopedic account of his career, "Arens, I. A." in *Voennaia entsiklopediia*, 3:17–18.

[19] RGVIA, f. 485, d. 355, l. 7.

[20] *Sankt-peterburgskie vedomosti* no. 285 (October 16, 1878); *Golos*, no. 305 (November 27, 1978); no. 328 (November 30, 1878).

[21] RGVIA, f. 485, d. 355, ll. 2–5.

[22] RGVIA, f. 485, d. 355, l. 1–10b.

the sufferings of those who captured Plevna, defended the Shipka mountain pass, and heroically marched through Bulgaria on empty stomachs to defeat the Turks. From the outset, the commission sided with the Commissariat, adopting the view that the Partnership was guilty of all the military's failures. In the commission's opinion, Varshavskii and Kogan were not entrepreneurs, but the criminal authors of the soldiers' hardships. The contractors bore responsibility for the famine endured by troops in San Stefano. Chief contractors Levitan, Levinson, and Pergament embezzled governmental property. Ironically, during the investigation, the Partnership was still in Bucharest, endeavoring to fulfill the terms and conditions of its contract. The vouchers its staff dispatched to St. Petersburg demonstrate that Greger, Kogan, and the others were not initially aware of the seriousness of the charges brought against them. They attempted to convince the authorities that the Commissariat had shifted its responsibilities onto the Partnership, making it the only agent for all deliveries, while retaining for itself the duty of control.[23]

Ultimately, the charges against the Partnership were reduced to three: its supplies were not always of good quality; its operations were poorly organized; and it artificially raised prices. In response, the Partnership attempted "to present unquestionable proof that, under existing conditions, it could not have done more than was actually done," and published two detailed reports: *The Account of the Activity of the Greger, Gorvits and Kogan Partnership in the Supply of Food to the Army in the Campaign of 1877–1878* and *The Civilian Commissariat Transport in the Turkish War of 1877–1878*. The Partnership succeeded in proving its diligence, responsibility, and efficiency. Loyalty and patriotism permeate the sober analysis of the reports. Both studies contained examples of military provisioning during European wars, numerous tables detailing the volume of purchases and deliveries, and copies of military orders. Both reveal that the poor supply was the result of two factors: the unwillingness of the Commissariat and the occupation authorities to assist the Partnership, and the specific local conditions in Romania and Bulgaria, unfamiliar both to the military authorities and to the Partnership. On April 11, 1880, the commission investigating the Partnership reported to War Minister Miliutin, faulting the commander of the occupation forces in Romania, Commissar Rossitskii, and the Partnership itself.[24] The report did not explicitly attribute blame to the Jewish purveyors. Consequently, Miliutin dissolved the commission and ordered a new investigation, under the military prosecutor Neelov.

The new report accused the Partnership of attempting to steal from the troops. On August 28, 1880, the commission found against the Partnership and demanded payment for its failure to deliver 17,210 rubles worth of provisions. In response, the Partnership submitted 101,723 receipts, for a total sum of 3,442,085.79 rubles (its cumulative expenditure for army supplies in the Balkan campaign); the military had reimbursed it for only 38,523.36 rubles. By the fall,

---

[23] RGVIA, f. 485, d. 355, l. 9, 29.
[24] RGVIA, f. 485, d. 360, ch. 1, ll. 15–180b.

the situation had not improved; the Partnership paid the forfeit. Any additional compensation under the contract now was out of the question.[25] According to Count Witte's vague account, intrigues on the part of Serebriannyi, an attorney, and Duchess Iurievskaia, the young wife of Alexander II, enabled the Partnership finally to recoup some of its losses.[26] Yet, in the eyes of the public, the Partnership remained the guilty party and represented the entire Russian Jewish community.

Alexander III, who had commanded the Rushchuk corps during the Balkan campaign, ascended the throne four months after the verdict of the War Ministry commission. Neither he nor his future war minister, Petr Vannovskii, doubted the Partnership's guilt; nor did they question the supposed inability of Russian Jews to serve the fatherland. Jews were obliged to pay for what a military historian described as the Russian army's "incompetence, dilatoriness, and amateurishness in the 1877 campaign."[27] When dismissing War Minister Miliutin, the new Russian emperor assured everyone that he condemned Jews alone for the poor supplies to the army; the War Ministry, the military Commissariat, and Miliutin himself all were held blameless. The culprit was "that unfortunate partnership."[28] General Levitskii, who served as chief of staff during the Balkan campaign, confirmed this opinion, observing that

the belief in the unscrupulousness of the Jewish contractors was so strong that they trusted every allegation of poor behavior by any supplier, without commissioning an audit; they concealed any embezzlement on the part of the military Commissariat or of any other supply agent. The consequence was a fast-growing irritation against Jews in general, especially noticeable among army personnel serving under the emperor's successor: the Crown Prince [future Alexander III] became deeply antisemitic. With this hostile attitude toward Jews, Alexander III assumed the throne.[29]

General Vannovskii was appointed as Miliutin's successor; he remained war minister for the next seventeen years. Immediately upon his appointment, he informed Alexander III that he had inherited from his predecessor the lawsuit brought against the Partnership.[30] It is possible that the scandal concerning the

[25] RGVIA, f. 485, d. 360, ch. 1, ll. 288–320.

[26] Witte, *Vospominaniia*, 1:317.

[27] See David Alan Rich, *The Tsar's Colonels: Professionalism, Strategy, and Subversion in Late Imperial Russia* (Cambridge, Mass.: Harvard University Press, 1998), 190.

[28] *Dnevnik D. A. Miliutina*, 4: 75. Miliutin probably paraphrased his interlocutor's speech, altering Alexander III's rude remarks against the Partnership. For the estimation of Alexander III's manner of speech, see P. A. Zaionchkovskii, *Rossiiskoe samoderzhavie v kontse XIX stoletiia* (M.: Mysl, 1970), 37, 43.

[29] General Levitskii's opinion is recorded in G. B. Sliozberg, *Dela davno minuvshikh dnei. Zapiski russkogo evreia* (Paris: Pascal, 1933), 1:115–116.

[30] On November 1, 1881, Vannovskii wrote to Alexander III, "On Tuesday, November 3, there will be hearings held at the committee of ministers on the amicable settlement of the transactions with the Partnership. Would it be possible for Your Imperial Majesty to allow me not to come that day with the report?" See RGVIA, f. 248, op. 1, d. 14, l. 10.

Partnership cemented his anti-Jewish bias and prompted his segregationist regulations regarding Jewish military service.

The Architect of Discrimination

Among Alexander III's ministers, Petr Semenovich Vannovskii was one of the most complex,[31] He could be portrayed as an opponent of liberal reforms, were it not for his choice as closest assistant of General Nikolai Obruchev, an architect of Miliutin's liberal innovations.[32] He might be regarded as an ignorant administrator or a bungling disciplinarian but for the belief held by many of his opponents that he was diligent, aware of his personal shortcomings, and capable of redressing the omissions in his education. He could pass for an extreme conservative but for the fact that he suddenly emerged as a democrat and a liberal when for a short term he became minister of education under Nicholas II.[33]

Although Vannovskii viewed the alien ethnic populations in the army with as much suspicion as did his ruler, he remained a cautious pragmatist who understood that the indiscriminate imposition of restrictions upon Jews did not benefit the military enterprise.[34] Nevertheless, during his tenure as war minister, Vannovskii created a complex system of prohibitions barring Jews (and Poles) from certain positions. His closest colleagues often failed to grasp the logic underlying these restrictions. While after the Polish rebellion of 1863–1864 the imperial administration had good reasons to consider Poles disloyal and restricted their career opportunities in the Russian military, there were no grounds for suspecting Jews of disloyalty, except some paranoid fancies, as John Klier put it. Yet restrictions against Poles now served Vannovskii as a blueprint for similar measures against Jews. The military posts closed to Jews included, among others, clerks, artisans, draftsmen, escorts, orderlies, munitions factory workers, engineering officers, engineers, millers, warehouse

[31] For the authoritative account of Vannovskii, see Zaionchkovskii, *Samoderzhaviie i russkaia armiia*, 57–69.

[32] For a detailed analysis of Obruchev's career, see David Alan Rich, *The Tsar's Colonel*, 46–52, 73. For the revolutionary illusions of Obruchev and his work under Miliutin and Vannovskii, see Menning, *Bayonets before Bullets*, 17–20, 97–98. Russian military historian Airapetov rejects the characterization of Obruchev as a staunch liberal; see O. R. Airapetov, *Zabytaia kariera "russkogo Moltke." Nikolai Nikolaevich Obruchev (1830–1904)* (SPb.: Aleteia, 1998), 72–75.

[33] *Voennaia entsiklopediia*, 5:234–235; Witte, *Vospominaniia*, 1:304–305; *Dnevnik Perettsa* (M.: Gosudarstvennoe izdatelstvo, 1927), 75; *Dnevnik gosudarstvennogo sekretaria A. A. Polovtsova*, 2 vols. (M.: Nauka, 1966), 1:79, 108; 2:131; *Vospominania Sukhomlinova*, pref. by V. Nevskii (M., L.: Gosudarstvennoe izdatel'stvo, 1926), 72.

[34] For the influence of Alexander III's conservative views upon Vannovskii, see the file "Zapiski Aleksandra III Vannovskomu," in RGVIA, f. 278, op. 1, d. 16, nos. 554, 580, 600, 629, particularly l. 25 (a commentary on Pobedonostsev's letter); l. 37 (a discourse on the nationalistic character of the Russian troops); l. 64 (a note on an article by "a most humble citizen," Count Meshcherskii).

inspectors, chemists, veterinary medical assistants, and doctors and medical assistants in the western districts.[35]

Notable among Vannovskii's harsh anti-Jewish decrees was the revocation of residence privileges for retired Jewish soldiers. Until 1885, the military maintained that Jewish soldiers who served on pre-1874 terms and retired had earned the right to reside anywhere in the empire, particularly if they served outside the Pale. This privilege liberated the Jewish soldier from the Pale of Settlement, the most glaring manifestation of Jewish inequality. Although this stance contravened the letter of the law, the police routinely permitted retired Jewish soldiers to settle outside the Pale. Yet, in the mid-1880s, the police suddenly refused to acknowledge Jewish soldiers' retirement certificates as according them the right of universal residence, and began driving them back into the Pale. The soldiers turned for protection to the War Ministry. On April 5, 1885, the governor of St. Petersburg forwarded to Vannovskii a petition by ten Jewish retired privates, appealing for permission to live in St. Petersburg.[36] This petition was rejected on the grounds that the Jewish soldiers had served under the 1874 statute, rather than under the conscription regulations of Nicholas I. On January 22, 1888, after two years of similar appeals, Obruchev prepared and Vannovskii approved a circular entitled "On barring the residence of retired Jewish soldiers in places closed to Jews." This circular marked the moment military service ceased to be a step toward equality for Russian Jews. Unlike those who had served under Nicholas I, Jewish soldiers in the last quarter of the nineteenth century were not permitted to settle in the interior of the empire, but instead were compelled to return to the Pale. Jews who had completed their service journeyed immediately to the place of their previous residence registration.[37]

The ministry then introduced a set of legal and quasi-legal restrictions barring Jews from various military positions, occupations, and regions. Jewish physicians were the first to feel the effects of these strictures. Count Totleben, the commander of the Vilna military district, alleged that Jewish military doctors practiced medicine for financial reasons exclusively, and were less diligent than Christians; therefore, their presence in the army must be strictly limited. At the time, Jews comprised 10 percent of military doctors (250 men).[38] Most of them served in the Vilna, Odessa, Warsaw, and Kiev military districts, and represented 20, 25, 11, and 12 percent of the medical staff, respectively. The number of Jewish doctors roughly corresponded to the percentage of Jews among the general population of the western provinces. Nikolai Manassein, the minister

---

[35] Numerous qualifications rendered the register even more complex. For a list of the positions from which Jews were excluded, see RGVIA, f. 400, op. 5, d. 1265, l. 69.

[36] RGVIA, f. 400, op. 5, d. 870, ll. 2–50b.

[37] RGVIA, f. 400, op. 5, d. 870, ll. 2–20b., 5–50b., 110b., 16–17. After the Russo-Japanese War, the Ministry of the Interior made another attempt to curtail the right of Jewish soldiers to settle beyond the Jewish Pale, see RGVIA, f. 400, op. 6, d. 1072, ll. 24–33.

[38] RGVIA, f. 400, op. 5, d. 1650, ll. 1–20b.

of justice, tried in vain to convince the War Ministry that it made no sense to blame Jewish physicians for the army's deplorable sanitary conditions.[39]

Although the military was critically short of doctors, Vannovskii concurred with Totleben's criticism and issued a circular "On measures restricting the influx of Jews into the army medical service."[40] The circular stipulated that Jewish doctors were required to serve in the interior provinces and not in the Pale of Settlement; the army allocated four and a half thousand rubles to transport them to Turkestan and to the East Siberian districts. Subsequent medical assistants and pharmaceutical students shared a similar destiny. Violating the 1874 statute, Vannovskii prohibited Jews from securing positions as medical assistants and apprentice pharmacists, despite a shortage of medical assistants in the army.

To the War Ministry's credit, the principal advocates of Jewish segregation within the army were in fact high-ranking officials in the Ministry of the Interior.[41] Military commanders, particularly local ones, preferred to retain Jews in posts that they officially were prohibited from occupying. Only when the War Ministry received a denunciation, protesting the illegal service of Jews in certain positions, did the commanders feel compelled to enforce the law.[42] On the other hand, Vannovskii willingly followed the Ministry of the Interior's initiative. In April 1887, Viacheslav Pleve, then deputy minister of the interior, asked Vannovskii to dismiss Jewish clerks (*pisaria*) from the regiments, claiming that they abused their authority to help their co-religionists evade the law. Without troubling to investigate the charges, Vannovskii forwarded Pleve's report to the Main Staff, with a note in the margin that read, "It is necessary to issue an order that they appoint no Jewish clerks in local brigades and local military administration; also, they should have no Catholic clerks in the Vistula region [a Russian bureaucratic euphemism for Poland] and western provinces."[43] Lieutenant General Mirkovich remarked that these restrictive measures should be introduced gradually, to allow time for the training of new clerks. Vannovskii summarily dismissed his comments, stressing the need for immediate action.

---

[39] See Manassein's reprinted article (originally published in *Voenno-meditsinskii zhurnal*) in *Russkii evrei*, no. 36 (1882): 1355–1357; for a discussion of Jewish doctors, see *Russkii evrei*, no. 44 (1882): 1653–1654.

[40] RGVIA, f. 400, op. 5, d. 1650, ll. 6–7, 70b., 80b., 90b.

[41] After Dmitrii Tolstoi's relatively neutral attitude toward Jews, the appointment of Durnovo as the minister of the interior resulted in a number of radically anti-Jewish regulations. See Hans Rogger, "Russian Ministers and the Jewish Question, 1881–1917," in his *Jewish Policies and Right-Wing Politics in Imperial Russia* (Berkeley and Los Angeles: University of California Press, 1986), 56–112; Zaionchkovskii, *Rossiiskoe samoderzhavie*, 131–188.

[42] RGVIA, f. 400, op. 5, d. 1438, ll. 2, 5, 9, 15, 17. Concerning Vannovskii's penchant for denunciations and "secret investigations," see *Voennaia entsiklopediia*, 5: 236.

[43] RGVIA, f. 400, op. 5, d. 883, ll. 2, 30b.-4, 12. Later, Vannovskii expanded and enforced this ban on Jews and Poles in all administrative and educational institutions, staff and army offices in the Kiev, Vilna, and Warsaw military districts. He also initiated the prohibition against Jews and Poles (Catholics) serving as armorers. Included in the ban were Jews and Orthodox Christians who married Catholic women. See RGVIA, op. 5, d. 1265, l. 5.

He agreed to a single exception: a Jew who was completing an additional term of service.[44] Vannovskii urged local commanders to enforce the restrictive regulations, and was dissatisfied with their failure to do so. He used any excuse to implement further limitations and to turn individual offences into examples of Jewish soldiers' collective guilt.[45] On October 16, 1899, he signed Secret Circular no. 1366, requiring the heightened supervision of Jewish soldiers, whom he suspected of intending to desert. The immediate cause of this harsh measure was a postcard advertising the Weinberg steamship line, engaged in transporting Jewish emigrants to America. It was received by Shlomo Gurevich, a private in the Nezhin regiment. An investigation revealed two similar post-cards, sent to other soldiers. This was sufficient for Vannovskii to consider all letters received by Jewish soldiers from transatlantic relatives as enticement to desert.[46] Obruchev sent a follow-up message to the Main Staff clerks, claiming that Jewish privates received letters from abroad urging them to run away to America; consequently, the War Minister deemed it necessary to monitor strictly all letters addressed to Jewish soldiers.[47]

Pragmatic military commanders of various ranks understood the damage that the secret circulars caused to the army, and disagreed with their regulations. They occasionally countered the repressive anti-Jewish measures. The deputy chief of the Main Staff, Lieutenant General Afanasiev, analyzed numerous War Ministry orders concerning Jewish doctors and observed that these restrictions contravened the law. In reply to a circular barring Jewish artisans from non-combatant army service, the commander of the Odessa military district wrote to the War Ministry, informing him that soldiers of peasant origin had no knowledge of handicrafts, whereas Poles and Jews, who inhabited the western provinces, were "in the majority, artisans, tailors, and shoemakers"; thus, the ban on Polish and Jewish artisans created a desperate situation. Energetic pro-tests on the eve of Vannovskii's resignation won the main engineering super-intendent a special concession: in June 1898, disregarding its own circular of 1894 that barred both Jews and Catholics from serving as telegraphers, the War Ministry permitted them to serve in this capacity. Even Vannovskii occasionally exhibited pragmatism: when division commanders requested that Jews remain at posts now barred to them, he acquiesced, declaring only that no Jews were to be appointed to these positions in the future.[48]

---

[44] RGVIA, op. 5, d. 1265, ll. 290b., 300b., 310b., 390b.-40.

[45] RGVIA, f. 400, op. 2, d. 5764, ll. 1–10b., 3, 7, 11.

[46] See RGVIA, f. 400, op. 2, d. 5764, l. 1–10b. From the few available letters, a very different picture emerges: Jewish emigrants wrote that a soldier's bread was much more easily obtained than that of an emigrant, and that it was preferable to serve in the army than to live in America. See Witold Kula et al., eds., *Writing Home: Immigrants in Brazil and the United States. 1890–1891* (Boulder, Colo.: East European Monographs; New York: distributed by Columbia University Press, 1986), 187–188. I am grateful to Jonathan Sarna for bringing this book to my attention.

[47] RGVIA, f. 400, op. 2, d. 5764, l. 11.

[48] RGVIA, f. 400, op. 5, d. 1650, ll. 45, 48, 58, 68–680b.; d. 1265, ll. 19–21; d. 1488; d. 1265, ll. 28, 350b., 38–39, 53, 55.

While Vannovskii's attitude toward Jewish soldiers mirrored Russian society's xenophobic turn, his desire to segregate them and to limit severely the positions available to them was based upon his conviction that Jews were out of place in the Russian army. A plethora of press publications, ethnographic studies, and ministerial commissions' reports had informed his opinion. The internal military scandal over the Partnership, and its profound social ramifications and cultural repercussions, adversely affected Jewish soldiers' rights and inspired harsh military regulations regarding them.

"Harmful to the Army"

Paradoxically, the concept of Jews as harmful to the army had civilian origins; Vannovskii was hardly responsible for it. This anti-Jewish concept insinuated its way into the War Ministry through ministerial commissions, influential Russian polemicists, and Russian literary xenophobes. Consider the state advisor Khomentovskii, marshal of the nobility from Minsk province, who served on the commission combating Jewish draft evasion. Khomentovskii was renowned for his diligence; his expert reports on Jews circulated among the ministry's hierarchy. In 1882, he sent the Main Staff a comprehensive analysis of what he saw as innate Jewish hostility toward military service. The responsibility for this antipathy, he asserted, rested squarely with the mysterious and all-powerful *kahal*, a self-governing Jewish body. Wealthy Jews endowed the *kahal* with money that was used to ensure the voluntary or forced conscription of recruits selected from disgraced or impoverished families. Various methods enabled other recruits to evade the call-up.[49] Although Khomentovskii's descriptions of the Jews' evasion practices resemble a satirical pamphlet rather than a scholarly sociological study, the military accepted them at face value; they corroborated the observations of Iakov Brafman, an apostate who, in the eyes of Russian officialdom, was the most influential nineteenth-century expert on the Jewish question.

Brafman plays a peculiar role in the history of Russian xenophobia. His blatantly anti-Jewish *Book of the Kahal* conveyed the same message to the late nineteenth-century Russian public as did *The Protocols of the Elders of Zion* to Europeans at the beginning of the twentieth. *The Book of the Kahal* reinforced basic anti-Jewish prejudices among the Russian reading public.[50] Brafman had exposed the invisible machinery that controlled the Jewish world: the *kahal*. A traditional Jewish, self-governing institution, the *kahal* no longer operated in the Polish Kingdom after 1822, nor in Russia after 1844. Yet Brafman's writings elevated this officially dismantled communal organization to the status of a contemporary secret world power. Brafman disclosed that the *kahal*'s decisions were based upon the Talmud. Thus, by means of the *kahal*'s administration, it was the Talmud that dictated international financial transactions and West

---

[49] See RGVIA, f. 400, op. 14, d. 15703, ll. 4–9.
[50] See Klier, *Imperial Russia's Jewish Question*, 261–262, 274–283.

European politics, while also exerting its influence on the psyche of the poorest Jew, the passportless tramp who wandered the Jewish Pale in search of alms.[51] The machinations of Brafman's omnipotent *kahal* accounted for all current political realities. When the War Ministry convened to discuss the introduction of universal military service, conservative members of its commission argued against conceding equal status to Jews because of their reputation as draft dodgers. Brafman contended that the *kahal* alone bore responsibility for this phenomenon; it meddled with the draftee lists and shielded from service those deemed the Talmudic aristocracy (Brafman's term).[52] He concluded unequivocally, "Among *the tens of thousands* of Jews who have entered the Russian army over the last forty years, there have been no aristocratic Talmudists."[53] His account furnished a simple solution to a vexatious problem. Russian bureaucrats used *The Book of the Kahal* as an authoritative encyclopedia on East European Jewry. To establish incontrovertibly the guilt of a junior doctor in the Ninth field engineers' battalion, Mark Volpert, who was charged in 1876 with issuing forged certificates of unfitness to Jewish conscripts, the assistant public prosecutor had only to refer to Brafman's book, which he remembered as *The Yids and the Kahal*.[54]

Relying chiefly upon Brafman's assertions, Khomentovskii declared that the *kahal*, the organized Jewish community, and any Jews comprising a unified and coherent entity were enemies of the draft. Since the *kahal* declared unfit the strong, healthy sons of rich Jews, "one never finds any strong Jews in the army."[55] The cunning Jews always managed to exploit a legislative loophole allowing them to evade military responsibility, and the *kahal* always found ways to exempt its brethren from their sacred Russian duty. Khomentovskii quoted Brafman to explain the failure to draft Jews; until 1877, he claimed, Jews simply did not appear for the call-up. In 1877, when the military introduced separate draft lists for Jews and Christians, Jews increasingly resorted to self-mutilation. Once the military decided, in 1881, to draft self-mutilators, the practice of mutilation ceased. However, Jews managed to obtain a year's leave, and up to 50 percent succeeded in avoiding service. When the military canceled the soldiers' leave, Jews adopted the practice of fasting for two weeks prior to

[51] Brafman recycled century-old ideas of western Christianity that Jews were the people of the Talmud, not of the Bible (and therefore were no longer the keepers of the tradition of God's revelation), and that the Talmud accounted for Jewish backwardness and isolation. See Jeremy Cohen, *The Friars and the Jews: The Evolution of Medieval Anti-Judaism* (Ithaca and London: Cornell University Press, 1982), 74; Gevin Langmuir, *History, Religion and Antisemitism*, 294–295.

[52] Klier, *Imperial Russia's Jewish Question*, 281–282, 340. Klier correctly assumes that the anonymous article in *Golos* was authored by Brafman, permeated as it was by primitive and easily recognizable metaphors.

[53] Brafman, *The Book of the Kahal*, 76. Italics in the original.

[54] See the selected rulings of the chief military court, *Voennyi sbornik*, no. 11 (1880): 62–67 (case no. 91, April 8, 1880). In fact, Volpert's lawyer claimed that he could not find any book containing a refutation of Brafman's statements, which demonstrates that it was easier to find Brafman's book than the writings of his critics.

[55] RGVIA, f. 400, op. 14, d. 15703, ll. 20b.-3, 12.

conscription, thus arriving for their initial examination in a state of complete exhaustion. Although it is difficult to ascertain whether Khomentovskii's reports circulated widely in the ministry, it is probable that he preached the same gospel at meetings of the Commission on Jewish Draft Evasion. His idea of the irreconcilable enmity between Jews and the military was intended to convince the military to purge the army of this undesirable element. "Why do we need this refuse in our troops?" he asked.[56]

While Khomentovskii advocated Brafman's views to War Ministry officials, Vsevolod Krestovskii disseminated his anti-Jewish gospel through the Russian conservative press and popular literature.[57] As one of the most widely read Russian novelists, and one who worked in close cooperation with the military, Krestovskii had long attracted scandal.[58] Before becoming a famous writer, he had been a student at the University of St. Petersburg and quite a talented imitator of Eugene Sue. At the height of the Great Reforms, Krestovskii broke off his relations with liberal circles and joined the army. Democratic writers such as Grigoriev, Dostoevsky, and Leskov condemned his behavior and ostracized him, but conservatives, especially those close to the court, took him under their wing.[59] Nonetheless, Krestovskii's reputation as a court military writer had grown to such an extent that he took orders directly from Alexander II; the emperor extended to him his personal guardianship. Alexander even served as proofreader of Krestovskii's volume on the history of His Majesty's Uhlan guard regiment. In addition to having penned a series of military sketches and articles published in *Svet*, and descriptions of his travels in the eastern and western borderlands of the Russian Empire in *Grazhdanin, Russkii vestnik*, and *Moskovskie vedomosti*, Krestovskii gained renown as a novelist.[60] A gifted writer who, unlike most Russian authors, knew some Yiddish, Krestovskii played a key role in shaping anti-Jewish ideology, primarily among the high- and middle-ranking army officers who formed his principal readership.

---

[56] RGVIA, f. 400, op. 14, d. 15703, l. 150b.

[57] Krestovskii accepted Brafman's fantasies at face value, publishing a highly positive review of Brafman's book; see *Zaria*, no. 11 (1870): 149. According to a Russian literary historian, Brafman's book subsequently became a major source for Krestovskii. See V. A. Viktorovich, "Krestovskii," in *Russkie pisateli, 1800–1917* (M.: Entsiklopediia, 1989), 3: 146–149.

[58] Russian biographers compared Krestovskii's popularity to that of Alexander Dumas; see I. S. Ruslanov, *Iz moikh vospominanii* (M.: Grzhebin, 1923), 51–52; one well-educated memoirist reread Krestovskii's novels twenty times; see V. Kelsiev, *Perezhitoe i peredumannoe: Vospominaniia* (SPb., Golovin, 1868), 74; Wolf, one of the largest Russian publishers, considered *Petersburg Slums* by Krestovskii an average low-brow novel, yet hailed it as "an outstanding piece of writing from the point of view of the seller and the general public." See S. F. Librovich, *Na knizhnom postu. Vospominaniia. Zapiski. Dokumenty* (SPb., M.: Wolf, 1916), 26.

[59] "Krestovskii, Vsevolod Vladimirovich," in *Voennaia entsiklopediia* (Pb.: Sytin, 1913), 12: 283–285; Viktorovich, "Krestovskii," 149; *Voennyi sbornik*, no. 10 (1876): 144–149; P. D. Boborykin, *Vospominaniia. Za polveka* (M.: Khudozhestvennaia literatura, 1965), 1: 393.

[60] Among his important works are an anti-Polish novel in two volumes, *Krovavyi puf* (The Bloody Padded Stool), and an anti-Jewish trilogy consisting of *T'ma Egipetskaia* (The Egyptian Darkness), *Tamara Bendavid* (Tamara Bendavid) and *Torzhestvo Vaala* (Baal's Triumph). For more detail on Krestovskii, see Savelii Dudakov, *Istoriia odnogo mifa* (M.: Nauka, 1993), 118–120.

In the 1870s, Krestovskii welcomed the rapprochement between the Jews and the army quartered in the Pale. He portrayed sympathetically, if somewhat satirically, the activities of the Jewish artisans who improved their poor economic situation by meeting the needs of the military. His Jews were devious and indispensable. His regimental tailor was "a rascal, albeit a good Yid."[61] Yet any more intimate interaction between the Jews and the army was inconceivable. An ignoble character, the Jew could never become a soldier, let alone an officer. While the liberal press in St. Petersburg reacted joyfully to the official decision that students of church seminaries and Jews who obtained certificates of maturity could become officers, Krestovskii's countered with a polemical pamphlet, "Po povodu liberal'nykh privetstvii" (With Regard to Liberal Rejoicing).[62]

In the pamphlet, Krestovskii begins by recalling his old friend, Itsko Mysh, a shtetl Jew, the owner of a grocery store. Mysh is a superficial liberal: he praises France as a civilized country that allows Jews to become generals, while criticizing barbaric Russia, which does not permit a Jew even to become an officer. Krestovskii sketches a brutal caricature of a Russian Jew promoted to the rank of officer:

Now imagine Reb Itsko Mysh in the army as an officer, not yet a general. Imagine him as the commander of a squadron. Imagine him riding a stallion, if he ever dares saddle one. Here he is, riding in front of a brave squadron, if only the squadron under his command could be as brave as he is. So, Major Mysh receives the order: "Canter!" and gives the command to his cavalry unit:
– Shquadron, eyes right, trothing martz!
Or, for example:
– Shquadron, from right, one by one, jumping, flanking, hurdling into galloping, martz-martz!
It is impossible to figure out how Reb Itsko Mysh looks during the battle at the moment of attack. However, it is quite possible to figure out what Reb Mysh does during an armistice and how he makes use of his squadron, of his measures of oats, of his poods of hay for his "gandel," for his delicate "geshefts," and for his "cummerce." Just imagine, what a brave sergeant major Itsko Mysh would appoint! I bet a hundred to one that this sergeant major is called Ioshka Berenshtamm, and that he is the right hand of his meritorious and courageous commander in every "gandel" and "gesheft." How wonderful will the Russian soldier's life be under Mysh and Berenshtamm![63]

Krestovskii's Major Mysh was comically grotesque, but in no way vile. This ambiguous portrayal of Jews defined Krestovskii's work until the end of the Russo-Turkish War, after which a very different tone emerged.

During the Balkan campaign, Krestovskii was appointed crown historian to the commander in chief of the Russian army.[64] Other sources posit that he also

[61] See V. V. Krestovskii, *Sobranie sochinenii*. 8 vols. (SPb.: Obshchestvennaia pol'za, 1899), 4:250–251.
[62] Krestovskii, *Sobranie sochinenii*, 4: 180–183.
[63] Krestovskii, "Po povodu liberal'nykh privetstvii," in his *Sobranie sochinenii*, 4: 182.
[64] Dudakov, *Istoriia odnogo mifa*, 118–120.

acted as correspondent in chief for the official periodical *Pravitel'stvennyi vestnik* (Governmental Herald).[65] Thus, he had access to a wide readership, both among high-ranking military officials and across Russia generally. He depicted Jews in his regular front-line reports and in his novel *Tamara Bendavid*. According to his accounts, Jews did not fight at the front, nor were there any Jewish soldiers worth mentioning.

Conversely, he reported at great length about the Jewish purveyors to the army.[66] Krestovskii presented Greger, Gorvits, Kogan, and Varshavskii as high-ranking gentlemen responsible, on the eve of war, for feeding the troops. He explained how this Partnership supplied bread, groats, grain, and other provisions to the army. Jewish and Romanian vendors and money changers cheated the Russian soldiers, he asserted. In a footnote to his reports, Krestovskii voiced serious concern that foreign journalists could easily purchase military secrets from Greger, Gorvits, Kogan, and their agents. Yet, in his notoriously antisemitic *Tamara Bendavid*, he transformed the Partnership into the international *kahal*'s pawn, used to humiliate Russia. Jews were responsible for feeding the Russian army; hence the hunger in the trenches, the rampant epidemics, and the unexpectedly high mortality rate. He rendered Greger, Gorvits and Kogan as supposed Russian Jewish patriots who managed to recruit governors, generals, and even senators by means of intrigues and deceit. Consequently, the Partnership was uniquely situated to rob the army. "The army was in Jewish bondage," claimed Krestovskii.[67]

No trace remained of Krestovskii's former playfulness; his Jews had become aggressive and dangerous, appearing as insolent impostors. They used their whips, which they once had brandished theatrically, to beat Russian wagon-drivers in order to "shupport the dishiplin." Krestovskii's Jewish characters supported anti-Russian political propaganda, arranged terrorist acts against government officials, appropriated valuables belonging to the Russian Orthodox Church, and plundered the Credit Society and the banks. The Partnership sold the army rotten oats, moldy bread, biscuits mixed with dirt, and diluted alcohol; in the end, it went bankrupt and ruined thousands of peasant families.[68] Krestovskii's summary clearly displayed his agenda:

It was here, near Tsargrad [Constantinople, Istanbul] that we – including those who had never thought about it before – unintentionally started to think about the "Jewish question in Russia." It was here that we found words to express our feelings in the warning: "The Yid is coming!" And this Yid seemed to be more frightening than any war, than any European coalition against Russia.[69]

[65] *Voennaia entsiklopediia*, 12: 284.

[66] Krestovskii, "Dvadtsat mesiatsev v deistvuiushchei armii v 1877–78 godakh," *Sobranie sochinenii*, 5: 135, 145, 269–273.

[67] Krestovskii, *Sobranie sochinenii*, 5: 18, 33, 157, 93, 62, 72 n.; 8: 217–218, 220.

[68] Krestovskii, *Sobranie sochinenii*, 8: 239, 287.

[69] Krestovskii, *Sobranie sochinenii*, 8: 288–89. Even such an ultraconservative as Katkov did not share Krestovskii's extreme views, and so kept a distance from him. See N. D. Tamarchenko,

After 1881, Krestovskii utterly rejected any idea of contact between the army and the Jews. Jews did not even have the right to be Russian patriots. The purported Jewish admiration of Russian military triumphs was nothing but the servile and hypocritical desire of a serf to appease his magnanimous master. The military campaign, maintained Krestovskii, had been of great financial benefit to the Jews, who would otherwise never have cared about pan-Slav unity or their oppressed Slavic brethren.[70]

Krestovskii was not the first Russian writer to portray the Jew as harmful both to society and to the army; his predecessor Faddei Bulgarin had done the same in *Ivan Vyzhigin*, the first popular Russian novel.[71] Officialdom constituted 30 percent of its readership, while army officers of higher and lower ranks accounted for another 25 percent.[72] Bulgarin pandered to their prejudices in depicting the conflict between Polish Jews and Russian army officers. The Jew in *Ivan Vyzhigin* is an insatiable exploiter who causes poverty and poor harvests in the district, a ruthless creditor, a smuggler who destroys the economy, an innkeeper and greedy informer who demoralizes the peasants, a traitor trading in "live goods" (prostitutes), and a cunning provider of news and drink to the Russian officers.[73]

Krestovskii succeeded in deftly combining Brafman's theory of the *kahal* with the boulevard novel genre of Bulgarin to highlight the damage Jews inflicted upon the army. His talented and prolific pen was one of the factors that influenced the Russian military in their adoption of the view that Jews were bloodsuckers, false patriots, and enemies of the army, who deserved only segregation.[74] It may well be that, just as Brafman had earned the *kahal* its notoriety, Krestovskii introduced the word *gesheft* as an anti-Jewish reference into the vocabulary of military bureaucracy. By the beginning of the twentieth century, it already had become a catchphrase with which any right-wing patriot could explain why a Jew would never be a good soldier.

Thus, by the mid-1880s, the army had established narrow parameters within which Jewish soldiers were permitted to serve, while conservatives tried to convince the army to segregate Jews altogether. Under such circumstances, it is

"Krestovskii," in *Russkie pisateli XIX veka. Biobibliograficheskii slovar* (M.: Prosveshchenie, 1996), 1: 385.

[70] Krestovskii, *Sobrannie sochinenii*, 8: 206.

[71] On *Ivan Vyzhigin*'s popularity, see A. I. Reitblat, ed., *Vidok Figliarin: Pis'ma i agenturnye zapiski F. V. Bulgarina v III-e otdelenie* (M.: Novoe literaturnoe obozrenie, 1998), 37.

[72] A. D. Thumim, "In the Spirit of the Government: Faddei Bulgarin and the Formation of the Middle Class in Russia, 1789–1859," (Ph.D. diss., Harvard University, 1995), 121, 123, 192, 210.

[73] See Bulgarin, *Ivan Vyzhigin* (M.: Vdova Plushar, 1829), 1: 31, 41, 68, 97, 99, 104–109, 125–126, 145, 157. In reality, a Jew had saved the lives of Bulgarin and his mother, rescuing them from Polish rebels. See F. Bulgarin, *Memuary: otryvki iz vidennogo, slyshannogo i perezhitogo* (SPb.: M. D. Olkhin, 1846–1849), 1:23–29.

[74] Dubnow asserted that Krestovskii "attempted to remind the present emperor and his generals about 'the Jewish crime' and to incite the government to mount new reprisals." See Dubnov, *Kniga zhizni*, 159.

important to examine the Jewish response and to determine whether their immediate commanders bowed to the anti-Jewish messages of the ascendant far right.

In the Service of Late Imperial Russia

Figures speak for themselves; the number of Jews in the army and their distribution among the troops disproved the contentions of the Ministry of the Interior, the conservative press, and literary xenophobes. In 1889, at the Warsaw conscription center, Jewish recruits constituted 35 percent of the total. In Polotsk province, more than 10 percent were Jews; in Petrokov (Piotrków), about 14 percent; in Radom, more than 15 percent; and in Lodz (Łódź), almost 17 percent, representing higher than average Jewish conscription for the Kingdom of Poland. In Kovno, Minsk, and Vitebsk provinces, within the Pale of Settlement – whose total Jewish population was 14 percent – Jews constituted 18, 19, and 12 percent, respectively, of all recruits. In the urban areas, Jews contributed an even higher proportion of conscripts, especially in Kovel (Kowel, 24 percent), Ponevezh (Poniewież, 20 percent), Novoaleksandrovsk (19 percent), Minsk (26 percent), Bobruisk (27 percent), Rechitsa (19 percent), Pinsk (24 percent), Vitebsk (22 percent), and Dinaburg (16 percent).[75] Jews outside the Pale of Settlement were better off financially; they either could pay off the service by obtaining exemption tickets or could receive exemptions as a result of their status as established doctors, lawyers, or guild merchants. Nonetheless, some of them chose to enter the army.[76] In 1888, after the newly inducted soldiers were assigned to their posts, Jews in the Kiev, Odessa, Moscow, Vilna, and Warsaw military districts numbered 2,300, 1,200, 1,350, 2,000, and 1,200, respectively.[77] Between 1889 and 1893, 27,144 Jewish soldiers served in these districts, a figure sufficient to compose five-seven infantry regiments at wartime strength.

In what capacity did these Jews serve? It is instructive to compare the distribution of Jewish recruits within the Pale of Settlement, outside it, and in the Kingdom of Poland, using as examples the St. Petersburg, Vilna, Warsaw, and Kiev military districts (Tables 12 and 13).

In the Vilna military district, between 84 and 90 percent of all Jews served in combat posts. The average number of Jewish cavalrymen in the early 1890s comprised between 1 and 7 percent of all Jews serving in the district. Some of them were engaged in crafts necessary to the cavalry, such as saddlery and metalwork; others served in combat positions. Between 8 and 21 percent of all Jewish troops served in the artillery. In 1893, there was a significant decrease in the number of Jews serving in the artillery and in the cavalry: 85 percent fewer in the cavalry and 50 percent fewer in the artillery. At the same time, there was a

---

[75] RGVIA, f. 400, op. 5, d. 1022, ll. 7, 9, 13, 30–31.

[76] Jews accounted for 1.49 percent in Tula district, for 0.3 percent in Orel province, and for 0.23 percent in Belgorod, Kursk province. See RGVIA, f. 400, op. 5, d. 1022, ll. 5, 13.

[77] RGVIA, f. 400, op. 5, d. 1254, ll. 9–11, 12–20, 17–21, 25–27, 28–30.

TABLE 12. *Distribution of Jewish Lower Ranks in the Vilna Military District, 1890–1893*

Units	1890	1891	1892	1893
16th infantry division	158	78	117	220
25th infantry division	179	51	135	271
26th infantry division	96	113	74	229
7th infantry division	89	169	147	243
2nd infantry division	89	38	113	227
29th infantry division	60	152	141	267
2nd sappers brigade	19	18	8	3
Railway brigade	1	5	2	18
45th reserve brigade	62	107	1	73
46th infantry brigade	40	67	48	113
5th local brigade	25	27	14	18
6th local brigade	11	40	60	57
Fortress sappers' company (Kovno)	1	2	2	–
Fortress infantry brigade (Ust-Dvinsk)	8	11	14	–
Total in the infantry	1,276	1,383	1,398	1,739
2nd cavalry division	17	31	42	11
3rd cavalry division	20	21	55	5
4th cavalry division	41	20	42	1
Total in the cavalry	78	72	139	17
1st artillery brigade	48	299	257	176
Mobile artillery parks	20	13	14	5
Horse-drawn artillery battalion	3	6	7	2
Independent artillery units	43	65	47	40
Hospitals	–	–	–	–
Total in the artillery	114	383	325	223
Military District Total	1,527	1,867	1,924	1,979

Source: RGVIA, f. 400, op. 6, d. 960, ll. 124–128.

continuous increase in the numbers of Jews in the infantry: 1,739 versus 1,398. About 76 percent of Jewish soldiers in the St. Petersburg district served in the infantry, just as they did in the Vilna district. From 4 to 14 percent of all Jewish troops served in the cavalry, with the same proportion in 1889 (230 men), and about an average of 6.5 percent for four years. From 6 to 11 percent of all Jews served in the St. Petersburg district artillery. From 1892 to 1893, as elsewhere, there was a decrease in the number of Jews serving in the cavalry, in the artillery, and in the number of Jewish servicemen (down from 10 to 5 percent) in local and reserve units.[78] The data for these two districts, Vilna and St. Petersburg, one inside the Jewish Pale and the other outside it, in many respects show identical trends. The overwhelming majority of Jews served in the

---

[78] RGVIA, f. 400, op. 6, d. 960, ll. 124–128.

TABLE 13. *Distribution of Jewish Soldiers in the St. Petersburg Military District, 1890–1893*

Units	1890	1891	1892	1893
5th infantry division	119	179	73	202
9th infantry division	303	99	50	190
11th infantry division	242	272	261	303
12th infantry division	200	212	168	285
19th infantry division	137	151	62	215
31st infantry division	316	122	36	207
32nd infantry division	190	111	98	212
33rd infantry division	247	127	100	152
Total in the infantry	1,754	1,273	848	1,766
9th cavalry division	8	5	66	70
10th cavalry division	10	31	83	–
11th cavalry division	25	8	43	12
12th cavalry division	49	20	33	–
5th brigade cavalry reserve	–	–	18	9
Total in the cavalry	89	125	230	91*
1st artillery brigade	84	229	189	125
Horse-drawn artillery brigade	1	7	2	4
Mobile artillery parks	16	14	12	6
Independent artillery units	29	24	39	108
Total in the artillery	130	274	242	243
3rd rifle brigade	130	40	111	60
3rd sappers' brigade	1	14	20	30
42nd infantry reserve battalion	118	99	77	30
47th infantry reserve battalion	40	73	72	71
12th local brigade	5	2	–	–
14th local brigade	48	30	35	13
Total in local and reserve brigades	211	204	184	114
Military District Total	2,318	1,930	1,635	2,233

Note: *Total figure of Jews in cavalry is mine, cf. three figures above.
Source: RGVIA, f. 400, op. 6, d. 960, ll. 124–128.

infantry. In the artillery, commanding officers testified unreservedly to the professionalism of the Jews. The fluctuations in the number of Jewish recruits in the artillery, the cavalry, and the infantry occurred in response to Vannovskii's circular letters to the district commanders rather than because of any changes in the Jewish population.

The Jewish presence in the army in the early 1900s was quite similar. In the Kiev military district, in the south of the Pale of Settlement, Jews served predominantly as combat troops (Table 14).

There were 4,661 Jewish enlisted men in 1908. Of all the Jewish men in the army, 96 percent served on combat positions (4,425 men); of these, 80 percent

ILLUSTRATION 5. Studio portrait of Jewish soldiers in the tsar's army, with props that include firearms and a loaf of bread: (left to right) A. L. Shepshelevitch, E. Pomul, L. Ya. Grif, M. M. Tshukasov, Ya. I. Pobermanski, B. R. Rubinshteyn; Troitskosavsk, December 1887. From the archives of the YIVO Institute, collection R1, catalog no. Troitsk 1, no. 3459.

TABLE 14. *Distribution of Jewish Lower Ranks in the Kiev Military District, 1908*

	Combat Positions		Noncombat Positions				
Troops	In Line	Musicians, Drummers, Buglers	Tailors, Hatters, Cutters	Military Hospitals Clerks	Pharma- ceutics	Trans- port Units	Other
Infantry	3,743	319	103	3	3	3	46
Cavalry	248	14	14	4	3	3	14
Engineers	66	4	–	–	–	1	1
Artillery	20	10	14	8	8	–	13
Others	–	1	–	–	–	–	1
Office	–	–	–	–	–	–	–
TOTAL	4,077	348	131	15	11	4	75

Source: RGVIA, f. 400, op. 6, d. 960, ll. 62–64.

TABLE 15. *Distribution of Jewish Lower Ranks in the Warsaw Military District, 1908*

| Troops | Combat Positions | | Noncombat Positions | | | | |
	In line	Musicians, Drummers, Buglers	Tailors, Hatters, Cutters	Military Hospital Clerks	Pharma- ceutics	Trans- port Units	Other
Infantry	5,555	423	43	1	1	10	64
Cavalry	312	16	11	5	1	–	15
Engineers	62	20	–	–	–	–	–
Artillery	562	41	9	5	–	–	14
Others	–	–	–	–	–	–	–
Office	–	–	–	–	–	–	–
TOTAL	6,491	499	63	15	2	10	93

Source: RGVIA, f. 400, op. 6, d. 960, ll. 124–128.

were in the infantry (3,743 men), 5 percent in the cavalry (238 men), 1.5 percent in the engineers (66 men), and less than 1 percent in the artillery (20 men); buglers, musicians, and drummers constituted the remainder, nearly 8 percent (348 men). Only 5 percent of all Jews served in noncombat positions, including 2 percent who were tailors, hatters, and uniform cutters. In 1908, again, there were 7,173 Jewish soldiers in the Warsaw military district, of whom 97 percent served in combat positions; 77 percent of the total were in the infantry, 4 percent in the cavalry, 1 percent in the engineers, and 8 percent in the artillery (Table 15).

The remaining 7 percent were buglers, musicians, and drummers. Only 3 percent of all Jewish soldiers in the Warsaw district served in noncombat posts, including tailors, hatters, and uniform cutters, who comprised roughly 1 percent. That same year, there were 5,050 Jewish soldiers in the Vilna military district, 97 percent of whom were in combat positions: 77 percent were in the infantry, 3 percent in the cavalry, 1 percent in the engineers, 10 percent in the artillery, and 6 percent served as buglers, musicians, and drummers (Table 16).[79]

The data explain why some district commanders believed that there were too many Jews in the army and why they petitioned for a reduction of Jewish recruits.[80] Interestingly, in 1889–1890, the War Ministry discussed a proposal for creating special Jewish noncombat detachments. An experimental Jewish battalion was to have included 688 enlisted men, 2 staff officers, 32 noncombat officers, and 58 corporals. This plan was ultimately rejected, as there were more Jews on service than the entire number of noncombat posts available in the army. To mollify the generals unhappy with the number of Jewish soldiers under their command, the War Ministry decided to resort to manipulation

[79] RGVIA, f. 400, op. 6, d. 960, ll. 62–64, 173–174.
[80] RGVIA, f. 400, op. 5, d. 1044, l. 2–20b.

TABLE 16. *Distribution of Jewish Lower Ranks in the Vilna Military District, 1908*

Troops	Combat Positions		Noncombat Positions				
	In line	Musicians, Drummers, Buglers	Tailors, Hatters, Cutters	Military Hospital Clerks	Pharma- ceutics	Trans- port Units	Other
Infantry	4,279	334	23	4	–	8	51
Cavalry	140	–	6	2	–	–	12
Engineers	69	12	–	–	–	–	–
Artillery	562	28	8	9	–	–	30
Others	–	–	–	–	–	–	–
Office	–	–	–	–	–	–	–
TOTAL	5,050	374	37	15	–	8	93

Source: RGVIA, f. 400, op. 6, d. 960, ll. 173–174.

of the data, and ordered a census of Jews in each unit. The Main Staff recommended dispersing Jews evenly among the detachments, at least on paper; the stringent limitations imposed upon Jewish soldiers made it impossible to do so in reality. The proposed reports would corroborate the convenient fiction.[81] Yet even such manipulation of military statistics failed to disguise the fact that the stereotype of the Jewish soldier unfit for combat duties was a gross misrepresentation. Furthermore, juggling with paper figures could hardly have fooled any commander complaining there were too many Jews in his brigade.

Clearly, the overwhelming majority of Jews, between 80 and 95 percent, were intended as cannon fodder. In three districts, the average percentages of Jewish troops were: infantry, 76 percent; cavalry, 4 percent; engineers, 1 percent; and artillery, 6 percent. Despite the strictest prohibition against Jews serving in the Guards regiments, every year one or two Jews were placed in the Guards infantry, and occasionally even in the cavalry. The fewest served in the engineers: in the St. Petersburg district, there were between two and eleven Jews in a battalion, on average. Between ten and fifty Jews served in an artillery brigade, 2 to 6 percent of the total in the ranks. In some cases, this figure was as high as 229 men in an artillery unit (more than 20 percent).[82] Only about 3 percent of Jews served in noncombat positions.

During Vannovskii's tenure, and throughout the revolutionary period of the 1900s, not only was the army determined to curtail the privileges Jews had

[81] RGVIA, f. 400, op. 5, d. 1044, ll. 2–20b., 3–4; d. 1711, l. 1.

[82] RGVIA, f. 400, op. 5, d. 1208, ll. 2–10; RGVIA, f. 400, op. 5, d. 1208, ll. 10–100b., 18–20, 23–35. More detailed data on the batteries of the Vilna and Warsaw military districts confirm these figures. For similar data on the number of the Jews in the troops between 1896 and 1903, see RGVIA, f. 400, op. 5, d. 1351, 1361, 1428, 1468, 1477, 1529, 1538, 1579, 1588; op. 6, d. 34, 35, 163.

enjoyed under the 1874 statute, it also subjected Jews to markedly harsher punishment for minor disciplinary infractions.[83] Accordingly, morale among the Jewish soldiers plummeted, and discipline deteriorated. Cases of desertion during new recruits' brief leave increased dramatically.[84] The military courts responded by classifying late return from leave as desertion.[85] The slightest departure from regulations was interpreted as insubordination.[86] In 1886, 1887, and 1889, Jews constituted about 7 percent of those under arrest.[87] In the 1900s, punishing Jews severely for the slightest misdemeanor became standard practice. The military court could barely cope with the enormous number of appeals, applications, and requests for reconsideration.[88]

The sharply increased number of offences reflected the heightened conflict between enlisted men and their immediate commanders, as well as the officers' evident anti-Jewish bias. They do not appear to indicate a rise in infractions of army discipline among Jewish soldiers. In absolute figures, the number of disciplinary violations among troops as a whole increased 2.2 times (from 5,577 to 12,108) between 1900 and 1909, while among Jewish soldiers infringements grew 3.2 times. And yet even this absolute increase in the crime rate among Jewish soldiers was insignificant in comparison with the crime rate in the army (Table 17).

In the period from 1900 to 1910, the military charged 158 officers and 9,074 soldiers of the lower ranks with political offenses: 233 of these were Jews.[89] Thus, during the revolutionary period, Jews composed 2.6 percent of

---

[83] For example, a private in the Fifty-eighth Prague regiment, Lipman Abramovich, received a sentence of six years' imprisonment solely for quarrelling with a corporal. RGVIA, f. 801, op. 43, 2 otd., 1 st., sv. 99, d. 77, l. 3–30b.

[84] See, for example, the case of Ida Shikhman, sentenced to fifteen months in a disciplinary battalion for returning late from his holiday, despite the fact that he had already been discharged into the reserves. The military rejected his parents' appeal. See RGVIA, f. 801, op. 43, 2 otd., 1 st., d. 82, ll. 2–20b., 40b., 11.

[85] See the case of Duvid Mikhel Bakhman, sentenced in 1884 to two years in a penal battalion by the Zhitomir temporary military court for desertion, when he was guilty only of unauthorized absence. The military rejected his appeal. See RGVIA, f. 801, op. 43, otd. 2, st. 1, d. 53, ll. 2–20b., 60b.-7.

[86] See the case of Bornshtein, punished with 200 lashes and sentenced to nine months' solitary confinement for "waving his arms" while talking to the company's staff captain, Kuchukov. RGVIA, f. 801, op. 1, 4 otd., 1 st., sv. 68, d. 111, ll. 1–10b., 8.

[87] In 1886, 243 out of 3,448; in 1887, 466 out of 6,295; and in 1889, 235 out of 3,430. See Afanasiev, "Distsiplinarnye bataliony," *Voennyi sbornik*, no. 7 (1890): 141.

[88] See, e.g., RGVIA, op. 14, otd. 4, st. 2, sv. 169–201, d. 37 (Geller); d. 41 (Feldman); d. 77 (Raskin); 115 (Gertsik); d. 179 (Umanskii); d. 192 (Goldshtein); d. 226 (Farberg); d. 295 (Fishman); d. 314 (Bluvshtein); d. 381 (Rozenberg), d. 384 (Bronfen); d. 405 (Epelbaum); d. 472 (Sandler); d. 583 (Birbraer); d. 619 (Levin); d. 661 (Preis); d. 691 (Podolskikh); d. 757 (Mindlin); d. 771 (Zigerbaum); d. 844 (Voiman); d. 851 (Makhlis); d. 861 (Vasserman), d. 1318 (Goltman), d. 1483 (Leison), d. 1513 (Neisis), d. 1702 (Finkelshtein), d. 1849 (Vainshtein), d. 1924 (Gershkovich).

[89] *Voina i evrei*, 228.

TABLE 17. *Crime Rate among the Jewish Lower Ranks, 1900–1909*

	In Disciplinary Battalions		In Military Prisons		% Jews in the Total Number		Male Jews (Number and % of Total Russian Male Population, 1907)	
Year	Total	Jews	Total	Jews	Disciplinary Battalions	Prisons	In Russia	In the Army
1900	5,577	341	4,086	286	6.11	6.99	2,471,000 4% of 62,477,000	53,000 4.94% of 1,076,000
1901	5,652	327	3,921	282	5.78	7.19		
1902	5,656	320	4,264	277	5.65	6.49		
1903	6,121	352	4,601	332	5.75	7.21		
1904	6,460	364	4,667	309	5.63	6.62		
1905	6,384	409	5,006	252	6.40	5.03		
1906	6,356	383	4,544	279	6.02	6.13		
1907	7,060	540	4,230	217	7.64	5.13		
1908	11,024	747	3,716	170	6.77	4.57		
1909	12,108	1,078	3,745	220	8.90	5.87		

Source: *Voina i evrei*, 131; *Gosudarstvennaia Duma. Statisticheskie otchety. Sessiia II*. Zasedanie 29 (sekretnoe), 17 aprelia 1907 goda (SPb.: Gosudarstvennaia tipografiia, 1907), 2177–2183.

those charged with political crimes, half of their proportion in the army.[90] The rise in the crime rate among the Jewish soldiers was closely related to the intensification of the persecution of Jews in society at large.

The Making of the Nonkosher Jew

While War Ministry officials sought ways to limit Jewish influence in the army, the Jewish leadership endeavored to contain a corrupt impact of the army on Jewish soldiers. Indeed, the post-reform Russian army had no intention of converting Jewish soldiers, who could enjoy their regular "rites of creed" unhindered. Often, Jewish soldiers were allowed to congregate in their own groups, to establish their own prayer quorums, to arrange their own celebration of major Jewish festivals in the regimental canteens and barracks, and to be granted leave to travel to nearby communities for the holidays. Some continued to abide by their traditions, while others did not, but until the very end of the

---

[90] Source: *Voina i evrei*, 131; *Gosudarstvennaia Duma. Sessiia II*. Zasedanie 29 (sekretnoe), 17 aprelia 1907 goda (SPb.: Gosudarstvennaia tipografiia, 1907), 2177–2183.

Russian Imperial Army, both observant and secular soldiers participated in the joint celebration of Jewish festivals. In some cases, some commanders allowed Jewish soldiers a reprieve from work on the Shabbat, while others compelled their Jews to participate in training or other activities. For many conscripts, if not for most, a religious holiday was a well-established pretext to request a day off to visit parents or a nearby community. Since, even without the pressure to convert, the army provided an array of opportunities to break with tradition, the Jewish communal leadership strove to foster traditional Jewish self-awareness, reconciling army service with the soldiers' values and practices.

To assist traditional yet relatively uneducated Jewish recruits in retaining elements of their religious observance, Rabbi Israel Meir Kagan (known as the Chafetz Chaim), a preeminent East European rabbinical authority, published his Hebrew book *Mahaneh Israel*.[91] The volume appeared in 1881, in Vilna, as a pocket-size digest of the basic laws of Judaism, intended for Jewish soldiers.[92] The work attempted to differentiate between integration, a necessary and therefore somewhat acceptable evil of the time, and assimilation, an imminent and insidious threat to Jewish continuity that was not to be tolerated even by Jews in the military.[93] Rabbi Kagan maintained that the Jew regarded himself, before the draft, as a social being anchored by his lifestyle and community, whereas in the barracks he considered himself theologically an orphan and socially an outcast. To defeat such a self-perception, *Mahaneh Israel* furnished the only easily portable compendium of answers to all legal and ethical questions likely to bother him.[94]

Rabbi Kagan observed that the psychological and social ramifications of a Jew's life in exile (*galut*) were doubly burdensome for him in the army, an exile within exile. Attempting to rescue the soldier from despair and to impart religious conviction, Rabbi Kagan argued that a soldier was neither banished theologically from the God of Israel nor excluded from the Jewish community;

[91] According to his memoirs, the idea of writing a book was prompted by Rabbi Kagan's meeting with a soldier who did not know how to deal with Jewish legal issues during Passover. See Moses M. Yoshor, *The Chafetz Chaim: The Life and Works of Rabbi Israel Meir Kagan of Radin* (New York: Mesora Publishers, 1997), 1: 225; the hypothesis that Rabbi Kagan wrote the book for yeshiva students who became subject to conscription under the new Military Statute of 1874 appears more likely. See Lester Samuel Eckman, *Revered by All: The Life and Works of Rabbi Israel Meir Kagan – Hafets Hayyim (1838–1933)* (New York: Shengold, 1974), 29–30.

[92] I am using the later edition: Israel Meir Hacohen, *Mahaneh Israel* (Bnei-Brak: Torah ve-dat, 1967–1968).

[93] Cf. the analysis of this book in hagiographic sources: Eckman, *Revered*, 25–47; Yoshor, *The Chafetz Chaim*, 235–246.

[94] In this sense, *Mahaneh Israel* became a paradigm for later guides on Jewish law for the Jewish soldiers. During World War II, Moses Yoshor, a disciple of Rabbi Kagan, published an English book, *Israel in the Ranks: A Religious Guide to Faith and Practice for the Jewish Soldier* (New York: n. p., 1943), which was "based upon the book *Machaneh Yisrael* by Rabbi Israel Meir Hacohen (Rabbi Kagan)."

the army was merely a test of his ability to survive as a Jew.[95] While trying to fulfill the religious commandments, the Jewish conscript was in the custody of his Creator and therefore safe, even if he were remiss in his observance of the law. The moral implications were clear: a Jew in the army should be no less observant than the average shtetl Jew. If he were not, no big deal – but he was obligated to make an effort and would be ultimately judged by his effort. A soldier's cleaving to tradition served him as a shield in battle, promoted his victory, and protected him from being taken captive. As 248 words of "Shema, Israel" prayer are equivalent to the 248 members of human body, regular recitation of this prayer would protect the physical body from the bayonets and bullets of the enemy. Rabbi Kagan elaborated how one could adapt the regimen of praying three times a day or pronouncing lengthy blessings to the circumstances of life in the barracks. He proclaimed that army service did not exempt the Jew from eating kosher food or from learning the Torah. In short, army service conferred no excuse for any kind of laxity.[96] The problem was how to circumvent obstacles and to combine the exigencies of military service with Jewish traditional requirements.

Rabbi Kagan declared that the Jewish soldier must be enterprising and inventive, employing his wits and ingenuity (*hithakhmot*) in a dedicated effort to observe the law, except when it directly contradicted the tsar's decree. He made an important allowance for military circumstances, equating the act of withstanding temptation with the performance of a positive commandment. Technically, a Jewish soldier had not committed a violation if it originated in imperial military legislation; nonetheless, he should try to avoid such transgressions. For one unable to counteract or to transcend the unfavorable circumstances in which he found himself, the doors of *teshuvah*, repentance, were open; even repentance a day before death could redeem a Jew's soul.[97] Therefore, on the eve of battle, the Jewish soldier should write a will, confess his sins, and repent.

Theological optimism offered another means of confronting the depressing military experience. Libertinism and card-playing, both notoriously common in the military, reflected discontent with life and an absence of gratitude, stated Rabbi Kagan. Thievery and heavy drinking similarly were manifestations of malaise, a negation of divine justice. A soldier should not complain about his fate. On the contrary, one who was capable of stoically enduring hardship distinguished himself as a true Jew. At the same time, Rabbi Kagan knew that a soldier who gracefully accepted his circumstances and held himself aloof from typical barracks behavior became a target of ridicule. Rabbi Kagan regarded

---

[95] Cf. "The more we are immersed in *galut*, the more we are obliged to fulfill God's will, especially in the army." See *Mahaneh Israel*, 7–9. To corroborate this view, Rabbi Kagan mentioned a *halakhah* (a legal ruling) according to which a Jew remained a Jew even if he sold himself as a slave to a non-Jew, quoting 2 Kings 5:18. Because the Jewish soldier was drafted and had not chosen to serve in the army, his Jewish essence remained undiminished; see *Mahaneh Israel*, 11, and a discussion of the biblical quote in the B. Talmud, *Sanhedrin*, 74b.

[96] *Mahaneh Israel*, 14, 20–23, 44–49, 56–59.

[97] *Mahaneh Israel*, 95, 104–114, 127.

the Jewish soldier as the biblical Joseph, isolated from his brethren, exiled to the military, and enticed by the low moral standards of life in the barracks. He assured his readers that the community embraced retired soldiers, and that one who maintained strict observance would be unconditionally accepted upon his return; this was a redemption. Even in the army, argued *Mahaneh Israel*, the Jewish soldier remained a communal being, as the community assumed responsibility for its drafted brethren; this observation was reiterated throughout the book. It was the soldier's duty as a Jew to avoid assimilation, to request kosher food from nearby communities and to arrange his accommodation with Jewish families over Passover. In turn, the community was obligated to provide the soldier with appropriate economic and moral support and to apprise itself of the Jewish draftees' situation.[98]

Although the Jewish community in the Pale was not particularly adept at helping its brethren in the service, some local communities did assume this responsibility. Rabbi Kagan regularly invited as Shabbat guests a group of Jewish soldiers from the Lida garrison.[99] The Borkov Crown Rabbi organized a Passover seder for one hundred Jewish soldiers. The communities of Korets, Ponevezh (Poniewież), Orsha, and other towns in the Pale and in the Kingdom of Poland arranged lunches for Jewish conscripts on the occasion of Alexander III's inauguration.[100] However, the paucity of evidence on the active role played by Jewish communities in assisting the recruits is instructive; care for Jewish soldiers, especially regarding their food, was the exception. In response to this communal neglect of the needs of conscript Jews, Rabbi Kagan published an appeal to the Jews of the Russian Empire to establish and maintain kosher kitchens for them.[101] Did it succeed? Consider how the communities organized the feeding of Jewish reserve soldiers during regular training.[102] In 1887 and 1888, Jews comprised 32 percent of the reserve troops in the Warsaw garrison. The Warsaw Jewish community prepared their food on its own initiative. The fifty Jewish soldiers stationed in the Poltava regiment ate separately, from a special pot, delivered to their barracks. In another (unspecified) regiment of the same military district, nine of the sixty-seven reserve soldiers were Jews. All of them refused to eat from the company pot (*rotnyi kotel*); they were grudgingly given cash in order to purchase their own produce. Of the 159 reserve soldiers

---

[98] *Mahaneh Israel*, 7, 51, 61–78, 95–102, 188. It is not known how widely *Mahaneh Israel* was read by Jewish soldiers. Rabbi Kagan himself was reported to give the book as a gift to young men who came to him before the draft; it appears that he also gave it to his yeshiva students to intimidate them if they did not follow his advice. See Yoshor, *The Chafetz Chaim*, 239. Rabbi Kagan claimed that he sent chapters of the book to soldiers at the Russo-Japanese front and that he received letters of gratitude from them, see *Mikhtevei Chafets Hayyim*, 20, and the hagiographic account in Eckman, *Revered*, 54.

[99] Yoshor, *The Chafetz Chaim*, 226.

[100] *Russkii evrei*, no. 14 (1882): 510; no. 21 (1883): 16.

[101] Yoshor, *The Chafetz Chaim*, 242–243.

[102] For lower ranks who served in the army less than three years, the training term was twenty-one days (order no. 86, 1889). See *Voennyi sbornik*, no. 3 (1890): 155.

in the Keksgolm grenadier regiment, 20 were Jews. The command allowed them to obtain meat from a Jewish purveyor and to do their cooking separately. Yet the reserves preferred to pocket the money earmarked for food and to send it to their families as compensation for their lost earnings; during the three days of training, they subsisted on herrings and tea. On the third day, the commanders decided to put an end to this undernourishment in the name of dietary restriction, and ordered the Jews to eat from the soldiers' common pot.[103]

Most Jewish soldiers in the reserves came from traditional Jewish families who kept kosher. They realized that their special diet entailed greater expense than the regular fare, and attempted to curtail their spending. The officers in charge of training the reserves often compelled them all to eat from a common pot. Since their service stint was brief, reserve Jewish soldiers could make do with onions, herrings, bread, and tea, exchanging the portion of kasha with pork suet for personal items. In some cases, perhaps, Jewish soldiers ate with their hosts or in neighboring communities. The relative freedom granted to local commanders and to Jewish soldiers was reduced abruptly at the end of the 1880s. Between 1887 and 1888, the commanders of the Moscow, Odessa, Caucasus, Vilna, Finland, and Turkestan military districts legally forbade Jews to eat separately, and prohibited other soldiers from driving Jews away from the company pot.[104] Only when fasting and feasting could Jews affirm their symbolic adherence to tradition.

Lomzha had some five thousand Jews; thirty-six Jewish soldiers, quartered with their regiment in the town, asked the local rabbi to find local families to feed them on a daily rotation basis, as was the usual practice for yeshiva students. The rabbi replied, if one believes the source: "I do not care; as far as I am concerned, you may eat even treif [forbidden, ritually unclean food]."[105] In other places, the communities entrusted with providing pots of food for Jewish soldiers allotted insufficient, if not meager, budgets for provisions. In Minsk, for example, communal donations yielded 2.5 kopeks daily per soldier. This allowed for a maximum of 0.8 ounces (23 grams) of mutton suet (the cheapest meat substitute available) in a soldier's kosher soup portion.[106] Jewish soldiers were confronted with a painful dilemma: either to suffer daily from hunger, or to eat from the common pot. Not surprisingly, they preferred to eat nonkosher soup with meat from the company pot than to starve. After all, it was the Jewish communities' poverty that caused their neglect of their drafted brethren. Under such conditions, neither Rabbi Kagan nor any other spiritual leader could have

---

[103] Luganin, "Zametki," *Voennyi sbornik*, no. 5 (1888): 136–137; anon., "Zametki po povodu uchebnykh sborov zapasnykh nizhnikh chinov," *Voennyi sbornik*, no. 4 (1889): 305–306.

[104] *Voina i evrei*, 48. Only one tendentious source with a reference to the commander of the Serpukhov regiment mentioned that in Minsk, in the 1890s, Jews illegally arranged "secret kitchens" for those soldiers who did not eat from the common pot; see A. Shmakov, *Minskii protsess: Delo o soprotivlenii evreiskikh skopishch voennym patruliam* (M.: Mamontov, 1899), 85–86.

[105] *Russkii evrei*, no. 16 (1881): 617–618.

[106] See Mkonon, "Koshernyi kotel dlia soldat-evreev," *Rassvet*, no. 4 (1880): 132–135.

prevented the rapid decline in daily observance among Jewish soldiers, particularly in the last decade of the nineteenth century. The Jewish soldier underwent training, served, fought, and ate alongside the Russian Orthodox soldier. His Judaism metamorphosed from a way of life into a creed, sustained by randomly observed rituals. And since, in nineteenth-century Russia, one's identity was primarily a religious issue, the Jewish soldier expressed his identity not through everyday practice but through the rites and symbols connecting him to his tradition. The more tenuous this connection, the more the Jewish soldier was prone to breaches of army discipline.

The War Ministry versus Military Pragmatism

Army officers who rejected the War Ministry's antisemitic prejudice and who did not blindly acquiesce in official policy understood how crucial it was for Jewish soldiers to maintain ties to their communities. As military discipline decreased, it became a matter of sheer pragmatism to foster such contacts, to ensure that conscripts engaged in supervised activities during their holidays. It was clear that the army created a rift between an individual and his community, whether Jewish or Christian, which the soldier filled with promiscuity, drunkenness, violence, and, later in the 1900s, with subversion. Encouraging communal self-awareness helped to neutralize any revolutionary ambitions among the lower Jewish ranks. Some commanders recognized the detrimental effects upon morale of the xenophobic military regulations, and perhaps believed that encouraging the Jewish soldier's religious activities demonstrated respect for his beliefs and instilled loyalty and obedience.[107] The Torah scroll was as potent a symbol for the Jews as the icon of St. George the Victorious was for the Russians. The legally sanctioned, pan-regimental celebration of a Jewish holiday might normalize relations between Jews and non-Jews in the regiment. However, even though the late nineteenth-century War Ministry considered Jewish militarization a social imperative, the army felt no obligation to acknowledge the validity of its soldiers' Judaism. Pragmatic officers who thought otherwise invariably incurred their superiors' wrath; higher military authorities swiftly disciplined them.[108] Jewish soldiers unwittingly triggered a

---

[107] Enhancing the Jewish recruit's sense of religious identification acquired particular significance because, under Alexander III, the army had adopted a new Slavic nationalism and began displaying its Christian symbols. See Richard Wortman, "National Narratives in the Representation of Nineteenth-Century Russian Monarchy," in Marsha Siefert, ed., *Extending the Borders of Russian History, Essays in Honor of Alfred Rieber* (Budapest and New York: Central European University Press, 2003), 57–61.

[108] Hereafter, the phrase "military intelligentsia" refers to the Russian army officers who did not share the higher command's mainstream ideology, yet did not themselves commit any actions against the government. In this respect, they distinguished themselves from the "military intelligentsia" (praetorians, to use the word of John Keep) of the beginning of the nineteenth century, such as the Decembrists, who rebelled against the tsar. See Keep, *Soldiers of the Tsar*, 244–247.

number of bitter conflicts between the more tolerant regimental commanders and the increasingly xenophobic War Ministry.

In May 1888, Vannovskii learned from Alexander III that Jewish soldiers in the Odessa military district had raised funds to commission a Torah scroll, which they had placed in a synagogue. Alexander ordered Vannovskii to furnish him immediately with a report explaining how such a disgraceful incident could have occurred. On June 11, Vannovskii sent a note to Obruchev, then commander of the Main Staff, requesting that he ascertain "who has allowed the collection of money; who has permitted Jews to solemnly transfer [the scroll to the synagogue], who took part in it, etc."[109] A few days later, Vannovskii cabled the mayor of Odessa asking for the same information. The Odessa mayor, General Roop, wrote that the actions of the regimental commander, Colonel Makeev, who had endorsed the ceremony, were "extremely tactless and unbecoming an officer." Yet, on purely pragmatic grounds, General Roop opposed the war minister's desire to discipline Makeev.[110] He explained, "Considering the heretofore unblemished service of Colonel Makeev and his good standing within the regiment, with particular regard to the commendable situation of both regimental economy and drill, I would consider it desirable to limit action in his case to a severe reprimand." Vannovskii disagreed: Makeev, he argued, had not asked for permission from his commanders and had sanctioned the arrangement of "a special solemn ceremony," which was totally unacceptable. The war minister demanded that Makeev be relieved of his post. On July 23, Alexander approved the minister's decision. Makeev was dismissed and transferred to the reserves, albeit with full pension.[111]

The Makeev case set the tone for the army's treatment of commanders who failed to display antisemitic attitudes. On May 21, 1897, the official Russian periodical *Varshavskii dnevnik* recounted the donation of a Torah scroll to the Forty-eighth dragoon corps. Somebody carefully clipped this article from the newspaper and sent it to the Main Staff, with a marginal note written in bold red: "Is the fraternization of Russian troops with Yids really desirable? Or is money involved?" Upon reading the account, Obruchev ordered an investigation into the case. He was particularly mystified by the statement that "the first letters of the Torah belong to the commander of the regiment." An angry, almost illegible note (probably Vannovskii's) circulated among the Main Staff, alleging "similar cases in the towns of Chudnov and Simferopol, which had both been mentioned in the newspapers."[112] The military command was indignant; this was not the first time that commanders' attempts to show favor toward Jews ended in scandal. The Main Staff condemned Makeev's "shocking

---

[109] RGVIA, f. 400, op. 15, d. 1092, l. 3.
[110] General Roop exhibited considerable courage in expressing opinions that often differed from those of his superiors. See Rediger, *Vospominaniia*, 1: 182.
[111] RGVIA, f. 400, op. 15, d. 1092, l. 7, 19.
[112] RGVIA, f. 400, op. 15, d. 1711, l. 2, 5, 3.

action" in a communiqué, as it did the "shocking actions" of the commander of the Third Turkestan line battalion, Colonel Kazantsev. The latter, in 1889, had allowed the Jews in his battalion to conduct a ceremony marking the establishment of a synagogue in Chardzhui. The Main Staff protested that Jews were no better than Russian sectarians (Old Believers), whom the law prohibited from publicly engaging in religious ritual.[113] Nor could Russian Christian sectarians participate in public "singing in the streets and squares, openly carrying icons, etc.," although high-ranking officers also were present at these public ceremonies.

The Main Staff tolerated its officers' misconduct, such as the embezzlement of state money, but it was not benevolent toward Jews. Consequently, Colonel Korbut, the commander of the Forty-eighth dragoon corps, who had endorsed the festival in Serpets, felt compelled to write a groveling apology for his actions. However, Vannovskii flatly rejected his arguments, resolving that army officers were not to participate in any Jewish ceremony or to countenance any public expression of Judaism. Specifically, he forbade the regiment to keep the Torah scroll, as if to do so constituted an effort to smuggle Judaism into the army. Nicholas II concurred, writing in the file's margin, "The Torah should not be allowed into the regiment, but kept in a synagogue." The War Ministry intended to reprimand Colonel Korbut "for disrespect." Fortunately, Adjutant General Prince Imeretinskii, the commander of the Warsaw district, came to Korbut's rescue. The prince was motivated by pragmatism, rather than any benevolent feeling toward the Jews. He wrote to the Main Staff, "I consider that the display of good relations between the army and the people is rather desirable, and deserving of comprehensive attention, in particular since it is undertaken in the name of the Emperor." Vannovskii observed bitterly, "Korbut has demonstrated his disrespect, but since the commander of the military district has approved his actions, it is obviously impossible to reprimand him."[114]

In other cases, there was nobody to support a regimental commander who also believed in the desirability of good relations between the army and the people. Officers adopting an impartial attitude toward Jewish soldiers were subjected to harsh rebukes. A pattern emerged: a sympathetic newspaper article led to an anonymous denunciation to the ministry, resulting in harsh reprisals meted out to a regimental commander. The case of the 159th Guriisk regiment provides one such illustration. On March 24, 1901, *Mogilevskie gubernskie vedomosti* (Mogilev Province Weekly) described the presentation of a Torah

[113] Although the governmental policy toward *raskol'niki* (Old Believers) vacillated significantly throughout the second half of the nineteenth century, this group was treated largely as were other tolerated aliens, despite their being Russian Christians. See the extensive analysis in Jackson Taylor, Jr., "Dmitrii Andreevich Tolstoi and the Ministry of the Interior, 1882–1889," (Ph.D. diss., New York University, 1970), 66–84.

[114] RGVIA, f. 400, op. 15, d. 1171, ll. 14, 150b.-16.

scroll by Jewish soldiers to the local synagogue. An anonymous note to the War Ministry followed:

Yids' trickery. According to the *Shulkhan Arukh*, they hate the Tsar as a *goy*. The Yids bribed everybody with their flattery or money. Where does the government look? The regimental commander is a friend of the rabbi. The Christian folk are confused. The Yids showed the soldiers how virtuous their religion is, and all commanders participated in the procession. Who permitted them to bring the Torah into the regiment? Why is it there? Where will they keep it? Rumors circulated that it would be carried along with the colors. Really, the time of the Yids has arrived. Are the Russian people dying out?[115]

It is probable that an officer in the regiment penned this note, since it included a detailed account of the ceremony and raised the problem of storage. Most likely, the author hoped to benefit from the disgrace of the regimental commander, Colonel Turkov. The Main Staff recommended disciplinary action against Colonel Turkov as the party principally responsible.

An idiosyncratic senior officer, Turkov was born to an upper-class, Russian Orthodox family. His career had progressed uneventfully.[116] Perhaps the 49-year-old colonel with a perfect service record represented an obstacle to a regimental officer's career plans and thus became the target of a jealous colleague. Another anonymous letter, signed "A Russian Lady," attacked Turkov and called for his punishment:

A resident of Rogachev in Mogilev province, I thought the behavior of the commander of the 159th Guriisk infantry, Colonel Turkov, and his friendship with alien elements and his moral oppression of his officers and soldiers offensive. Jewish soldiers, without informing the company's commanders, wrote a Torah in the house of an influential Jew, Ginsburg, and cunningly dedicated its completion to the recovery of the emperor. Turkov actively participated in the ritual dedication of the Torah scroll, carried it himself and forced his officers to take part in the ceremony. He also wanted to involve the regimental band in the Torah procession, despite the fact that the musicians were fasting. The priest failed to convince the colonel not to play music. Sarcastic stories circulated in the city that they would carry the Torah with the regimental banners. Such a disgrace can occur in Russia without any punishment of those guilty because from the quartermaster to the Senate, everything and everyone has been bought by the Yids' gold. Are there really any strong and respected people at the top who can lead Russia out of the Yids' captivity and evil?[117]

---

[115] RGVIA, f. 400, op. 15, d. 1171, l. 1, in margin.

[116] Upon graduation from the Odessa infantry college, he served as a private in the Fifty-second Vilna regiment. In 1868, he became a corporal; later, he served as an ensign in the Fiftieth Belostok infantry regiment. In 1875, his commander promoted him to staff captain; in 1881, to captain; and in 1887, to colonel. He served twenty-eight years and was awarded for his professional service with the Cross of Franz-Joseph, third class, and a St. Vladimir third-class decoration. In 1899, he became the regimental commander. See RGVIA, f. 400, op. 15, d. 2053.

[117] RGVIA, f. 400, op. 15, d. 2053, l. 1–10b.

The Main Staff clerk underlined the last sentence with a red pencil. Further investigation and more anonymous denunciations offer a reconstruction of events, demonstrating the divergence in stance of various officers on the Jewish question.

Once the scribe had completed the writing of the scroll, Turkov granted his Jewish soldiers a day off, and invited all officers and the regimental band to participate in the festivities. This was a direct attempt to turn a Jewish celebration into a public event. Several officers disapproved and refused to join in. Andrei Bekarevich, the regimental chaplain, explained to Turkov that the musicians were fasting because of the advent of Lent, and therefore could not take part in the synagogue celebrations. "No," responded Turkov. "Firstly, I have promised. And secondly, [if you do not allow the musicians to perform in the ceremony] in the eyes of the Jews you will be considered a fanatic." Father Bekarevich took offence: Turkov had given his word to the rabbi and had rejected the request of a Christian priest. However, during the investigation Bekarevich confirmed that neither the regimental band nor the Jewish military musicians had been involved in the celebration. Instead, a small string orchestra was hired, most likely a klezmer band. Other senior officers considered the celebration a Judaization of the military. Lieutenant Colonel Popov remarked to Lieutenant Colonel Berdiaev, "Vasilii Mikhailovich, the staff officers should insist that there be no Yids' celebration." Popov and Berdiaev approached Turkov. Afterward, Popov related to his comrades, "He did not listen to us and so bears full responsibility for his actions." Lieutenant Colonel Sudnikov was of the same opinion as Popov and Berdiaev: "It is impossible that the Jews invite us to render homage to their holy relics." But Lieutenant Colonel Fliorkovskii was of a different mind. While he did not attach much importance to the event, he was aware of similar Jewish festivities in other regiments. He observed that "the officers and the colonel unwrapped the scroll and observed the calligraphic art with amazement." Lieutenant Colonel Berdiaev also refused to play any role in the Torah dedication ceremony, but his stepdaughter attended.[118]

Despite repeated accusations by means of anonymous letters, Turkov acted with dignity and resolutely fought off all charges. He observed, "Three months after the dedication of the Torah scroll, the author of those letters has at last touched the 'Russian' conscience, shamefully hiding his name in his secret report, which certainly is not the behavior of a true Russian. The lengthy time interval positively proves that the accusation is the result of personal animosity."[119] At the same time, to quell rumors in the regiment, Turkov issued an internal order obliquely calling upon his detractors to reveal their identities:

The anonymous letters that I have repeatedly received indicate that certain people ignorant of the spirit of military decency and nobility interfere with the life of the regiment. To terminate this ruinous corruption of moral principles, I consider it

---

[118] RGVIA, f. 400, op. 15, d. 2053, l. 16–18.
[119] RGVIA, f. 400, op. 15, d. 2053, ll. 7–80b.

necessary to inform all ranks that I will destroy these letters without reading them. Army officers should protect their rights according to the laws of the military rather than cowardly hiding their names.[120]

Major Nikolai Valgin, of the Vilna military district headquarters, conducted an investigation. He determined that, while Turkov did not force any officers to participate in the Torah scroll's dedication ceremony, he had strained the limits of mutual tolerance and had also failed to keep an eye on illegal fund-raising in the regiment. He suggested that Turkov be charged with two offenses and required to pay a fine. The war minister insisted upon a more severe punishment: either transfer Turkov to a similar post in another district, or discharge and demote him to the infantry reserves. Nicholas II concurred with Vannovskii, and Turkov was duly transferred to the infantry reserves.[121]

This case study amply demonstrates the disparity in attitudes toward Jews in the Russian army. While Nicholas II and the war minister were xenophobes, in among military intelligentsia there were as many temperate and pragmatic men as there were antisemites. On September 12, 1900, Nikolai Valgin, a case investigator and close friend of the war minister, wrote a personal letter to Vannovskii: "Dear Petr Semenovich! As an old classmate, I seek to support the prestige of the regimental commander. Turkov is scrupulous and resolute, does not seek popularity, yet has provoked enmity. Any measure against Turkov undermines the prestige of authority and encourages the authors of anonymous letters, rather than serving justice." Vannovskii did not respond, and soon retired from his position. In late December 1901, a letter from the town of Rogachev, from Lieutenant Colonel Popov's widow, Antonina Popova, arrived at the War Ministry. Popova requested that Turkov be pardoned, and asserted that the "Russian woman" who had written the denunciations had been forced by her husband to make the slanderous allegations. The husband then had departed for St. Petersburg, where he accomplished the removal of the regimental commander from his post.[122]

The Russian army's responses to its Jewish soldiers varied from individual to individual and ranged across the entire spectrum: neutral, sympathetic on either moral or pragmatic grounds, inclined toward xenophobia, blatantly antisemitic, or employing antisemitic parlance to pursue selfish goals. The War Ministry considered sympathy for Jewish soldiers to be antithetical to the spirit of the army, and consistently removed those who dared publicly to manifest pragmatic, and therefore tolerant or welcoming, attitudes. Like Makeev, Kazantsev, and Turkov, almost all officers who endorsed Jewish festivities paid for their goodwill by being discharged. Colonel Korbut was spared only by the intercession of a superior officer. In the wake of the 1905 Russian Revolution, twenty-five officers in the Kiev military district found themselves under arrest and trial "for criticizing the operation of the troops engaged in suppressing the

[120] RGVIA, f. 400, op. 15, d. 2053, ll. 11–13.
[121] RGVIA, f. 400, op. 15, d. 2053, l. 31.
[122] RGVIA, f. 400, op. 15, d. 2053, ll. 5–70b., 34.

anti-Jewish disturbances in Kiev." The military accused them of having published a letter of protest in the newspaper *Kievskie otkliki*, in which they demanded an immediate investigation of the criminal actions of the police and troops who had taken no action to suppress the 1905 pogrom in Kiev.[123]

After 1905, the conflict between the zealots in the War Ministry and the more tolerant and pragmatic army officers leaked into the press. The question of whether or not the army should make accommodation for its Jews stirred hot public debate. Commanders found themselves apologizing for their public display of sympathy toward Jews, not to placate Main Staff clerks but to protect themselves against attacks in the far right press. Now officers such as Major General Annushkin, the commander of the Fortieth artillery brigade, had to publicly justify their benevolent attitude to the celebration of Jewish holidays granted to Jewish soldiers.[124]

Conclusion

The era of Alexander II changed Russian Jews' attitude to the army, bolstered their patriotic fervor and a new political self-awareness, and inspired some patriotic-minded Jewish contractors to support the pan-Slavic cause – the War for the Liberation of Slavs, or the Russo-Turkish War. This was the unique point in the nineteenth century when the symbiosis between Russian Jews and the Russian army reached its highest momentum. It manifested the Russian Jews' readiness for complete integration with society at large; it coincided with the ministerial discussions about the possibility of lifting the Pale of Settlement restrictions, a major manifestation of Jewish inequality in the Russian empire. Yet part of the Russian administration found the Russian–Jewish symbiosis unacceptable and spared no effort to demonstrate that Jewish assistance was redundant and that the greedy Jews sought nothing but embezzlement at the Russian army's expense. Starting in the late 1870s–early 1880s, the conservatives used every pretext to prove that Jews were corrupt contractors, disloyal subjects, and poor soldiers. Those commanders who thought otherwise were traitors to the noble Russian cause.

The new War Ministry's Judeophobia stemmed from rising Russian nationalism and ignored the grassroots reality. Jewish soldiers were overrepresented in the Russian army when compared with their percentage of the overall male population. They served predominantly in the infantry, while some also served in the artillery and engineer troops. While there were many Jews in noncombat posts – for example, in regimental orchestras or among the regimental artisans – the overall numbers of Jews in these posts did not exceed 2 to 3 percent of Jews in military service. The other 97 percent of Jews served in

[123] *Kievskie otkliki*, no. 292 (October 31, 1905); RGVIA, f. 400, op. 15, d. 3158, ll. 1–2.
[124] Annushkin endorsed the celebration of Passover by the Jewish troops in the Skobelev military camp in Nesvizh, Belorussia, see RGVIA, f. 400, op. 15, d. 3521, l. 164–164ob.

combat posts – as infantry privates. Despite their skills and educational status, they were deemed cannon fodder.

Consistent attempts at further curtailing the rights and privileges of Jewish soldiers, as well as those of Catholics and other alien creeds, could not significantly worsen their singular situation in the military, only too obvious to the neutral observers. Yet the late nineteenth-century anti-Jewish restrictions in the army and in society at large provided high-ranking Russian Judeophobes with excellent grounds for persecuting pragmatic-minded army commanders and for attempting to instill debate in the military about the harmful impact of Jews on the troops.

6

The Revolutionary Draft

Russia's accelerated industrialization at the turn of the nineteenth century reconfigured its social landscape and profoundly affected Russian Jewry. Minister of Finance Count Witte's initiatives generated a dramatic advance in the development of Russian capitalism and resulted in an increase in the absolute number of workers, especially among Jews. The worsening economic and political situation in the country compelled Jews to flee overseas: some 1,250,000 emigrated between the 1880s and the second decade of the twentieth century. At the same time, a constant flow of migrant Jews moved to areas of industrial growth: to Lodz (Łódź) and to other centers of the Polish textile industry; to the northwestern industrial centers of the Russian Empire, such as Minsk, Vilna, and Dvinsk; and to the rapidly developing southeastern regions, like Ekaterinoslav.[1] Those who relocated to the cities joined the organized economic and political struggle of the Russian proletariat.[2] An unprecedented growth in the Jewish population in the second half of the century created a surplus in the working force, exacerbating labor market problems. Moreover, the emerging light-industry factories in the western and northwestern regions of

---

[1] Shaul Stampfer, "Patterns of Internal Jewish Migration in the Russian Empire," in Yaakov Roi, ed., *Jews and Jewish Life in Russia and the Soviet Union* (Ilford, Essex: F. Cass, 1995), 28–47.

[2] N. A. Bukhbinder, *Istoriia evreiskogo rabochego dvizheniia v Rossii* (L.: Akademicheskoe izdatel'stvo, 1925); "Bund," in *Politicheskie partii Rossii: Konets XIX-pervaia tret' XX v. Entsiklopediia* (M.: ROSSPEN, 1996), 92–94; A. D. Kirzhnits, ed. *1905. Evreiskoe rabochee dvizhenie. Materialy i dokumenty* (M., L.: Gosudarstevennoe izdatel'stvo, 1928); Ia. Leshchinskii, "Evreiskoe naselenie Rossii i evreiskii trud," in *Kniga o russkom evreistve ot 1860 gg. do revoliutsii 1917 g.* (New York: Soiuz russkikh evreev, 1960); Moshe Mishkinsky, *Reshit tenu'at ha-po'alim ha-yehudit be-rusia* (Tel-Aviv: Ha-kibbuts ha-me'uhad, 1981); Yoav Peled, *Class and Ethnicity in the Pale: The Political Economy of Jewish Workers' Nationalism in Late Imperial Russia* (London: Macmillan, 1989); M. Rafes, *Ocherki po istorii Bunda* (M.: Moskovskii rabochii, 1923); Henry Tobias, *The Jewish Bund in Russia: From Its Origins to 1905* (Stanford, Calif.: Stanford University Press, 1972); Jonathan Frankel, *Prophecy and Politics: Socialism, Nationalism, and the Russian Jews, 1862–1917* (Cambridge: Cambridge University Press, 1981), 134–257.

the empire rendered obsolete the handcrafted goods of Jewish artisans, who now joined the unemployed in search of work.

At the beginning of the twentieth century, organized workers' movements revolutionized the country's population. Strikes by Russian proletarians spread increasing unrest into rural areas. Although the Russo-Japanese war (1904–1905) unfolded far away, conscription aggravated the predicament of the Russian peasantry, which was now obligated to provide the army with 80 percent of its reserve troops. The drafted men were reluctant to abandon their families to engage in conflict in the Far East. They expressed their indignation by getting drunk at railway stations and near conscription points and triggering hundreds of pogroms. Often, Jewish petty traders and store owners found themselves victims of the recruitment drive. The Mobilization Department maintained that Jewish reserves behaved defiantly during the call-up and dispatch of the troops.[3] The war did not impede the growing revolutionary movement. The loss of the navy fleet near Tsusima and the disastrous military defeat near Port Artur and Mukden significantly affected the stability of the regime. With skyrocketing poverty rates and a 20 percent decline in workers' wages, social clashes became inevitable.

The Bloody Sunday massacre of January 9, 1905, when troops opened fire during a peaceful workers' demonstration in St. Petersburg, killing 100 and wounding 300, marked the beginning of the 1905 Russian Revolution. The intelligentsia and middle-class bourgeoisie organized the Union of Unions, demanding the establishment of a constituent assembly. Peasants resorted to the illegal seizure and redistribution of land, to looting the gentry's estates, and to violence, particularly in the Samara, Grodno, Kovno, and Minsk provinces. In more than 3,000 cases, the regime deployed the army to suppress rural unrest. Yet the army was less reliably loyal than formerly: soldiers refused to suppress the revolution, and instead advanced their own demands. In some cases, they took up arms against the regime. This turmoil reached its zenith in June 1905 with the mutiny on the battleship *Potemkin*. Numerous military revolts, the well-organized proletarian strikes in European Russia's industrial centers, and the pan-Russian railway workers' strike in October paralyzed the empire. A reluctant Nicholas II issued the October Manifesto, granting basic freedoms to the populace. While the bourgeoisie and empire constitutionalists welcomed the manifesto, the left-wing parties rejected it, precipitating the December Uprising in Moscow. After brutally suppressing the rebels, the tsar went some way toward pacifying the country in 1906 by establishing the First State Duma. This was a semi-parliamentary, consultative body with limited power. The consequent legalization of the far right parties prompted the regime to enlist their help in launching a counter-revolutionary attack. The country's urban population was intimidated by pogroms orchestrated against the Jews in major urban centers, particularly in Odessa, Kiev, and Belostok. Drafted into the army

---

[3] See RGVIA, f. 400, op. 5, d. 1588 ("O nariade konvoia dlia partii evreiskikh novobrantsev," March 1904), ll. 19–220b.

at the turn of the nineteenth century, Jewish soldiers were dismayed to find themselves in the first decade of the twentieth century in the midst of the country's revolutionary upheaval.

The Draft Pool at the Turn of the Century: The Jewish Proletariat

By the end of the nineteenth century, the social stratification of Russian Jews underwent significant upheaval. Within the Jewish Pale, in 1897, 660,000 out of 1,197,175 working Jews were employed in industrial positions, while only 412,000 remained in trade. Approximately 55 percent of the Jewish population underwent the process of proletarianization.[4] The influx of peasants from rural to urban areas and the entry of other ethnic minorities into trades considerably worsened the situation for Jewish artisans and traders alike.[5] Jewish industrialists were reluctant to hire their co-religionists, who, consequently, were compelled to seek low-paid employment in ecologically hazardous industries, such as cigarette and match factories. This further aggravated Jewish poverty. Because of police reluctance to accept or to extend artisans' licenses, the number of Jewish craftsmen evicted from internal provinces who returned to the Pale of Settlement increased steadily between 1894 and 1900.[6] The rampant industrialization also had a sweeping effect upon traditional Jewry. By the end of the nineteenth century, numerous "workers'" synagogues sprang up throughout the Pale of Settlement: their congregants were masons, cobblers, tailors, tinsmiths, tanners, shoemakers, hatters, and others. The workers' *kassy*, mutual aid funds and rudimentary labor unions supporting workers during strikes, emerged throughout the Pale of Settlement, replacing Jewish informal guilds and occupational alliances. *Skhodkes* (Yiddish for informal assemblies of workers) emerged among Jewish proletarians as a new means by which they could strive to attain basic economic rights. The transition of Jewish labor from craft to factory work had a devastating impact upon the traditional modes of Jewish social life, eventually alienating the increasingly radicalized younger generation.[7]

In the 1890s, the first organized manifestation of the Jewish proletariat was a massive Jewish workers' movement, at whose head stood the Bund, a socialist alliance for Jewish proletarians in Lithuania, Poland, and Russia. Officially

---

[4] Arcadius Kahan, *Essays in Jewish Social and Economic History*, ed. Roger Weiss (Chicago and London: University of Chicago Press, 1986), 6–9; Kirzhnits, *Evreiskoe rabochee*, 25–27.

[5] In the Kingdom of Poland, this process was even more rapid, see Leshchinskii, *Evreiskoe naselenie*, 204; Mendelsohn, *Class Struggle*, 21; Rafes, *Ocherki Bunda*, 201.

[6] For the list of cases, see Ia. I. Gimpelson, and L. M. Bramson, eds., *Zakony o evreiakh: Sistematicheskii obzor deistvuiushchikh zakonopolozhenii o evreiakh s raz'iasneniiami pravitel'stvuiushchego Senata i tsentral'nykh pravitel'stvennykh ustanovlenii* (SPb.: Iurisprudentsiia, 1914), 122–138.

[7] Bukhbinder, *Istoriia dvizheniia*, 90, 177; Kirzhnits, *Evreiskoe rabochee*, 129, 355–356; Mendelsohn, *Class Struggle*, 40–44, 105; Rafes, *Ocherki Bunda*, 199–210, 363; Tobias, *Bund*, 257.

founded in 1897 from several grassroots groups, the Bund found massive support and acquired a sterling political reputation among Jews in the empire's industrially developed regions. While the Russian Social Democratic Workers' Party (RSDRP) had scarcely begun discussing the need to oversee the workers' movement, the Bund already was successfully managing Jewish labor strikes. Industrialists were frequently forced to make concessions, reducing the number of working hours and increasing salaries. In 1899, 72 percent of Jewish laborers' strikes ended in victory. In 1903, out of ninety-five strikes sponsored by the Bund, eighty yielded positive results. Jewish workers' strikes before the 1905 Revolution achieved their zenith in the town of Krynki, in Grodno province, where for several days the town was run by tinsmiths, who had secured the support of the local population.[8] Thousands of laborers supported the Bund; between May 1903 and June 1904 its fund-raising yielded 191,132 rubles from workers and over 100,000 rubles in donations from wealthy Russian and American Jewish families. Although some of these funds covered the party's activities and expenses, the lion's share was spent on revolutionary leaflets, pamphlets, and periodicals. In 1896, the Bund's *Der Yiddisher Arbeter* had a circulation of a thousand copies. By 1900, the Bund printed about 74,750 copies of brochures and papers; and in 1902–1903, 347,150 copies; by the beginning of 1905, if one believes somewhat self-serving Bundist data, an astronomical 808,000 copies of various publications were distributed.[9]

During the 1905 Russian Revolution, the Bund was unquestionably the driving force among the Jews, responsible for 288 strikes. The largest of these took place in Kovno (Kowno) and in Dvinsk, with as many as 3,000 participants in each city; in Revel, with about 10,000 participants; and in Lodz, with 70,000 participants. The Program of the Socialist Revolutionary Party (SR), published in the first 1901 issue of the *Vestnik russkoi revoliutsii* periodical, boasted that the laborers' movement was the best organized of the Jewish movements in the western region.[10] Even Moisei Rafes, a Marxist historian of the workers' movement in the 1920s and a former Bundist, admitted that this body was extremely efficient and disciplined, and more democratic than the RSDRP. The Bund frequently offered itself as a mediator between warring social democratic groups. It succeeded in retaining its independence within the framework of the revolutionary movement as a party of the Jewish proletariat until the Bolshevik Revolution. Criticized by the political right for its excessively Marxist leanings, and by the left for its championing of narrowly ethnic interests, the Bund continued to move from a proletarian platform toward a greater emphasis upon nationalistic principles. After the 1905 Russian Revolution, and in spite of its formal reunification with the RSDRP, the Bund

---

[8] See the archival sources vividly illustrating these events, which were monitored by the army, in RGVIA, f. 400, op. 3, d. 8, ll. 10, 16; op. 15, d. 1834, ll. 2, 5, 13.

[9] Kirzhner, *Evreiskoe rabochee*, 48–49; Tobias, *Bund*, 158, 244.

[10] Cited in *Partiia sotsialistov-revoliutsionerov: Dokumenty i materialy, 1900–1907.* In 2 vols. (M.: ROSSPEN, 1996), 1:57.

adopted an aggressively anti-assimilationist position. It made inroads into the larger Jewish community through hundreds of literary societies, officially recognizing Yiddish as the national Jewish language. Furthermore, the Bund effectively addressed the economic concerns of the traditional-minded Jews. The new Jew who emerged from the midst of the proletarian movement combined traditional values with the socialist metaphor, a cultural bilingualism peculiar to Jewish draftees of the 1900s. Rafes regarded the Jewish laborer as a nondescript representative of the masses, an anonymous apprentice, who suddenly raised his voice to declare his rights and who boldly faced his enemies.[11]

Transforming Proletarians into Soldiers

At the turn of the nineteenth century, the imperial authorities decided to uproot the growing revolutionary movement and to discipline the unruly youths in the barracks. Their actions eventually sowed revolution in the army.

In 1899, an official circular letter was sent to all governors, demanding that mutinous students and workers be drafted.[12] Jewish workers were overrepresented among them. Provincial governors' reports to War Minister Kuropatkin of a new levy also proved an influx of Jewish socialist proletarians into the troops. Edid Sokolianskii fostered revolutionary sentiment among workers in Slonim; consequently, he was arrested and sent to serve in an infantry regiment. Shimon Vysotskii, from Plotsk (Płock), Zalman Freidan, from Chernigov, and Avrum-Ovsei Srulevich, from Makhnovka, all members of the Kiev Union of Struggle for the Liberation of the Working Class, soon found themselves in the army: in the Thirty-seventh artillery brigade, the Brest artillery battalion, and the Warsaw fortress infantry regiment, respectively. Shlomo Davidovich and Viktor Zhilinskii, political agitators who stashed illegal literature in their homes, were inducted into the Twenty-eighth Polotsk infantry regiment and the Warsaw telegraph service. Berko Leibovich Khavkin, from Vitebsk, who oversaw a fund supporting striking Jewish artisans in Vitebsk, was sent into the Twenty-second artillery brigade in Novgorod. The military drafted Leiba Grin and Izrail Tsitlin, participants and organizers of a Minsk artisans' society, assigning them as cannoneers to the Twenty-eighth artillery brigade and to the First mortar artillery brigade. Abram Vitezon, from Orsha, an organizer of strikes in Vilna, was conscripted into the Kronstadt fortress regiment.[13]

The same fate befell Abram Breida, Tsalko Levit, and Meier Kvit, participants in the Krynki uprising. Breida, as the indictment stated, endorsed

---

[11] Bukhbinder, *Istoriia dvizheniia*, 366–371; Kirzhnits, *Evreiskoe rabochee*, 323–337; Mendelsohn, *Class Struggle*, 109–110, 118–123; Rafes, *Ocherki Bunda*, 21, 158, 211–214.

[12] Fuller, *Conflict*, 107–108; B. M. Kochakov, "Sotsial'nyi sostav soldat tsarskoi armii," in *Iz istorii imperializma v Rossii* (M., L.: Akademiia Nauk SSSR, 1959), 352–353.

[13] RGVIA, f. 400, op. 3, d. 8, ll. 2, 19.

revolutionary violence and had been among the organizers of a secret workers' circle. Tsalko Levit, who had come from the town of Derezin in the Slonim district in search of employment, was one of the most active participants in the Krynki revolt. In 1897, he raised funds for the strikers, and visited factory and plant owners to present the employees' demands for a salary increase and a shorter workday. The police dispatched Breida and Kvit to the Sixty-fifth Moscow Imperial infantry regiment and to the 172nd Lida infantry regiment, respectively. Abram Dymshits, dispatched to the Libava fortress battalion and later commissioned, incited workers to initiate a strike and also to demand a shorter workday. Alter Drabkin, from Kremenchug, a cannoneer who trained workers to conduct strikes, was similarly conscripted.[14]

Scores of Jewish participants in the workers' movement ended up in the army at the behest of the government and the police. Movsha Epshtein and Girsh Sheperzon, forced to choose between arrest and military service, both joined the army: Epshtein was sent to the 197th Lifland infantry regiment in Dvinsk, and Shapiro to the 191st Dragich infantry reserve regiment in Warsaw province.[15] Both soldiers had experience in organizing revolution. In 1898–1899, Epshtein had worked as a lithographer and conducted clandestine activities: under an alias, *Alter*, he became a member of the Dvinsk Jewish social-democratic committee, known to be one of the most efficient among Jewish political associations. After the suppression of the workers' movement, Epshtein moved to Riga, where he established a society for propagating socialist ideas among Jewish artisans. He organized five study groups, attended by tailors, hatters, cobblers, tinsmiths, and lithographers. Later, he united the tinsmiths into the Riga Central Committee of the Jewish Social and Democratic Movement. At his apartment, he conducted "readings," intensive studies of revolutionary literature. Shapiro joined the group and assumed responsibility for maintaining contacts between the central committee's leadership and its members.

Neither Epshtein nor Shapiro was able to transfer his experience as a political activist to life in the barracks. Both regarded the army as too backward and entirely unsuitable for propaganda purposes. Thirsty for revolutionary work, Epstein served for two years, after which he deserted, sneaked across the border, and joined a foreign-based branch of the Jewish Socialist Workers' Party.[16] Shapiro remained in the same regiment, although he considered the army a burdensome but unavoidable duty, rather than a field of social experiment.[17]

In 1898, the minister of the interior's report to War Minister Kuropatkin included lists of drafted agitators: in sixteen cases out of twenty, they were of

[14] RGVIA, f. 400, op. 15, d. 1757, ll. 10–14, 16–16ob., 38, 48; op. 3, d. 8, ll. 10, 16; f. 801, op. 15, d. 1834, ll. 2, 5, 13.
[15] RGVIA, f. 801, op. 4, otd. 5, sv. 1, d. 32/20, ll. 1–2.
[16] For Epshtein's escape, see *Poslednie izvestiia*, no. 135, June 9, 1903.
[17] RGVIA, f. 801, op. 4, otd. 5, sv. 1, d. 32/20, l. 5.

proletarian Jewish origin. The police conscripted not only the dangerous strike organizers but also activists who merely distributed handouts. For example, Shlema Novomeiskii, a nineteen-year-old worker at a brush factory in Verzhblov (Wierzbołów), was accused of inciting the laborers of the Suvalki and Kovel industrial regions. He was arrested and sent to the Eightieth Kabardin infantry regiment, which later created revolutionary unrest among the soldiers and workers of Kutaisi province. Khaim Leibush Golberg found himself a gunner in the Fifth battery of the Thirty-fourth artillery regiment, as a result of having argued publicly that the land should belong to landless peasants. The police hoped that sending seditious laborers to the army would effectively neutralize them, while in fact the tactic served to destabilize the army. Although Jews were not the only ones guilty of revolutionary agitation, some of them became powerful catalysts in the early 1900s. In its "Address to All Jewish Workers, Male and Female, on the Army Call-Up," the Bund called upon Jewish conscripts to orchestrate class struggle within the army. It assured its drafted activists that social-democratic ideals, if implemented, would improve the lot of the ignorant and maltreated soldiers. The Bund encouraged its members to rally the soldiers under its red banners in a revolutionary struggle against the tsarist autocracy.[18]

The Warsaw and Vilna military authorities swiftly realized the danger in drafting revolutionary activists, and determined to transport seditious soldiers to distant military districts. Shmul Mordukhovich Chuzhovskii, who worked in Vilna's Bloch hosiery factory, participated in a demonstration near the Vilna Theater; for this offense, the police exiled him to East Siberia, where he was placed under surveillance. Two years later, he returned, and skillfully sowed revolt among the factory employees. They treated him with great respect, electing him as manager of the strikers' *kassa*; indeed, the investigation report described Chuzhovskii as the main organizer of a hosiery-factory workers' strike. In September 1906, the police conducted a search of his house at 15 Evreiskaia Street, and confiscated 434 copies of the *Soldatskaia zhizn* (Soldiers' Life) newspaper, five copies of the *Nasha dolia* (Our Destiny) leaflet, and 21 booklets of *Biulleten Profsoiuza* and *Soldatskii Biulleten* (Professional Union Bulletin and Soldiers' Bulletin, the latter published by the Military-Revolutionary Union of Lithuania and Belorussia). Consequently, Chuzhovskii was drafted and assigned to the Third Finland regiment, quartered outside the Pale of Settlement. In another court case, the secret police reported that Shlomo Gordon (Gordin) was involved in a clandestine revolutionary workers' group, and that he had made inflammatory antigovernment speeches and had sung songs of punishable content. On September 22, 1901, he was arrested while on an off-duty errand and was found to have in his possession a Bundist leaflet extolling the steadfastness of the Shereshevski factory employees in Grodno,

---

[18] RGVIA, f. 400, op. 15, d. 1757, ll. 1–10b., 17–170b., 19–190b., 38, 48; RGVIA, f. 400, op. 15, d. 1757, l. 37; RGVIA, f. 400, op. 3, d. 8, ll. 21. Also see *Poslednie izvestiia*, no. 44, April 1901, and Petrov, *Ocherki*, 112.

ILLUSTRATION 6. Ekhil Khilbartovich, a locksmith at the Kharkov locomotive repair plant, private of the 184th infantry regiment, and participant in the Russo-Japanese War; Kharkov, 1908. Courtesy of the Judaica Institute of Ukraine.

where eight hundred women had staged a strike. The police recommended transferring Gordon to a military unit stationed outside the Pale, and at a distance from any industrial area.[19] He was promptly conscripted into the First Warsaw fortress regiment.

[19] RGVIA, f. 1964, op. 1, d. 49, ll. 1–20b., 122; RGVIA, f. 801, op. 4, d. 1, ll. 1–5.

Although Jewish recruits joined local Bund societies in order to incite workers to rebel, they were less successful in fostering sedition in the army. Converting peasant soldiers into Marxists proved difficult; both Chuzhovskii and Gordon had attempted to return to their previous places of employment precisely because they considered the military too impenetrable an institution for revolutionary efforts to bear fruit. Other cases supported this conclusion. In 1900, Itsik Gelchinskii, a private in the Twelfth dragoon Mariupol regiment, stationed in the town of Trostiany (Troscianka) in the Belostok district, joined a discussion group of Jewish workers. The group discovered an informer in its midst and appointed Gelchinskii to punish him. Upon fulfilling his duty, the hapless soldier was arrested and imprisoned for two months, after which he was returned to the regiment under close surveillance. His supervisors found no evidence that he intended to become a revolutionary activist among the troops.[20]

Just as the military cited the conscripts' civic duty, the Bund also had urged its activists to join the troops – albeit with vastly different goals. One of the Bundist leaflets read, "More than police brutality or persecutions, our organized workers increasingly are concerned with mandatory army service. The days of being drafted into the army are almost upon us. It is difficult for qualified and well-organized workers to give up their struggle against autocracy and to become blind instruments of tsarism. A farewell party recently was organized to say goodbye to those who were about to leave for the army. About sixty comrades were present; there were toasts and speeches about the necessity of working among the soldiers and about the undesirability of abandoning organized workers and fleeing abroad to avoid the call-up."[21] Long before the revolutionary events had begun to unfold, the Bund emphasized that inciting soldiers to rebel, even if such efforts were spontaneous and poorly organized, yielded immediate results. Alarmed, the army issued a strict order that anyone who discovered inflammatory leaflets should deliver them to senior officers. The Bund was aware that privates obeyed the order more reluctantly than did junior officers; the former studied the leaflets before surrendering them. Although non-Jewish soldiers also read these tracts, senior officers chose to take more drastic measures against Jews in their attempt to suppress revolutionary provocation.[22]

Outside the army, Bundist agitators spread their Marxist gospel in Yiddish; when addressing the troops, they dispensed with their Jewish accents. One of the 1902 Bund proclamations portrayed the soldier as a worker in a trench coat, although in fact not more than 15 to 20 percent of the troops were of proletarian origin. The proclamation enjoined soldiers to preserve class solidarity, declaring that the barracks should serve as a school for arms training; those arms later could be turned against the rulers. Soldiers should become gravediggers for tsarism, not its defenders. The proclamation did not allude to

[20] RGVIA, f. 801, op. 4, otd. 5, sv. 1, d. 50/34, ll. 2–5.
[21] *Poslednie izvestiia*, no. 91, October 26, 1902.
[22] *Poslednie izvestiia*, no. 71, May 29, 1902; no. 95, November 20, 1902.

specific Jewish issues such as the dissolution of the Pale or the introduction of Jewish equality. In Zhitomir, two days before Jewish recruits joined the army, the Bund held a gathering in a nearby forest, which ended in a demonstration by Bundists, who marched through the streets of the town singing Russian revolutionary songs. War Minister Kuropatkin complained, in his circular letter of August 12, 1902, that the Bund sent its brochures as regular mail to junior officers and privates. This universal propaganda was effective. In mid-1902, Kuropatkin had received reports from the commander of the Warsaw military district concerning political provocation among the officers of the 116th Maloiaroslavets, 141st Mozhaisk, and 133rd Simferopol regiments, and about the spread of revolutionary materials in the barracks of the Sixty-fifth Moscow, Sixty-sixth Butyrsk, Twenty-first Belorussia dragoon, and Thirteenth infantry regiments. Kuropatkin was bewildered that "individuals currently on active military duty" were inciting the troops, and repeatedly asked the commander of the Warsaw military district whether he had taken measures to prevent the army's being infiltrated by agitators.[23]

The Bundist press's readership in the barracks continued to grow, sometimes with the unwitting assistance of the commanders. On June 21, 1903, the Vitebsk Bund society distributed several hundred copies of two proclamations, "To the Soldiers" and "To the Officers," in the camps of the 163rd Lenkoran-Pasheburg and the 164th Zakatal infantry regiments. Conscripts gathered into groups of about a dozen people each to read the proclamations aloud and to debate them. The commanders realized, too late, that an unsanctioned activity was taking place. A sergeant major who found a copy of the proclamation read the title and mistook it for a regimental order. Assembling his company, he read the proclamation to the ranks, if one believes the self-serving Bundist report, with increasing consternation. At last, deducing that something was seriously wrong, he stopped abruptly and, in a thunderous voice, dismissed the company.[24]

Because the printed word lent the impression of an official legal document, commanders had always allowed their men to read whatever printed matter was available. This changed only before the Russo-Japanese war, when the Bund disguised its materials as brochures issued by the Ministry of Education. Consequently, in June 1904, the commander of the Twenty-ninth artillery brigade ordered his junior officers to examine everything read by enlisted men and not to be deceived by misleading covers.[25]

The Bund attempted to transform soldiers into responsible socialists, and ignored the fact that some of its mottoes increased hostility in the army toward Jews. Its exposure of imperial wartime chauvinism was replaced by calls for class struggle against, among other enemies, the conservative-minded Jews.

---

[23] *Poslednie izvestiia*, no. 94, November 13, 1902; no. 101, December 10, 1902; no. 92, October 30, 1902; RGVIA, f. 801, op. 4/64, otd. 5, sv. 2, d. 65/49, l. 2–20b.

[24] *Poslednie izvestiia*, no. 136, July 16, 1903.

[25] *Poslednie izvestiia*, no. 197, October 29, 1904.

Leaflets listed among the most vicious enemies of the Jewish proletariat the pseudo-patriotic Jewish bourgeoisie, Zionists who joined in the jingoistic chorus, and rabbis who condoned Jewish soldiers' participation in the butchery that was the Russo-Japanese War.[26] Jewish soldiers and Russian recruits perceived Bundist phraseology very differently. Russians found their anti-Jewish prejudice confirmed, and regarded every Jewish trader as an exploiter and bloodsucker. Once Russia began sending its reserves to the Far East, soldiers' riots devastated hundreds of Jewish stores.[27] It is plausible that the Bundist instigation of class struggle played a role in sparking the riots.

Soldiers who supported the Bund and smuggled subversive literature into the barracks were motivated by the principle of international proletarianism, and did not concern themselves with ethnic differences. By 1905, the Bund controlled workers' units in Chenstokhova (Częstochowa), Vitebsk, Vilna, Grodno, Riga, Zhitomir, and Gomel, where troops consisted of Orthodox Russians, Jews, and Poles. Between 300 and 500 leaflets were distributed to each regiment. By the end of 1905, the number of circulated handouts may have been as high as 3,500. Such large-scale activity required the participation of soldiers of various origins, who ensured that the handouts found their way into barracks, kitchens, offices, and military camps and hospitals. The Częstochowa Revolutionary Military Branch, for instance, had Polish and Jewish members distributing its literature in the Polotsk brigade. Menashe German (Gershkhorn), a Jew, and Aleksandr Fedorchuk, a Ukrainian, both of whom were regimental scribes, distributed a Yiddish leaflet calling upon soldiers to respond to the Duma with the slogan "Down with autocracy; long live a democratic republic!" The socialist message transcended ethnic barriers. The Riga Revolutionary Combat Committee worked on a nonparty basis under the Federal Committee of the Latvian Branch of the Russian Social-Democratic Workers' Party (RSDRP) and the Bund. In 1904–1905, this committee distributed leaflets in the Viazma, Staraia Russa, Maloiaroslavets, and Staryi Torzhok infantry regiments and in the Twenty-ninth artillery brigade. The sheer number of leaflets (exceeding seven hundred per regiment) attests to the involvement of many soldiers, not all of them Jews. The Bund Revolutionary Combat Committee in Grodno attempted to influence the Chuvash, Cheremis, and Tartar enlisted men, traditionally considered too passive and bigoted. By the end of the summer of 1905, after several years of effort, weekly gatherings attracted 110 soldiers, who represented the regimental revolutionary soldiers' committees of the Perm, Viatka, and Petrozavodsk infantry, part of the Ustiug infantry, and the Twenty-sixth artillery brigade, all of them multiethnic in composition.[28]

---

[26] *Poslednie izvestiia*, nos. 94, 143, 169, 189, 191, 197, 198, 252, 255.

[27] See John Bushnell, "The Specter of Mutinous Reserves: How the War Produced the October Manifesto," John W. Steinberg et al., eds., *The Russo-Japanese War in Global Perspective: World War Zero* (Leiden: Brill, 2005), 335–339.

[28] *Poslednie izvestiia*, no. 194, October 5, 1904; no. 243, July 20, 1905; no. 252, October 10, 1905; RGVIA, f. 1872, op. 1, d. 316, ll. 3, 50b., 8, 9, 38, 102.

During the prerevolutionary period, many activists were drafted from the Jewish workers' movement. Yet these soldiers found fomenting political agitation in the barracks a challenging job, and were compelled to universalize their message and to expand their network. Consequently, they identified less and less as Jews. Caught between the revolution and the army, they underwent an accelerated process of acculturation. The need to encompass soldiers of diverse ethnic and national backgrounds obliged the Bundists to resort to the Russian language more often than to Yiddish. A still more pronounced alienation of Jewish soldiers from their ethnic identities occurred among those who joined socialist parties and groups other than the Bund.

Radicalizing Jewish Soldiers

Jews caught up in the vortex of the 1905 Russian Revolution found themselves cast upon new political shores. Like their brethren in the Pale of Settlement, these soldiers aligned themselves with distinct political groups and parties. Sometimes they chose to espouse revolutionary propaganda on behalf of a socialist body other than the Bund; in other cases, they joined the local organization closest to their regiment, because the Bund was less active in the southern Pale of Settlement and beyond. Some participated in several revolutionary cells. Once they had chosen to affiliate with the Socialist Revolutionaries (SRs) or with the Socialist Democrats (SDs), Jewish soldiers found themselves among conscripts who shared a party agenda rather than an ethnic identity. In the process, they unwittingly surrendered their Jewish interests. The equality that had eluded them in Russian society and that they could not obtain in the army was, ironically, acquired when they offered themselves as conscientious revolutionaries. Socialist bodies welcomed the skills, literacy, and networks of the Jewish enlisted men.

Initially, the SRs regarded the army as an enclave of peasants unresponsive to propaganda. One of the first SR groups, the Minsk Workers' Party for the Liberation of Russia, criticized socialist parties for neglecting their revolutionary work with the soldiers. The SRs focused their attention on oppressed regions and upon social groups impatient for change. Paradoxically, the propaganda of the far right convinced left-minded soldiers of peasant background that Jewish privates were to be considered close associates. In at least one instance, involving Meir Pilipovskii and Khaim Barats from Berdichev, SR and Bundist agitators cooperated in smuggling leaflets into the barracks.

During the Russo-Japanese War, the SRs boasted at a congress in Amsterdam that they had committees in twenty-six towns, including Vilna, Kursk, Nizhnii Novgorod, Minsk, and Sevastopol. An SR circular letter, sent to all its committees in December 1904, claimed that the war had created conditions particularly conducive to a struggle against the tsarist regime; conscripts were judged to be ready to explode into violence. Provocateurs capitalized upon the anger of troops unwilling to proceed to the Far East. The SRs reexamined their priorities, placing agitation and the dissemination of propaganda ahead of terrorist activity. At the Second Extraordinary SR Congress, in 1907, the party affirmed that it would be glad to share at an international convention its experience in the distribution of illegal literature.[29]

Jewish soldiers contributed to the SRs' clandestine work, although their impact upon the mutinies was scant and their Jewish self-awareness certainly was compromised.[30] Out of twenty court martial cases concerning membership in revolutionary military groups and civilian combat organizations in Kiev, seven involved Jews. Lazar Shkliar and Itsko Rybak, cannoneers of the Fourteenth artillery brigade, distributed the SR newspaper *Voennyi listok* amongst the gunners, organized gatherings in forests across the Dnieper River, and participated in the Kiev garrison revolt.[31] The Kiev SR Military Revolutionary Committee instigated unrest in the Forty-first Selegin regiment and in the Twenty-first Engineer battalion, which turned into mutiny, occurring two days after the dissolution of the Second Duma (on June 3, 1907). After a brief exchange of fire with security forces, the Twenty-first Engineer battalion laid down its arms. The secret police arrested eighty-five of the most active revolutionary members, while the military district's acting commander ordered an immediate suppression of the disturbances. The Kiev military district commander, General Sukhomlinov, reported to Nicholas II that he had successfully defeated an attempt to stage an armed uprising in the Kiev garrison.[32] A police investigation identified those responsible: in the spring of that year, the SRs had sparked unrest among the privates in the Selegin regiment when it moved from its barracks to a camp on the river Syrets.

The SRs had planned to rise up against the regime on the very day of the Duma's dissolution; the combat committee's regimental representatives were to have coordinated the effort. Five participants of the abortive uprising, all from the Twenty-first Engineer battalion, Shevchenko, Dontsov, Kalinin, Gubanov and Sukhareltidze, received capital punishment. Of thirty-five members of the soldiers' revolutionary cell of the Selegin regiment, at least seven were

---

[29] V. V. Shelokaev, ed., *Partiia sotsialistov-revoliutsionerov: dokumenty i materialy* (M.: ROSSPEN, 1996), 39, 56, 61, 167, 507, 547; M. Perrie, ed., *Protokoly Pervogo S'ezda Partii Sotsialistov-Revoliutsionerov* (Millwood, N.Y.: Kraus, 1983), 313; RGVIA, f. 801, op. 6/ 66, t. 8, otd. 5, sv. 42, d. 6/62, l. 20–200b; RGVIA, f. 400, op. 5, d. 1153, l. 89; RGVIA, f. 801, op. 4/64, otd. 5, sv. 2, d. 89/69, ll. 1–20b., 40b.-5.

[30] For example, Khaim-Nokhum Belostok, a private in the Fiftieth Irkutsk dragoon regiment, deserted after a year of service, joined the SR branch in Kherson, and changed his name to Andrei Miklashov to make working among peasants easier. See RGVIA, f. 801, op. 6/66, otd. 5, t. 8, sv. 42, d. 6/62, ll. 3–5.

[31] RGVIA, f. 801, op. 6/66, t. 8, otd. 5, sv. 42, d. 6/62, ll. 32.

[32] V. M. Katsnelson, "Revoliutsionnoe dvizhenie v voiskakh Kievskogo voennogo okruga," in V. I. Konovalov, *Revoliutsionnoe dvizhenie v armii v gody pervoi russkoi revoliutsii* (M.: Politicheskaia literatura, 1955), 245–247. Rosenblum mistakenly designates the Kiev military committees as RSDRP. According to the above sources, they were organized predominantly by SR. See K. Rosenblum, *Voennye organizatsii bol'shevikov 1905–1907 gg.* (M., L.: Gosudarstvennoe sotsial'no-ekonomicheskoe izdatel'stvo, 1931), 61.

Jews: Aron Lazovskii, Ovsei Shapsis, Avram Tsvetanskii, Abram Kirponos, Aron Domashnitskii, Gribis, and Kutsekon. None of them had taken up arms. Shabsis had agitated for the overthrow of the tsar, and Tsvetanskii transported revolutionary leaflets he had received in the city to the barracks, where he distributed them and read them to the soldiers. These leaflets probably came from the SR Regional Ukrainian Committee's printing press. Jewish participants in the conspiracy received four to six years of hard labor, a sentence reflecting the belief that Jews were low-ranking SRs. The SR Revolutionary Committee in Belaia Tserkov, which maintained close ties with the Selegin regiment, also contained Jewish agitators, who assisted in organizing the soldiers of the Ninth Uhlan and Bug infantries, and of the Sixth and Seventh mortar artillery battalions. When the committee's activities were curtailed by the police, it was learned that five of its eleven members were Jews; they had distributed propaganda leaflets but had not participated in the mutiny.[33] Jewish activists in the SR committees comprised but a tiny percentage of the 2,600 to 2,800 Jewish soldiers in the Kiev military district. All the rest apparently chose either loyalty or a more acceptable form of social protest.

Jewish soldiers who joined the Socialist Democrats were more profoundly radicalized. Initially, the Bolshevik wing of the Russian Socialist Democratic Workers' Party (the SD) had understood its task only vaguely, envisioning armed civilians bent upon revolution rather than a revolutionized regular army. In the party's eyes, the army itself was of no intrinsic value to the socialist revolution. Bolshevik handouts were laced with bombastic phrases urging soldiers, who were viewed as the tsar's servants, to join the workers in their struggle.[34] The narrow partisan approach and the pompous clichés characteristic of this literature often proved irritating to the intended audience.[35] Lenin larded his 1905–1907 essays with references to a revolutionary army, speaking of the necessity of dividing it into small units and of rousing it to action. Yet he was alluding to an armed populace, a people's militia. Any attempt at involving the army in revolutionary tasks Lenin regarded as Menshevik, and therefore bourgeois.[36] Only in November 1905 did he change his view.[37] However, no

---

[33] RGVIA, f. 801, op. 6/66, d. 47, no. 312, ll. 55–610b., 76–78.

[34] Menshevik propaganda was less bombastic but hardly more effectual, see *Mensheviki. Dokumenty i materialy. 1903–1917* (M.: ROSSPEN, 1996), 97–98, 176–177, 206–207, 337.

[35] The Bolshevik leaflets harshly demanded that soldiers side with the general populace, asserting that they otherwise would bear the shameful stigma of being enemies of the people. Some leaflets even threatened soldiers with ignominious death. See *Listovki bolshevistskikh organizatsii v pervoi russkoi revolutsii 1905–1907*, 3: 199–200, 240–243, 272–275, 438–440; M. Pokrovskii, ed., *1905: Bolshevistskie proklamatsii i listovki po Moskve i Moskovskoi gubernii* (M.: Gosudarstvennoe izdatel'stvo, 1926), 304–306.

[36] V. I. Lenin, "Boikot bulyginskoi Dumy i vosstanie," in *PSS* (M.: Politicheskaia literatura, 1960), 11: 174; "Zadachi otriadov revoliutsionnoi armii," in *PSS*, 11: 339–343; "Ot oborony k napadeniiu," in *PSS*, 11: 261–271; "Zamretki k statie 'Mobilizatsiia armii proletariata,'" in *PSS*, 9: 403–404; 335–344.

[37] In the immediate aftermath of the *Potemkin* mutiny, Lenin did include soldiers and sailors in his "revolutionary army," but they had disappeared again by August 1905. Bogdanov, at the

party directives addressed this. The most significant military revolts, in St. Petersburg and in Sevastopol, merited only his ex post facto praise.[38]

Nonetheless, Lenin determined that exposure to propaganda should commence before a soldier's recruitment. Regarding soldiers as unreceptive to the SD slogans, the Bolsheviks gladly ceded the revolutionary work to the SRs, who sought to incite a peasants' revolt, and to the Bund, which possessed its own ethnic network. The Bolshevik periodical *Proletarii* (no. 9, 1906) published an article citing a prevalent attitude expressed at the First Conference of Combat and Military SD Organizations, in Tammerfors. It related how a Menshevik joined the SD outfit and the activists resolved to get rid of him by consigning him to marginal revolutionary work – or so they thought – in the military. Few Bolsheviks understood the impact of incitement. Perhaps former Russian army soldier Emelian Iaroslavskii was the only one to criticize sharply what he described as the dismissive attitude toward agitation in the army. He was convinced that the party had lost an opportunity to use the soldiers' revolutionary potential.[39]

Emelian Iaroslavskii (born Meita-Iuda Izrailevich Gubelman, 1878–1943) was a close associate of Lenin. He served as a private in the Eighteenth Eastern Siberian regiment, where he began inciting revolt. Perhaps to avoid arrest, he deserted after two years of service. At the age of twenty, he joined the SDs subsequently organizing a revolutionary workers' group, the first of its kind in the Zabaikalie area. In 1901, he smuggled Socialist Democratic pamphlets from abroad into Russia. In 1904, he spent six months under arrest for his membership in the SD, and in 1905 he initiated his political agitation among the soldiers in St. Petersburg. When arrests of Bolsheviks began there, Gubelman left the city. Under the assumed name Stepan Krasilnikov, he joined the Odessa SD committee, and later resumed his career as a political agitator in Tula and Iaroslavl (where he chose his revolutionary pseudonym of Iaroslavskii). At the end of 1905, he arrived in Moscow and launched a new SD military organization; in November 1906 he introduced it at the First Conference of Military Combat Organizations. He also presented reports in his capacity as the organizer of SD military revolutionary committees in Iaroslavl, Ekaterinoslav, and Rostov.[40] In the same year, he joined an outfit in St. Petersburg that was well connected with the locally quartered troops. In the 1920s, after the Bolshevik Revolution, he became the head of the Central Control Commission of the Russian Communist Party.

Iaroslavskii maintained his position despite enjoying little support among influential social democrats. At the Fourth SD Congress, he defied the majority of

---

Third Congress of the SD, April 1905, called for revolutionary work in the army, but was ignored. See Bushnell, *Mutiny*, 58–64.

[38] V. I. Lenin, "Voisko i revoliutsiia," in *PSS*, 12: 111–114.

[39] Rosenblum, *Voennye organizatsii*, 82–83, 148–149, 183.

[40] E. Iaroslavskii, *Pervaia konferentsiia voennykh i boevykh organizatsii RSDRP* (M.: Partizdat, 1932), 365; RGVIA, f. 801, op. 6, otd. 5, sv. 35, d. 10, ll. 262, 268ob.

delegates, who failed to appreciate the importance of political agitation in the army, and he convinced participants to demand a separate conference for revolutionary military units. His understanding of the army's value and his willingness to establish nonparty divisions within it made him unusual among the SDs.[41] His participation in the creation of the St. Petersburg revolutionary military body proved decisive. In 1906, the St. Petersburg SD Military Organization included Boris Vorob'ev, Moisei Zundelevich, and Boris Sergievskii, all students. Altogether, the group had twenty-one active propagandists, eight of them Jewish. Iakov Vishniak, the only Jew to come from the upper bourgeoisie, incited sedition among the soldiers of the Second urban district, as did Iosif Shmulevich Veller, a student from Baku. Moisei Zundelevich, a St. Petersburg University student, agitated among soldiers in the Vyborg and Petersburg districts; Moisei Lazurkin, who studied law at St. Petersburg University, worked as an agitator in the Aleksandr-Nevsky regiment. Khana Magaril, an obstetrics student from Vitebsk, agitated in the barracks of the Okhta district, as did Sara Kornblit in the Petersburg district. David Gershanovich, a typesetter, propagandized among the soldiers of the St. Petersburg fortress. Zalman Liberman, a journalist and pharmacist, who studied at Moscow University, was not assigned to any specific section.[42] Thus, in St. Petersburg, more than one-third of the members of the SD military organization were Jews, most of them civilians.

Despite police arrests in November and December of 1906, particularly after a rebellion by enlisted men at the St. Petersburg electro-technical school, the number of Jews in the SD military organization was undiminished. The reconstituted SD committee resumed its propaganda efforts. Iaroslavskii was responsible for reestablishing ties with the army. After ten weeks, he succeeded in creating a committee of thirty-three people. By February 1907, 310 soldier-activists had infiltrated the barracks. Included in the multiethnic committee were Jews Meir Trilisser, Leizer Bravo, Iosif Lazovskii, and Mera Fisher; the Lutheran Ivan Feldman; and Russian Orthodox Stanislav Bogonosov, Mikhail Agibalov, and David Agibalov. Twenty-year-old Leizer Bravo was an assistant to the propaganda organizer of the Novocherkassk regiment, which the Soviet historian Akhun described as a school for revolutionary soldiers. Bravo regularly visited the electro-technical school, where he operated in the corridors during breaks between classes.[43] With the help of Iosif Lazovskii, formerly a bookbinder and now a private in the 145th infantry regiment, Bravo distributed propaganda to the regiment's reserve battalion. Private Isai Epshtein received booklets and leaflets from Bravo and delivered them to the Novocherkassk

[41] *Protokoly s'iezdov*, 126, 134.

[42] RGVIA, f. 801, op. 6, otd. 5, sv, 35, d. 10, l. 4–40b.

[43] The students of the St. Petersburg electro-technical school played an important role in supporting the mutinies in the northern Russian capital. See Korabliov, "Revoliutsionnoe dvizhenie v voiskakh Peterburgskogo voennogo okruga," 124–127; Akhun and Petrov, *Bolsheviki i armiia*, 34–38; Petrov, *Ocherki po istorii dvizheniia*, 285–286; Pokrovskii, *Materialy*, 22, 98.

regiment. Movsha Tilman, a private in the 198th Aleksandr-Nevsky regiment, dispersed leaflets in his regimental barracks and in the courtyard of the regimental barracks. Stanislav Frumov, a former pharmacist who was now a private in the same regiment, brought in propagandist Eva Gurevich, who smuggled pamphlets into the barracks. Bravo himself visited the town of Sestroretsk to inspire rebellion among the artillerymen.

The revolution compelled most Jewish SD activists to conceal their identities, both for security reasons and to facilitate outreach to the soldiers. Sara Kornblit distributed the Iaroslavskii-edited *Kazarma* (Barrack) newspaper using her revolutionary pen name Krizhanovskaia. Gubelman became Iaroslavskii; Iosif Veller introduced himself to recruits as Nikolai; and Khana Berlin called herself Dunia. Jewish soldiers espoused a revolutionary, multiethnic, Marxist platform that broached no specifically Jewish issues. The "Address of the St. Petersburg Garrison Troops to Members of the State Duma" was composed solely of general Socialist Democratic demands. Committee representatives who went to Duma deputy Ozol's apartment to deliver the document to thirty-five deputies of the People's Freedom faction consisted of four Russians and one Jew: Aleksei Arkhipov, a sailor in the guards' crew; Konstantin Koliasnikov, a private First Class of the aeronautic unit; Ivan Kutyrev, a private in the electro-technical company; Isai Epshtein, a private of the Novoingermanland regiment; and Timofei Dolgov, a private of the First Khoper Cossacks regiment. The St. Petersburg military organization used its Jewish connections as a cover for its socialist activities. In this respect, St. Petersburg's Jewish community differed little from that of Vilna or Warsaw; ethnic connections were more efficient and more reliable than those of social class. Frida Radzilovskaia and Avgusta Neiman offered their apartment as military organization headquarters, while Askinazi and later Bliuman used their apartments to store the printing press for propaganda. Weekly gatherings for soldiers were held in various locations across town, but often at 129 Fontanka Street, in an apartment belonging to Mera Breina Fisher, the daughter of a Jewish reserve soldier. Gavriil Polosin, a janitor and police stool pigeon also living at this address, was suspicious that so many Jewish soldiers came to see Fisher; however, they replied that they came for kosher food. The relationship between SD agitators and local Jews was perhaps the only indication of the revolutionaries' Jewish identity.[44] The blithe cynicism with which the soldiers outwitted the janitor disguised the fact that their only kosher food was hard-boiled socialism.

The authorities, disregarding the SDs' multiethnic and class-based character, attempted to portray political agitation as an exclusively Jewish enterprise. Soldiers of the fortress battalion of the Seventh Finland regiment, such as

---

[44] RGVIA, f. 801, op. 6/66, t. 8, otd. 5, sv. 35, d. 10, ll. 210b., 22, 250b.-26; d. 6/11b., l. 163; d. 6/62, ll. 124–130, 139. For the political context of this SD group activities, see Ascher, *The Revolution of 1905*, 2: 340–347; *Gosudarstvennaia Duma: Stenograficheskii otchet. Sessiia II. Zasedanie 52, zakrytoe* (SPb.: Gosudarstvennaia tipografiia, 1907), 1482–1502; Akhun, *Bolsheviki i armiia*, 49.

Russians Aramilev, Shcherbakov, and Filippov, and Jews Rozental, Neishtadt, Aronsid, Pivovarov, and Tregubov, met regularly at a coffee shop in the main square of Vyborg. They were frequently joined by two others: Poliakov, a choir musician, and Matsievich, a baker, both of Jewish origin. The coffee shop was a legal gathering place for agitators with an international, anti-imperialist agenda. They discussed primarily Russo–Finnish relations, the dissolution of the Finnish troops, and SD support for Finnish independence.[45] Seeking supporters for a civilian combat brigade, Tregubov traveled from Vyborg to Williamstrand, where he found someone he believed to be sympathetic: Petr Osipov, a Russian instructor of the First Company of the Finland regiment. Tregubov tried to persuade Osipov to incite the soldiers to rebellion and to supply the combat brigade with ammunition. Osipov reported Tregubov to the military police, who ambushed and arrested him; eighty-three privates in Tregubov's Vyborg garrison were also arrested. The army investigator, deviating from military-court practice, insistently emphasized the detainees' ethnic background: "Jew Tregubov and Jew Sorokin regularly got together at a Jewish apartment." Tregubov's activities cost him nine years of hard labor; the others received prison terms of between three and six years. The Main Staff concluded that the Socialist Democrats, some of whom were Jews, were instigating revolt and pushing the empire toward collapse. The Vyborg revolutionary cell's patently amateur methods, its utter disregard of ethnic issues, and its multiethnic composition all were proof to the contrary.[46]

Jewish soldiers involved in the SD and SR revolutionary groups underwent a dramatic change in self-definition. They continued to rely upon their ethnic networks, perhaps sometimes employing Yiddish as a secret means of communication. If accused of underground activities, they cited Jewish customs as an excuse. Yet they were committed to Russian revolution far more than to Jewish emancipation. Jewish soldier-socialists appeared ready to support any national initiative, whether Finnish or Polish, rather than a Jewish agenda. To be Jewish signified a ghettoized, backward, religious, and contemptibly bourgeois identity. Jewish soldiers with a revolutionary bent had integrated themselves thoroughly into the Russian socialist movement – as had previously the cantonists in the battalions of Nicholas's army or privates in the regiments under Alexander II. Their use of pseudonyms also manifested their intent to sacrifice their Jewish self-awareness on the altar of Russian revolution. In rescinding their Jewishness, they felt entirely modernized, if not emancipated, and their like-minded brethren accepted them as full-fledged Russian citizens.

---

[45] For the Russian-Finnish tensions in the military context and the rise of the Finnish independence movement, see Pertti Luntinen, The *Imperial Russian Army and Navy in Finland, 1808–1918* (Helsinki: SHS, 1997), especially 158–166.

[46] RGVIA, f. 801, op. 6/66, otd. 5, sv. 35, d. 6/11b., ll. 78–790b., 84, 860b.-87, 90–900b.

Integrating the Revolutionary Culture

While some Jewish soldiers crept from the barracks to attend clandestine party meetings, most of them, even the revolutionary-minded, stayed in their quarters with their non-Jewish colleagues. Perhaps a sense of duty, among other reasons, impelled them to remain loyal to their military oaths. Although they differed from their compatriots in origin, social status, sometimes in financial opportunity, and quite often in language and religious tradition, they shared the Russian revolutionary culture with Muslim, Russian Orthodox, Catholic, and Lutheran conscripts. Few Jews expressed their quest for Russian citizenship through party affiliation or political incitement. Those who faced court martial subscribed to views regarded as suspicious, voiced solidarity with a subversive cause, or criticized state politics and the army. However, they did not formulate any program, belong to a particular political group, or impose the Bundist, SR, or SD agenda upon their fellow soldiers. They preferred to recite revolutionary poems and to sing revolutionary songs, both of which they perceived as part of their heritage and of obvious appeal. The songs inspired them with rebellious fervor without requiring them to manifest or to conceal their immediate class, ethnic, or political affiliation.

Most of the soldiers were of peasant background, while the majority of Jews were urban. The army was a corporate entity with its own hierarchies, which did not always coincide with rank and with social class. Attempts to introduce the concept of class distinctions for the purpose of propaganda yielded meager results. Conversely, the soldiers' favorite songs fostered a sense of solidarity, of belonging to a cultural group sharing the same language, value system, passion, and purpose. As military court documents demonstrate, soldiers carried revolutionary poems with them to the detention cell and to the guardhouse, to military gatherings and to the barracks. Subversive songs, political satire, and anonymous, antigovernment poems were found during almost every police raid or search, far more often than were Bundist handouts or SD newspapers. Recruits also received texts of poems and lyrics legally, by mail, to the extent that in January 1908, the chief of the Main Staff, General Aleksei Evert, complained to the Warsaw district commander, General Georgii Skalon, that he saw an advertisement in the *Iasnaia Polaiana* newspaper explaining how to obtain, legally, the booklet *Podpol'nye pesni i rasskazy* (Underground Songs and Stories).[47]

Whether as Pale of Settlement Jews or as soldiers, Jews did not feel like full-fledged citizens; yet singing revolutionary songs with their fellows made them feel like genuine Russian Jews. Unexpectedly, the cultural heritage of the Russian revolution imparted a sense of belonging that the state, the army, and the socialist parties had been unable to confer. Military court data alluded to "criminal singing" and to "revolutionary propaganda spread by means of subversive songs" as the most typical seditious activity. A police report to War

[47] RGVIA, f. 1872, op. 1, d. 400, l. 40.

Minister Rediger mentioned Jewish, Polish, and Estonian soldiers suspected of singing revolutionary songs and of waving red flags while in a train with recent conscripts along the Warsaw–Vilna railway. Among the seven soldiers arrested, the report named Vladislav Shleptsak, from the Fifth Caucasus battalion; Gersh Pudoler, David Abramovits, Nusin Goltser, and Ian Lakhura from the 155th regiment; and Ían Kherkhel from the Eighteenth East Siberian regiment. Another case mentioned Girsh Kamenetskii, a Jewish private in the Medvedsk disciplinary battalion, and Vassili Voidanov, a Russian private. The police discovered on Voidanov's person the texts of the revolutionary songs "Vy zhertvoiu pali" ("You Have Fallen Victim") and "Smelo, tovarishchi, v nogu!" ("Comrades, March Bravely, in Step!"); Kamenetskii had a poem on the revolution, the end of the Russo-Japanese War, Bloody Sunday, and the Krondshtadt revolt. The poem related the tale of a soldier who returned from war to find that none of his family had survived: his wife had perished after joining thousands of others who marched to the tsar's palace on Bloody Sunday; Cossacks had lashed his mother to death; his son had been killed, and his brother, a sailor, had died at the hand of an officer. The poem concluded that soldiers should not wage war on foreign states, but should fight evildoers at home, in Russia.[48]

The less they alluded to class struggle, the more the leaflets reflected national sympathies. Volf Ginzburg, a twenty-two-year-old private from Mogilev province, drafted into the Fourteenth Engineer battalion, was arrested in May 1907 while deployed on the outskirts of Vilna. NCO Kotkov, Private First Class Elovskii, and Lieutenant Serdiuk, his immediate superiors, considered him a bright soldier who had served well. After six months of service, Ginzburg had departed for Vilna without asking permission, and there he received a batch of leaflets. Upon his return, his commanders detained him and found two poems he was carrying. One, entitled "What Have You Done, Soldier; Why Have You Killed a Child?" condemned punitive governmental measures and exposed the brutality of a soldier who aimed his weapon at his own people:

> Come, soldier, to your senses,
> It's high time you woke up,
> Don't commit executioner's offenses,
> Join forces with the peasants,
> March to freedom, break down all defenses![49]

The court martial determined that the poem did not represent a threat to the army, and Ginzburg received a short term in the detention cell for having been absent without leave.

However, an officer discovered a pad under the soldier's mattress containing the poem "Two Sermons." The poem described a priest who addressed peasants in a church. He accused the Jews of stealing everything in the village and of making the peasants' lives intolerable. He exhorted the peasants to beat up all

---

[48] RGVIA, f. 400, op. 15, d. 3052, l. 14; f. 801, op. 6, sv. 50, d. 10, l. 176.
[49] RGVIA, f. 801, op. 6/66, d. 14, l. 49.

the Jews and to cut their bodies into pieces. One of the peasants left the church
and delivered a very different speech, condemning landowners and bureaucrats.
He reassured the peasants that they would identify their true enemies and oust
them from power. "We are the breadwinners of Russia, we are the plowmen,
and we will plow them into the ground, starting from the black coats up to
the tsar," he proclaimed.[50] Apparently, Ginzburg, a nonpartisan Jew, realized
that he could more efficiently convey an antipogromist message by means of
a poem.[51]

The Jewish soldier shared with his Christian fellow-in-arms a fear of the
oppressive regime's hatred and violence. Jews and non-Jews alike frequently
discussed regicide. Privates in the Ninety-sixth Omsk regiment, serving sentences
in the guardhouse's detention cell, probably listened to Isak Samuilov recounting
how he was going to run away to Krasnoe Selo (one of the tsar's residences) and
kill the tsar, adding that his friend had promised him a large sum of money for
this. Three Russians and two Jews were among Samuilov's audience: Nikanorov,
Nikolaev, Ivanov, Kats, and Goldshtein. Private Nascrent, of uncertain ethnic
background, informed on them. The court acquitted Samuilov for lack of
evidence, which implies that such conversations and informer's reports were
regular occurrences. Furthermore, it is evident that Samuilov did not represent
the SR or any other political group promoting individual terror, but instead
spoke for himself.[52]

Like most non-Jewish soldiers, Jewish enlisted men were consumers of revolutionary propaganda rather than producers of it. Urban dwellers with a
markedly high degree of literacy, Jews were avid readers and sometimes the
distributors of proclamations. While aggregated reports did not record the
names of detained or suspected soldiers who had picked up leaflets in the street,
some reports identified an unnamed distributor as a Jew. A report from the
Warsaw military district headquarters stated that a private in the Sixty-fourth
infantry possessed a pamphlet that a Jew had shoveled into his pocket. Another
Jew threw three leaflets into the open window of a barracks of the 196th Zaslav
infantry. Shapiro, a young soldier in the Twenty-third Nizovsk infantry, was
found to have a brochure and two leaflets.[53]

Group readings and the discussion of revolutionary brochures brought Jews
and non-Jews together, for political debate or simply to vent their emotions. In
August 1905, the deputy minister of the interior reported to War Minister
Rediger about the situation in Tiflis. He asserted that subversive propaganda
had spread from the army into private homes and that several propagandists

[50] RGVIA, f. 801, op.6/66, d. 14, l. 42–42ob.
[51] An amateur poem of pro-Jewish content also was seized from Gorin, a Russian private in the
103rd infantry regiment. For its Russian original, see Petrovskii-Shtern, *Evrei v russkoi armii*,
241–242. A leaflet of similar content was found following the arrest of Ivan Kutyrev, one of the
leaders of an abortive revolt by the St. Petersburg electro-technical soldiers, see Akhun,
Bolsheviki i armiia, 38.
[52] RGVIA, f. 801, op. 6, sv. 50, d. 10, l. 136–136ob.
[53] RGVIA, f. 400, op. 3, d. 15, ll. 78, 113.

had been detained, among them privates Khaskel Ansel, Abram Kats, Linga Balyga, Shinbinashvili, Abrazhank, and David Frenkel, NCOs Rudov and Tsendzadskii, all of them from the Fifteenth Tiflis grenadier regiment; and privates Esheulov, Goldman and Epshtein, of the Sixteenth Mingrel grenadier regiment. The list demonstrates that common revolutionary concerns united Jews, Georgians, Russians, and perhaps even Yakuts and North Caucasians.[54]

The ways in which Jewish soldiers engaged their comrades-in-arms in conversation is telling. Rediger, after a fierce discussion of the issue with Witte, decided to redeploy the Fifty-second Vilna regiment stationed in Feodosia, in order to weaken or intimidate the regimental revolutionary committees.[55] The Vilna regiment was a typical example of how troops reacted to the call to suppress the revolution, corresponding to the pattern described by John Bushnell as "mutineers and chastisers." During the mutiny on the battleship *Potemkin*, the Vilna regiment riflemen obeyed orders to open fire upon the *Potemkin*'s sailors as the latter attempted to load coal in the Feodosia harbor. Yet the Vilna regiment had its own martyrology, in which the martyr-hero was Iosif Mochedlober, a Jewish private. On June 25, 1905, Colonel Gertsik ordered the Vilna regiment to assemble on the parade-ground. He publicly expressed his thanks to the soldiers who had demonstrated their loyalty to the government by opening fire on the *Potemkin*'s sailors. As the colonel spoke, Iosif Mochedlober attempted to assassinate him. The private was immediately arrested, tried, and sentenced to be shot by firing squad. On October 6, 1905, he was executed. However, Mochedlober's attempt upon the commander's life had made such a profound impression upon the soldiers and the SD military societies that a leaflet was issued to commemorate the event.[56]

Two months later, on December 18, 1905, a company in the Vilna regiment refused to mount guard, and presented Colonel Gertsik with their demands: courteous treatment of soldiers; a discharge for those whose terms of service had ended; new and better uniforms; the payment of money promised for assisting civil authorities; exemption from police duties; and an amnesty for those who had introduced these demands. The colonel tried, without avail, to compel the soldiers to abandon their petition. He then ordered that a unit armed with machine-guns storm the barracks and arrest those responsible for such insubordination. The mutinous company was arrested and its members disarmed. The entire regiment appeared at the top of a list of the most suspect regiments in the Odessa garrison.[57] The military responded by moving the regiment to Crete.

Even this measure failed to quash the unit's revolutionary fervor. Three Jewish privates – Gessel, of unknown origin; Leizerzon, a locksmith; and Meir Litvin, a bookkeeper – figured prominently among the agitators. Leizerzon,

---

[54] RGVIA, f. 400, op. 3, d. 40, ll. 53, 3200b., 3210b.
[55] For a discussion of the polemics around the relocation of the troops, see Fuller, *Conflict*, 138–141.
[56] Petrov, *Ocherki dvizheniia*, 150.
[57] Pokrovskii, *Armiia*, 226–227; Petrov, *Ocherki dvizheniia*, 306, 334.

whom his commanders considered a good and honest soldier, regularly drew his fellow soldiers into seditious conversation. At impromptu gatherings, he declared that the government crippled the soldiers' self-esteem by circulating objectionable books and antisemitic papers.[58] He also strove to organize a discussion group to foster independent thinking. For instance, on a September Saturday in 1907, the soldiers spoke of the uprising that was likely to erupt in Crete, and then observed that Russia was in a constant state of rebellion and that nobody wanted the tsar any longer. In his own account, Leizerzon damned the monarch with faint praise, finding him pitiable. Craftily employing the soldiers' traditional belief in the tsar as an important Russian cultural symbol, Leizerzon constructed a shrewd syllogism designed to justify revolution. Soldiers, he said, believed in the tsar. But the government had spread rumors that all those who insisted upon justice were, in fact, defying the tsar. Moreover, the government had purposely lied, to incite the ignorant against the revolutionaries, who were the true champions of justice and freedom. Most of the soldiers became engaged in a discussion about the fate of the Russian autocracy, while Leizerzon discreetly steered the exchange.

Private Murashko, ignorant and impetuous, flew into a rage and threatened to kill everybody who opposed the tsar. He attempted to relate to the soldiers the contents of a Black Hundred – a militant far-right grouping – propaganda brochure that embodied a blind hatred of Jews, liberals, intellectuals, and democrats; it would be excellent, he shouted, if the government were to allow the murder of Jews and liberals. He spoke in an atrocious mixture of Russian and Ukrainian, neither of which he had mastered. How dare all those editors of journals and newspapers, all those no-good, dime-a-dozen wordmongers, tell Father Tsar what to do! Then, rushing at Leizerzon, who probably was the only Jew present, Murashko raised his fist and screamed, "I know you're all against the tsar; all of you should be hanged!" Several soldiers grabbed Murashko and pulled him away.[59] A day or two later, Leizerzon wrote to his friend Boris Freidson, in Ekaterinoslav, describing in minute detail the entire episode. From this blunder, one may surmise that Leizerzon was a solitary agitator rather than a professional revolutionary. Following a raid on Freidson's house and the discovery of the letter from Crete, the police ordered Leizerzon's arrest. He was sentenced to eight years of hard labor.

Unlike Mochedlober, most Jewish soldiers did not resort to arms; they merely talked of revolution. The Russian revolutionary language held a more powerful attraction for them than did a Berdan rifle. Khaim Khazetskii, a private in the Forty-fifth Azov regiment, wrote to his girlfriend, Basia Gutman. In one letter, he complained about having been transferred to a new unit and having to start from scratch after having already established a relationship with the soldiers that had laid the groundwork for his incendiary conversations. Vulf

---

[58] RGVIA, f. 801, op. 6/66, t. 8, otd. 5, sv. 42, d. 6/62, l. 61.
[59] RGVIA, f. 801, op. 6/66, t. 8, otd. 5, sv. 42, d. 6/62, ll. 64–69.

Blinder, a private in the 122nd Tambov regiment, befriended three NCOs and tried to convince them to be disrespectful and mistrustful toward their superiors. Iosif Pabis, a private First Class of the Voronezh regiment, hid a notebook with the text of the song "To the Barricades!" in his trunk, and held revolutionary conversations with the other men in his unit. Shulim Galperin, a private in the Seventy-fourth Stavropol infantry, maintained contact with agitator Daniil Tsitsiashvili from Georgia. The latter gave him handwritten texts of satirical, revolutionary songs such as "Kak nash Trepov Tsariu ugodil" ("How Our Trepov Has Conceived the Idea to Please the Tsar"), "Vikhri vrazhdebnye" ("Menacing Whirlwinds"), and "Otrechemsia ot starogo mira" ("Let's Renounce the Old World").[60] A court martial acquitted Khaim Khazetskii for lack of criminal evidence, sentenced Blinder to exile for his refusal to stand on duty, briefly sent Galperin to a detention cell, and exonerated Pabis, whose colleagues insisted that he was not guilty of propaganda activity. These comparatively mild punishments reflected the belief that words were less harmful than revolutionary acts.

Because they were more concerned with the skyrocketing crime rate among the troops, commanders often refused to accept denunciations against Jewish soldiers who discussed sensitive political topics or who disseminated socialist literature. This was especially so when the alleged agitation occurred before a soldier's arrival to the regiment. Nonetheless, Itska-Zalman Leman, cannoneer of the Fortieth artillery brigade, was subjected to formal investigation, as were Gershon Birkovskii, a private in the Ust-Dvinsk infantry regiment, and Aron Miliavskii, a private in the Twenty-ninth Chernigov regiment. These three individuals had pasted illegal proclamations "To Comrade Recruits!" on the town walls after the military call-up but before their arrival in the regiment. The Military Courts Department recommended the dismissal of their cases, since the police had presented no convincing evidence. Lieutenant General Masliukov refused to impose the vigilant secret surveillance on Jewish recruits that the department had recommended. In another case, Kushakov, an officer in the Forty-ninth Brest regiment, learned from a stool pigeon that two arrested Jewish privates, Kremer and Rubinstein, had engaged in revolutionary conversation in their prison cell. Dismissing the denunciation, he warned the Jewish soldiers about the traitor in their cell. Likewise, Company Commander Egulov and Lieutenant Colonel Komarovskii, from the Vilna regiment, advised Private Leizerzon that his company members were too backward to comprehend his propaganda and that he should cease his activities.[61] Local military commanders realized that Jewish soldiers presented little threat to the army; after all, everybody now was talking revolution and singing revolution.

---

[60] RGVIA, f. 801, op. 6/66, d. 47, no. 312/(3), l. 11; no. 1716, ll. 109, 137; no. 1764, ll. 115–116ob., no. 2547, l. 155–155ob.
[61] RGVIA, f. 801, op. 4, otd. 5, sv. 3, d. 23/15, ll. 1–3, 67, 95–95ob., 98.

Enemies of the Imperial Army

Some imperial officials were aware that Jewish involvement in revolutionary incitement was predicated upon the degree of Jewish emancipation. In 1906, a state official writing anonymously to Nicholas II cited three reasons why Jews merited full and immediate civil equality. Firstly, Jews understood that the risk entailed in participating in the revolution paled in comparison with the advantages that the revolution seemed likely to afford them. Secondly, the abolition of anti-Jewish laws might result in an end to what the government viewed as Jewish agitation within the army. Thirdly, the 1906 recruits, who were susceptible to revolutionary activism, would replace the obedient former cadre and might become an explosive element, if drastic measures were not taken. Nonetheless, the authorities turned a deaf ear toward this advice. At the same time, they closely monitored the revolutionary cells' activity. On October 31 of that year, War Minister Rediger issued Secret Circular no. 2319, identifying to military district commanders the three revolutionary parties disseminating propaganda in the army: the SDs, the SRs, and the Bund. He also took note of the independent, nonpartisan All-Russian Union of Military Servicemen, a body that encouraged the participation of all ranks in an anti-government struggle. Several military groups in urban centers were planning a coup d' état, he asserted.[62] Rediger realized the threat to the army represented by the socialist movement and by urban areas. While he did not assign blame for mutiny to any particular ethnic, class, or party group, the rising Russian far right did. Responding to accelerated modernization and the radicalization of society, this political segment attempted to incite the army against the Jews, whom they viewed as implacable foes.

Rampant antisemitism in the Russian army's upper echelons was an early twentieth-century phenomenon; there had been no anti-Jewish violence by the military during the previous century. During the pogroms of the early 1880s, soldiers had attempted to protect the Jews. Archival military sources still awaiting proper contextualization confirm that, between 1881 and 1884, army commanders, responding to requests by civil authorities, expediently dispatched troops to suppress anti-Jewish riots.[63] The troops' lateness in arrival was the result of a cumbersome civil management system, an understaffed and inadequately trained police force, and a lack of experience in managing urban riots, rather than any reluctance to defend the Jewish population.

Relations between the army and the Jewish community at the turn of the nineteenth century changed dramatically. In the late 1890s, a few radical journalists claimed that the entire Pale of Jewish Settlement had risen up against

---

[62] RGVIA, f. 970, op. 3, d. 1128, ll. 33–38; f. 400, op. 5, d. 1153, ll. 88–89.

[63] For reports on military responses to anti-Jewish riots (Second brigade of the Fifth infantry division; Fourteenth company of the Oldenburg regiment; 111th infantry Don regiment; Twenty-second Nizhegorodsk regiment), see RGVIA, op. 15, d. 750, ll. 102–103; d. 751, ll. 59–590b., 720b.-73; d. 752, ll. 10, 14, 49, 800b.; d. 836, l. 19; d. 1755, l. 2.

the Russian army. Two clashes, in Medzhibozh in 1896 and in Minsk in 1897, were offered as illustration of a new model for relations between the military and the Jews. Officers of the Thirty-fifth Belgorod dragoon regiment had been billeted in the Medzhibozh vicinity. Drunken Lieutenant Bakunin quarreled with local Jews, lost his epaulet during the ensuing fight, and provoked a pogrom in which seventy soldiers and officers beat up Jews. The Kiev military district's commander, while expressing distaste for this "extremely violent event," nevertheless articulated his own justification for it. Echoing insinuations in the conservative, anti-Jewish press, he maintained that the hostile and insolent Jewish attitude toward the troops had triggered exasperation, bitterness, and animosity.[64] On April 15 of the following year, drunken soldiers in the 119th Kolomna infantry regiment argued with Jewish shopkeepers at the Nizhnii marketplace in Minsk. The soldiers contended that Jews evaded military service and that they made poor soldiers. Jews affirmed the opposite, and the resulting dispute escalated. An army patrol arrived and used force, whereupon the Jewish merchants resorted to self-defense. Fourteen Jews were arrested. The prosecution charged them with demonstrating a hostile attitude toward the army and toward the Christian population. It presented a radically different version of events: Jews had attacked unarmed soldiers in the market and had beaten them with iron bars. When the soldiers sought to escape, a crowd surrounded them, threw them to the ground, and beat them mercilessly. The Jewish crowd then attacked the arriving patrol soldiers and beat them, one by one.[65]

During the court hearings, juror Aleksei Shmakov represented the 119th Kolomna infantry regiment. According to a famous Russian Jewish lawyer, Shmakov was "a not very malicious man, but his antisemitic views completely obsessed him."[66] Shmakov recycled Brafman's ideas, tied the charges to a religious and political conspiracy, and claimed that Jews had beaten the soldiers on the orders of the Paris-based Jewish *kahal*. The motive was an innate Jewish hatred of Christians, especially of Russian Orthodox soldiers. The soldiers, new Christian martyrs, offered remarkable resistance, he declared.[67] Shmakov's speech had its desired effect: five Jews ended up in prison.[68] Six years later, when the troops had acquired experience of anti-Jewish violence, Shmakov described pogroms as the resistance of small groups of soldiers beset by insolent

---

[64] On August 14, 1896, Nicholas II read the file and said he could not allow it to be heard in a courtroom. He suggested that Lieutenant Bakunin be forcibly retired; that all thirteen officers who had participated in the pogrom be demoted to the rank of privates; and that the Jewish community's claim for 3,645 rubles in compensation be denied. Instead, only the loss of 151 rubles 85 kopecks was acknowledged, and responsibility for its payment was placed upon the officers. See RGVIA, f. 400, op. 15, d. 1647, ll. 7–8.

[65] *Minskii protsess. Delo o soprotivlenii evreiskikh skopishch voennym patruliam* (M.: A. Mamontov, 1899), 3–13.

[66] O. O. Gruzenberg, *Vchera: Vospominaniia* (Paris: Izd. avtora, 1938), 119.

[67] *Minskii protsess*, 23, 27, 31, 32–40, 44, 47, 55, 74.

[68] S. M. Ginsburg, "Bor'ba s evreiskoi raznuzdannost'iu," *EV* (1928): 92.

and well-armed masses of Jews. In the wake of revolutionary riots, he asserted that Jews had declared war not upon the government, but upon the Russian people.[69] In the prerevolutionary years, far-right journalists did much to convince younger officers, and through them the soldiers, that the principal domestic enemies of the throne and the homeland were, in Alexander Kuprin's words, "mutineers, students, horse thieves, Yids and Poles."[70] The first Russian revolution and the legalization of parties across the political spectrum served to introduce the propaganda of the far right into the army.

Late in 1905, immediately after the legalization of the far-right parties, journalists from the Union of Russian People (URP) approached military officials to convince them that Jews were destroying both society and the army. Georgii Butmi, a principal mouthpiece of the Russian radical right, declared that the Japanese and the Jews represented two armies fighting the Russian state and the Russian people: the first on the battlefield; the second subversively. Jews were responsible for the Russian army's defeat in the Far East, he asserted; their presence among the troops caused the army's dissolution and the collapse of its traditions. Shmakov declared Jewish treachery on the battlefield, asserting that, of 18,000 Jews in the Manchurian army, 12,000 had defected to the Japanese side or had surrendered. Jews purportedly avoided the front lines, committed crimes, spread panic, and generally demoralized the army. Butmi agreed that the presence of Jews in the ranks seriously affected discipline and paralyzed the Russian soldier's will.[71] These ideas, published in government-sponsored, although unpopular, books, found their way into the War Ministry's cabinets through the leading figures of the Union of the Russian People (URP).

The URP's leadership enjoyed considerable influence among the highest military officials.[72] In 1906, the URP chairman, Prince Emmanuil Konovnitsyn,

---

[69] A. S. Shmakov, *Svoboda i evrei* (M.: Gorodskaia tipografiia, 1906), CCCIII, CCCXXXI, CCCLXVIII, DLVIII, DCLI.

[70] This was the reply to the message of private Ovechkin, a victim of far-right propaganda, in Kuprin's *The Duel*. See A. I. Kuprin, *Sobraniie sochinenii* (M.: Khudozhestvennaia literatura, 1957), 3:414–415.

[71] G. Butmi, *Konstitutsiia i politicheskaia svoboda* (SPb.: Tip. uchilishcha glukhonemykh, 1906), 15; G. Butmi, *Iudei v masonstve i revoliutsii* (SPb.: Tip. uchilishcha glukhonemykh, 1906), VII–VIII; G. Butmi, *Vragi roda chelovecheskogo* (SPb.: Tip. uchilishcha glukhonemykh, 1907), VII–VIII; Shmakov, *Svoboda i evrei*, CCCLXXI, CCCLXXXVII.

[72] For example, representatives of the far-right factions in the Duma conducted meetings with War Minister Sukhomlinov to discuss military matters; Duma deputies Zamyslovskii, Krupenskii, and Volkonskii secretly asked the chairman of the Duma to restrain from censoring their speeches against the Jews; General Gershel'man petitioned for the provision of workplaces for URP employees; URP's chairman Dubrovin discussed with the war minister's assistant Polivanov ways to spread Black Hundred propaganda among the troops; Prince Meshcherskii urged the war minister to adopt the decision and to allow all army ranks to join the club of the nationalists; Grand Duke Nikolai Nikolaevich discussed with the war minister's assistant how to remove from the Main Staff individuals whom he identified as Jews with Russian family names – that is to say, the liberals. See A. A. Polivanov, *Iz dnevnikov i vospominanii po dolzhnosti voennogo ministra i ego pomoshchnika* (M.: Vysshii voennyi redaktsionnyi sovet, 1924), 1: 31, 55, 68–71, 73, 79, 89, 94, 97.

addressed a letter to the war minister in which he expressed his satisfaction with the regular appearance in the army of new branches of the union, and requested the ministry's endorsement. Konovnitsyn attached to his letter a URP brochure, which he offered to distribute among the troops. Based upon the ideas of the *Protocols of the Elders of Zion*, which Butmi subsequently published in a book edition, this brochure expressed views of the extreme right that bordered upon racial hatred. The URP demanded a ban on all political parties, reasoning that loyal subjects of the tsar did not need them. The union proclaimed the Orthodox Church's renewed dominance, unlimited imperial autocracy, and the exclusive rights of the Russian people. In the domain of nationality policy, the union recognized the rights of three peoples only: the Great Russians, the Little Russians (Ukrainians), and the White Russians (Belorussians). Its stance on national minority issues was unequivocal: the Russian people should resist the attempts by Jews and by other non-Russians to enslave Russians under the guise of civil equality.[73]

The War Ministry perceived the URP as a useful counterbalance to revolutionary heresy and to socialist propaganda in the army.[74] The military considered revolutionary sentiment a foreign heresy, infiltrating the barracks only to destroy the empire. To prevent this from happening, enlisted men were forbidden to read any newspapers other than those of the far right, such as *Den'* or *Znamia*. Soldiers complained to the Duma that the officers permitted them to read only the Black Hundred periodicals (*chernosotennaia pressa*). Furthermore, the military distributed to enlisted men thousands of antisemitic leaflets similar to the URP brochure. Military district headquarters provided printing presses to produce these leaflets, and to fulfill orders for antisemitic associations. The SD newspaper *Kazarma* timidly opposed the military-sponsored attacks upon the revolution and Jews, but its convoluted language was no match for the crude propaganda of the far right.

Word was followed by deed. The Odessa military district headquarters printed thousands of copies of a far-right leaflet and distributed it among the soldiers of the Kazan, Vladimir, and Uglich regiments. The leaflet, a typical example of radical propaganda, accurately replicated the imagery and metaphors of the *Protocols of the Elders of Zion*. It equated Zionism, the French

---

[73] RGVIA, f. 400, op. 15, d. 3521, ll. 81, 84–85.

[74] From 1906 to 1908, the Main Staff regularly demanded that its troops subscribe to right-wing radical papers. Circular no. 2566 ordered that the *Armiia* newspaper be delivered. In Circular no. 8,455, Polivanov obliged the army to subscribe to the newspaper *Russkoe chtenie*. On March 21, 1907, the Main Staff again confirmed that the *Armiia* newspaper should be dispatched to the troops. See circulars of the Main Staff in RGVIA, f. 400, op. 5, d. 1153, ll. 55–56, 72–720b., 91, 99, 117, 128. See also requests of the far-right activists for the governmental subsidies to cover the publication expenses of the new patriotic periodicals which would "fight the revolution until it is completely defeated." RGVIA, f. 970, op. 3, d. 1128 (["Petitions to Count Geiden,"] 1906, 1907), ll. 2–5, 26–27, 29–30.

Revolution, emancipation, and Jews.[75] Targeting "brethren soldiers" (*bratsy*), it appealed to enlisted men with patriotic, familial language. The brochure contended that Jews had lost their Zion and had been wandering ever since, searching for another empire to seize and to proclaim Zionist. Russia's revolutionary turmoil was simply the consequence of a Jewish attempt to make Mother Russia a new Zionist empire. The leaflet exclaimed, "Away with red Yids' equality and brotherhood!"[76] Despite lacking a call to action, this appeal resonated among the troops. A later amendment was noticed immediately by liberal Jewish Duma deputy Vinaver: the clarion final call read, "Rise up, wake up, Russian people, stand up to fight the enemy!" In April and May 1906, the military produced several hundred thousand copies of this leaflet and distributed it to soldiers of the Sixteenth infantry division deployed in Belostok and its environs.[77]

The Sixteenth division soldiers regarded the leaflet as constituting an order. Their commanders issued a reinforcing order, introducing extended service for troops stationed in the town. Forces under the command of Colonel Voitsekhovskii occupied the northern part of the city, while a regiment under the command of Lieutenant Colonel Bukovskii took the southern part. The soldiers believed that they were preparing for action against a menacing enemy. After the Belostok pogrom of June 1906, in which at least seventy-eight men perished, most of them Jews, the Duma's "Commission of Thirty-three," established to investigate the pogrom, accused the police of organizing this atrocity, and the army of implementing it. Deputy Stakhovich insisted that the Duma did not have the right to accuse the army. Yet Deputy Arakanskii, the head of the commission, furnished convincing evidence that the troops had participated directly in the pogrom. Ostrogorskii, the deputy from Belostok who had been in town at the time of unrest and had tried vainly to prevent bloodshed, confirmed that the soldiers had conducted the pogrom rather than protecting peaceful residents. Deputy Vinaver was still more outspoken, avowing that the army and the police had sought to intimidate revolutionaries by murdering the innocent.[78] Nobody doubted the innocence of the victims. Even Purishkevich, whom Hans Rogger called "the father of Russian fascism," joined the deputies when the Duma commemorated the Belostok victims. However, the Duma's liberals had neglected a key point: the pogrom corresponded to the agenda of

---

[75] On the other hand, army commanders exacted punishment for the possession and distribution of any revolutionary literature deemed dangerous, but considered Zionist publications harmless. See the file of Isaac Levi's case: he was accused of keeping a brochure and the *Semaphor* newspaper, which were "revolutionary propaganda," while a Zionist brochure by Gordon, *Zionism and the Christians*, the court considered innocuous; see RGVIA, f. 801, op. 6/66, st. 1, otd. 2, d.. 6/62, l. 1180b.

[76] RGVIA, f. 400, op. 15, d. 2696 (2), prilozhenie. See also *Vek*, no. 77, June 28, 1906.

[77] *Gosudarstvennaia Duma. Stenograficheskie otchety. Sessiia I* (SPb.: Gosudarstvennaia tipografiia, 1906), 2: 1735.

[78] *Gosudarstvennaia Duma. Stenograficheskie otchety. Sessiia I*, 2: 734, 952–960, 1577–1603, 1623–1645, 1727–1747, 1755–1792, 1806–1844.

the far right. The commander of the Vilna military district, in "apologizing" for the Belostok disorder, made a direct reference to the far-right conceptualization of the conflict when he informed the war minister that responsibility resided with the Jews fighting the troops.[79]

Even in revolutionary Russia, the army's newly acquired antisemitic bias sometimes clashed with practical considerations. The commander of the Sixty-second infantry division from Dvinsk complained that Jews were openly handing proclamations in the street to privates from the garrison, and that policemen were shirking their duties, failing to assist soldiers in detaining malefactors. His enlisted men, he continued in a fit of pique, were incensed by the seditious Jews. The Dvinsk chief of police dismissed the accusations. When the division commander insisted that the police interfere to prevent Jews from distributing leaflets to soldiers, the police chief retorted that the military should have prevented its men from loitering in the streets of the town.[80] In this way, he signaled his knowledge that the soldiers had gone deliberately to the Jewish section of town to acquire these leaflets; instead of blaming the Jews, the division commander should have taken measures to improve military discipline.

Prior to demanding the removal of Jews from the army, the far right succeeded in inculcating suspicion of Jewish enlisted men. Extreme conservatives proclaimed that the Jews were a Trojan horse among the troops. The class-based, Marxist-biased Russian socialists did not feel like defending the Jews and were remarkably reticent about acknowledging anti-Jewish violence. The only antipogrom appeal issued for the entire Moscow military district came from a nonparty group of artillery officers. In the eighteen months from early 1906 to mid-1907, SD bodies released only two leaflets referring to Jewish pogroms: significantly, they cited those in Kazan and Tver, situated far from the Jewish Pale. Under such conditions, Jewish soldiers were powerless to prevent pogroms, even within the Pale of Settlement or in Poland.[81]

The dread of pogroms was scarcely affected by the establishment of ties between the growing Jewish workers' movement and the Jewish soldiers. In Vitebsk, several days after police had disrupted a gathering of Jewish workers, the local garrison held its military parade. During the procession, Colonel Botsianov ordered all Jewish soldiers to step forward. When they complied, he threatened that if their civilian coreligionists did not stop meddling in political affairs, he would not send a single soldier to defend the Jews if ever they should need protection. This announcement was received as threat of a pogrom, and the shaken Jewish soldiers sent a deputation to the colonel to ascertain his intentions.[82] When pogroms occurred elsewhere, Jewish conscripts sometimes

---

[79] RGVIA, f. 400, op. 15, d. 2696/1, l. 201.

[80] RGVIA, f. 400, op. 3, d. 40, l. 4.

[81] For the SR reaction to the Belostok pogrom and to other anti-Jewish riots, see the article "Soldaty-razboiniki" in *Soldatskaia gazeta*, no. 2 (1906): 14–15. On Black Hundreds as instigators in the military, see *Soldatskaia gazeta*, no. 4 (1906): 7–8, 12; no. 136 (1907): 12–13; no. 5 (1907): 3–5.

[82] *Poslednie izvestiia*, no. 75, June 20, 1902.

tried to rescue their brethren, but these instances only emphasized the general rule: by trying to protect other Jews, the Jewish soldier risked provoking a pogrom directed against his own unit. In July 1903, a Jewish private defended Jewish vendors at a market near the Skobelev military camp, and stopped senior NCO Shuiskii, an aggressive orderly in the 119th Kolomna regiment, from smashing the vendors' stalls. The military accused the Jew of having beaten up the orderly, instructing him that he should be defending soldiers, not Jews. When the soldier retorted that he had never pledged to beat his brethren, he incurred the wrath of all his superiors: the regiment commander, the second in command, officers, and even the regiment's military investigator. A lieutenant in the Thirteenth company issued permission to arrest any Jewish soldier found in a Jewish shop. However, military commanders considered the presence of Jewish soldiers an obstacle to punitive expeditions. Therefore, whenever the military planned a full-scale pogrom, commanders sent not only units whose loyalty was uncertain but also individual Jewish soldiers to distant locales. For instance, in June 1905, several days before the pogrom in Lodz, local authorities sent 180 Jewish soldiers from the garrison out of town.[83] It is not clear whether they intended to place their Jewish troops beyond reach of the orchestrated violence to protect them or to circumvent their involvement on behalf of the Jewish community.

The Outcome of the Revolutionary Draft

The activity of Jewish soldier-agitators achieved results considerably different from those they had anticipated. After the 1905 Revolution, the Russian military accelerated the army's modernization. The War Ministry ordered that the daily portion of meat in soldiers' meals be tripled. The soldiers' mess began serving tea and sugar. Soldiers received new boots and underwear. The commanders allowed recruits under arrest or in disciplinary units to sing and to smoke. In Circular no. 1172, the War Minister ordered the military district heads to address the economic demands of the enlisted men. Circular no. 25651 forbade officers to humiliate corporals or privates. Circular no. 7249 stipulated that government undertakings be explained to the soldiers. To suppress revolutionary unrest and improve soldier–officer relations, the officers were advised to read to their men various patriotic brochures, such as regimental histories. The Warsaw military district secretly instructed its regimental commanders to take greater care to provide a variety of food to the privates during holidays, and to encourage soldiers to socialize with the local population and to attend theatrical performances organized by the officers. Soldiers could even be served beer during holidays, and officers were encouraged to learn basic socialist ideas. Adjutant General Evert, the head of the Central Headquarters of the First Manchurian Army, ordered General Skalon, the commander of the Warsaw

---

[83] *Poslednie izvestiia*, no. 152, November 7, 1903; no. 240, June 10, 1905; no. 241, June 17, 1905.

military district, to ensure that officers acquired a proper understanding of the origins and aims of socialism and were able to argue against them.[84] Jewish soldiers who began their careers as activists in the workers' movement perhaps could congratulate themselves upon the success of their mission. Although they did not secure for themselves a better position in the army and were not accorded full military privileges, they contributed to the army's modernization.

By late 1907, the Ministry of the Interior was striving to convert the army into a coercive apparatus and to suppress the revolutionary unrest with its help. A special circular was issued calling for cooperative effort and mutual understanding between police and military commanders. The minister of the interior allowed the police to search draftees, particularly factory workers and Jews, each time they returned to their units after having been granted leave, and to seize any proclamations or other illegal publications they might be carrying. Prime Minister Petr Stolypin ordered that conscripts under suspicion be kept under secret but close police surveillance. Stolypin read reports on SR and SD activity in the army, and informed Deputy Minister of War Polivanov and military district heads of any plans by revolutionary cells. At the same time, the SDs and SRs learned, through their own network of informers in army head-quarters, what military countermeasures they could expect. Stolypin forbade the Warsaw military district commander to use staff clerks in preparing secret circulars for mailing, or to use regimental scribes to seal envelopes. Only staff officers were permitted to handle outgoing and incoming documents concerning revolutionary propaganda among the troops. There were to be no unsanctioned gatherings, and junior officers were to monitor soldiers' reading materials. Their correspondence, too, would be under secret surveillance.[85]

These attempts to impose police functions upon the army caused an increasing rift between the state's senior officials and the military. The army emerged with a new understanding of its professional, nonpartisan character. The tsarist regime and the Main Staff ceased to trust the troops. Civilian authorities could no longer rely entirely upon the army, which openly circumvented the police functions imposed upon it. However, the army proved that its cohesive character was not conducive to the class framework that the partisan revolutionaries had tried to prescribe.[86]

Even before the postrevolutionary changes, Jews fitted well into this new, professional army. Although Russian society evinced little sympathy for the Russo-Japanese War, most Jewish soldiers performed commendably in battle. Some Russian newspapers dismissed the ever-circulating rumors of Jewish soldiers' cowardice. Instead, they praised Jews as "excellent, brave, and entrepreneurial," noting that many Jews were awarded St. George Crosses (for instance, Margolin, Genzel, Shteinberg, and Voisvol, among others), some of

---

[84] RGVIA, f. 400, op. 5, d. 1153, ll. 49, 56, 59, 60, 70, 128; RGVIA, f. 1872, op. 1, d. 400, ll. 20–240b., 34–37, 40.

[85] RGVIA, f. 1872, op. 1, d. 400, ll. 3–4, 10–14, 20–21, 24, 34.

[86] Fuller, *Conflict*, 146–154; Bushnell, *Mutiny*, 228.

them twice and some three times. Moreover, the award recipients were selected by members of the company, rather than by the commanders. Some 2,030 Jews perished at the front in the Far East, while another 913 were lost in action. War correspondents wrote extensively about the self-abnegation of the Jewish artillerist Lazar Likhtmakher, who lost his hand during the Mukden battle. They also lavishly praised the drummer Shmul Simanovskii, who helped to organize the evacuation of wounded men under fierce enemy fire; Mikhael Chernomordik, who saved an entire battalion from Japanese encirclement; and two Jewish musicians who assisted the regimental priest in holding aloft a golden cross during the Turechensk battle.

Lance Corporal Zakharovich, a defender of Port Artur and an envoy of General Kondratenko, was scandalized by the far right's accusations against the Jews. He demanded rhetorically, "What did Jews do in Port Artur? Did they not suffer like the rest of the soldiers? Who prepared the cartridges? Who worked in the labs? Who went into attacks beside the others? Of what faith were the gun-layers on the Golden Mountain, the Tiger peninsula, and other land and navy batteries? Who were the best telegraph operators? Who were the Port Artur heroes if not Trumpeldor, Ostrovskii, Fridman, Grinshpun, Prezherovskii and others? Why do you suppose they received St. George Crosses?" Combat officers, who had witnessed Jews in action during the Russo-Japanese war, had no complaints about their performance and in no way singled them out. The anonymous author of *Voina i evrei* (War and Jews) maintained that "the silence of the army signifies that the Jewish question does not exist in the front lines."[87]

Nevertheless, it existed in the commanders' offices. Some high-ranking military officials chose to attribute military failure to the Jewish soldiers' purported ineptitude and treason.[88] And at the height of the 1905 unrest, the regime hit upon the idea of associating revolution with the Jews, thus conferring official status upon the agenda of the far right.[89] From then on, unequivocal antisemitic phraseology permeated official military reports and circulars. A culprit guilty of all the army's troubles and misfortunes had been identified at last. War Minister Rediger circulated a secret notice in the army, which declared that Jews engaged in political provocation because they believed themselves to be fighting for their own civil freedoms. Such expectations he labeled wishful thinking, contending that Jews were shameless, dishonest

---

[87] Anon., *Voina i evrei*, 68.

[88] See, for example, General Alekseev's diary notes, in which he accused Jews, particularly Jewish doctors, of the spread of revolutionary corruption among the troops; V. Alekseeva-Borel, *Sorok let v riadakh russkoi imperatorskoi armii. General M. V. Alekseev* (SPb.: Belveder, 2000), 202, 204, 215.

[89] For this agenda, see the newspaper clippings amassed by the War Ministry on various issues related to the revolutionary activities in the army: RGVIA, f. 400, op. 15, d. 2734 ("Vyrezki iz gazet po delam Voennogo ministerstva"). On the image of the Jew as the enemy alien during the Russo-Japanese War created by the Russian right-wing press, see L. V. Zhukova, "Formirovanie 'obraza vraga' v Russko-iaponskoi voine 1904–1905 gg.," *Voenno-istoricheskaia antropologiia. Ezhegodnik. 2003/2004* (M.: ROSSPEN, 2005), 259–275, here 261.

malefactors who had no regard for the tsar or for the Russian Fatherland.[90] Although Jews were not the driving force behind the 1905–1906 military revolts, nor even among the key organizers or participants, the military charged them with responsibility for all subversive activity in the army. Before 1905, the ideas of the founder of modern racism Arthur de Gobineau found their ways to the office of the War Ministry Navy Department; now they shaped the minds of many high-ranking military bureaucrats.[91]

Conclusion

Russia's rapid modernization at the turn of the nineteenth century exacerbated the empire's political, economic, and social contradictions. It also gave birth to the Russian and Jewish proletariat, brought about the 1905 Russian Revolution, and triggered a wave of bloody pogroms. Jewish soldiers did not respond to these events with violence. Nor did they turn their backs on military service, as their performance during the Russo-Japanese War proved. Although a minority among various political groups, Jews were the first to point to the urgent need to bring revolutionary propaganda into the army. In the army, some Jews took on the secondary role of revolutionary agitators. In the barracks, Jewish soldiers distributed leaflets, talked politics, recited revolutionary verse, and sang revolutionary songs – as did many of their Russian fellow-soldiers in the revolutionary period. Perhaps, as privates of predominantly proletarian origin in a peasant-soldier milieu, Jews were overrepresented among the revolutionary agitators within and outside the barracks, due to their educational status and class. Yet, with minor exceptions, Jews did not join the instigators of the army mutinies. Jewish soldiers successfully absorbed Russian revolutionary culture, in most of its genres, but not its call to arms.

The revolution altered the self-identification of those Jewish soldiers who joined it. For the radical-minded, being Jewish contradicted the class-based Marxist worldview and was unacceptable. Joining the revolution signified leaving Jewishness behind. For those who chose to bring a revolutionary gospel to the soldiers of peasant origin, their Jewish self-awareness presented a hindrance which needed to be overcome. The Russian military authorities monitoring the situation in the army did not realize that the revolutionary milieu gave Jewish soldiers what they lacked elsewhere in society: emancipation, at least of a type which was cultural and circumscribed by the borders of the revolutionary cells.

[90] RGVIA, f. 400, op. 3, d. 40, l. 433.
[91] See the unsigned report repeating the key anti-Jewish accusations of Markov II, Dubrovin, Shakov, Butmi, and others (falsehood of the Jewish military oath, dodging the draft, Jews as the "secret society" and "Judaic hydra"), in RGAVMF, f. 29, op. 1, d. 7 ("Chernovoi nabrosok mer, napravlennykh k ogranicheniiu rasprostraneniia evreiskogo vliianiia na politicheskuiu, ekonomicheskuiu i dukhovnuiu zhizn' russkogo gosudarstva," 1904), ll. 173–1880b.

While the assertion of some commanders that any "too clever" soldier was a Jew and a revolutionary was not ungrounded, the claim that Jews were the only ones responsible for the revolutionary corruption of the troops defied reality. Nonetheless, following the formulations of the far right, top military officials argued that Jews themselves bore the guilt for the pogroms as the sole socialist agitators. For Jews, perhaps the most fateful consequence of the revolution was this attitude, which prevailed until the adoption, in 1912, of a new statute concerning military duty.

7

Banished from Modernity?

"The Talmud provides us with innumerable passages clarifying how observant Jews avoid the fulfillment of any promise or oath. The Jews mock and jeer at oaths. If a soldier does not respect an oath, violates an oath and considers that his religious cult allows him to disdain the oath, it is obvious that we can expect from him nothing but evil. It is shocking that the War Ministry hesitates to cut this sore out of the noble pure body of the Imperial Russian Army."[1] This assessment belongs to Duma deputy Markov II, a politician of the Russian extreme right who later became an advisor to Nazi Germany's Propaganda Department.[2] Markov pronounced this observation on December 2, 1911, as the Duma discussed a new military service statute. He maintained that the army could do handsomely without Jews, since Jewish soldiers, like all Russian Jews, obeyed the regulations of a secret international Jewish government whose precepts were based upon the Talmud. This view was similar to that of many conservative Duma members and War Ministry officials, to whose fertile imaginations Markov appealed. He alluded to *The Book of the Kahal*, with its omnipotent Talmud, and to the *Protocols of the Elders of Zion*, with its secret international Jewish government. At the turn of the century, the military was subject to a growing xenophobia that mirrored developments in Russian society as a whole.[3] The War Ministry's numerous anti-Jewish circulars of the 1880s had, by the late 1890s, set the stage for charges against Jewish soldiers of

---

[1] *Gosudarstvennaia Duma. Stenograficheskie otchety. III sozyv. Sessiia V.* Zasedanie 35 (SPb.: Gosudarstvennaia tipografiia, 1911), 3082.

[2] See R. Ganelin, "N. E. Markov 2-oi na svoem puti ot chernosotenstva k gitlerizmu," in *Evrei v Rossii. Istoriia i kul'tura*, 211–218.

[3] Marc Raeff, *Political Ideas and Institutions in Imperial Russia* (Boulder, Colo.: Westview Press, 1994), 140; Hans Rogger, "Reforming Jews – Reforming Russians," in Herbert Strauss, ed., *Hostages of Modernization, 1870–1933/39* (Berlin: Walter de Gruyter, 1993), 1225. Concerning the repressive politics against people of alien beliefs in the army, see P. A. Zaionchkovsky, *Samoderzhavie i russkaia armiia na rubezhe XIX-XX stoletii. 1881–1903* (M.: Mysl, 1973), 196–202.

insubordination (*raznuzdannost'*).[4] The far right's assertion of the Jews' implacable hostility toward the army culminated in a 1912 military duty statute and in disputes in the Duma about Jewish soldiers.

Banishing Jews from the Army

In the second decade of the twentieth century, Russian–Jewish discourse focused upon Jewish military service. The far right demonized the Jews in an attempt to poison the rest of society with the same virulent antisemitism. One fabrication was the blood libel against Menahem-Mendel Beilis, accused of using the blood of a Christian boy, Andrei Iushchinskii, to bake unleavened bread for Passover. The Beilis trial sparked a controversy as heated as the Dreyfus case had been in late nineteenth-century France. In the courtroom, Beilis described himself as a reserve soldier, believing that his patriotism would arouse the jury's sympathy. Vociferous antisemites jumped on this characterization, claiming knowledge of other incidents of ritual murder by Jewish soldiers.[5] Between 1911 and 1913, a series of pamphlets was published, offering examinations of similar alleged crimes, including the revitalized Saratov case.

Among the accused in the 1853–1860 Saratov blood libel case were Iushkevicher, a Jew living with a family of converts to Christianity; his son Iurlov, a Christian; and several Jewish soldiers from the Saratov garrison, who apparently were the only observant Jews in town. The Christian experts consulted in the case – including Daniil Khvolson (Chwolson), a Jewish convert to Christianity and a leading Russian authority on Semitic studies – repeatedly protested the absurdity of the charges, yet a guilty verdict was rendered nonetheless.[6] In 1911, the Duma deputy Georgii Zamyslovskii, a man "of great capacity, but totally shameless," according to Oskar Gruzenberg, cited this case involving Jewish soldiers in his pamphlet *Zhertvy Izrailia* (The Victims of Israel).[7]

Journalism proved very profitable for Zamyslovskii: he already had received 75,000 rubles from a special state fund for his brochure purportedly proving that the Jews of Kiev, particularly Beilis, had tortured Iushchinskii to death. Having acted as the prosecuting civil attorney for the Beilis case, Zamyslovskii now argued that Jewish soldiers corrupted the local Christian community, "the victim of Israel." There were forty-four Jews in the town's battalion, which, opined Zamyslovskii, was "the major nursery of the Saratov Yids." Jewish soldiers were insolent and unruly, they embezzled state property, used religious rites with criminal purpose, attempted unsuccessfully to convert others to Judaism, and treated Christians as their stooges, only to betray them later. In Zamyslovskii's hands, Bulgarin's imaginary convert in *Ivan Vyzhigin* was

---

[4] See S. M. Ginsburg, "Bor'ba s evreiskoi raznuzdannost'iu," *Evreiskii vestnik* (1928): 92–107.

[5] *Vestnik Soiuza Russkogo Naroda*, no. 157 (October 27, 1913): 9.

[6] On the Saratov case, see Dubnov, *History*, 150–153; Iulii Gessen, *Istoria evreev v Rossii* (SPb.: Ganzburg, 1914), 267–270.

[7] O. O. Gruzenberg, Vchera. *Vospominaniia* (Paris: Izd. avtora, 1938), 120.

transformed into a real-life renegade, Daniil Khvolson, who employed the same duplicitous means to disguise ritual murder.[8] Zamyslovskii held that the true perpetrators of the murder were not converts but Jewish soldiers from the Saratov garrison such as Berlin, Berman, Fogelfeld, and Zaidman. The chief culprit was Shliferman, an army barber. Investigators found in one soldier's possession a Sephardic Passover Haggadah, in Ladino, with an etching of Pharaoh bathing in the blood of Jewish boys. Zamyslovskii convinced his readers that the scene depicted a ritual murder: a Jew bathing in the blood of Christians. Professor Zalesskii, reviewing the Saratov case, supported the allegations, stating that the soldiers had "confessed their guilt."[9] Once the jury had exonerated Beilis, Zamyslovskii sought to use the Saratov case in his appeal. His objective was to convince the Russian public and the Russian army that Jews represented a mortal threat to society: Beilis was a murderer and, quite literally, a bloodsucker, as were the Jewish soldiers.

The far right strove to convince the military to banish Jews from its ranks. It postulated that the abolition of Jewish military service would serve as proof of the Jews' fundamental incompatibility with modern Russian society. More severe anti-Jewish measures followed, such as the ejection of Jews from all higher educational establishments, a ban on their practicing law or medicine, a boycott of Jewish trade, and the expropriation of Jewish assets purportedly stolen from the army. Far-right periodicals openly discussed these issues, cognizant that Jewish military service represented a serious obstacle to the creation of a nationalist (*natsional'naia*) Russian army, free of alien elements. As Hans Rogger observed, "the attempt of the maniacs to impose their will on the state" was partially successful.[10]

The far-right agenda informed the views of top military officials, a fact reflected in a 1912 secret survey on Jews in active service. Although the military did not implement the survey's conclusions, the questionnaires themselves are instructive. The War Ministry dispatched them to high-ranking clerks, to military district commanders, and to corps and division generals, all of whom were well aware of the War Ministry's and the imperial court's view of Jews. Middle-ranking officers, who had direct contact with Jewish soldiers, did not receive the questionnaires. It is possible that the responses scrawled by Nicholas II in the margins of military surveys calling for Jewish expulsion from the army ("I agree;" "yes, and one more time, yes;" "I am of the same opinion") were known to senior military officials.[11] In any case, the latter sympathized with the conservative Congress of the United Nobility, which, at its 1911 meeting, voted for the army to expel all its Jews.

---

[8] G. G. Zamyslovskii, *Zhertvy Izrailia. Saratovskoe delo* (Kharkov: Mirnyi trud, 1911), 7, 12, 19, 22, 47, 54.

[9] V. F. Zalesskii, *Taina krovi. K voprosu o ritual'nykh ubiistvakh* (Kharkov: Mirnyi trud, 1912), 45–47.

[10] Hans Rogger, "The Beilis Case: Anti-Semitism and Politics in the Reign of Nicholas II," in Herbert Strauss, ed., *Hostages of Modernization*, 1273.

[11] See RGVIA, f. 400, op. 19, d. 38, l. 18.

Predictably, twenty-eight respondents to the survey strongly favored the removal of Jews from the army. Their principal argument was that Jews caused revolutionary unrest, thus undermining the army's combat capacity. Sixteen respondents opposed expulsion, suggesting instead that problematic Jewish soldiers be replaced and that a special tax be imposed upon them in lieu of personal military service. These officers reasoned that military service was a sacred duty, and that the exclusion of Jews would send the wrong message to other ethnic minorities; they even suggested that some civilians might adopt Judaism in order to evade military service. Sixteen "neutral" respondents regarded Jews as "a necessary evil," and resolved "to leave in force all restrictions regarding the Jews and to let them remain in the ranks." Six army commanders proposed segregation: to reduce the Jews' harmful impact upon the troops, Jews should be removed from combat service and placed in specially created Jewish artisan squads. Many respondents supported the opinion of General Malyshevskii, who claimed that it was necessary first to resolve Russia's Jewish question, and only then to consider the military context.

On January 12, 1913, War Minister Sukhomlinov summarized the survey's findings and ruled as follows: "Initially, I wished to recommend the complete removal of all Jews from the army."[12] Although many influential politicians shared this vision, the more balanced approach won.[13] While the war minister was hardly an ally of the Russian Jews, he was disgusted by the violence against them, and had even been accused of having sympathized with them during the 1905 pogroms. On the eve of the adoption of the 1912 statute, Sukhomlinov refused to endorse a discussion of the expulsion of Jews from the ranks.[14] The Duma's left-wing faction considered the 1912 statute antisemitic; yet the leading far-right politicians thought it was too liberal. Paradoxically, in view of the potential result of the secret survey never made public, the opinion of the Russian right appears to be a more accurate assessment.

The 1912 Statute on Military Duty

Even before public debate ensued over the new statute, the question of Jewish military service engendered a heated dispute in the Duma. The draft in general

---

[12] See RGVIA, f. 400, op. 19, d. 38 ("Dokladnaia zapiska nachal'nika General'nogo Shtaba, generala ot kavalerii Ia. G. Zhilinskogo voennomu ministru, general-adiutantu, generalu ot kavalerii V. A. Sukhomlinovu ob otnoshenii evreev k voinskoi povinnosti"), ll. 1–18.

[13] In 1928, V. Shulgin, the publisher of the *Kievlianin* newspaper, a former Duma deputy and a Union of the Russian People associate, maintained that there was no benefit in having Jews in the army; "Who contributes less, gets less." See V. V. Shulgin, *Chto nam v nikh ne nravitsia. Ob antisemitizme v Rossii* (M.: Khors, 1992–1994), 260–261.

[14] *Vospominaniia Sukhomlinova* (M., L.: Gosudarstvennoe izdatel'stvo, 1926), 102–103, 108–109. For the far right's accusations of Sukhomlinov's sympathetic attitude toward Jews, see Polivanov, *Iz dnevnikov*, 65. For a nuanced portrayal of Sukhomlinov's stance on Jewish issues and the accusations against him, see William Fuller, Jr., *The Foe Within: Fantasies of Treason and the End of Imperial Russia* (Cornell University Press: Ithaca and London, 2006), 45–46.

and the draft of Jews in particular remained a key issue all the way through World War I. In 1907, the army had proposed that the Duma adopt an administrative bill approving an increase in the number of recruits. In response, the Duma requested an analysis of annual quota shortfall figures. Deputy Rein, from Volhynia province, presented the data for the previous three years, offering two reasons for the deficits: the rejection of unfit candidates, and Jewish draft dodging. According to Rein, in 1906, 19,998 of 76,000 absentees were Jews; in 1907, the shortfall was 21,000, of which 11,270 were Jews. Rein pointed out that the shortfall of Jewish recruits exceeded by six times the shortfall of recruits from other ethnic groups. Upon hearing these figures, Deputy Lashkarev, from Minsk province, suggested the ejection of all aliens, including Poles and Jews, from the army. "It is better to have an open enemy than a secret one," he asserted. However, deputy Abramson, from Kovno province, argued that the "paper shortage" of Jewish recruits merely reflected the army's desire to overestimate the number of Jewish draftees required. The Ministry of the Interior, he argued, provided incorrect data, enabling the military to request an additional 11,722 men annually, which the Jewish population was utterly unable to provide. These data, obtained from local police authorities, failed to recognize the erroneous duplication of names, or Jews who had emigrated or died. Abramson, who knew from experience that such attempts at explanation were useless, declined to comment upon the accuracy of the data collection. Instead, he compared the percentage of Jews in Russia with the number of Jewish soldiers, demonstrating that, while Jewish men comprised 4 percent of the population (2,471,000 out of 62,477,000), 4.94 percent of the army's enlisted men (53,000 out of 1,076,000) consisted of Jews. When the Jewish male population was compared exclusively with the empire's male population of draft age, this percentage was even higher.[15] These figures eloquently proved that the supposed lack was a fiction; to the contrary, Jews were overrepresented in the army.

Further public debate about Jewish military service attracted new voices on both sides. To foster a positive image of Jews in the military, the academic *Evreiskaia starina* printed a series of articles and memoirs portraying Jews as victims of Nicholas's harsh conscription. In 1911, Saul Ginsburg, one of the leading Russian Jewish historians, published a book entitled *Otechestvennaia voina 1812 goda i russkie evrei* (Patriotic 1812 War and Russian Jews), presenting examples of early Jewish allegiance to the Russian army during Napoleon's invasion. Two other monographs appeared that, for the first time, examined Jewish military performance. *Evrei v armii* (Jews in the Army, 1911) was authored by M. Usov (a pen name of Moisei Lvovich Trivus); *Voina i evrei* (War and the Jews, 1912), a more scholarly work, was published

---

[15] *Gosudarstvennaia Duma. Stenograficheskie otchety. Sessiia II.* Zasedanie 28 (sekretnoe), 16 aprelia 1907 goda (SPb.: Gosudarstvennaia tipografiia, 1907), 2130, 2188, 2156–2157; *Gosudarstvennaia Duma. Statisticheskie otchety. Sessiia II.* Zasedanie 29 (sekretnoe), 17 aprelia 1907 goda (SPb.: Gosudarstvennaia tipografiia, 1907), 2177–2183.

anonymously.[16] Both authors strove to refute the accusations of the far right and to prove the Jews' strong sense of military duty and their loyalty to Russia. An odd combination of reliable statistics and biased analysis, Usov's study provided a gloomy picture of Jewish service in the Russian army.[17] Antisemitism dogged the Jewish soldier constantly. Usov presented hard data to dispel the myth of the Jewish conscript's unfitness and unreliability. Yet his extensive use of apologetics rather than of impartial analysis undermined his argument, and drew sharp responses.

Russkii invalid, no longer the pro-Jewish daily it had been in the late 1850s, printed a lengthy response to Usov by the xenophobic General Apukhtin. He contended that a Jew could not be promoted to the rank of officer because Christian soldiers would always address him as "Yid" rather than as "Commander." Jews could become officers only if their religious teaching was "without the blemish of the Talmud." Jews from the Pale of Settlement did not merit the equality that would enable them, among other things, to enter the Moscow chapel to see inscribed the names of the six Jewish soldiers who, along with Russian grenadiers, died in battle at Plevna. Apukhtin cynically asked, "Should we change the law directed against six million because of six men?"[18] Even Jewish military doctors were useless, he declared. Apukhtin acknowledged that he was not qualified to comment upon Usov's data. Although he recalled examples of his own benevolence toward Jewish soldiers, ultimately Apukhtin's conservative bias won out; the tone of his article was primarily negative.

Other rebuttals of Usov's monograph followed. Smirnov, an experienced officer, expressed his conviction that the attitude toward Jews in the army was profoundly hostile, that Jews were ill-suited to defend the fatherland and were undesirable even in noncombatant posts. Kovalevskii proposed to "relieve the army of Jews" and to introduce a special tax to counter the heavy burden imposed on the state treasury by the search for Jewish recruits. Polianskii claimed that Jewish soldiers slandered Russia. A regimental aide-de-camp, he nonetheless relied upon his reading (of Brafman and Krestovskii) to inform his opinions. He asserted, "It is common knowledge that Jews neither recognize nor fulfill military duty; it is no secret that behind each Jew stands the kahal, a mysterious and powerful institution that despotically controls its members." Tifon Dalinskii, a prolific military journalist, responded to Usov with a series of articles that appeared in *Voennyi sbornik*, the military's heavy academic monthly. He rejected the figures painstakingly amassed by Usov as "unreliable," "unscientific," and "prejudiced." The repressive measures against Jews in the 1890s he regarded as necessary, while considering Jewish

---

[16] *Voina i evrei* (SPb.: n. p., 1912).

[17] M. Usov, *Evrei v armii* (SPb.: Razum, 1911), 83. He culled his examples from a variety of sources, including Nikitin's "Vek prozhit'," the memoirs published by *Evreiskaia starina*, and antisemitic material from *Vilenskii voennyi vestnik* (The Vilna Military Bulletin) and *Russkii soldat* (The Russian Soldier).

[18] A. N. Apukhtin, "Evrei v armii," *Russkii invalid*, no. 102 (May 13, 1911); no. 103 (May 14, 1911).

emigration an attempt to evade military service. In his view, all Jews were cowards; soldiers, officers and other loyal subjects of the emperor were indiscriminately murdered, "shot from behind corners by the conscientious Semites." Jewish soldiers also were alleged to engage in ritual murder; Dalinskii could not resist alluding to the Saratov case, which demonstrated the extent to which the far right's propaganda had found fertile soil in the army. Except for the cautious, equivocating Apukhtin, all the military polemicists agreed that "there is no room for Jews in the army."[19] And yet the military retained its pragmatic stance.

The 1912 statute was a last legal attempt to curtail the rights of Jewish soldiers. Duma members spoke of the SR Evno Azef as a provocateur of Jewish origin; of Dmitrii Bogrov, whom they called the Jew Mordke, as the murderer of Stolypin; and of Mendel Beilis, still on trial, as examples of the destructive roles Jews played in Russian society and as arguments against Jewish equality. And yet, for all the statute's supposed severity, only 9 of its 150 new paragraphs (in comparison with the preceding statute) were obviously restrictive in nature. The statute made no mention of the purging of Jews from the army. The military's objective was to transform Russian subjects into serfs of the War Ministry; a male above the age of fifteen could not "opt out of Russian citizenship" unless he had completed his army service. This amendment clearly targeted Jewish emigration, although it did not mention Jews specifically. Other amendments restricted previously granted privileges. For instance, Article 23 provided for the recruitment of Jews in the first exemption category if there was an insufficient number of Jews in the second, third, and fourth categories. Article 25 deprived all first-category conscripts of their privileges if they did not support their relatives financially. Article 28 abolished the right of a Jew to replace his enlisted brother, cousin, or stepbrother. Article 46 removed rabbis from the list of clergymen exempt from military duty (despite the fact that the list included all Christian clerics, senior Muslim clergymen, and elders of Old Believers' communities). Article 74 stipulated that Jews should address their complaints to the Ministry of the Interior, which effectively meant that these would be ignored. Article 145 provided for the punishment of those who avoided military duty, including Jews who had returned temporarily, even though they might be foreign citizens.[20] The War Ministry authorized imposing fines of up to 300 rubles upon relatives of Jewish recruits who had deserted the army. Two separate draft lists were to be compiled: one for Jews and another for all other conscripts.

---

[19] A. Smirnov, "Evrei v armii," *Russkii invalid*, no. 122 (June 10, 1911); F. Kovalevskii, "O evreiakh v armii," *Russkii invalid*, no. 134 (June 24, 1911); M. Polianskii, "O evreiakh v armii," *Russkii invalid*, no. 196 (September 11, 1911); Tifon [Dalinskii], "Po povodu knigi 'Evrei v armii,'" *Voennyi sbornik*, no. 12 (1911): 75–84.

[20] See "Proekt zakona ob izmenenii Ustava o voinskoi povinnosti" in *Osoboe prilozhenie no. 2 k stenograficheskomu otchetu 153-go zasedaniia Gosudarstvennoi Dumy. Gosudarstvennaia Duma. III Sozyv. 1912 god. Sessiia 5. Chast' 4* (SPb.: Gosudarstvennaia tipografiia, 1912), 2–47.

The liberals in the Duma vigorously protested. Deputies Petrovskii from Voronezh, Babaianskii from Perm, and Garusevich from Lomzha advised the Duma to repeal the anti-Jewish amendments as illegal, inadmissible, and contradictory to the spirit of Russian military legislation. If the statute's intent was to establish common ground for service, they demanded, how could one justify incorporating the wording "except for people of Judaic faith" into its numerous amendments? Since the modernized penal code presupposed personal responsibility, how could the medieval principle of collective responsibility be introduced for Jewish families obliged to pay a fine for a deserter? The liberals pointed out that these were civil issues. "The only son in a Jewish family," remarked deputy Garusevich, "emigrated to America solely because he needed to support his family; otherwise he would have had to serve [in the army], regardless of his first-category exemption. This was not a Jewish issue. It was a question of justice, pure and simple."[21]

Deputy Minister of the Interior Lykoshin brusquely replied to these and similar objections: all paragraphs complied with the general legislation concerning Jews; it was impossible to revoke them. Lykoshin admitted that the attempt to pass restrictive rules governing Jewish military service resulted from the perceived need to place Russian Jews under a separate legal framework. The military was simply following a general legislative trend. A lawyer with excellent academic training, Lykoshin had assisted in the rescue of an innocent Jew serving in the front line who, at the height of the 1915 antisemitic paranoia, was accused of espionage. He also arranged for the punishment of Colonel Iakhontov, a blatant antisemite who had ordered the secret murders of Jewish privates awarded the St. George Cross.[22]

Deputy Nisselovich tried to persuade the Duma that the proposed revisions punished the entire Jewish population. However, the Duma accepted the army's reasoning and voted, although by a narrow margin (106:101), to adopt all the amendments. Consequently, the 1912 statute embodied most of the anti-Jewish restrictions established in numerous War Ministry circulars from the early 1880s to the end of the 1900s.[23] The view of Jews as draft dodgers and bad patriots was now legally sanctioned, furnishing the conservative Fourth Duma with compelling arguments against Jewish emancipation. Deputy Purishkevich cynically asked: "What is the reason for expanding the rights of those who refuse to execute their sacred duty to protect their native land?"[24] Jews found their lives in the army circumscribed, as they had been in the Pale, by legal and

---

[21] *Gosudartsvennaia Duma. Stenograficheskie otchety. Sessiia 5.* Ch. 2, zasedanie 86 (zakrytoe), 17 marta 1912 goda (SPb.: Gosudarstvennaia tipografiia, 1912), 580–581, 760–762. For a discussion of antisemitism in the Third Duma, see Ben-Zion Pinchuk, *The Octobrists and the Third Duma* (Seattle and London: University of Washington Press, 1974), 172–174.

[22] Gruzenberg, *Vchera*, 79–81, 88–89.

[23] Gimpelson, *Zakony o evreiakh*, 2: 471.

[24] Purishkevich' argument was predicated upon faulty military statistics calculated by G. G. Zamyslovskii. See *Gosudartsvennaia Duma. Stenograficheskie otchety. Sessiia IV.* Zasedanie 6, 29 oktiabria 1913 g. (SPb.: Gosudarstvennaia tipografiia, 1913), 445.

psychological barriers that they could not surmount. Yet the Russian far right remained dissatisfied. By refusing to oust Jews from the army, the War Ministry had manifested a combination of moderation and common sense that clashed with the expectations of senior army officers and of numerous statesmen. Perhaps the military found it was more significant to retain the status quo in the western provinces with their five million Jews: Russian's western borderlands were the most likely arena of potential military conflicts with Austria or Germany, or with both; the draft of the local dwellers helped the military to exercise control of these territories. Besides, the military simply could not afford to loose fifty thousand soldiers on the eve of a major military conflict. The extent to which the army committed itself to retain universal liability to military duty can be illustrated by the following example. When World War I broke out, the military required that all Russian subjects of military age, including those of Jewish origin, immediately return to Russia and present themselves to military authorities.[25] Pragmatic reasoning seems to have trumped ideology and the principles of the draft took precedence over the biases of the regime.

In April 1914, several months before the outbreak of World War I, the Duma's Commission on Military and Naval Affairs made a final attempt to ameliorate the conditions under which Jews served. Despite Markov II's renewed antisemitic diatribes, discussion in the Duma was more temperate than it had been two years earlier. Count Bennigsen, who considered Jewish emigrants to be deserters, conceded that emigration's legal aspects merited reexamination. Deputies Bomash and Rodichev objected to the Ministry of the Interior's "Jesuitical statistics" concerning Jewish draft dodgers. Deputy Fridman, a commission member, demonstrated that the alleged 1913 deficit of 9,000 Jews was fictitious, and that the War Ministry's demand that 6.7 percent of the male Jewish population be recruited was preposterous when one considered that the ratio of Jews to the empire's male population was 4.1 percent. Emigration, he affirmed, largely accounted for what he dubbed the "paper shortages." He proved that the number of Jews in the army exceeded the proportion of Jewish males in the population. The question of the Jewish draft, Fridman announced, reflected the larger problem of Jewish inequality in society at large. This he movingly illustrated by alluding to a group of retired Jewish soldiers, all of whom had fought in the Russo-Japanese War and had been awarded St. George Crosses for their bravery. Upon their arrival in St. Petersburg, they applied for permanent residence. The authorities denied their petition, even though the law permitted Jewish war veterans to settle in the interior Russian provinces. Fridman continued:

Do you really think that a young Jew forbidden to spend one night in a city where he had served for many years; that this young Jew, who knew nothing but humiliation and

---

[25] For analysis of a group of Russian subjects of Jewish origin (more than three thousand) who preferred to obey and return to Russia to join the troops, see Harold Shukman, *War or Revolution: Russian Jews and Conscription in Britain, 1917* (London and Portland, Oreg.: Vallentine Mitchell, 2006), 67–100.

insult during his service; that this young Jew returning from his tour of duty as devoid of civil rights as he had been before entering the army – do you really think that he is a sort of a superman, capable of meeting superhuman requirements? Entirely deprived of rights, can he be both a patriot and a brave soldier? Do you not see that this makes no legal or human sense?[26]

Interrupted by angry shouts from the right, Fridman appealed to the Duma: once they dissolved the Pale of Settlement, they would acquire many grateful and patriotic Jewish soldiers. The Duma chose to preserve the status quo, neither granting Jewish equality nor ejecting Jewish soldiers.

Russian Jews and the Great War

In the first year of World War I, frustrated by their strategic failures and seeking a convenient scapegoat, the military authorities chose to adopt the ideology of the Russian far right. Although their hatred extended to other ethnic alien minorities whom they accused of espionage and disloyal conduct, such as the Poles, Lithuanians, Germans, and gypsies, they reserved a particular animosity for the Jews. Once Russian troops had occupied Galicia, which was densely populated by emancipated, Yiddish-speaking Jews, the army's command decided to identify Jewish civilians as Austrian spies. It also charged Jews in the Pale with collective betrayal of the Russian cause. If Russian Jews were spies, reasoned the military, their family and communal networks might be exploited to undermine Russia's war plans. Under direct orders from the Main Staff, the occupational authorities in Galicia initiated mass deportations of the allegedly disloyal and treacherous Jews from areas near the military front. The army commanders initiated the same in the western parts of the Pale of Settlement. The goal was to expel as many Jews as possible from the newly captured territories, not only to the east but also to the west, to Germany and Austria, thus enabling the creation of a Russian borderland "free of Jews." By the summer of 1915, more than a quarter of a million Jews had been deported.

The Jewish population's forcible relocation triggered a number of pogroms. As Eric Lohr noted, "[t]he army clearly initiated the violence in nearly every case."[27] Later that year, the military changed to a policy of hostage taking. The targets were primarily wealthy Jews and the so-called spiritual rabbinic leaders (whose salaries were not paid by the state), who would forfeit their lives if any Jew in the community were implicated in a case of treason or espionage.[28]

---

[26] *Gosudartsvennaia Duma. Stenograficheskie otchety. Sessiia IV.* Ch. III, zasedanie 64 (zakrytoe), 24 aprelia 1914 g. (SPb.: Gosudarstvennaia tipografiia, 1914), 155–160.

[27] For a concise and well-substantiated account of the army's ignominious role in anti-Jewish violence, see Eric Lohr, *Nationalizing the Russian Empire: The Campaign against Enemy Aliens during World War I* (Cambridge, Mass.: Harvard University Press, 2003), 137–150, here 147.

[28] See William Fuller, Jr., *Foe Within*, 175–176; M. Lemke, *250 dnei v tsarskoi Stavke* (Pg.: Gos. Izd-stvo, 1920), 204.

The Main Staff suspected the Jewish press of secretly passing military information to the Germans and Austrians. Accordingly, it ordered the closure of all Yiddish and Hebrew newspapers, including *Haynt, Ha-Tsefirah, Dos volk, Vilner togblat, Di yiddishe velt, Unzer lebn,* and *Ha-Shiloakh.* Even *Der moment* was shut down, despite its having more than a hundred thousand subscribers. This "suppression of all expressions of opinion deemed unfavorable to the national interests" was common in many countries during the war, but in Russia it manifested as a specifically anti-Jewish (and more broadly, anti-alien) measure.[29] Because the volume of Jewish soldiers' correspondence exceeded the capacities of the military censors (who were unfamiliar with Yiddish script), the army forbade Jewish conscripts from writing in Yiddish. Jews complained in vain to Duma deputy Bomash that a Jew in the trenches or in the hospital was not permitted to send his Yiddish-speaking mother greetings or a farewell note.[30]

By late 1914, the War Ministry's internal documents, reports from the front line, and regulations governing civilian Jews all revealed anti-Jewish slander. The Main Staff, "in the grip of anti-Semitic frenzy," as characterized by Fuller, was convinced that Jewish soldiers were not only bad patriots, but were also spies. In several military districts far from the front line, commanders ordered the removal of Jewish specialists; Jewish engineering and metalwork experts from the army's automobile companies in St. Petersburg and Moscow were transferred to the front line.[31] Since all Jewish soldiers were regarded as potential secret agents, the press was prohibited from making any positive references to them. When *Minskaia kopeika* dared to describe the heroic deeds of a Jewish soldier, the Minsk military district's senior aide-de-camp, Colonel Dessino, angrily demanded of the editor how such information could have leaked into the press. He wrote, "I ask you to notify me of the source of your information on the heroic action of the Jew Appel, as described under the title 'The Jewish Hero,' which was prohibited by the military censor, Lieutenant

---

[29] For an analysis of the European context, see Pierre Purseigle, "Warfare and Belligerence: Approaches to the First World War," in Pierre Purseigle, *Warfare and Belligerence: Perspectives in First World War Studies* (Leiden and Boston: Brill, 2005), 1–38, here 32. For the attitudes of wartime Russian authorities to ethnic minorities, see Peter Gatrell, *Russia's First World War: A Social and Economic History* (Harlow, Essex: Pearson Longman, 2005), 30–31, 180–181; Lohr, *Nationalizing the Russian Empire,* 26–27, 129–137; Fuller, *Foe Within,* 180–182, 201–202; for censorship orders forbidding publications and correspondence in Hungarian, German, and Yiddish, see M. Lemke, *250 dnei v tsarskoi Stavke* (Pg.: Gos. Izd-stvo, 1920), 412–415.

[30] GARF, f. 9458, op. 1, d. 168, l. 2.

[31] A telegram to Fridman disclosed that Jewish specialists had worked in the automobile companies for about ten months. According to their immediate commanders, they executed their duties "fully and honestly." The Main Staff was engaged in a dispute with Sekretov, the automobile company's chief engineer, who did not wish to dismiss Jews from the service. However, ultimately he was helpless against the orders of the Main Staff. See RGVIA, f. 13251, op. 5, d.12, l. 1.

Colonel Meltikov, on July 13, 1915."[32] The chief chaplain of the army and navy recalled these circumstances:

For the failures which have affected us, the front-line troops accuse the Main Staff and the war minister; the Main Staff accuses the war minister; and the front troops and the war minister place the blame on Grand Duke Nikolai [Nicholas II's uncle, the army's chief-in-command]. All these prosecutors, who simultaneously are the accused, have fastened upon a more blameworthy group, in whose condemnation they have shown unanimity: the Jews.[33]

The war minister studied the reports on Jewish espionage and mass desertions submitted by the army's chief of staff, General Ianushkevich, and wrote, "It is time to expel the Jews from the army."[34] Although Jews remained in the Russian army until the February Revolution, the attitudes of its top generals toward them continued to deteriorate. Explaining the paradoxical situation, a historian of the Russian army has observed that the military leaders "preached (and believed in) the long-term goal of a multi-ethnic nation while practicing short-term imperial policies of ethnic discrimination."[35]

Grand Duke Nikolai Nikolaevich, the Russian army's commander in chief at the beginning of the war, was personally responsible for inciting anti-Jewish hysteria; his subordinates considered his widely circulated xenophobic statements to be wartime directives.[36] Ianushkevich, also known for his rabid anti-semitism, portrayed Jews as guilty of any failure of military operations on the western front. The chief of the Seventh army staff reported that Austrian spies had established contacts with local Jews, and that local Jews, in turn, had contacts with Jewish enlisted men in the rear and transport units. Suspicious staff officers either requested permission to send Jews to front-line battalions or recommended strict controls over Jews dispatched to the front regiments.[37] The northwestern front headquarters were instructed not to employ local Jews; it was thought that they used their privilege of free movement to spy for the enemy.[38] In December 1914, the head of the Northwestern army supplies

---

[32] See RGVIA, f. 13251, op. 5, d.12, ll. 2–3. See also *Minskaia kopeika*, no. 1036, June 15, 1915.

[33] G. Shavel'skii, *Vospominaniia poslednego protopresvitera russkoi armii i flota*, 2 vols. (New York: Izd. im. Chekhova, 1954), 2: 271.

[34] See RGVIA, f. 400, op. 19, d. 105, l. 32.

[35] Joshua Sanborn, *Drafting the Russian Nation: Military Conscription, Total War, and Mass Politics, 1905–1925* (DeKalb.: Northwestern Illinois University Press, 2003), 71.

[36] For a military hagiography of Grand Duke Nikolai, see R. M. Portugal'skii, P. D. Alekseev, V. A. Runov, *Pervaia mirovaia v zhizneopisaniakh russkikh voenachal'nikov* (M.: Elakos, 1994), 11–51. For a contemporary depiction of his antisemitism and nationalism and their consequences, see M. Lemke, *250 dnei v tsarskoi Stavke* (Pg.: God. Izd-stvo, 1920), 81, 108–111; Mark G. [Talpern], *Bol'she pravdy, chem fantazii (Zapiski Burzhuia)* (Paris: Russkoe knigoizdatel'stvo, 1919), 16–17. For a description of how misunderstanding transforms into hatred and hatred into suspicion that Jews are sympathizing with the enemy, see B. N. Sergeevskii, *Perezhitoe* (Belgrade: n. p., 1933), 74.

[37] CAHJP, HMF/585A-H. For the original, see GARF, f. 9458, op. 1, d. 162, l. 40b.

[38] RGVIA, f. 2049, op. 1, d. 390, l. 102.

ILLUSTRATION 7. A Jewish private of the 97th Lifland infantry regiment, ca. 1915. Courtesy of the Judaica Institute of Ukraine.

complained that "Jews store provisions for the German troops," and so forbade any dealings with Jewish middlemen. As the result of these and other restrictions, the army suffered badly from the absence of food and, later, of cartridges. A chronicler depicting this failure compared the situation to Dante's Hell.[39]

---

[39] A. I. Verkhovskii, *Rossiia na Golgofe* (iz pokhodnogo dnevnika 1914–1918 g.) (Pg.: Delo naroda, 1918), 38–40. For Grand Duke Nikolai's order prohibiting all Jews from providing supplies to the troops, see M. Lemke, *250 dnei v tsarskoi Stavke*, 325.

When patriotic Moscovite contractors Struzer and Gofshneider offered to provide the troops with relatively inexpensive products, the army's Chief Controller resolved to confiscate their supplies.[40] All officials of Jewish descent in the Western Front Zemstvo Union who had assisted nongovernmental organizations at the front were ordered replaced.[41] Jews found themselves regarded as the "enemy alien," to use Eric Lohr's term, and as an internal threat to society. As such, they deserved neither mercy nor civilized treatment. On May 27, 1915, the head of the Minsk military district banished innumerable Jewish civilians to Chita province, confiscating their possessions "as recompense for the damage those people caused the state in such a difficult time." Russian officialdom echoed the sentiments of the Duma's conservatives. In a succinct statement to the Main Staff, the chief of the Minsk police summarized the concerns of the collapsing regime: "Jews are harmful and dangerous to the Russian people."[42]

Russian Officers and Jewish Soldiers: A Front-Line Perspective

S. Ansky, an eye-witness and chronicler of the events, accurately recorded the swift spread of slanders against Jews among the Russian state officials, some of whom viewed 90 percent of the entire Russian Jewry as traitors and 10 percent as spies. Ansky noted that '[t]he rumors found particularly fertile soil among the troops on the front line and especially the officers and the commanders, who got their ideas about Jews from *Novoye Vremya* and other newspapers that supported the Black Hundreds. Indeed, the officers' corps was thoroughly permeated with profound hatred for Jews."[43] A Yiddish letter written by a certain Abram, who had exerted himself to obtain a release from the draft, supports Ansky's ominous picture. Abram wrote: "God only knows how long our brothers will have to suffer. There are 80,000 Jews fighting in the army, yet Jews become the victims of the pogroms. Our brothers spill their blood on the battlefield, while the Poles beat peaceful Jews in Poland and Cossacks mercilessly persecute them. You cannot imagine what a Jewish soldier feels and thinks when he goes into battle, while his fellows call him a 'Yid' and constantly mock him as if he were a coward."[44] While there is little reason to doubt the accuracy of such reports, the entirety of the Jewish soldier's situation proved more complex. Ansky, the Jewish writer, and Abram, the Jewish draft dodger, were repeating clichés that did not reflect the experience of most Jewish soldiers.

At the beginning of the war, the Russian army comprised 1,423,000 troops. After mobilization, this figure leaped to 6.5 million. During the nineteen

---

[40] RGVIA, f. 2049, op. 1, d. 390, ll. 96, 167–168.
[41] M. Lemke, *250 dnei v tsarskoi Stavke*, 792–793.
[42] RGVIA, f. 2049, op. 1, d. 390, l. 203, 357.
[43] S. Ansky, *The Enemy at His Pleasure: A Journey through the Jewish Pale of Settlement during World War I*, ed. and trans Joachim Neugroshcel (New York: Metropolitan Books, 2003), 4–5.
[44] A copy of an intercepted letter of January 27, 1915, sent from the town of Sartana, Ekaterinoslav province, to the United States. GARF, f. 102, op. 1915, d. 165 (t. 1), l. 1–10b.

ILLUSTRATION 8. German Ioffe, private of the 166th Rovno infantry regiment; Tarnov, ca. 1914. An inscription on the back reads: "To my dear brother M. Ioffe from his brother German." Courtesy of the Judaica Institute of Ukraine.

conscription drives conducted between 1914 and March 1917, some 16 million males were pressed into service, 13 million of whom were of peasant origin. Soldiers of workers' origin constituted 3 to 3.5 percent of the troops: about 500,000 people. At least half of these were Jews.[45]

As Russia's forces faltered on the western front, the military command became intent upon identifying Jewish "cowards" and "whiners" as the cause of the martial defeat.[46] The War Ministry was in a quandary: if Jewish civilians

---

[45] *Rossiia v mirovoi voine 1914–1918 gg. (V tsifrakh)* (M.: 1925), 4, 17, 18, 49.

[46] Sanborn, *Drafting the Russian Nation*, 116–122. David Rich's doubts "about the realism of any of Russia's military and strategic thought" are borne out by the Main Staff's antisemitic paranoia during World War I. See his *Tsar's Colonels*, 228.

were spies, how should Jewish soldiers be dealt with? Were they reliable? Were they indeed cowards, plotting their desertion or their escape to America, or opting for easy, noncombat posts? Ianushkevich requested precise data concerning local Jews' and Jewish soldiers' attitudes to the war. In response, Baron Diterikh sent a cable to Count Geiden requesting immediate reports on any Jewish soldiers violating the oath and on any local Jewish civilians who might have spoken against the Russian troops or might have voiced sympathy for the enemy.[47]

The Main Staff asked regimental commanders for extensive data regarding Jewish soldiers who had been wounded, killed, or lost in action, as well as those who had earned medals or who had deserted. Additionally, it investigated Jews accused of engaging in such activities as antigovernment propaganda, separatism, or self-mutilation, and scrutinized those thought to have displayed physical ineptitude or scorn toward Russian troops. The questionnaire was not intended to elicit an objective picture of the situation in the ranks, but instead to corroborate the high command's worst suspicions. Yet, despite knowing what their superiors expected them to say, unit commanders reported just the opposite.

The Russian army was a complex entity; not everyone in its hierarchy bowed to the aggressive, state-orchestrated antisemitism. As the anti-Jewish disturbances in Galicia spread, the governor of Warsaw province firmly declared that Jews were innocent of any criminal activity. General Alekseev, one of the highest military commanders, penned a bold reply to General Ianushkevich's antisemitic innuendo, asserting that neither the army nor the state would receive any benefit from the eviction of Jews from areas near the front line. To the contrary: according them permission to remain in their places of residence "would be of greater benefit to the fighting troops."[48]

Most of the commanders responding to the questionnaire portrayed Jews as obedient soldiers, whose performance, conduct, and reliability demonstrated that they had successfully integrated into the army. The responses to the questionnaire matched the opinions of the combat officers, participants in the Russo-Turkish War, who saw Jews in the battle and praised their performance. The commander of the Twenty-first infantry division maintained that, while Jews did not possess the stamina (*vynoslivost'*) of their Christian brethren, they "fulfilled their duty satisfactorily," and made no attempt to avoid the hardships of service.[49] In short, their comportment was entirely normal. The commander of the Eighth division reported that 828 of his Jewish soldiers had been killed, 2,947 wounded, and 1,194 taken as POWs since the outbreak of the war; 2,813 Jews remained under his auspices. Many of them, he affirmed, were excellent soldiers and outstanding scouts, and those in noncombat posts were skilled and

[47] CAHJP, HMF/585A-H (Original in GARF, f. 9458, op. 1, d. 162, ll. 60, 70).
[48] GARF, f. 9458, op. 1, d. 162.
[49] RGVIA, f. 2113, op. 2, d. 68, l. 349.

useful artisans. The commander of the 237th Graivoron infantry regiment reported that his Jewish soldiers in no way differed from the other enlisted men, "therefore it is impossible to provide the required data, even for certain periods of time." None were deserters, he continued, adding that there were "cases of excellent, brave, and efficient soldiers among them, awarded St. George crosses and medals." The commander of the Sixtieth infantry Zamost regiment was even stauncher in his support. To the military authorities' biased queries, he replied that he would like to retain, on the front line, his nine Jewish telephone operators, eight company scribes, and one medical assistant, "because they deserve nothing but praise." Jews in the artillery, he claimed, had established telephone lines under enemy fire, while Jewish scribes were the only ones well informed regarding the composition of the troops. The commander of the Seventy-first artillery brigade held a similarly high opinion of his eleven Jewish enlisted men, informing the army's headquarters that he and other commanders firmly "stand by them." Jews "perfectly fulfill their service in the front lines," he avowed, noting that four out of the eleven had received the St. George Cross.[50] The commander of the Fourth artillery division related that Jews served under his command as telephone operators and as gun-layers; there were virtually no cases of flight or desertion among them. Jewish soldiers "fulfill their duties as diligently as the enlisted men of other nationalities," he announced.[51] The Briansk regiment commander wrote that Jews fought as well as non-Jews; they evinced no sympathy toward German troops; and there were no cases of voluntary surrender among them. As if to mock the military's anti-Jewish bias, the commander of the Volhynia infantry regiment declared that he had sent nineteen men, one of them a Jew, on a reconnaissance mission; eighteen were lost in action, and only the Jew returned with a report.[52]

The army considered Russian Orthodoxy an important resource in ensuring the troops' psychological wellbeing. The military mobilized some two thousand Russian orthodox priests; by the end of World War I there were some five thousand chaplains in the army. Priests greeted and blessed the troops, the regiments conducted regular services, and the military embraced the concept of a Christ-loving army.[53] This new religious emphasis may have helped to maintain the soldiers' morale and discipline. There were no complaints from Jewish soldiers that they felt humiliated or ostracized because of the

---

[50] CAHJP, HMF/585A-H. For the original, see GARF, f. 9458, op. 1, d. 162, l. 74–74a, 161, 164.

[51] RGVIA, f. 2134, op. 2, d. 543, l. 22.

[52] GARF, f. 9458, op. 1, d. 162, l. 12.

[53] For a description of Russian Orthodox prayer during wartime, see A. Ksiunin, *Narod na voine (Iz zapisok voennogo korrepsondenta)* (Pg.: Suvorin, 1916), 232–33. Regarding the wartime conceptualization of Russian troops as Christ-loving, see S. Broiakosvkii, *Voina chetyrnadtsatogo goda (po rasskazam uchastnikov i ochevidtsev)* (Kiev: Dukhovnaia beseda, 1915), 19–20. For pictures of Christian army services, see E. A. Vertsinskii, *Iz mirovoi voiny: boevye zapisi i vospominaniia komandira polka i ofitsera General'nogo Shtaba za 1914–1917 gody* (Tallinn-Revel: Izd. Soiuza Tsarskosel'skikh strelkov, 1931), inserted photos between pp. 96 and 97, 160 and 161.

intensification of Russian Orthodox activities; they seem to have recognized this as primarily a political or ideological measure. Available documents indicate a camaraderie and mutual respect between Jewish and Christian soldiers, and make no mention of any attempt by Russian soldiers to isolate their Jewish

ILLUSTRATION 9. Vladimir Shneiderman at Russia's World War I western front, December 1914. The picture follows a letter congratulating the Shneidermans on Hanukkah. Courtesy of the Judaica Institute of Ukraine.

fellows-in-arms.[54] Photographs by military journalists, published in the Russian Jewish press, attest to the Jewish soldiers' celebration of religious rites in the barracks, on the front line, and in military hospitals. Middle-ranking officers and colonels appear among the Passover seder participants.[55] The War Ministry does not appear to have reprimanded officers for publicly taking part in Jewish rites, as had been the case during War Minister Vannovskii's tenure.

Chroniclers' accounts alternately describe Jewish soldiers as sickly and useless, and as good and obedient soldiers.[56] Officers' personal experience determined their treatment of Jews: The staff officers susceptible to state propaganda dealt with them scornfully, while the combat officers better acquainted with Jews in the trenches regarded them neutrally or even accorded them respect, a blasphemy in Ianushkevich's view. A Russian propaganda booklet published in the first months of the war cited a letter from a Jewish soldier named Jacob, who said he was unable to look calmly upon the great events unfolding before his eyes. Another episode spoke of Private Martsel Rabinovich, a volunteer and a junior student at Kiev University, who fought in Galicia, participated in successful reconnaissance missions, and obtained an Austrian horse in recognition of his sterling performance.[57] Colonel Vevern, commander of the Sixth artillery division, recalled Jewish boys in Lwów who assisted Russian officers, and an obedient if workaholic Jewish smith who served under his auspices in the artillery.[58] Military doctor N. Davydov, a conservative who had subscribed to anti-Jewish propaganda, nonetheless felt compelled to admit that Jewish soldiers served diligently and that Jewish civilians selflessly aided wounded Russian soldiers in military hospitals. A Russian company commander with eight Jewish reservists comprehended, during their first battle, that "a Jewish soldier was a real soldier; he manifested well-developed selflessness, courage, and contempt for death." Company Commander Captain Virsky wrote to the parents of the wounded soldier Esaye, the only son of a wealthy merchant near Elisavetgrad, "I loved him; he was an outstanding soldier, brave, clever, and industrious. You should be proud of your son as a soldier." An immediate commander of Private Aizik Raikhenshtein, from Minsk province, wrote to the conscript's parents that their son was the most courageous soldier in his company. An artillery battery commander recounted how Bombardier

[54] A Jewish memoirist recalls entrepreneurial Jews among Russian soldiers in the Austrian POW camp: violinist Kogan, actors and singers Aizenberg and Epstein, opera singer Liberman, speaker and former lawyer Goldberg, tailors Levit and Mazel, and barber Borukhov. He portrays a fruitful symbiosis between Russian and Jewish POWs, who organized a church choir in the camp, with Jewish tenors and Russian basses. See Kirill Levin, *Zapiski iz plena* (Moscow: Federatsia, 1931), 36, 39, 40, 41, 56, 132–134.
[55] *Voina i evrei*, no. 2 (1914): 3; no. 8 (1914–1915): 7, 8.
[56] Sof'ia Fedorchenko, *Narod na voine* (M.: Sovetskii pisatel, 1990), 45–46; L. Ostrover, *V seroi shineli. Zapiski polkovogo vracha* (M., L.: Gosudarstvennoe izdatel'syvo. 1926), 7, 13, 99–100, 103–104, 117–118.
[57] *V ogne. Boevye vpechatleniia uchastnikov voiny* (Petrograd: Gramotnost, 1914), 17, 62–63.
[58] B. V. Vevern, *6-ia batareia 1914-1917 gg. Povest' o vremeni velikogo sluzhenia Rodine* (Parizh, n. p., 1938), 18–19.

Lebedinsky induced infantry soldiers to rise from the trenches in order to check
the enemy's charge: "He did not know fear. I had to hold him back." Oskar
Gruzenberg visited the front and recalled that officers by and large praised the
Jewish soldiers, who "fought excellently."[59]

Russian officer A. Brekalo wrote the following letter to Jewish lance corporal
Faivush Polisskii on the occasion of the latter's being awarded the St. George
Medal: "I hereby present you with this award. During the battle at the village of
Likhovka, although you were seriously wounded in both legs and had broken
a bone, and despite fierce and incessant rifle and machine-gun fire by the
Germans, you continued to shoot and remained in your position until nightfall.
Only then were you carried from your post, exhausted and semi-fainting.
Certainly, you will enjoy the rights of citizenship. The company is saddened to
learn of your distress and sends you its best wishes. May God grant you hap-
piness and strength till the end of your life. Please write more often and don't
forget us. Orekhov, Saveliev, Pankov, Sidorov, [and] Veselovskii send you their
personal greetings."[60] This letter is illuminating for several reasons. It pro-
claims the heroism of a Jewish soldier who enjoyed the respect of his commanding officer and of his non-Jewish comrades-in-arms. It also attests to their
sympathy for him and their belief that his patriotic fervor and his combat
performance would necessarily earn him civil equality and citizenship. It is
significant that the connection between the soldier's selflessness on the battlefront and the promise of civil equality appears in an apparently private letter,
rather than in political correspondence. If Brekalo's communication was a reply
to a letter from Polisskii that no longer is extant, Polisskii's note possessed a
remarkable awareness of the direct connection between full emancipation and
military duty. Perhaps Nahum Sabsay, who served in the Russian army during
World War I, deftly captured this connection in conversation. He once arrived
at a distant Galician hut and met a Ukrainian family unable to comprehend
how he, a humiliated and segregated Jewish soldier, could serve xenophobic
Russians. He replied, "Sometimes you have to do things you hate to do."[61]

The more democratically minded military commanders appreciated the
Jews' patriotism, professional skills, and proverbial wit. Notwithstanding the
Ministry of the Interior's statistics, they knew that Jews were overrepresented in
the Russian army, and that they deserved better treatment. When confronted
with the dilemma of how to continue his military career after February 1917,
Lieutenant Colonel Kurzenev, the commander of the Fifth battery of the Thirty-
second artillery brigade, remarked, "It would be a most pleasant task to be a
commander of a Jewish battery. If they are going to form any of this type, I shall
apply for the post immediately."[62]

---

[59] *Voina i evrei*, no. 2 (1914) : 9–10; 3 (1914–1915): 4, 9, 12; no. 4 (1914–1915): 13.
[60] CAHJP, HMF/585A-H (original in GARF, f. 9458, op. 1, d. 162, l. 22).
[61] Nahum Sabsay, *A Moment of History: A Russian Soldier in the First World War* (Caldwell,
Iowa: privately printed, 1960), 87–88.
[62] V. Milodanovich, "Polevoi zhid i ego kollegi," *Voennaia byl'*, no. 93 (1968): 14.

In the Trenches on Russia's Western Front

Bruce Lincoln once observed that "Jews continued to fight and die bravely for the homeland that persecuted them."[63] Indeed, during the war, Jewish patriotism was the norm rather than the exception. Once hostilities had broken out, the Warsaw rabbinate issued an appeal to all synagogue and prayer-house congregations, alluding to Russia as "our fatherland," and praising "our brothers and sons" who enlisted in order to fight the enemy. It was a sacred Jewish duty to welcome the Russian troops and to assist them, regardless of the cost.[64] Influential rabbinic leaders praised Jewish soldiers. They sent an open letter to the Russian civil and military administrations, arguing that Jews "have never been traitors of the fatherland and would never be traitors; they proved that with their selfless loyalty to the motherland which sheltered them and will be happy to prove that to their Russian fatherland on the battlefield."[65] The self-abnegation of Jewish soldiers inspired Russian film-makers, actors, writers, and poets, who depicted Jews sympathetically as "good soldiers who fight for the might and glory of Russia."[66]

The military inadvertently proved the Jewish soldiers' patriotism. It had ordered its censors to monitor their correspondence, paying particular attention to attitudes toward the army and the war. Having amassed a representative body of evidence, consisting of copies of and excerpts from several thousand letters, the censorship commission summarized its results in a memorandum. The conclusions were surprising: It was impossible to identify Jewish soldiers' attitudes. Jews scarcely touched upon such themes; they did not complain; and they wrote very cautiously. A selection of nineteen letters that directly discussed the war yielded nine containing positive attitudes and five that were negative. Excerpts quoted in the aggregate report underscored Jews' patriotic fervor,

---

[63] It is difficult, however, to agree with Lincoln that the army "proclaimed Jews unfit to receive the Cross of St. George, and noncommissioned officers felt free even to shoot Jews in uniform for no good reason." See W. Bruce Lincoln, *Armageddon: The Russians in War and Revolution, 1914–1918* (New York: Simon and Shuster, 1986), 140.

[64] S. Broiakovskii, *Voina chetyrnadtsatogo goda (po rassskazam uchastnikov i ochevidtsev)* (Kiev: Dukhovnaia beseda, 1915), 31. The Russian philosopher Stepun, who served in the artillery during World War I, vividly contrasted the patriotism of the subservient imperial press that celebrated multiethnic Russian brotherhood with the reality at the front, where officers cruelly humiliated Jewish civilians; see Fedor Stepun (N. Lugin), *Iz pisem praporshchika-artillerista* (Tomsk: Vodolei, 2000), 75–76.

[65] RGVIA, f. 2049, op. 1, d. 455, ll. 27–30 ("Obrashchenie vilenskogo, varshavskogo, novodvorskogo ravviniov," 1915).

[66] For the first sound approach to this misunderstood theme, see Hubertus F. Jahn, *Patriotic Culture in Russia during World War I* (Ithaca and London: Cornell University Press, 1995), 113, 133, and a short filmography, 197–198, here 133. However, some folkloric representations of the Jewish war experience "highlighted the essential incompatibility between Russian military service and the Jewish way of life." See Aviel Roshwald, "Jewish Cultural Identity in Eastern and Central Europe during the Great War," in Aviel Roshwald and Richard Stites, eds., *European Culture in the Great War* (Cambridge: Cambridge University Press, 1999), 89–126, here 97.

pronounced self-awareness, and desire to fight and die for the Russian military cause. "My soul strives to fight in the first rows and defend my beloved fatherland," stated one of the letters. "Don't think I am showing off – I talk seriously since I loved and love my fatherland." Another letter claimed that Mitia (Dmitrii), who had been awarded a St. George Medal, "participated in reconnaissance missions eleven times, as a volunteer, to disprove the rumors about Jews."[67] Participation in the most dangerous missions appears to have been regarded as a matter of honor for others as well as for Russian Jews. To Jews in the Austrian army, for instance, it "served the useful purpose of giving the lie to anti-Semitic canards about Jewish cowardice."[68]

The war galvanized Jewish teenagers, predominantly those from accultur-ated bourgeois families. Many were reported to have volunteered. Thirteen-year-old Iakov Sharfinovich, from Nikolaev, ran away from home to join the army, was sent back, fled once again, and at last succeeded in joining the troops. He had sent the commander in chief a petition in which he begged to be accepted as a volunteer into "the glorious Russian troops" because he wanted to be of help and to "kill a big enemy." Another runaway Jewish boy, fourteen-year-old Iosif Guttman, the son of the Russo-American Trade Society's director, joined the front-line troops and excelled in reconnaissance. When he was wounded in action, Colonel Golovin wrote to his father, "Your son, Iosif Guttman, was very helpful to our army, demonstrating his courage and brav-ery. The Ninth army commander awarded him with the silver medal of St. George, inscribed 'For Courage.'"[69]

A specialist in Russian military awards has calculated scrupulously that at least 1,957 Jews received St. George crosses during World War I; about twelve of them were "Full Cavaliers," awarded all three ranks of this highest soldier's decoration.[70] This is a disproportionately high number for Jews in the Russian army. Even so, it scarcely reflects the true levels of Jewish patriotism and hero-ism. A cautious comparative analysis of selected military divisions reveals that, during World War I, Jews received proportionately half as many awards as did non-Jews. About 10 percent of the Ninth infantry division's non-Jewish soldiers received St. George medals, whereas only 6 percent of Jews did. In the Briansk regiment, 13 percent of soldiers received the St. George Cross and 4 percent

[67] See CAHJP, HM 2/8344 (original in RGVIA, f. 400, op. 19, d. 106, "So svedeniami, postupivshimi iz Glavnoi voenno-tsenzurnoi komissii ob otnoshenii evreev k voinskoi povinnosti v voinu Rossii s Germaniei i Avstro-Vengriei, 10 marta–15 maia 1915 g."), l. 3–30b.

[68] See Marsha Rozenblit, *Reconstructing a National Identity: The Jews of Habsburg Austria during World War I* (New York: Oxford University Press, 2001), 91.

[69] *Voina i evrei*, no. 1 (1914): 11; 2 (1914): 9; no. 4 (1914): 1; no. 4 (1914): 1.

[70] See http://sammler.ru/index.php?showtopic=5114&st=100#entry85839 (accessed January 1, 2008). Other sources report some 3,000 Jews who received St. George Cross by 1917. See I. Levitas, "Georgievskie kavalery," *Evreiskie vesti*, no. 13–14 (July, 1995); "Voennaia sluzhba," in *Kratkaia evreiskaia entsiklopediia*, 10 vols. (Jerusalem: Keter, 1976), vol. 1 (dop 2), part 1: 682–691 and part 2: 286–291. Among the "Full Cavaliers" of St. George Cross was firefighter Leiser Pekhovich of the Thirty-second artillery brigade, see RGVIA, f. 16180, op. 7, d. 75, l. 284.

ILLUSTRATION 10. Volunteer Shimon Meirovich Shtern (Semen Vasil'evich Petrovsky, 1897–1972), Odessa, 1916. From the author's archive.

were issued St. George Medals. Among Jews (about one hundred), the figures were less than half that: 4 percent were presented with the St. George Cross, and 3 percent with medals.[71] In 1915, the War Ministry considered this difference a clear indication of the Jews' lack of military fitness. Yet, in light of the virulent antisemitic propaganda in the country, the ongoing pogroms against the Jewish population on the western front, and the association of purported civilian Jewish spies with Jewish soldiers, the mere fact of the Jews' having so distinguished

[71] RGVIA, f. 2113, op. 2, d. 68, ll. 95–96.

themselves in service as to have been accorded such recognition powerfully attests to their dedication and to their ability.

While during the war the military censorship introduced a ban on any publications about Jewish heroic behavior, the Russian Jewish periodical *Voina i evrei* (War and the Jews) regularly informed its readership about the valiant deeds and the altruism of their brethren at the front.[72] The journal sought simultaneously to inspire Jewish volunteers, to educate Russian public opinion about Jewish goodwill and patriotism, and to counteract the slanderous anti-Jewish publications of the conservative press. It published a portrait photo of Yosef Trumpeldor on its cover, offering him as a role model. Trumpeldor appears as a clean-shaven, modern Jew in the uniform of an NCO, with four St. George crosses and a St. George Medal adorning his chest. Several accounts of Jewish heroism at the front appeared in the periodical: Volunteer Mikhels was involved in fierce combat against German and Austrian troops, near Peremyshl. His company had to provide cover for Russian forces that were holding back the advancing enemy troops. After accomplishing their objective, they counterattacked. Mikhels was wounded, but refused to abandon the ranks until his commander sent him back. In another battle, Mikhels and two other soldiers retrieved and set up a machine gun under savage enemy fire. For these two deeds, he received two St. George orders. Alperovich, a pious Jew from Vilna province, worked as a *melamed* (instructor) in a Jewish elementary school and dreamed of a rabbinic career. When war erupted, he volunteered for the front-line troops. During his first reconnaissance, he disabled German artillery guns. His commanders promoted him to the rank of an NCO, and awarded him the St. George Order. Kh. N. (whose last name was erased by a censor), a sickly Jew relegated to a transport unit, managed to convince his company commander to transfer him to the front line. During his first reconnaissance outing, he detected a camouflaged Austrian artillery battery and helped the Russian artillery to destroy it. Il'ia S. (whose last name was also erased by a censor) captured a German officer while out on a reconnaissance mission and brought him to headquarters, receiving a second-rank St. George Order for his pains. Sh.-M. Zelkovich saved a company commander from enemy fire during combat in Lodz; while out on reconnaissance operations, he captured seventeen German telegraph devices. He was honored with a St. George Medal, and later with a St. George Cross for having spent three days cutting the enemy's barbed wires to facilitate the advance of the Russian troops. A certain Yosif, from Berdichev, connected severed telephone wires under enemy fire, thus reestablishing the connection between the artillery battery and the observation post; for this, he was presented with a fourth-rank St. George Order. Vulf Shvarts was decorated for excellence in action with three St. George Crosses of various ranks; twice

---

[72] For more detail on the Russian military censorship, see Eric Lohr, "The Russian Press and the 'Internal Peace' at the Beginning of World War I," in Troy R. E. Paddock, ed., *A Call to Arms: Propaganda, Public Opinion, and Newspapers in the Great War* (Westport, Conn.: Praeger, 2004), 91–114.

wounded, he recovered and twice requested to be returned to the front. *War and the Jews* also regularly published photos and brief biographies of Jews recognized for bravery. Among them were Abram Landau, a graduate of Moscow University's Law Department; V. A. Nurenberg, a lawyer; and V. Vilenkin, a legal assistant; all received fourth-rank St. George decorations for excellence in combat. Wolf Vinokur-Kogen received four St. George Crosses and an Order of St. Anna, and was nominated for a Large Golden Medal; Osher Hanukaev received three St. George crosses and a medal for bravery during combat.[73]

Despite the Jewish soldiers' patriotic fervor, the regime became increasingly hostile toward them. Moreover, the military's lack of upward mobility meant that Russian Jews gained virtually nothing in return for their exemplary combat performance. The constant anxiety engendered by active duty sometimes resulted in psychological instability. At the turn of the century, military data disclosed that Jews suffered two to three times as many cases of depressive psychosis as did recruits as a whole. Officers, physicians, and battle eyewitnesses remarked on the unstable psyches of Jewish soldiers. A supervisor of reserve soldiers observed that they were agitated during night training sessions: the Jews particularly so.[74] Others noticed that previously fearful Jews showed reckless bravery in action. Vadim Belov, a Russian officer active during World War I, concurred in this view of the Jewish soldier's unstable conduct.[75] A newspaper correspondent related a curious incident in which a Jewish conscript, Abramka, overcame his own cowardice, outwitted a group of Austrian soldiers, and forced them to surrender.[76] Russian artillery officer V. Milodanovich corroborated these views, observing similar tendencies in Jewish soldiers and artillerymen. He portrayed operator Leizer Pukhovich, junior fireworker Shmul' Sonts, and gunner Mendel Lapshun as Jewish enlisted men exhibiting both indecisiveness and heightened personal responsibility. A characteristic example was the conduct of Shmul Sonts, who was ordered to restore telephone communication under intense enemy fire:

– Oh, Your Honor, the line broken!
– Then fix it!
– (In complete despair) Your Honor! Well, how will I go?

---

[73] The journal's data regarding Jewish heroism at the front appears to be trustworthy; most of it was obtained through non-Jewish military correspondents or reprinted from the Russian press. See *Voina i evrei*, no. 1 (1914): 16; no. 2 (1914): 5; no. 4 (1914–1915): 5; no. 7 (1914–1915): 11; no. 8 (1914–1915): 7; no. 9 (1914–1915): 7–8; no. 13 (1914–15): 10.

[74] Luganin, "Zametki," *Voennyi sbornik*, no. 4 (1888): 320.

[75] Vadim Belov, *Evrei i poliaki na voine. Rasskaz ofitsera-uchastnika* (Pg.: Biblioteka Velikoi Voiny, 1915), 3–26, 78–85. Cf. Aleksandr Stepanov, an eyewitness to the Russo-Japanese war and son of a participant, who wrote about Zaiats, a Jewish soldier from Sventsiany (Święciany), "Zaiats was a characteristic psychological type, sometimes cowardly and intimidated, but ultimately fearless and heroic." A. Stepanov, *Port-Artur*. 2 vols. (M.: Khudozhestvennaia literatura, 1988), 1:35–36, 44, 453–454; 2: 608.

[76] I. Tonkonogov, *Epizody voiny. Sbornik rasskazov uchastnikov voiny i korrespondentov razlichnykh periodicheskikh izdanii* (Petrograd: Imperatorskaia Voennaia Akademia, 1916), 93–95.

[Kurzenev, a senior officer, laughing] – It is already your business. I will not help you.

Shmul Sonts disappeared again, fixed the communication and received the fourth-rank St. George's Cross. (Subsequently, for a similar action, he was decorated with a third-class cross and later promoted to junior artillery NCO).[77]

While chroniclers noted Jewish soldiers' strange behavior before and during action, one wonders whether the commanders' impressions before battle may have been colored by antisemitic propaganda, whereas their attitude after combat was informed by their eyewitness experience.

If assimilation by means of conscription was intended to foster loyalty, to impart military technique, and to create devoted citizens, these goals largely were achieved for the Jews. The anti-Jewish campaign imposed upon the military did not prevent middle-ranking commanders from seeing Jewish conscripts as well trained and loyal, hopeful of becoming full-fledged citizens of their fatherland. The regime itself was to blame for having replaced its vaunted "military-based citizen-building process" with a system of increasing Jewish segregation.[78]

The Militant Jew

The wholehearted Jewish support of Russia's military cause rendered segregation in the Pale of Settlement particularly painful. That Jews who chose to fight and to die for their fatherland were not permitted to settle freely beyond the fifteen overcrowded western provinces was an outrage to the Jews in the trenches, to the liberals in the Duma, and to the military journalists at the front. The brutal and haphazard wartime deportation of Jews did not entirely solve the problem posed by the Pale; Jewish military performance made emancipation a burning issue. Russian Jewish public opinion demanded radical change. It was clear to Jews in Poland and Russia that military veterans would enjoy residential and employment equality. Count Eugene Trubetskoi argued that "Russia should prove that she is a mother rather than a stepmother to all the nationalities and ethnicities that she comprises. This is important not only to the aliens but, above all, for her own salvation, wellbeing, and greatness."[79]

The military experience established a new perception among Russian Jewish soldiers, who felt themselves de facto Russian citizens by the time the February 1917 Revolution changed their status de jure. As soon as the Provisional Government abolished all legal restrictions against Jews, opened the Pale of Settlement, and offered, among other things, access to military schools, thousands of Jewish volunteers took advantage of the unprecedented privilege.

---

[77] V. Milodanovich, "Polevoi zhid i ego kollegi," *Voennaia byl*, no. 93 (1968): 9–14.

[78] Among similar cases of ethnic segregation, the Russian model seems rather extreme. According to a historian of Austrian Jewry, the interaction during the war "did not lead to a further integration of Jews into Austrian society." See Rozenblit, *Reconstructing a National Identity*, 82.

[79] *Voina i evrei*, no. 1 (1914): 2.

Deputy Fridman promised the State Duma members that, should the government introduce true civil equality, Russia could expect to harvest a rich crop of Jewish patriots. The previously suppressed and neglected Jews cast off their humiliating restraints and rushed to enroll for military service. By the end of August 1917, Jews comprised 50 to 60 percent of the students in military schools in Kiev and Odessa. In June 1917, some 131 Jewish students in the Constantine Military School, Kiev, obtained officer rank. By late summer, some 160 Jewish students received officer rank in Odessa military schools. In Moscow and St. Petersburg, Jews formed several officers' brigades, which received new shoulder-straps bearing the Golden Star of David. The Petrograd-based Union of Zionist Soldiers developed plans for special units in the Caucasus army, to participate in the liberation of Palestine. (They later created self-defense detachments on their bases.) Trumpeldor arrived to assist in bringing these plans to fruition; apparently they were discussed in the War Ministry.[80]

Historian Mark Von Hagen maintains that World War I militarized the empire's nationalities, creating "the rise of a mass movement for nationalization of the military during 1917."[81] This was as true for Jews as for other nationalities in the Russian empire. Underestimated as soldiers before 1917, Jews became a significantly overrepresented minority group among officers in the Red Army after 1917, as if trying to compensate for one hundred years of exclusion.[82] The nationalization of the military eventually triggered the militarization of the national minority. At a time when desertion on the western front during World War I reached epidemic proportions, a group of young Jewish boys from Mogilev province wrote enthusiastic letters to the Jewish detachment of the British army founded by Ze'ev Jabotinsky and Yosef Trumpeldor and placed under the command of Colonel Patterson: "We are ready to join your struggle at any minute." The militarization of the Jewish mentality made some rabbinic leaders such as Rabbi Yitzhak Yaakov Reines look at Jews not only as the People of the Book but also as the People of the Sword.[83] The experience of World War I taught violence to the Jew as it did to the Russian soldier.[84] The Jewish spirit of readiness for military action

[80] Mikhail Beizer, *Evrei Leningrada: 1917–1939. Natsional'naia zhizn' i sovetizatsia* (M., Jerusalem: Mosty kultury; Gesharim, 1999), 47–48.
[81] Mark Von Hagen, "The Limits of Reform: The Multiethnic Imperial Army Confronts Nationalism, 1874–1917," in David Schimmelpenninck van der Oye and Bruce Menning, eds., *Reforming the Tsar's Army*, 34–55, here 55.
[82] See Arthur Ruppin, *The Jews in the Modern World* (London: Macmillan, 1934), 224. Cf.: F. D. Sverdlov, *Evrei-generaly vooruzhennykh sil SSSR: kratkie biografii* (M.: n. p., 1993).
[83] See Elie Holzer, "The Use of Military Force in the Religious Zionist Ideology of Rabbi Yitzhak Ya'akov Reines and His Successors," in Peter Y. Medding, ed., *Jews and Violence: Studies in Contemporary Jewry. An Annual*, XVIII (New York: Oxford University Press, 2002), 74–94.
[84] See O. S. Porshneva, "Mental'nyi oblik i sotsial'noe povedenie soldat russkoi armii v usloviiakh pervoi mirovoi voiny (1914-fevral' 1917 gg.)," in *Voenno-istoricheskaia antropologiia. Ezhegodnik. 2002* (M.: ROSSPEN, 2002), 252–267, here 260–264.

ILLUSTRATION 11. Nikolai Trotsky (a revolutionary pseudonym), a Jewish sailor, December 1917. Courtesy of the Judaica Institute of Ukraine.

transformed the experience acquired in the Russian army into a tool for implementing Zionist and socialist endeavors.[85] The Russian army had taught politically engaged Jews that modernization was inseparable from military

[85] For the spread of the Zionist ideology in the postrevolutionary Russian army and the formation of the units of Zionist-minded soldiers, see RGVIA, f. 2049, op. 1, d. 35 ("Delo o evreiakh-sionistakh"); GARF, f. 579, op. 1, d. 2038 ("Stat'ia o sozdanii evreiskoi armii dlia osvobozhdenia Palestiny, 1917 g."); for the appeals of the Zionists to the Jewish soldiers in the army and attempts to monitor their activities, see RGVIA, f. 3596, op. 1, d. 18 ("Delo 4-go mariupol'skogo polka," 1918), ll. 97–99.

craft. The founders of the *Haganah*, which later became the Israeli Defense Force, were predominantly Russian Jews, some of whom had fought in the Russo-Japanese War and in World War I.[86] After a century of militarization of the Jews, those Russian Jews who joined either Marxists or Zionists finally sought to claim the military as their own.

Conclusion

In the years following the 1905 Russian Revolution, the newly established nationalist parties, contaminated with racial and political antisemitism, suggested ridding the Russian army of what they considered its most harmful element: the Jews. Russian nationalists agitated aggressively among the troops and exerted pressure on the War Ministry, trying to prove at any cost that Jews were incompatible with the army. They brought their discourse on Jewish military service into the fulcrum of the Duma debates, as if the alleged anti-patriotism of Russian Jews was one of the key questions of national security. Russian nationalists also managed to inculcate the military with the most vicious Judeophobia. But although they were supported by the highest officials, top generals, and the tsar, Jews remained in the military service until the end of the Old Regime. Albeit the 1912 statute legitimized all anti-Jewish restrictions and regulations approved since the 1880s, military officials ruled out the nationalists' proposal solely on pragmatic grounds: not because of their philosemitic stance, but because the imperial vision of a multiethnic army superseded the nationalist, ethnically pure version. Whatever proof the nationalists could show for their case, Jews were regarded as one of the integral constituencies of the imperial army and could not be dismissed from it. Yet there was a bitter irony in that the Russian military discussed the expulsion of Jews from the troops, while even Germany – following Italy, France, and Austria – had finally endorsed upward mobility for Jewish soldiers, opening military careers for them.

Nationalist paranoia could not check the wave of Russian Jewish patriotism during World War I. Jews accepted the wartime draft as yet another state duty they would have to fulfill with dignity. While top military authorities blamed the Jews for campaign failures and expelled Jewish civilians from Russia's western front, Jews fought in the trenches on a par with Russian soldiers, were distinguished for their performance, and particularly excelled as artillerymen, telegraphists, and scouts. That Jews were awarded highest soldiers' awards testified that the best among them were as good as the best among Russian soldiers and that the immediate commanders of the units where Jews served, unlike top army officials, were much less contaminated with Judeophobia. Their reports, contradicting the intent of the biased questionnaires, portrayed

[86] Z. Schiff, *A History of the Israeli Army, 1874 to the Present* (New York: Macmillan, 1985), 3–7.

Jews as obedient, disciplined, and resourceful soldiers with only one peculiar feature worth mentioning: normalcy.

The increasing segregation of Jewish soldiers failed to prevent the emergence of a Russian Jewish citizen; in the army, as nowhere else, Jews swiftly realized the connection between their sacred duty to the state and the state's duty to grant them civil equality. Jews shared similar expectations with other ethnic minorities in belligerent armies: they hoped that the end of the war would bring them a long-sought-for emancipation, which they, now patriotic and selfless soldiers, fully deserved.

Conclusion

The army performed a pivotal role in the integration and acculturation of East European Jews. The 1827 law on Jewish conscription pursued a goal expressed by enlightened monarchs elsewhere in Europe: to "improve" the Jews through their enforced military service. Yet Nicholas I's plans to transform this purportedly alien and harmful population into loyal and useful subjects brought unexpected results: more than any other imperial policy, and long before the educational reforms, enlistment made East European Jews into Russian Jews.

As elsewhere in Europe, military duty in Russia signified a threefold transformation of the Jews. Firstly, joining the military was tantamount to what Jacob Katz described as coming "out of the ghetto"; the army integrated Jews into gentile society and radically changed their ghettoized perceptions. Secondly, whether in France, Russia, or Austria, the presence of numerous Jewish soldiers altered the larger society's conception of Jews. Thirdly, by reshaping Jewish perspectives on the values and patterns of their society of origin, the army served as a catalyst for the genesis of Jewry as a modern nation.

The goal of the imperial project was to turn Jewish soldiers into loyal subjects despite the state administration's requirement that the military treat them as disloyal aliens. The military did not necessarily and not always acquiesce to the monarch's demands. Jews were not inept cowards languishing in the rearguard; nor was the Russian army a blatantly antisemitic institution whose only intent was to alienate Jews from their faith or to orchestrate pogroms. In as multilayered a society as imperial Russia, the Jewish military experience served as one, but not the only, model of modernization. No doubt, future historians of East European Jewry will compare this model and integrate it with others, such as modernization through education or politics. At present, students of Jewish and of Russian history do not appear to have a theoretical framework to accomplish this task. Not all of the five million East European Jews served in the Russian military, and the army was not synonymous with the Russian state at large, although some contemporary Russian romantic poets would like one to think otherwise.

Like the Russian peasants, Jews initially resented the draft, and bemoaned having to send their sons, believing them consigned to an unknown and miserable fate. Yet, despite their being less prepared for military service than their Russian Orthodox counterparts, Jews endured the army's hardships surprisingly well. Both adults and minors proved competent soldiers, meeting the army's expectations of training, behavior, and performance. Some were indispensable as military artisans, while the majority saw active service in the infantry and artillery. Jews excelled on the battlefront, fighting as bravely as their Russian fellows. Their immediate commanders, particularly the combat officers, considered Jews disciplined, literate, and resourceful soldiers: genuine assets. On the contrary, the high-ranking commanders who had never dealt with Jewish soldiers more often than not shared anti-Jewish bias and kowtowed to rabid antisemitism.

Accommodated in the military as a distinct religious group, Jewish soldiers developed dual loyalties: toward traditional Jewish values, and toward the Russian army and state. Theirs was a dual identity. They emerged from the army as robust, strong-willed, reliable, Russian-speaking individuals, who, like modernized Jews in Western Europe, considered Judaism a religion rather than the way of life. Before the 1880s, Jewish soldiers were permitted to establish themselves outside the Pale of Settlement, in interior Russia. Thus, the army provided benefits to Jewish soldiers that enlightened Jews had sought to attain through progressive education for every Jew in the Pale of Settlement.

The army made Jews equal with the rest of the population in respect of state duties, not civil rights. The fact that Jews were not allowed upward mobility in the military was a result of the regime's bias rather than of poor performance or of antisemitism in the War Ministry. While, in practice, the army failed to grant Jews equality before the law, a Jew was generally no worse off than a simple Russian soldier, a peasant, or a factory-worker. The conditions of Jewish conscription and military service became a focus of the struggle for emancipation and equality. The army taught Jews the importance of equal duties. Jewish heroism on the front lines during World War I showed that most Jewish soldiers shared a patriotic, imperial vision. Before Russia extended their citizenship to them de jure, Jews serving in the army already had construed themselves to be de facto Russian soldiers of the Mosaic faith, aware of their shared Russian fate and values. The conscription of East European Jews thus became a historical crucible, producing the integrated, acculturated, modernized Jew aware of his nonemancipated status, particularly acute in the army. Jewish soldiers shared this awareness with the rest of Russian soldiers and with the majority population of Russia – modernized, culturally integrated, but not legally emancipated.

Bibliography

Archival Sources and Collections

Russian State Military Historical Archive *(Rossiiskii gosudarstvennyi voenno-isto-richeskii arkhiv*, Moscow, Russia)
  Fond 1– Chancellery of the War Ministry
  Fond 278 – P. S. Vannovskii
  Fond 324 – Department of Military Schools
  Fond 395 – Inspectors' Department
  Fond 400 – Main Staff
  Fond 405 – Department of Military Settlements
  Fond 485 – Department of Military Supply
  Fond 801 – Department of Military Courts
  Fond 846 – Military Research Archive
  Fond 970 – Odessa Military District
  Fond 1769 – Kiev Military District Attorney
  Fond 1872 – Chancellery of Warsaw District Military Court Prosecutor
  Fond 1964 – Military Court of Vilna District
  Fond 1965 – Chancellery of Vilna District Military Court Prosecutor
  Fond 2049 – Chancellery of the Head of Supply of the Western Front Armies
  Fond 2113 – Headquarters of the Third Army
  Fond 2134 – Headquarters of the Eighth Army
  Fond 2641 – Vitebsk infantry regiment (27th)
  Fond 2649 – Briansk infantry regiment (35th)
  Fond 12651 – Central Office of the Russian Red Cross
  Fond 13251 – Central Military Industry Committee
State Archive of the Russian Federation (*Gosudarstvennyi Arkhiv Rossiiskoi Federatsii*, Moscow, Russia)
  Fond 109 – Third Department of His Majesty's Chancellery
  Fond 579 – P. N. Miliukov
  Fond 728 – Winter Palace
  Fond 2271 – Nicholas I
  Fond 9458 – M. Kh. Bomash
  Fond P-9534 – A. S. Katsnelson

Russian State Archive of the Navy (*Rossiiskii gosudarstvennyi arkhiv voenno-mors-kogo flota*, St. Petersburg, Russia)
  Fond 33 – Navy General Supervisor of the Military Courts
  Fond 170 – Chancellery of the Navy Minister
  Fond 256 – Office of the Astrakhan Port
  Fond 283 – Inspectors' Department of the Navy Ministry
  Fond 410 – Chancellery of the Navy Ministry
  Fond 627 – Headquarters of the Third Division of the Baltic Fleet
  Fond 968 – Office of the Northern District of the Navy Construction
Russian State Historical Archive (*Rossiiskii gosudarstvennyi istorichockii arkhiv*, St. Petersburg, Russia)
  Fond 560 – Chancellery of the Ministry of Finance
  Fond 796 – Chancellery of the Holy Synod
  Fond 821 – Ministry of the Interior, Department of Spiritual Affairs of Foreign Creeds
  Fond 822 – Roman Catholic Collegium of the Ministry of the Interior
Russian State Museum of Ethnography (*Russkii gosudarstvennyi muzei etnografii*, St. Petersburg, Russia)
  Fond 2 – S. Ansky Collection
Central State Historical Archive of Ukraine (*Tsentral'nyi derzhavnyi istorychnyi arkhiv Ukrainy*, Kyiv, Ukraine)
  Fond 442 – Chancellery of Kiev, Podol, and Volhynia Governor General
  Fond 533 – Kiev Governor General
State Archive of Vinnitsa District (*Derzhavnyi arkhiv Vinnyts'koi oblasti*, Vinnytsia, Ukraine)
  Fond 222 – Litin District Court
  Fond 391 – Vinnitsa State Magistrate
  Fond 468 – Lypovets Lower Zemskii Court
  Fond 471 – Gaisin District Court
  Fond 472 – Mogilev-Podols'k District Court
  Fond 473 – Bratslav District Court
  Fond 475 – Mogilev-Podols'k City Magistrate
Central Archive of Old Documents (*Archiwum Główne Akt Dawnych*, Warsaw, Poland)
  Zb. I Rada Stanu Królestwa Polskiego
  Zb. Sekretariat Stanu Królestwa Polskiego
  Zb. Kancelaria Senatora Nowosilcowa
  Zb. Policja Tajna w. kn. Konstantego
State Archive in Lublin (*Archiwum Państwowe w Lublinie*, Lublin, Poland)
  Fond 136 – Prefektury Departamentów: Lubelskiego i Siedleckiego, Dyrekcje Skarbu
  Fond 109 – Chełmski Zarząd Duchowny (Helm Office of Spiritual Affairs)
Central Archive of the History of the Jewish People (Jerusalem, Israel)

Newspapers and Periodicals

Armiia
Den
Der Yiddisher Arbeter

Evreiskaia biblioteka
Evreiskaia starina
Evreiskii mir
Evreiskii vestnik
Golos
Golos soldata
Grazhdanin
Ha-Karmel
Ha-Magid
Ha-Melits
Ha-Tsefirah
Istoricheskii vestnik
Kazarma
Khroniki Voskhoda
Kievlianin
Minskaia kopeika
Mogilevskie gubernskie vedomosti
Moskovskie vedomosti
Novoe vremia
Novorossiiskii telegraf
Otechestvennye zapiski
Poslednie izvestiia
Pravitel'stvennyi vestnik
Proletarii
Rassvet
Razvedchik
Russkaia starina
Russkii arkhiv
Russkii evrei
Russkii invalid
Russkii vestnik
Russkoe chtenie
Sankt-Peterburgskie vedomosti
Soldatskaia beseda
Soldatskaia gazeta
Soldatskaia zhizn
Soldatskii listok
Varshavskii dnevnik
Vestnik Soiuza Russkogo Naroda
Voennaia byl
Voenno-meditsinskii zhurnal
Voenno-statisticheskii sbornik
Voennyi listok
Voennyi sbornik
Voskhod
Zaria
Znamia

Dissertations and Theses

Geifman, Anna. "Political Parties and Revolutionary Terrorism in Russia." Ph.D. diss., Harvard University, 1990.

Kipp, Jacob. "The Grand Duke Konstantin Nikolaevich and the Epoch of the Great Reforms, 1855–1866." Ph.D. diss., Pennsylvania State University, 1970.

Kraız, Samuil. "Batei-sefer ha-yehudiim be-safah ha-rusit be-rusia ha-tsarit." Ph.D. diss., Hebrew University, 1994

Mendelovits, Yosef. "Ne'arim yehudim be-mosdot tsava rusi, 1827–1856." M.A. thesis. Jerusalem: Touro College, 2001.

Sanders, Joseph. "The Moscow Uprising of December 1905: A Background Study." Ph.D. diss., University of Washington, 1981.

Taylor, Jackson Jr. "Dmitrii Andreevich Tolstoi and the Ministry of the Interior, 1882–1889." Ph.D. diss., New York University, 1970.

Thumim, A. D. "In the Spirit of the Government: Faddei Bulgarin and the Formation of the Middle Class in Russia, 1789–1859." Ph.D. diss., Harvard University, 1995.

Wcislo, Francis W. "Bureaucratic Reform in Tsarist Russia: State and Society, 1881–1914." Ph.D. diss., Columbia University, 1984.

Weeks, Richard G. "Peter Andreevich Shuvalov: Russian Statesman." Ph.D. diss., University of Minnesota, 1977.

Bibliographies and Archival Guides

Altshuler, Mordechai, Pinkus, Benjamin, and Greenbaum, Alfred Abraham, eds. *Russian Publications on Jews and Judaism in the Soviet Union, 1917–1967: A Bibliography.* Jerusalem: Society for Research on Jewish Communities, 1970.

Archiwum Główne Akt Dawnych. Przewodnik po zasobie. 2 vols. Warsaw: DiG, 1998.

Greenbaum, Alfred Abraham. *The Periodical Publications of the Jewish Labour and Revolutionary Movements in Eastern and Southeastern Europe, 1877–1916: An Annotated Bibliography.* Jerusalem: Ben Zion Dinur Center, 1998.

Hundert, Gershon D., and Gershon C. Bacon. *The Jews in Poland and Russia: Bibliographical Essays.* Bloomington: Indiana University Press, 1984.

Kelner, V. E., Eliashevich, D. A., eds. *Literatura o evreiakh na russkom iazyke, 1890–1947: knigi, broshiury, ottiski statei, organy periodicheskoi pechati: bibliograficheskii ukazatel'.* SPb.: Akademicheskii proekt, 1995.

Lyons, M. *The Russian Imperial Army. A Bibliography of Regimental Histories and Related Works.* Stanford, Calif.: Stanford University Press, 1968.

Raskin D., Sukhanova, O. *Fondy rossiiskogo gosudarstvennogo istoricheskogo arkhiva.* SPb.: RGIA, 1994.

Russkaia voennaia periodicheskaia pechat', 1702–1916: bibliograficheskii ukazatel'. M.: Gosudarstvennaia Biblioteka im. V. I. Lenina, 1959.

Sistematicheskii ukazatel' literatury o evreiakh na russkom iazyke so vremeni vvedeniia grazhdanskago shrifta (1708 g.) po dekabr' 1889 g. SPb.: A. Landau, 1892.

Vasiliev, A. A. *Obzor dokumental'nykh istochnikov po istorii evreev v Fondakh RGVIA.* Evreiskii Arkhiv. Vyp. 2. M.: Jewish Heritage Society, 1995.

Zaionchkovskii, P. A., ed. *Spravochniki po istorii dorevoliutsionnoi Rossii: Bibliograficheskii ukazatel'.* Compiled by G. A. Glavatskikh et al. M.: Kniga, 1971–1978.

Encyclopedias

Encyclopedia Judaica. 16 vols. Jerusalem: Encyclopedia Judaica; New York: Macmillan, 1972.

Evreiskaia entsiklopediia: svod znanii o evreistvie i ego kul'turie v proshlom i nastoiashchem. 16 vols. SPb.: Izd. Ob-va dlia nauchnykh evreiskikh izdanii i Izd-va Brokgauz-Efron, 1906–1913.

Krasnov V. *Russkii voenno-istoricheskii slovar'*. M.: OLMA-Press, 2001.

Politicheskie partii Rossii. Konets XIX–pervaia tret' XX v. Entsiklopedia. Edited by V. V. Shelokaev. M.: ROSSPEN, 1996.

Voennaia entsiklopediia. Edited by V. F. Novitskii. 18 vols. Pb.: 1911–1915.

Published Documents

Anarkhisty: dokumenty i materialy, 1883–1935. 2 vols. Edited by V. V. Kriven'kii. M.: ROSSPEN, 1998.

Gosudarstvennaia Duma. Stenograficheskie otchety. Sessiia 1. SPb.: Gosudarstvennaia tipografiia, 1906.

Gosudartsvennaia Duma. Stenograficheskie otchety. Sessiia II. SPb.: Gosudarstvennaia tipografiia, 1907.

Gosudarstvennaia Duma, Stenograficheskie otchety, III Sozyv. SPb.: Gosudarstvennaia tipografiia, 1911.

Gosudarstvennaia Duma. Stenograficheskie otchety. III Sozyv. SPb.: Gosudarstvennaia tipografiia, 1912.

Gosudartsvennaia Duma. Stenograficheskie otchety. IV Sozyv. SPb.: Gosudarstvennaia tipografiia, 1914.

Khristoliubivoe voinstvo. Pravoslavnaia traditsiia Russkoi Armii. Edited by A. Savinkin. M.: Voennyi universitet, Russkii put', 1997.

Listovki bolshevistskikh organizatsii v pervoi russkoi revolutsii 1905–1907. 3 vols. M.: Politicheskaia literatura, 1956.

Mensheviki: dokumenty i materialy, 1903-fevral 1917 gg. Edited by S. V. Tiutiukin. M.: ROSSPEN, 1996.

1905. Bolshevistskie proklamatsii i listovki po Moskve i Moskovskoi gubernii. Edited by M. M. Pokrovskii. L.: Gosudarstvennoe izdatelstvo, 1926.

Partiia sotsialistov-revoliutsionerov: dokumenty i materialy. Edited by N. D. Erofeev. M.: ROSSPEN, 1996.

Pervaia konferentsia voennykh i boevykh organizatsii RSDRP. Edited by E. Iaroslavskii. M.: Partizdat, 1932.

Polnoe sobranie zakonov Rossiiskoi imperii: sobranie pervoe; sobranie vtoroe; sobranie tret'e. SPb.: Tip. II otdelenia E. I. V. Kantseliarii, 1830–1916.

Pravye partii: dokumenty i materialy, 1905–1917. 2 vols. Edited by Iu. I. Kirianov. M.: ROSSPEN, 1998.

Protokoly pervogo s'ezda Partii sotsialistov-revoliutsionerov. Edited by M. Perrie. Millwood, N. Y.: Kraus, 1983.

Rasporiazheniia Pravitelstvuiushchego Senata. SPb., n.d.

Rukovodstvennye dlia pravoslavnogo dukhovenstva ukazy Sviateishego pravitel'stvuiushchego Sinoda. 1721–1878. M.: Tip. M. Lavrova, 1879.

Stoletie voennogo ministerstva. 13 vols. SPb.: Glavnyi shtab, 1902–1912.

Ubiistvo Stolypina. Svidetel'stva i dokumenty. Edited by A. Serebrennikov. New York: Telex, 1991.
Ulozheniia o nakazaniiakh ugolovnykh i ispravitel'nykh. SPb.: E. I. V. Kantseliariia, 1845.
Ustav o voinskoi povinnosti, so vsemi dopolneniiami i raziasneniiami, posledovavshimi so vremen obnarodovaniia ego. SPb.: Gogenfelden, 1875.
Ustav o voinskoi povinnosti. 4 vols. SPb.: Gosudarstvennaia tipografiia, 1886.
Ustav o polevoi sluzhbe. Voinskii ustav o pekhotnoi sluzhbe. SPb.: Voennaia tipografiia, 1846.
Vidok Figliarin. Pis'ma i agenturnye zapiski F. V. Bulgarina v III-e otdelenie. Edited by A. I. Reitblat. M.: Novoe literaturnoe obozrenie, 1998.
Voenno-statisticheskii sbornik. 4 vols. SPb.: Glavnyi shtab, 1869–1871.
Voinskii ustav o pekhotnoi sluzhbe. SPb.: Voennaia tipografiia, 1836.
Writing Home: Immigrants in Brazil and the United States, 1890–1891. Edited by Witold Kula et al. Boulder, Colo.: East European Monographs; New York: distributed by Columbia University Press, 1986.
Zhurnal Vysochaishe utverzhdennoi komissii dlia rassmotreniia proekta voinskogo ustava o nakazaniiakh. SPb.: Gosudarstvennaia tipografiia, 1865.

Russian Legislation on Jews

Fride, I. E. *Zakony o pravie zhitel'stva evreev v cherte ikh osedlosti i vne onoi.* SPb.: n.p., 1909.
Gessen, I. V., Fridstein I. *Sbornik zakonov o evreiakh: s raz'iasneniiami po opredieleniiam Pravitel'stvuiushchago Senata.* SPb.: Iuridicheskii knizhnyi magazin Martynova, 1904.
Gimpelson, Ia. I., and L. M. Bramson, eds. *Zakony o evreiakh. Sistematicheskii obzor deistvuiushchikh zakonopolozhenii o evreiakh s raz'iasneniiami pravitel'stvuiushchego Senata i tsentral'nykh pravitel'stvennykh ustanovlenii.* SPb.: Iurisprudentsiia, 1914.
Levanda, V. O. *Polnyi khronologicheskii sbornik zakonov i polozhenii kasaiushchikhsia Evreev, ot ulozheniia Tsaria Aleksieia Mikhailovicha do nastoiashchago vremeni, ot 1649–1873 g.* SPb.: K. V. Trubnikov, 1874.
Mysh, M. I. *Rukovodstvo k russkim zakonam o evreiakh.* Izd. 3-e, peresmotrennoe i znachitelno dopolnennoe. SPb.: M. P. Frolov, 1904.
Mysh, M. I. *Rukovodstvo k russkim zakonam o evreiakh: dopolnenie; uzakoneniia i senatskiie raz'iasneniia za 1903–1909 gody.* SPb.: n.p., 1910.
Orshanskii, I. G. *Russkoe zakonodatelstvo o evreiakh: ocherki i issledovaniia.* SPb.: Landau, 1877.
Pozner, S. V. *Evrei v obshchei shkole: K istorii zakonodatelstva i pravitelstvennoi politiki v oblasti evreiskago voprosa.* SPb.: Razum, 1914.
Rogovin, L. *Sistematicheskii sbornik deistvuiushchikh zakonov o evreiakh: po Svodu Zakonov, Prodolzheniiam 1906, 1908, 1909 i 1910 gg. i Sobraniiu Uzakonenii 1911, 1912 i 1913 gg. (po 1 iiunia).* SPb.: n.p., 1913.
Sbornik reshenii ravvinskoi kommisii sozyva 1910 goda. SPb.: Ministerstvo vnutrennikh del, 1912.
Vainshtein, E. V. *Deistvuiushchee zakonodatelstvo o evreiakh: po svodu zakonov s Raz'iasneniiami.* Kiev: Radomysl, 1911.

Vashkevich, V. V. *Sbornik uzakonenii, kasaiushchikhsia evreev*. SPb.: n.p., 1884.
Vetlugin, G. M. *Polnaia spravochnaia kniga o pravakh evreev s raz'iasneniiami, opredeleniiami i resheniiami Pravitel'stvuiushchego Senata*. SPb.: E. M. Nikitenko, 1913.

Memoirs and Diaries

Alekseeva-Borel, V. *Sorok let v riadakh russkoi imperatorskoi armii: general M. P. Alekseev*. SPb.: Belveder, 2000.
Ansky, S. *The Enemy at His Pleasure. A Journey through the Jewish Pale of Settlement During World War I*. Edited and translated by Joachim Neugroshcel. New York: Metropolitan Books, 2003.
Beilin, S. "Vospominaniia o poslednikh godakh rekrutchiny," *Evreiskaia starina*, no. 2 (1909): 115–120; 3–4 (1914): 458–464.
Belov, V. *Evrei i poliaki na voine. Rasskaz ofitsera-uchastnika*. Pb.: Biblioteka Velikoi Voiny, 1915.
Boborykin, P. D. *Vospominaniia*. 2 vols. M.: Khudozhestvennaia literatura, 1965.
Broiakosvkii, S. *Voina chetyrnadtsatogo goda (po rasskazam uchastnikov i ochevidtsev)*. Kiev: Dukhovnaia beseda, 1915.
Brusilov, A. A. *Moi vospominaniia*. M.: Voennoe izdatelstvo Minoborony SSSR, 1963.
Bulgarin, F. *Memuary: otryvki iz vidennogo, slyshannogo i perezhitogo*. 2 vols. SPb.: M. D. Olkhin, 1846–1849.
Dubnow, S. *Kniga zhizni; vospominaniia i razmyshleniia*. Riga: Jaunatnes Gramata, New York: Soiuz Russkikh Evreev, 1934–1957.
Epanchin, N. A. *Na sluzhbe trekh imperatorov: vospominaniia*. M.: Nashe nasledie, 1996.
Fedorchenko, S. *Narod na voine*. M.: Sovetskii pisatel, 1990.
Ginsburg, S. *Minuvshee*. Pg.: Izd. avtora, 1923.
Grulev, M. *Zapiski generala-evreia*. Paris: Izd. avtora, 1930.
Gruzenberg, O. O. *Vchera: Vospominaniia*. Paris: Izd. avtora, 1938.
Itskovich, I. "Vospominaniia arkhangelskogo kantonista," *Evreiskaia starina*, no. 1 (1912): 54–65.
Kelsiev, V. *Perezhitoe i peredumannoe: Vospominaniia*. SPb.: Golovin, 1868.
[Kotik, Yekhezkel]. *Journey to a Nineteenth-Century Shtetl: the memoirs of Yekhezkel Kotik*. Edited. by David Assaf. Translated by Margaret Birstein. Detroit: Wayne State University Press in cooperation with the Diaspora Research Institute, Tel Aviv University, 2002.
Kretchmer, M. A. "Vospominania," *Istoricheskii vestnik*, no. 3 (1–3) (1888): 631–653; no. 32 (4–6) (1888): 125–141, 361–380.
Ksiunin, A. *Narod na voine (Iz zapisok voennogo korrespondenta)*. Pg.: Suvorin, 1916.
Lamsdorf, V. N. *Dnevnik. 1891–1892*. Ed. by F. Rotshtein. M., L.: Academia, 1934.
Lemke, M. *250 dnei v tsarskoi Stavke*. Petrograd: Gosudarstvennoe izdatel'stvo, 1920.
Levin, K. *Zapiski iz plena*. M.: Federatsiia, 1931.
Librovich, S. F. *Na knizhnom postu: Vospominaniia. Zapiski. Dokumenty*. SPb., M.: Volf, 1916.
Martynov, E. I. *Vospominaniia o iaponskoi voine komandira pekhotnogo polka*. Plotsk: Gubernskoe pravlenie, 1910.

Merimzon, M. "Rasskaz starogo soldata," *Evreiskaia starina*, no. 3 (1912): 290–301; no. 4 (1912): 406–422; no. 6 (1913): 86–95; no. 11 (1913): 221–232.

Mikhail Dmitrievich Skobelev: slovo Belogo generala, slovo sovremennikov, slovo potomkov. Sost. S. N. Semanov. M.: Russkii mir, 2000.

[Miliutin, D. A.]. *Dnevnik Miliutina*. Edited by P. A. Zaionchkovskii. 4 vols. M.: Gosudarstvennaia Biblioteka imeni Lenina, 1949.

Nemirovich-Danchenko, V. I. *God voiny: dnevnik voennogo korrespondenta*. 2 vols. SPb.: Suikin, 1878.

Ostrover, L. V *seroi shineli. Zapiski polkovogo vracha*. M., L.: Gosudarstvennoe izdatel'stvo, 1926.

[Peretts, E. A.]. *Dnevnik Perettsa*. M.: Gosudarstvennoe izdatel'stvo, 1927.

Polivanov, A. A. *Iz dnevnikov i vospominanii po dolzhnosti voennogo ministra i ego pomoshchnika*. 2 vols. M.: Vysshii voennyi redaktsionnyi sovet, 1924.

[Polovtsov, A. A.]. *Dnevnik gosudarstvennogo sekretaria Polovtsova*. 2 vols. M.: Nauka, 1966.

Rediger, A. *Vospominaniia voennogo ministra*. 2 vols. M.: Kanon-Press, Kuchkovo pole, 1999.

Rusanov, I. S. *Iz moikh vospominanii*. M.: Grzhebin, 1923.

Sabsay, Nahum. *A Moment of History: A Russian Soldier in the First World War*. Caldwell, Iowa: privately printed, 1960.

Serebrianskii, M. *Dnevnik polkovogo sviashchennika, sluzhashchego na Dal'nem Vostoke*. M.: Otchii Dom, 1996.

Sergeevskii, B. N. *Perezhitoe*. Belgrade: n.p., 1933.

Shavel'skii, G. *Vospominaniia poslednego protopresvitera russkoi armii i flota*. 2 vols. New York: Izd. im. Chekhova, 1954.

Shchit: literaturnyi sbornik. Edited By Maxim Gorky and Leonid Andreev. Izd. 3., dop. M.: Russkoe obshchestvo dlia izucheniia evreiskoi zhizni, 1916.

Shpigel, M. "Iz zapisok kantonista," *Evreiskaia starina*, no. 1 (1911): 249–259.

Sliozberg, G. B. *Baron G. O. Gintsburg. Ego zhizn' i deiatelnost'*. Paris: Pascal, 1933.

Sliozberg, G. B. *Dela davno minuvshikh dnei. Zapiski russkogo evreia*. 3 vols. Paris: Izd. avtora, 1933.

Sobolev, S. "Russko-Turetskaia voina v Bolgarii," *Russkaia starina*, vol. 54, no. 6 (1887): 761–84; vol. 55, no. 7 (1887): 183–202; no. 8 (1887): 339–376.

Stepun, F. (N. Lugin). *Iz pisem praporshchika-artillerista*. Tomsk: Vodolei, 2000.

[Sukhomlinov, V. A.]. *Vospominaniia Sukhomlinova*. Preface by V. Nevskii. M., L.: Gosudarstvennoe izdatelstvo, 1926.

Tonkonogov, I. *Epizody voiny. Sbornik rasskazov uchastnikov voiny i korrespondentov razlichnykh periodicheskikh izdanii*. Pg.: Imperatorskaia Voennaia Academia, 1916.

Tornau, F. F. *Vospominaniia russkogo ofitsera*. M.: AIRO-XX, 2002.

Verkhovskii, A. I. *Rossiia na Golgofe (iz pokhodnogo dnevnika 1914–1918 g.)*. Pg.: Delo naroda, 1918.

Vertsinskii, E. A. *Iz mirovoi voiny: boevye zapisi i vospominaniia komandira polka i ofitsera Generalnogo Shtaba za 1914–1917 gody*. Tallinn-Revel: Soiuz Tsarsko-selskikh strelkov, 1931.

Vevern, B. V. *6-ia batareia 1914–1917 gg. Povest o vremeni velikogo sluzhenia Rodine*. Paris: n.p., 1938.

Vitte, S. Iu. *Vospominaniia*. 3 vols. M.: Izd. sotsialno-ekonomicheskoi literatury, 1960.

V ogne. Boevye vpechatleniia uchastnikov voiny. Pg.: Gramotnost', 1914.

[Zotov, P. D.]. "Zapiski generala ot infanterii P. Zotova. Voina za nezavisimost' slavian 1877–1878," *Russkaia starina*, vol. 49, no. 1 (1886): 213–240; vol. 49, no. 2 (1886): 425–450.

Primary Sources: Books and Articles

Afanasiev, V. "Distsiplinarnye bataliony i roty," *Voennyi sbornik*, no. 7 (1890): 116–120.

Agapiev, P. "Mundirnaia odezhda v polkovom khoziaistve," *Voennyi sbornik*, no. 5 (1891): 168–183.

Akhun, M. I. *Bol'sheviki i armiia v 1905–1917 gg. Voennaia organizatsiia pri Peterburgskom komitete RSDRP(b) i revoliutsionnoe dvizhenie v voiskakh Peterburga.* L.: Krasnaia gazeta, 1929.

Akhun, M. I., and V. A. Petrov. *Bolsheviki i armiia v 1905–1907 gg.* L.: Krasnaia gazeta, 1929.

Anon. "Piat' mesiatsev na Shipke v 1877 godu. Iz vospominanii ofitsera Podol'skogo pekhotnogo polka," *Voennyi sbornik*, no. 4 (1883): 289–299; no. 5: 139–170; no. 6: 298–330.

Anon. "Dmitrii Alekseevich Miliutin vo vremia upravleniia ego voennym ministerstvom, 1861–1881 gg.," *Russkaia starina*, no. 49 (1886): 240–256.

Anon. "Zametki po povodu uchebnykh sborov zapasnykh nizhnikh chinov v 1888 godu." *Voennyi sbornik*, no. 4 (1889): 298–321.

Anon. *Voina i evrei.* SPb.: n.p., 1912.

Arkhipov, A. "Zametki o sanitarnom sostoianii russkoi armii za 1869–1885 goda," *Voennyi sbornik*, no. 8 (1888): 383–405.

Batsevich, Ruppenheit. *Ocherk voennyx deistvii, v kotorykh uchastvoval 35-yi pekhotnyi polk v kampanii 1877–1888 gg.* Kharkov: n. p., 1886.

Ben-Ami [Rabinovich, Haim Mordekhai]. "Ben-Yukhid. Byl' iz vremen lovchikov," *Voskhod*, no. 1 (1884): 151–161; no. 2 (1884): 131–156.

Beskrovnyi, L. *Russkaia armiia i flot v XVIII veke: ocherki.* M.: Voennoe izdatel'stvo, 1958.

Beskrovnyi, L. *Russkaia voenno-teoreticheskaia mysl' XIX i nachala XX vekov.* M.: Voennoe izdatel'stvo, 1960.

Beskrovnyi, L. *Russkaia armiia i flot v deviatnadtsatom veke. Voenno-ekonomicheskii potentsial Rossii.* M.: Nauka, 1973.

Beskrovnyi, L. *Russkoe voennoe iskusstvo XIX veka.* M.: Nauka, 1974.

Bogrov, G. I. *Zapiski evreia.* 3 vols. Odessa: Sherman, 1912–1913.

Brafman, Ia. *Kniga kagala: vsemirnyi evreiskii vorpos.* SPb.: Dobrodi, 1888.

Brant, P. "Zhenatye nizhnie chiny," *Voennyi sbornik*, no. 12 (1860): 357–378.

Brock, Peter, and John L. Keep, eds., *Life in a Penal Battalion of the Imperial Russian Army: The Tolstoyan N. T. Iziumchenko's Story.* York: William Sessions, 2001.

Brutskus, B. *Ocherki po voprosam ekonomicheskoi deiatelnosti evreev Rossii.* SPb.: Ganzburg, 1913.

Budnitskii, O. *Evrei i russkaia revoliutsiia. Materialy i issledovaniia.* Jerusalem: Gesharim, 1999.

Bukhbinder, N. A. *Istoriia evreiskogo rabochego dvizheniia v Rossii.* L.: Akademicheskoe izdatelstvo, 1925.

Bulgarin, F. *Ivan Vyzhigin*. 2 vols. M.: Vdova Pliushar, 1829.
Butmi, G. *Iudei v masonstve i revoliutsii*. SPb.: Tip. uchilishcha glukhonemykh, 1906.
Butmi, G. *Konstitutsiia i politicheskaia svoboda*. SPb.: Tip. uchilishcha glukhonemykh, 1906.
Butmi, G. *Vragi roda chelovecheskogo*. SPb.: Tip. uchilishcha glukhonemykh, 1907.
Byt russkoi armii XVIII– nachala XX veka. Sost. S. V. Karpushchenko. M.: Voennoe izdatelstvo, 1999.
Dagaev, [polkovnik generalnogo shtaba]. "K voprosu o prodovolstvii voisk pod Plevnoi v 1877 godu," *Voennyi sbornik*, no. 12 (1887): 305–318.
[Dalinskii], Tifon. "Po povodu knigi 'Evrei v armii,'" *Voennyi sbornik*, no. 12 (1911): 75–84.
Dubnow, S. "Kak byla vvedena rekrutskaia povinnost dlia evreev v 1827 g.," *Evreiskaia starina*, no. 2 (1909): 256–265.
Ein Stuck von uns: deutsche Juden in deutsche Armeen 1813–1976: e. Dokumentation. Mainz: v. Hase und Koehler, 1977.
Fedorov, A. V. *Russkaia armiia v 50–70-kh gg. XIX veka*. L.: n. p., 1959.
Garashchenko, A. "Kratkaia istoriia kamennogo zdaniia sinagogi v Irkutske," *Sibirskii evreiskii sbornik*. Irkutsk: Arkom, 1992.
Gessen, V. Iu. *K istorii Sankt-Peterburgskoi evreiskoi religioznoi obshchiny: ot pervykh evreev do XX veka* SPb.: Tema, 2000.
Gessen, Iu. *Istoriia evreiskogo naroda v Rossii*. Izdanie ispravlennoe. 2 vols. M., Jerusalem: Gesharim, 1993.
Ginsburg, S. M. *Historishe verk*. 3 vols. New York: Shoyl Ginzburg 70-Yohriger Yubiley Komitet, 1937.
Ginsburg, S. M. "Borba s evreiskoi raznuzdannostiu," *Evreiskaia biblioteka* (1928): 92–107.
Ginsburg, S. M. "Mucheniki-deti (iz istorii kantonistov-evreev)," *Evreiskaia starina*, no. 13 (1930): 50–79.
Ginsburg, S. M., and P. S. Marek. *Yiddish Folksongs in Russia*. Edited by Dov Noy (photo reproduction of the 1901 St. Petersburg edition). Ramat Gan: Bar Ilan University Press.
Herschberg, A. *Pinkes Byalistok: grunt-materyaln tsu der geshiktate fun di Yidn in Byalistok biz nakh der Ershter Velt-Milhome*. 2 vols. New York: Aroysgegebn fun der Gezelshaft far geshikhte fun Byalistok, 1949–1950.
Imeretinskii, N. K. "Iz zapisok starogo preobrazhentsa," *Russkaia starina*, no. 77 (1–3) (1893): 313–339, 531–558; 78 (4–6) (1893): 21–50.
Isaichikov, F. "Brianskii polk na Shipke," *Brianskii Kraeved*, no. 5 (Briansk, 1973): 171–175.
Kagan, I. I. *Ocherk istorii evreev Orenburzh'ia v XIX-nachale XX vv.* (Orenburg: Gosarkhiv orenburgskoi oblasti, 1996).
Kagan, Israel Meir. *Mahaneh Israel*. Bnei-Brak: Torah ve-dat, 1967–1968.
Kaufman, A. E. "Evrei v russko-turetskoi voine 1878–1879 gg.," *Evreiskaia starina*, no. 1 (1915): 56–72; no. 2 (1915): 176–182.
Kersnovskii, A. A. *Istoriia russkoi armii*. 6 vols. Belgrade: Tsarskii vestnik, 1933–1938.
Kirzhnits, A. D., ed. *1905. Evreiskoe rabochee dvizhenie. Materialy i dokumenty*. M., L.: Gosudarstvennoe izdatelstvo, 1928.
Kleinberg, L. *Rechi, proiznesennye v vilenskoi sinagoge v dni prochteniia Vysochaishego manifesta ot 12 aprelia 1877 g., prazdnovaniia vziatiia Plevny 2 dekabria*

1877 g. i 25 fevralia g. po povodu radostnoi vesti o preliminarnom traktate. Vilna: n. p., 1878.

Konovalov, V. I., ed. *Revoliutsionoe dvizhenie v armii v gody pervoi russkoi revoliutsii.* M.: Politicheskaia literatura, 1955.

Korngold, S. E. "Russkiie evrei na voine 1877/78," *Russkii evrei,* no. 7 (1879): 227–230; 384–387.

Korobkov, Kh. "Evreiskaia rekrutchina v tsarstvovanie Nikolaia I," *Evreiskaia starina,* no. 6 (1913): 70–85, 233–244.

Korolenko, V. G. *Sobranie sochinenii.* vol. 2. *Povesti i rasskazy.* M.: Khudozhestvennaia literatura, 1954.

Krestovskii, V. V. *Sobranie sochinenii.* SPb.: Obshchestvennaia polza, 1899.

Kritikus [S. Dubnow], "Literaturnaia letopis," *Voskhod,* no. 9 (I) (January 1891): 24–41.

Kuropatkin, A. "Blokada Plevny," *Voennyi sbornik,* no. 2 (1885): 185–256.

Lalaev, M. *Istoricheskii ocherk voenno-uchebnykh zavedenii podvedomstvennykh Glavnomu upravleniiu. Ot osnovaniia v Rossii voennykh shkol do iskhoda pervago dvadtsatipiatiletiia tsarstvovaniia gosudaria imperatora Aleksandra Nikolaevicha, 1700–1880.* SPb.: Tip. Stasiulevicha, 1880.

Lenin, V. I. *Polnoe sobrabie sochinenii.* M.: Politicheskaia literatura, 1960.

Leshchinskii, Ia. "Evreiskoe naselenie Rossii i evreiskii trud," in *Kniga o russkom evreistve ot 1860 gg. do revoliutsii 1917 g.* 183–206. New York: Soiuz russkikh evreev, 1960.

Levshinovskii [kapitan]. "O sberezhenii nog nizhnikh chinov, o portiankakh i sapogakh," *Voennyi sbornik,* no. 6 (1891): 351–368.

Libenzon, Z. Kh., ed. *Evrei Nizhnego Novgoroda.* Nizhnii Novgorod: Dekom, 1993.

Lipschitz, Y. *Zikhron Ya'akov.* 3 vols. Bnei-Brak: n. p., 1968.

Liubavskii, A. *Russkie ugolovnye protsessy.* 4 vols. SPb.: Obshchestvennaia polza, 1866.

Lossovskii [kapitan]. "Zametka ob usloviiakh pitaniia nashego soldata," *Voennyi sbornik,* no. 6 (1887): 201–215; *Voennyi sbornik,* no. 7 (1887): 85–108.

Luganin A. "Zametki po povodu uchebnykh sborov zapasnykh nizhnikh chinov v 1887 godu," *Voennyi sbornik,* no. 5 (1888): 131–169.

Mandelkern, S. *Slovo, proiznesennoe v odesskoi glavnoi sinagoge po povodu perekhoda russkikh voisk cherez Dunai.* Odessa: n. p., 1877.

Marek P. *Ocherki po istorii prosveshcheniia evreev v Rossii (dva vospitaniia).* M.: Obshchestvo rasprostraneniia pravilnykh svedenii o evreiakh i evreistve, 1909.

Milodanovich, V. "Polevoi zhid i ego kollegi," *Voennaia byl,* no. 93 (1968): 9–14.

Nevzorov, N. *Istoricheskii ocherk upravleniia dukhovenstvom voennogo vedomstva v Rossii.* SPb.: F. Eleonskii, 1875.

Nikitin, N. V. "Mnogostradalnye. Ocherki byta kantonistov," *Otechestvennye zapiski,* no. 8 (1871): 351–396; no. 9 (1871): 69–120; no. 10 (1871): 407–440.

Nikitin, N. V. "Vek prozhit' – ne pole pereiti," *Evreiskaia biblioteka,* no. 3 (1873): 164–214.

Nikitin, N. V. *Byt voennykh arestantov v krepostiakh.* SPb.: Kolesov i Mikhin, 1873.

Nikolaev, F. "Issledovaniie soldatskikh sukon," *Voenno-meditsinskii zhurnal,* no. 8 (CXIV) (1872): 183–200.

Ocherk deiatel'nosti Tovarishchestva Greger, Gorvits i Kogan po prodovolstviu deistvuiushchei armii v Vostochnuiu voinu 1877–1878 godov. Bucharest, 1878.

Opisanie Russko-turetskoi voiny 1877–1878 gg. Na Balkanskom poluostrove. 9 vols. Ed. by I. Gerua. SPb.: Voennaia tipografiia, 1901–1913.

Pekhota. Spravochnaia Kniga Glavnoi Kvartiry. SPb.: n.p., 1913.

Petrov, V. A. *Ocherki po istorii revoliutsionnogo dvizheniia v russkoi armii v 1905 g.* M., L.: Nauka, 1964.

Pokrovskii, M., ed. *1905. Armiia v pervoi revoliutsii.* L.: Gosudarstvennoe izdatel'stvo, 1927.

Portugal'skii, R. M., P. D. Alekseev, and V. A. Runov. *Pervaia mirovaia v zhizneopisaniakh russkikh voenachal'nikov.* M.: Elakos, 1994.

Pozner, S. "Kak podgotovlialas i provodilas konferentsiia voennykh i boevykh organizatsii," in *Pervaia konferentsia voennykh i boevykh organizatsii RSDRP.* M.: Partizdat, 1932.

Rabinovich, G. M. *Statisticheskie etiudy. Otnoshenie prizyvnogo vozrasta ko vsemu muzhskomu naseleniu v Evropeiskoi Rossii, osobenno u evreev.* SPb.: Izd. avtora, 1886.

Rabinovich, O. *Sochineniia.* 3 vols. Odessa: Trud, 1888.

Rafes, M. *Ocherki po istorii Bunda.* M.: Moskovskii rabochii, 1923.

Raskin, D. "Evrei v sostave rossiiskogo ofitserskogo korpusa v XIX-nachale XX veka." In *Evrei v Rossii. Istoriia i kultura. Sbornik nauchnykh trudov,* Edited by D. Eliashevich, 170–174. SPb.: Peterburgskii evreiskii universitet, 1998.

Rozenblum, K. *Voennye organizatsii bolshevikov 1905–1907 gg.* M., L.: Gosudarstvennoe sotsialno-ekonomicheskoe izdatelstvo, 1931.

Ryndziunskii P. G. *Gorodskoe grazhdanstvo doreformennoi Rossii.* M.: Izd. AN SSSR, 1958.

Schiper, Ignacy. *Dzieje handlu żydowskiego na ziemiach polskich.* Warsaw: Nakladem Centrali Związku kupców w Warszawe, 1937.

Schneersohn, J. I. *The Tzemach Tzedek and the Haskalah Movement in Russia.* New York: Kehot, 1962.

Serebrianskii, M. *Dnevnik polkovogo sviashchennika, sluzhashchego na Dalnem Vostoke.* M.: Otchii Dom, 1996.

Shatzky, Jacob, *Di geshikhte fun yidn in Varshe.* New York: YIVO, 1947.

Shavrov, K. "Gramotnost' v voiskakh," *Voennyi sbornik,* no. 5 (1892): 191–196.

Shavelskii, G. *Vospominaniia poslednego protopresvitera russkoi armii i flota.* New York: Izd. im. Chekhova, 1954.

Shilder, N. K. *Imperator Nikolai Pervyi, ego zhizn i tsarstvovanie.* SPb.: A. S. Suvorin, 1903.

Shkurko, E. A. *Ocherki istorii evreev Bashkortostana.* Ufa: n. p., 1999.

[Shmakov]. *Minskii protsess. Delo o soprotivlenii evreiskikh skopishch voennym patruliam.* M.: Mamontov, 1899.

Shmakov, A. S. *Svoboda i evrei.* M.: Gorodskaia tipografiia, 1906.

Shulgin, V. V. *Chto nam v nikh ne nravitsia. Ob antisemitizme v Rossii.* M.: Khors, 1992–1994.

Slutsky, Y. and M.. Kaplan,, eds. *Hayalim yehudim be-tsivot Eropa [Ha-lohem ha-yehudi be-tsivot ha-olam].* Tel-Aviv: Ma'arakhot, 1967.

Soloveichik, H. "Rupture and Reconstruction: The Transformation of Contemporary Orthodoxy," *Tradition,* vol. 28, no. 4 (1994): 64–130.

Stanislavskii, S. "K istorii kantonistov," *Evreiskaia starina,* no. 4 (1909): 266–268.

Tager, A. S. *Tsarskaia Rossiia i delo Beilisa. K istorii antisemitizma.* M.: OGIZ, 1933.

Tsitron, Sh. *Me-ahorei ha-pargod. Momrim, bogdim, mitkahashim.* 2 vols. Vilna: Tsevi Mats, 1923.

Tutundzhan, T. *Vosstanie turkestanskikh saperov v 1912 godu.* Tashkent: Gosudarstvennoe izdatelstvo UzSSR, 1960.

Usov, M. [M. L. Trivus]. *Evrei v armii.* SPb.: Razum, 1911.

Vasil'kovskii [poruchik], Grigorovich [kapitan], *Pamiatka o stoletnei sluzhbe 35-go pekhotnago Brianskogo General-Ad'iutanta Kniazia Gorchakova polka.* Kremenchug: n. p., 1909.

Viatkin, M. P. *Iz istorii imperializma v Rossii.* M., L.: Akademiia Nauk SSSR, 1959.

Vol'nonaiemnyi intendantskii transport v Turetskuiu voinu 1877–1878 gg. Bucharest: n. p., 1878.

Yoshor, Moshe. *The Chafetz Chaim: The Life and Works of Rabbi Israel Meir Kagan of Radin.* New York: Mesora Publishers, 1997.

Zalesskii, V. F. *Taina krovi. K voprosu o ritualnykh ubiistvakh.* Kharkov: Mirnyi trud, 1912.

Zamyslovskii, G. G. *Zhertvy Izrailia. Saratovskoe delo.* Kharkov: Mirnyi trud, 1911.

Zborowski, M., and E. Herzog. *Life Is with People: The Culture of the Shtetl.* New York: Shocken Books, 1972.

Zolotarev, A. M. "Materialy po voennoi statistike Rossii: Boleznennost, smertnost i ubyl armii za period 1869–1884 god," *Voennyi sbornik,* no. 2 (1888): 323–341; no. 3 (1888): 177–193; no. 4 (1888): 351–365; no. 11 (1888): 159–176.

Zolotarev, A. M. "Materialy po voennoi statistike Rossii: Naselenie Rossii kak istochnik komplektovaniia ee armii," *Voennyi sbornik,* no. 4 (1888): 351–365; no. 11 (1888): 157–176; no. 5 (1889): 98–141; no. 6 (1889): 334–359.

Zubarev, [Poruchik]. "Nashi polkovye sudy," *Voennyi sbornik,* no. 5 (1892): 167–171.

Zvegintsov, V. *Khronologia Russkoi Armii, 1700–1917.* 3 vols. Paris: Viraflay, 1961–1962.

Secondary Sources

Airapetov, O. R. *Zabytaia kariera "russkogo Moltke": Nikolai Nikolaevich Obruchev (1830–1904).* SPb.: Aleteia, 1998.

Antonov, V. I. *Imperatorskaia gvardiia v Sankt-Peterburge.* SPb.: Glagol, 2001.

Aronson, Michael. *The Troubled Waters: the origins of the 1881 anti-Jewish pogroms in Russia.* Pittsburgh, Penn.: University of Pittsburgh Press, 1990.

Asher, Abraham. *The Russian Revolution of 1905.* 2 vols. Stanford, Calif.: Stanford University Press, 1988–1992.

Assaf, David. *The Regal Way: The Life and Times of Rabbi Israel of Ruzhin.* Translated by David Louvish. Stanford, Calif.: Stanford University Press, 2002.

Avrekh, A. Ia. *P. A. Stolypin i sud'by reform v Rossii.* M.: Politizdat, 1991.

Baron, Salo W. *The Jewish Community. Its History and Structure to the American Revolution.* 3 vols. Philadelphia: Jewish Publication Society of America, 1942.

Baron, Salo W. *Russian Jews under Tsar and Soviets.* New York: Macmillan, 1964.

Bertaud, Jean-Paul. "The Revolutionary Role of the Army: To Regenerate Man, to Form a Citizen, a Model for Civil Society?" In *Culture and Revolution: Cultural Ramifications of the French Revolution,* edited by George Levitine, 18–39. College Park: University of Maryland at College Park, 1989.

Beyrau, Dietrich. *Militär und Gesellschaft in Vorrevolutionären Russland*. Cologne and Vienna: Bohlau, 1984.

Brubaker, Rogers. *Ethnicity without Groups*. Cambridge, Mass.: Harvard University Press, 2004.

Bushnell, John, "Peasants in Uniform: The Tsarist Army as a Peasant Society," *Journal of Social History*, no. 13 (1980): 565–576.

Bushnell, John. "The Tsarist Officer Corps, 1881–1914: Customs, Duties, Inefficiency," *American Historical Review*, no. 86 (1981): 753–780.

Bushnell, John. *Mutiny amid Repression: Russian Soldiers in the Revolution of 1905–1906*. Bloomington: Indiana University Press, 1985.

Caban, Wiesław. *Służba rekrutów z Królestwa Polskiego w armii carskiej w latach 1831–1873*. Warsaw: DiG, 2001.

Cohn, Norman. *Warrant for Genocide. The Myth of the Jewish World Conspiracy and the "Protocols of the Elders of Zion."* London: Serif, 1996.

Cooper, Frederick. *Colonialism in question: theory, knowledge, history*. Berkeley: University of California Press, 2005.

Coquin, F., and C. Cervais-Francelle, eds. *1905. La Première Révolution Russe*. Paris: Sorbonne et Institut d'études slaves, 1986.

Curtiss, John Shelton. *The Russian Army under Nicholas I, 1825–1855*. Durham, N.C., Duke University Press, 1965.

Deák, István. *Beyond Nationalism: A Social and Political History of the Habsburg Officer Corps, 1848–1918*. New York and Oxford: Oxford University Press, 1990.

Deák, István. *Jewish Soldiers in Austro-Hungarian Society: Leo Baeck Memorial Lecture*, no. 34. New York: Leo Baeck Institute, 1990.

Dubin, Lois C. *The Port Jews of Habsburg Trieste: Absolutist Politics and Enlightenment Culture*. Stanford, Calif.: Stanford University Press, 1999.

Dubnow, Simon. *History of the Jews in Russia and Poland*. Translated by I. Friedlaender. 3 vols. Philadelphia: The Jewish Publication Society of America, 1918.

Dudakov, S. *Istoriia odnogo mifa. Ocherki russkoi literatury XIX-XX veka*. M.: Nauka, 1993.

Eckman, Lester Samuel. *Revered by All: The Life and Works of Rabbi Israel Meir Kagan–Hafets Hayyim (1838–1933)*. New York: Shengold Publishers, 1974.

Eisenbach, Arthur. *Kwestia równouprawnienia Żydów w Królestwie Polskim*. Warsaw: Książka i Wiedza, 1972.

Eisenbach, Arthur. *Z Dziejów ludności żydowskiej w Polsce w XVIII i XIX wieku*. Warsaw: Państwowy Instytut Wydawniczy, 1983.

Eisenbach, Arthur. *The Emancipation of the Jews in Poland, 1780–1870*. Edited by Antony Polonsky, translated by J. Dorosz. Oxford and Cambridge, Mass.: Basil Blackwell, 1991.

Eliashevich, D. A. *Evreiskaia periodicheskaia pechat' i russkaia tsenzura*. M. and Ierusalem: Gesharim-Mosty kul'tury, 1998.

Elting, John R. *Swords around a Throne: Napoleon's Grande Armée*. New York: Da Capo Press, 1997.

Endelman, Todd M. "Memories of Jewishness: Jewish Converts and Their Jewish Pasts." In *Jewish History and Jewish Memory: Essays in Honor of Yosef Haim Yerushalmi*, edited by Elisheva Carlebach et al., 311–329. Hanover, N.H.: University Press of New England, 1998.

Engelman, Uriah Zevi. "Sources of Jewish Statistics." In *The Jews: Their History, Culture, and Religion*, edited by Louis Finkelstein. 2 vols, 2: 1510–1535. Philadelphia: Jewish Publication Society of America, 1966.

Farnsworth, Beatrice. "The *Soldatka*: Folklore and Court Record," *Slavic Review*, no. 49 (1) (1990): 58–73.

Fischer-Galati, Stephen, and Béla K. Király, eds. *Essays on War and Society in East Central Europe, 1740–1920*. New York: Boulder and Columbia University Press, 1987.

Fischer, Horst. *Judentum, Staat und Heer in Preussen im frühen 19. Jahrhundert: Zur Geschichte der staatlichen Judenpolitik*. Tübingen: J. C. B. Mohr, 1968.

Fishman, David. *Russia's First Modern Jews: the Jews of Shklov*. New York: New York University Press, 1995.

Foà, Salvatore. *Gli ebrei nel Risorgimento italiano*. Assisi and Rome: Carucci, 1978.

Frank, Steven. *Crime, Cultural Conflict, and Justice in Rural Russia, 1856–1914*. Berkeley: University of California Press, 1999.

Frankel, Jonathan. *Prophecy and Politics: Socialism, Nationalism, and the Russian Jews, 1862–1917*. Cambridge: Cambridge University Press, 1981.

Freeze, Gregory. "The Soslovie (Estate) Paradigm and Russian Social History." *The American Historical Review*, vol. 91, no. 1 (1986): 11–36.

Freeze, Gregory, ed. *Russia: A History*. Oxford and New York: Oxford University Press, 1997.

Fuller, William, Jr. *Civil-Military Conflict in Imperial Russia. 1881–1914*. Princeton, N. J.: Princeton University Press, 1985.

Fuller, William, Jr., *The Foe Within: Fantasies of Treason and the End of Imperial Russia*. Ithaca and London: Cornell University Press, 2006.

Gatrell, Peter. *Russia's First World War: A Social and Economic History*. Harlow, Essex: Pearson Longman, 2005.

Ganelin, R. "N. E. Markov 2-oi na svoem puti ot chernosotenstva k gitlerizmu." In *Evrei v Rossii. Istoriia i kultura*, edited by D. Eliashevich, 211–218. SPb.: Peterburgskii evreiskii universitet, 1998.

Gartner, Arie. "Hagirah he-hamonit shel yehudei europa, 1881–1914." In *Hagirah ve-hityashvut be-yisrael u-va-amim: kovets ma'amarim*, edited by Shinan Avigdor, 343–383. Jerusalem: Merkaz Shazar, 1982.

Gerachi, Robert P., and Michael Khodarkovsky, eds. *Of Religion and Empire: Missions, Conversion, and Tolerance in Tsarist Russia*. Ithaca and London: Cornell University Press, 2001.

Geyer, Dietrich. *Russian Imperialism: The Interaction of Domestic and Foreign Policy, 1860–1914*. New Haven and London: Yale University Press, 1987.

Glushkov, V. V. *Na karte general'nogo shtaba – Manchzhuriia*. M.: Institut politicheskogo i voennogo analiza, 2000.

Greenberg, Louis. *The Jews in Russia*. 2 vols. New Haven and London: Yale University Press, 1965.

Hagar-Lau, I. *He-hayal ve-ha-hosen. Tsava u-milkhamah be-ha-emek davar u-ve-meshekh khokhmah*. Jerusalem: Or Etsion, 1989.

Halpern, Israel. *Yehudim ve-yahadut be-mizrakh europa. Mekhkarim be-toldotehem*. Jerusalem: Magness Press, 1968.

Hamm, Michael, ed. *The City in Late Imperial Russia*. Bloomington: Indiana University Press, 1986.

Healy, Ann Erickson. *The Russian Autocracy in Crisis, 1905–1907*. Hamden, Conn.: Archon Books, 1976.

Horn, Maurycy. *Powinnośći wojenne Żydów w Rzeczypospolitej w XVI i XVII wieku*. Warsaw: Panstwowe Wydawnictwo Naukowe, 1978.

Israel, Jonathan. *European Jews in the Era of Mercantilism, 1550–1750*. Oxford: Clarendon Press, 1989.

Jahn, Hubertus F. *Patriotic Culture in Russia During World War I*. Ithaca and London: Cornell University Press, 1995.

Judson, Pieter M. and Marsha L. Rozenblit, eds *Constructing Nationalities in East Central Europe*. New York: Berghann Books, 2005.

Kagan, Frederick. *The Military Reforms of Nicholas I: The Origins of the Modern Russian Army*. New York: St. Martin's Press, 1999.

Kagan, Frederick, and Robin Higham, eds. *The Military History of Tsarist Russia*. New York: Palgrave, 2002.

Kahan, Arcadius. *Essays in Jewish Social and Economic History*, edited by Roger Weiss. Chicago and London: University of Chicago Press, 1986.

Kaplan, Robert Elliot. "Making Sense of the Rennes Verdict: The Military Dimension of the Dreyfus Affair," *Journal of Contemporary History*, no. 34 (4) (1999): 499–515.

Kappeler, Andreas. *The Russian Empire: A Multi-ethnic History*, translated by Alfred Clayton. Harlow, Essex, and New York: Longman, 2001.

Kappeler, Andreas, Zenon E. Kohut., Frank E. Sysyn, and Mark Von Hagen, eds. *Culture, Nation, and Identity: The Ukrainian-Russian Encounter (1600–1945)*. Edmonton and Toronto: Canadian Institute of Ukrainian Studies Press, 2003.

Keep, John L. *Soldiers of the Tsar: Army and Society in Russia, 1562–1874*. Oxford: Clarendon Press, 1985.

Keep, John. "The Origins of Russian Militarism," *Cahiers du Monde Russe et Soviétique*, vol. 26, no. 1 (1985): 5–20.

Keep, John. "Justice for the Troops: A Comparative Study of Nicholas I's Russia and France under Louis-Philippe," *Cahiers du Monde Russe et Soviétique*, vol. 28, no. 1 (1987): 31–54.

Keep, John. "No Gauntlet for Gentlemen: Officers' Privileges in Russian Military Law, 1716–1855," *Cahiers du Monde Russe et Soviétique*, vol. 34, nos 1–2 (1993): 171–192.

Kieniewicz, S. *Powstanie Styczniowe*. Warsaw: Panstwowe Wydawnictwo Naukowe, 1972.

Kimerling Wirtschafter, Elise, "Soldiers' Children, 1719–1856. A Study of Social Engineering in Imperial Russia," *Forschungen zur Osteuropaischen Geschichte*, no. 30 (1982): 61–136.

Kimerling Wirtschafter, Elise. *From Serf to Russian Soldier*. Princeton, N.J.: Princeton University Press, 1990.

Kimerling Wirtschafter, Elise. *Structures of Society: Imperial Russia's "People of Various Ranks."* DeKalb: Northern Illinois University Press, 1994.

Kimerling Wirtschafter, Elise. *Social Identity in Imperial Russia*. DeKalb: Northern Illinois University Press, 1997.

Klier, John. *Imperial Russia's Jewish Question, 1855–1881*. Cambridge: Cambridge University Press, 1995.

Klier, John. *Rossiia sobiraet svoikh evreev. Proiskhozhdenie evreiskogo voprosa v Rossii.* M. and Jerusalem: Mosty Kultury and Gesharim, 2000.

Klier, John, and Shlomo Lambroza, eds. *Pogroms: Anti-Jewish Violence in Modern Russian History.* Cambridge: Cambridge University Press, 1992.

Klier, John. "What Exactly Was a Shtetl." In *The Shtetl: Image and Reality*, edited by Gennady Estraikh and Mikhail Krutikov, 23–35. Oxford: Legenda, 2000.

Koropeckyj, I. S., ed. *Ukrainian Economic History. Interpretative Essays.* Cambridge, Mass.: Harvard University Press for Harvard Ukrainian Research Institute, 1991.

Kuznets, Simon. "Immigration of the Russian Jews to the U.S.: Background and Structure," *Perspectives in American History*, no. 9 (1975): 35–124.

Langmuir, Gavin. *History, Religion and Antisemitism.* Los Angeles: University of California Press, Center for Medieval and Renaissance Studies, 1990.

Lederhendler, Eli. *The Road to Modern Jewish Politics.* New York and Oxford: Oxford University Press, 1989.

Lederhendler, Eli. "Modernity without Emancipation or Assimilation? The Case of Russian Jewry." In *Assimilation and Community: The Jews in Nineteenth-Century Europe.* Edited by Jonathan Frankel and Steven Zipperstein, 325–343. Cambridge: Cambridge University Press, 1992.

Leslie, R. *Reform and Insurrection in Russian Poland. 1856–1865.* London: Athlone Press, 1962.

Lestchinsky, Jacob. *Ha-tefutsah ha-yehudit: ha-hitpathut ha-hevratit ve-ha-kalkalit shel kivutsei ha-yehudim be-Eropa u-va-America ba-dorot ha-aharonim.* Jerusalem: Mosad Byalik, 1960.

Lestschinsky, Jacob, "Jewish Migrations." In *Jews: Their History, Culture and Religion*, edited by Louis Finkelstein. 2 vols, 2:1597–1666. Philadelphia: The Jewish Publication Society of America, 1966.

Levin, Alfred. *A Study of the Social-Democratic Party and the Russian Constitutional Experiment.* Hamden, Conn.: Archon, 1966.

Lincoln, W. Bruce. *Nikolai Miliutin: An Enlightened Russian Bureaucrat of the 19th Century.* Newtonville, Mass.: Oriental Research Partners, 1977.

Lincoln, W. Bruce. *Nicholas I: Emperor and Autocrat of All the Russians.* Bloomington: Indiana University Press, 1978.

Lincoln, W. Bruce. *The Great Reforms: Autocracy, Bureaucracy, and the Politics of Change in Imperial Russia.* DeKalb: Northern Illinois University Press, 1990.

Litvak, Olga. *Conscription and the Search for Modern Russian Jewry.* Bloomington: Indiana University Press, 2006.

Lohr, Eric. *Nationalizing the Russian Empire: The Campaign against Enemy Aliens During World War I.* Cambridge, Mass.: Harvard University Press, 2003.

Löwe, Heinz-Dietrich. *Antisemitismus und Reaktionare Utopie. Russischer Konservatismus im Kampf gegen den Wandel von Staat und Gesellschaft, 1890–1917.* Hamburg: Hoffman und Campe, 1978.

Löwe, Heinz-Dietrich. "Political Symbols and Rituals of the Russian Radical Right, 1900–1914," *SEER*, vol. 76, no. 3 (1998): 441–466.

Lvov-Rogachvskii, V. *Russko-evreiskaia literatura i evrei.* M.: Moskovskoe otdelenie gosudarstvennogo izdatelstva. Also available in English: Lvov-Rogachevskii, Vasilii. *A History of Russian Jewish Literature.* Edited and translated by Arthur Levin. Ann Arbor, Mich.: Ardis, 1979.

Manning, Roberta. *The Crisis of the Old Order in Russia, Gentry and Government.* Princeton, N.J.: Princeton University Press, 1982.

Mayzel, Matitiahu. "The Formation of the Russian General Staff, 1880–1917: A Social Study," in *Cahiers du Monde Russe et Soviétique,* no. 16 (1975): 297–321.

McReynolds, Louise. "Imperial Russia's Newspaper Reporters: Profile of a Society in Transition, 1865–1914," *SEER,* vol. 68, no. 2 (1990): 277–293.

Markov, O. D. *Russkaia armiia: 1914–1917 gg.* SPb.: Galeia, 2001.

Mendelsohn, Ezra, *Class Struggle in the Pale; The Formative Years of the Jewish Workers' Movement in Tsarist Russia.* Cambridge: Cambridge University Press, 1970.

Menning, Bruce W. *Bayonets before Bullets: The Imperial Russian Army, 1861–1914.* Bloomington: Indiana University Press, 1992.

Miller, Forest A. *Dmitrii Miliutin and the Reform Era in Russia.* Nashville, Tenn.: Vanderbilt University Press, 1968.

Mishkinsky, Moshe. *Reshit tenuat ha-poalim ha-yehudit be-rusia.* Tel-Aviv: Ha-kibbuts ha-me'uhad, 1981.

Opalski, Magdalena, and Israel Bartal. *Poles and Jews: A Failed Brotherhood.* Hanover and London: Brandeis University Press, 1992.

Orbach, Alexander. *New Voices of Russian Jewry. A Study of the Russian-Jewish Press of Odessa in the Era of Great Reforms, 1860–1871.* Leiden: E. J. Brill, 1980.

Orlovsky, Daniel. *The Limits of Reform: The Ministry of Internal Affairs in Imperial Russia, 1802–1881.* Cambridge, Mass.: Harvard University Press, 1981.

Pacan, Ilaria. *Il Comandante: la vita di Federico Jarach e la memoria di un'epoca, 1874–1951.* Milan: Proedi, 2001.

Peled, Yoav. *Class and Ethnicity in the Pale: The Political Economy of Jewish Workers' Nationalism in Late Imperial Russia.* London: Macmillan, 1989.

Petrovsky-Shtern, Yohanan. " 'The Guardians of Faith,' or Jewish Self-Governing Societies in the Russian Army: The Case of Briansk 35th Regiment." In *The Military and Society in Russia, 1450 to 1917,* edited by Eric Lohr and Marshall Poe, 413–434. Leiden: Brill, 2002.

Petrovsky-Shtern, Yohanan. "The Jewish Policy of the War Ministry in Late Imperial Russia: The Impact of the Russian Right," *KRITIKA: Explorations in Russian and Eurasian History,* no. 2 (2002): 217–254.

Petrovsky-Shtern, Iokhanan. *Evrei v russkoi armii, 1827–1914.* M.: Novoe literaturnoe obozrenie, 2003 (Series *Historia Rossica*).

Petrovsky-Shtern, Yohanan. "Dual Identity Revisited: The Case of Russian-Jewish Soldiers," *Jews in Russia and Eastern Europe,* no. 1 (2004): 130–144.

Petrovsky-Shtern, Yohanan, "On Solzhenitsyn's 'Middle Path,' " *Polin,* no. 18 (2005): 381–392.

Petrovsky-Shtern, Yohanan, "Vrag roda chelovecheskogo:' o 'protokol'noi' paradigme v russkom obschestvennom soznanii." In *Obraz vraga, edited by* Lev Gudkov, 102–126. Moscow: OGI, 2005.

Petrovsky-Shtern, Yohanan, "Military Service in Russia." In *The YIVO Encyclopedia of Jews in Eastern Europe.* 2 vols. (New Haven: Yale University Press, 2008), 2:1170–1174.

Pinchuk, Ben-Zion. *The Octobrists and the Third Duma.* Seattle and London: University of Washington Press, 1974.

Pintner, Walter McKenzie. *Russian Economic Policy under Nicholas I.* Ithaca, N.Y: Cornell University Press, 1967.

Pipes, Richard. *Russian Revolution.* London: Harvill Press, 1990.

Pipes, Richard. *Russia under the Old Regime.* London: Penguin, 1995.

Portugal'skii, R. M. *Verkhovnye glavnokomanduiushchiie otechestva.* M.: Istfakt, 2001.

Porshneva, O. S. "Mental'nyi oblik i sotsial'noe povedenie soldat russkoi armii v usloviiakh pervoi mirovoi voiny (1914-fevral' 1917 gg." In *Voenno-istoricheskaia antropologiia. Ezhegodnik.* 2002, 252–267. M.: ROSSPEN, 2002.

Presniakov, A. *Emperor Nicholas I of Russia: The Apogee of Autocracy, 1825–1855.* Edited and translated by Judith C. Zacek. Gulf Breeze, Fl.: Academic International Press, 1974.

Purseigle, Pierre. *Warfare and Belligerence: Perspectives in First World War Studies.* Leiden and Boston: Brill, 2005.

Purves, J. G., and D. A. West., eds. *War and Society in Nineteenth-Century Russian Empire.* Toronto: New Review Books, 1972.

Raeff, Marc. *Political Ideas and Institutions in Imperial Russia.* Boulder, Colo.: Westview Press, 1994.

Reese, Roger, ed. *The Russian Imperial Army, 1796–1917.* Burlington, Vt.: Ashgate, 2006.

Riasanovsky, Nicholas. *Nicholas I and Official Nationality in Russia, 1825–1855.* Berkeley and Los Angeles: University of California Press, 1959.

Riasanovsky, Nicholas. *A History of Russia.* New York, Oxford, 2000.

Rich, David. "Imperialism, Reform and Strategy: Russian Military Statistics, 1840–1890," *SEER,* vol. 74, no. 4 (1996): 621–639.

Rich, David. *The Tsar's Colonels: Professionalism, Strategy, and Subversion in Late Imperial Russia.* Cambridge, Mass.: Harvard University Press, 1998.

Rieber, A. J. *Merchants and Enterpreneurs in Imperial Russia.* Chapel Hill: University of North Carolina Press, 1982.

Rogger, Hans. *Jewish Policies and Right-Wing Politics in Imperial Russia.* Berkeley and Los Angeles: University of California Press, 1986.

Rogger, Hans. "The Beilis Case: Anti-Semitism and Politics into the Reign of Nicholas II." In *Hostages of Modernization, 1870–1933/39,* edited by Herbert Strauss, 1257–1273. Berlin: Walter de Gruyter, 1993.

Roi, Yaakov, ed. *Jews and Jewish Life in Russia and the Soviet Union.* Ilford, Essex: Frank Cass, 1995.

Roshwald, Aviel, and Richard Stites, eds. *European Culture in the Great War.* Cambridge: Cambridge University Press, 1999.

Rosman, Murray J. *The Lords' Jews: Magnate-Jewish Relations in the Polish-Lithuanian Commonwealth during the Eighteenth Century.* Cambridge: Harvard University Press and Harvard Ukrainian Research Institute, 1990.

Rovighi, Alberto. *I militari di origine ebraica nel primo secolo di vita dello stato italiano.* Rome: Stato maggiore dell'esercito, Ufficio storico, 1999.

Rozenblit, Marsha. *Reconstructing a National Identity: The Jews of Habsburg Austria during World War I.* New York: Oxford University Press, 2001.

Ruppin, Arthur. *The Jews in the Modern World.* London: Macmillan, 1934.

Sablinsky, Walter. *The Road to Bloody Sunday: Father Gapon and the St. Petersburg Massacre of 1905.* Princeton, N.J.: Princeton University Press, 1976.

Sanborn, Joshua. *Drafting the Russian Nation: Military Conscription, Total War, and Mass Politics, 1905–1925.* DeKalb: Northwestern Illinois University Press, 2003.

Saunders, David. *Russia in the Age of Reaction and Reform, 1801–1881.* London and New York: Longman, 1992.

Schechter, Ronald. *Obstinate Hebrews: Representation of Jews in France, 1715–1815.* Berkeley: University of California Press, 2003.

Schiff, Ze'ev. *A History of the Israeli Army: 1874 to the Present.* New York: Macmillan, 1985.

Schimmelpenninck van der Oye, David, and Bruce Menning, eds., *Reforming the Tsar's Army: Military Innovation in Imperial Russia from Peter the Great to the Revolution.* Washington, D.C., and Cambridge: Woodrow Wilson Center and Cambridge University Press, 2004.

Schwierz, Israel. *Für das Vaterland starben: Denkmäler und Gedenktafeln für jüdische Soldaten in Thüringen: Dokumentation.* Aschaffenburg/Main: Krem-Bardischewski, 1996.

Shatsillo K. F. *Ot portsmutskogo mira k Pervoi mirovoi voine: generally i politika.* M.: ROSSPEN, 2000.

Shokhat, Azriel. "Han'hagah be-kehilot rusia im bitul ha-kahal," *Zion*, no. 42 (1977): 143–233.

Shukman, Harold. *War or Revolution: Russian Jews and Conscription in Britain, 1917.* London and Portland, Oreg.: Vallentine Mitchell, 2006.

Siefert, Marsha, ed. *Extending the Borders of Russian History, Essays in Honor of Alfred Rieber.* Budapest and New York: Central European University Press, 2003.

Simonsohn, Shlomo. *History of the Jews in the Dutchy of Mantova.* Jerusalem: Kiryat Sefer, 1977.

Simonsohn, Shlomo. "Teguvot ahadot shel yehudey italiya al 'ha-emantsipatsiya ha-rishonah.'" In *Italia judaica: gli ebrei in Italia dalla segregazione alla prima emancipazione: atti del III convegno internazionale*, 47–68. Rome: Ministero per i beni culturali e ambientali, 1989.

Sliuchenko Iu. I. *Brianskii polk: 200 let na strazhe otechestva.* M.: Reitar, 2000.

Slutsky, Yehuda. *Ha-itonut ha-yehudit-rusit ba-me'ah ha-tesha-esreh.* Jerusalem: Mosad Bialik, 1970.

Stampfer, Shaul. *Ha-yeshivah ha-litait be-hithavutah.* Jerusalem: Zalman Shazar, 1995.

Stanislawski, Michael. *Tsar Nicholas I and the Jews: The Transformation of Jewish Society in Russia. 1825–1855.* Philadelphia: Jewish Publication Society of America, 1983.

Stanislawski, Michael. *For Whom Do I Toil?: Judah Leib Gordon and the Crisis of Russian Jewry.* New York: Oxford University Press, 1988.

Stanislawski, Michael. *Psalms for the Tsar: A Minute-Book of a Psalms-Society in the Russian Army.* New York: Yeshiva University, 1988.

Strauss, Herbert, ed. *Hostages of Modernization, 1870–1933/39.* Berlin: Walter de Gruyter, 1993.

Taylor, Brian, D. *Politics and the Russian Army: Civil-Military Relations, 1689–2000.* Cambridge: Cambridge University Press, 2003.

Tobias, Henry. *The Jewish Bund in Russia: From Its Origins to 1905.* Stanford, Calif.: Stanford University Press, 1972.

Tomaszewski, Jerzy, ed. *Najnowsze dzeje Żydów z Polsce w zarysie.* Warsaw: Wyd. Państwowe Naukowe, 1993.

Van Dyke, Carl. *Russian Imperial Military Doctrine and Education, 1832–1914.* New York: Greenwood Press, 1990.

Von Laue, T. H. *Sergei Witte and the Industrialization of Russia.* New York: Columbia University Press, 1963.

Wandycz, Piotr. *The Price of Freedom. A History of East Central Europe from the Middle Ages to the Present.* London and New York: Routledge, 1992.

Weeks, Theodore R. *Nation and State in Late Imperial Russia: Nationalism and Russification on the Western Frontier, 1863–1914.* DeKalb: Northern Illinois University Press, 1996.

White, Charles Edward. *The Enlightened Soldier: Scharnhorst and the Militärische Gesellschaft in Berlin, 1801–1815.* New York: Praeger, 1989.

Wistrich, Robert. *Antisemitism: The Longest Hatred.* London: Methuen, 1991.

Zaionchkovskii, P. A. *Voennye reformy 1860–1870 godov v Rossii.* M.: Izdatel'stvo Moskovskogo Universiteta, 1952.

Zaionchkovskii, P. A. *Rossiiskoe samoderzhavie v kontse XIX stoletiia. Politicheskaia reaktsiia 80-kh-nachala 90-kh godov.* M.: Mysl', 1970.

Zaionchkovskii, P. A. *Samoderzhavie i russkaia armiia na rubezhe XIX-XX stoletii. 1881–1903.* M.: Mysl, 1973.

Zalkin, Mordechai. "Bein 'bnei elohim' li-'vnei adam': rabanim, behurei yeshivot ve-ha-giyus la-tsava ha-rusi ba-me'ah ha-19." In *Shalom u-milhamah ba-tarbut ha-yehudit,* edited by Avriel Bar-Levav, 165–222. Jerusalem: Zalman Shazar, 2006.

Zhukova, L.V. "Formirovanie 'obraza vraga' v Russko-iaponskoi voine 1904–1905 gg.," *Voenno-istoricheskaia antropologiia. Ezhegodnik. 2003/2004,* 259–275. M.: ROSSPEN, 2005.

Zinberg, I. *Istoriia evreiskoi pechati v Rossii.* Pg.: I. Fleitman, 1915.

Zinberg, Israel. *A History of Jewish Literature.* 12 vols. Cincinnati and New York: Hebrew Union College Press and Ktav, 1978.

Index of Names

Index of Places

Index of Regiments and Military Units

Subject Index